COBOL

Elements
of
Programming
Style

The Art of Programming
IBM Personal Computers Series

The Art of Programming IBM Personal Computers series consists of comprehensive texts for beginning programmers that present, by example, the essential skills necessary to write complete, clear, and practical programs using the IBM PC, XT, or AT. More than 75 field-tested program examples are featured in each activity-rich text, enabling the PC user to become fluent in a particular programming language while learning even the most sophisticated concepts.

FORTRAN 77: Elements of Programming Style
An introduction for beginning programmers that prepares users to handle sophisticated business applications—from microeconomics to corporate business simulations—and to use and adapt many prewritten statistical programs.

COBOL: Elements of Programming Style
An in-depth introduction to one of the most widely used business data processing languages, COBOL (Common Business Oriented Language). This text shows how to manipulate data and write business programs.

True BASIC: Elements of Programming Style
A step-by-step exploration of an enhanced version of a classic language, BASIC (Beginner's All-purpose Symbolic Instruction Code). You'll learn about conditional branching, loop constructs, arrays, subroutines, functions, data files, and more.

FORTH: Elements of Programming Style
A complete introduction to FORTH (FOuRTH generation language) data structure development with information on the FORTH dictionary, stack manipulation, arithmetic operators, data declarations, variables, constants, arrays, and more.

COBOL

Elements of Programming Style

William M. Fuori

Stephen Gaughran • Louis Gioia • Michael Fuori

Hayden Book Company
A DIVISION OF HAYDEN PUBLISHING COMPANY, INC.
HASBROUCK HEIGHTS, NEW JERSEY

To my Uncle Thomas

   William M. Fuori

To my wife, Claire, and my family—Steve, Maureen, Kathy M.,
Tricia, Sheila, Coleen, Kathy D., and Jenny

   Stephen Gaughran

To my parents, Gloria and Michael, and Ann and Thomas in great
appreciation for their support

   Louis Gioia

To the memory of my grandmother

   Michael Fuori

Acquisitions Editor: RON POWERS
Production Editor: ALBERTA BODDY
Design: JIM BERNARD
Composition: ART, COPY & PRINT
Manufacturing: THE MAPLE-VAIL BOOK MANUFACTURING GROUP

Library of Congress Cataloging-in-Publication Data

COBOL: elements of programming style.

   (The Art of programming IBM personal computers)
   Includes index.
   1. COBOL (Computer program language) 2. IBM Personal
Computer—Programming. I. Fuori, William M. II. Series.
QA76.73.C25C623   1986   005.265   86-3086
ISBN 0-8104-6396-2

IBM Personal Computer is a registered trademark of International Business Machines Corp., which is not affiliated with Hayden Book Company.

Printed in the United States of America

1	2	3	4	5	6	7	8	9	
86	87	88	89	90	91	92	93	94	YEAR

PREFACE

Welcome to the world of COBOL. Since you have purchased this book, we assume that you are as committed to learning COBOL as we were to producing a self-instructional, easy-to-read, and error-free book.

The authors of this book have written a number of books over the years, each of which has been the result of our frustrations with what is available in the marketplace or from computer or software manufacturers. Our belief has always been that a book should be understandable to any reader with a strong desire to learn and a minimum level of preparation. Therefore, we elected to write this book, assuming very little preparation on the part of the reader and to build from there. As such, you might find some parts of this book very basic, but once we reach your level of preparation, you will find the presentation interesting and understandable. To make certain that the presentation would be clear to all levels of readers, this book was extensively field-tested—using readers with various and diversified backgrounds—and continuously modified until the authors were certain that they had the very best book possible on the subject.

We realized that the presentation and illustrations in this book had to be perfectly clear and absolutely free from defects because the reader will most likely be alone with the book and his or her computer. Hence, there would be no one around to answer any questions that might arise during a learning session. You can be certain of one thing—*every program or program segment shown in this book has been thoroughly tested and run on an IBM PC, XT, and AT.* In addition, complete programs are presented after each and every major concept so that you can reinforce your understanding of that concept. The authors have learned long ago that program segments can never take the place of complete programs. It is also important that the programs presented not be complicated by asides and extraneous material. These programs had to focus on the concepts presented. Once you have run some programs illustrating the basic concepts presented, you should be ready to tackle the exercises presented at the end of each chapter. We have provided you with numerous problems that are representative of the type encountered in actual practice. Your mission, should you decide to accept it, is to complete all the exercises in the book.

One of the frustrating parts of learning a programming language is that the learning process is constantly being interrupted by the need to key in programs to verify your understanding of certain concepts. This is absolutely necessary to the learning process, since there is no better way to learn than by actually playing with the computer. Thus, programs must be written, entered into the computer, compiled, and executed. You will need to use a text editor or word processor to enter your programs before you can use your COBOL diskettes to compile them. EDLIN, the text editor supplied with DOS (or a separate word processing package, if you have one), can be used for this purpose. EDLIN is not covered in this text but is explained in your DOS manual. Once the basic program is operational, there is no better way to master the concepts than to begin experimenting on your own. Take the basic version of the program and modify it to determine what affect this or that change will have on the outcome. To save the reader the many hours of keying necessary to enter these programs into the computer, we have done this for you. These programs are provided on supplemental disks, which are available separately. In addition, these supplemental disks contain all illustrated programs and the answers to the end-of-chapter questions and programs. Altogether, there are more than 100 files available for your study and use.

We hope that you will enjoy reading and learning from this book as much as we enjoyed writing it. Please write us directly or in care of the publisher and let us know your reactions. We enjoy hearing from our readers and welcome any comments that can be used to improve our books.

William M. Fuori   Stephen Gaughran   Louis Gioia   Michael Fuori

CONTENTS

CHAPTER 1

CHAPTER 2

CHAPTER 7

CHAPTER 8

CHAPTER 9

CHAPTER 10

CHAPTER 11

CHAPTER 12

CHAPTER 13

EQUIPMENT NEEDED

To use the programs in this book on an IBM Personal Computer (PC), you will need the following equipment:

Hardware

IBM PC with a minimum of 64K

Two disketter drives, one high-capacity diskette drive (1.2MB), or one diskette drive and a hard disk

Video display (80 columns)

Printer (optional, but recommended)

Software

COBOL compiler

DOS 2.0 or later revision (with EDLIN editor), or a word processor.

1

INTRODUCTION TO IBM COBOL

The introduction of the computer into the business world brought with it many new and complex problems. Prior to that event, computers had been used only for scientific purposes. Consequently, computer manufacturers and users were faced with developing a data processing system that would be both usable on existing computers and applicable to the newer, larger, more powerful computers with minimal conversion, reprogramming, and retraining costs. They were also faced with developing a single business-oriented computer language that would be usable on virtually all computers and that would replace the multitude of nonstandard computer languages that existed at the time. This new language had to be easy enough to use so that a programmer could write a typical business application program in a reasonably short period of time with all necessary documentation. As it was to be heavily used in business, it would also have to be a language that noncomputer-oriented personnel, such as accountants and auditors, could read and understand with a reasonable amount of training.

To fulfill these needs, development began on a suitable and standardized commercial programming language. In May, 1959, a committee of computer users named CODASYL (Conference On DAta SYstem Languages) was formed consisting of computer manufacturers, representatives of the federal government, and other interested parties. In April, 1960, the committee produced a report titled *COBOL (COmmon Business Oriented Language)*. A CODASYL COBOL Maintenance Committee was formed and charged with the responsibility of making needed modifications to the language. In order to make the language universally acceptable to the business community, this founding group granted unrestricted use of the language specifications to all users.

COBOL was received with tremendous success in the business world and it was apparent that the language was going to have a long and bright future. Realizing this, the United States of America Standards Institute (USASI) set out to produce COBOL specifications that were to be consistent with CODASYL specifications and were to be used as the standard COBOL by computer manufacturers. In August, 1968, their efforts resulted in USASI COBOL, or, as it is now known, ANS (American National Standard) COBOL.

One of the most significant changes of concern to programmers in general was the introduction of top-down program design. This revolutionary program design concept changed the emphasis from how to code a program to how to design a program prior to the actual coding so that the program will be as error free, reliable, easy to read, easy to modify, and easy to maintain as possible.

The COBOL language is an easy-to-learn, easy-to-read, high-level programming language principally designed for use in business or commercial applications. Some of the advantages and features of this language are:

1. COBOL programs are written using precise, easily learned English words and phrases.

2. COBOL is usable on virtually all computer systems from the small microcomputer to the largest mainframe computer system. Most recently, COBOL has been provided for microcomputers running under PC-DOS or CP/M.

3. COBOL programs written for use on one computer are usable on other computers with a minimum of change. Some COBOL compilers (Ryan McFarland's, for example) are available with run-time systems so that a COBOL program written for one of these compilers can be run on virtually any computer system with no modifications.

4. COBOL programs are written utilizing common business terminology and are therefore easily read by nonprogrammer personnel such as accountants, auditors, or business executives with only a minimal background in data processing.

5. COBOL is easily learned by individuals who do not have extensive training in high-level mathematics.

6. COBOL facilitates program testing so that programs can be tested efficiently and thoroughly.

7. Documentation of a COBOL program is relatively simple. In many cases, the COBOL program itself provides much of the documentation required.

8. COBOL is suited to top-down program design techniques.

How to use this book

This book is designed for the beginning COBOL programmer but will prove useful to the experienced COBOL programmer as well. All examples found in the book should be entered, compiled, and executed. None should be skipped since each example is designed to demonstrate a different feature of the language. There is no better way to learn COBOL than to read about a language feature and then test it immediately on your machine. Your IBM PC, XT, AT, or compatible should be within arms reach when you are reading this book so that you can gain the maximum benefits from the presentation.

After you have learned some basic concepts in the first few chapters, you should be able to write some simple programs. To make this task both interesting and challenging, special real-life problems have been provided at the end of each chapter to test your understanding of the material and, at the same time, provide interesting and thought-provoking diversions. You may choose to accept the challenge, skip it completely, or simply defer it to a later date. If you skip or defer the challenge, you can still progress to the next chapter and topic.

For your convenience, a supplemental disk is available separately that will support the presentation in the book. This disk will contain all illustrative programs together with the solutions to the end-of-chapter problems. This will save you substantial time and effort keying in and correcting the sample and review programs.

The book is written so that you may progress at your own pace. However, it is essential that you do not move on to new material without fully understanding the material just read. You should stay with a chapter or section until you understand the concepts being presented. If you do jump ahead, you may find yourself in situations that are difficult to get out of. In such cases it may be necessary to reset your computer and go back and start your session again.

This book will not simply provide an overview of the COBOL language, as so many books on the subject do. There is little point in studying a language unless you study in detail those features that set the language apart from other programming languages. Therefore, we shall study COBOL in detail.

Each of the chapters in the book is followed by review programs. If you desire more than just an overview of the COBOL language, it will be necessary for you to attempt to code and run a majority of these programs. If you don't have time to complete each of the exercises, then review the programs on the supplemental disk available separately.

GETTING STARTED

Hardware Requirements

Due to the nature of the COBOL language and of the software features supported by it, a COBOL compiler requires a certain amount of hardware resources. Typical of these requirements are those for IBM Personal Computer COBOL (Microsoft):

- 64K (kilobytes) of RAM (random access memory)
- Two diskette drives, one high-capacity diskette drive (1.2 MB), or one diskette drive and a hard disk
- Video display (80 columns)
- Printer (optional, but essential for the convenience of reviewing program listings and of course for output)

Software Requirements

- COBOL compiler
- DOS 1.1 or a later revision (with EDLIN editor); or a word processor such as WordStar, VisiWord, or WordPerfect—for use in writing the programs

To compile and execute a COBOL program requires three sets of programs:

- Compiler programs
- Link programs
- Runtime programs

The **compiler** translates the COBOL source program into the object code. The **link** program brings together any needed library modules or subroutines and your compiled program to form a relocatable object program. In *mainframe* versions of COBOL this is sufficient to execute a program in conjunction with the appropriate operating system. Most microcomputer versions of COBOL also require a **runtime** program which is resident in RAM every time the program is executed. These programs will be discussed later, but they are a significant factor affecting both the execution time of your program and, more important, the amount of RAM necessary to run the program. IBM PC COBOL requires 32K for the runtime system.

All of the above-mentioned programs are included with your COBOL compiler. Runtime programs may be acquired separately in the event that you intend compiling your programs on one personal computer and executing them on another. For the remainder of this text, we shall assume that an IBM PC, XT, AT, or compatible system will be used for both purposes.

Additional Software Aids

In order to prepare your COBOL program, you must first create a COBOL source file. If you have written BASIC programs for your PC, XT, or AT you should know that COBOL is handled differently than BASIC. In BASIC, each statement is interpreted as it is entered. If a statement is entered correctly, it will be inserted into the program appropriately so that the program is created in line-number sequence. COBOL, however, is a **batch** language. That is, an entire or complete program (complete according to the rules for a complete program) must first be entered into a file just as if it were data. This may be done with the EDLIN text editor provided with your DOS, or with a word processor such as WordStar, VisiWord, etc.

Since most personal computer users will have a word processor program for other purposes, and since we believe that program preparation is easier using a word processor, the authors recommend this method.

Important Hint: *If you use a word processor, be certain to create your programs with the nondocument feature so that no special text formatting characters are inserted into the program.*

While you are creating your source file, you will not be interacting with the COBOL compiler; as was mentioned above, such interaction occurs only when you have finished writing your program and begin the compilation step. During the create operation (typing in your program) you will be creating a text file that will become your COBOL source program. This source program will not be checked for syntax or coding accuracy until you actually compile it.

Protecting Your Investment

As you have already discovered, the purchase of a COBOL compiler is a significant investment. The first thing you want to do is to *back up* or make a copy of your original disks and put the original disks in a safe place. You can use the COPY utility as described in your DOS manual. If you have enough disk capacity (a double-sided, double-density drive or a high-capacity (1.2 MB) drive), you can get all of the COBOL programs (compiler, link, and runtime) on the same disk. This will make it much more convenient to compile, link, and run your programs.

We are assuming that you have two disk drives or a disk drive and a hard disk.* If you are copying your original COBOL COMPILER diskettes to one or two backup diskettes, follow the instructions on the opposite page at the left. If, however, you wish to copy the original COBOL diskettes onto a hard disk, follow the instructions at the right.

RUNNING A SAMPLE PROGRAM

We have included a sample COBOL program as Fig. 1–1. This first program is a simple one that will calculate the future value of an investment with interest calculated yearly. The input will be three quantities:

1. The original balance, a five-digit integer

2. The interest rate, a two-position decimal fraction

3. The number of years, a two-position integer

The output will be the new balance at the end of the number of years specified.

Note that Fig. 1–1 (page 8) shows the program on a COBOL coding sheet. This has been done to emphasize the importance in COBOL of following the specified format for COBOL statements. This will be ex-

---

*If you have a PC AT system with a high-capacity drive (1.2 MB) only, follow the instructions in the Application Setup Guide that is provided with DOS 3.0 or higher.

plained later in Chapter 2. As you can see, certain entries begin in column 8 whereas others begin in column 12. This format *must* be followed in creating the source program; you can use either the space bar or the tab feature of your text editor to move over the required number of columns. You will also observe that certain words contain the hyphen character (-). This observation is also important, because *spaces are not permitted within COBOL words.*

Two-Drive System	One Drive, One Hard Disk
1. Format one DS/DD or high-capacity diskette or two SS/DD diskettes. Be certain to copy the system onto each of these. If you are not familiar with this procedure, refer to your DOS manual.	**1.** If you intend to make a sub-directory (DOS 2.0 or higher), then you must set up the subdirectory and then change the current directory to this subdirectory by typing in the following:

2. Place the COBOL COMPILER diskette in the default drive A and a formatted scratch diskette in drive B.	`C: <CR>`
	`C>`
	
	`MD your directory name <CR>`
	`C>`
	
	`CD your directory name <CR>`
	`C>`

3. Type in `COPY *.* B: <CR>` This will copy all files from the COBOL diskette to your scratch diskette in drive B with the *same filenames and extensions.* (Note: \<CR\> stands for carriage return and is accomplished by pressing the [↵] key.)	If you do not want a subdirectory, then simply type: `C: <CR>`
4. If you have DS/DD drives and diskettes, leave the scratch diskette in B, but if you are using SS/DD drives or diskettes, then put a new formatted scratch diskette in B. In either case, place the COBOL LIBRARY diskette in drive A and again type in `COPY *.* B: <CR>`	**2.** Place an original COBOL diskette in drive A. **3.** Type in `COPY A:*.* <CR>` **4.** Repeat step 2 for the remaining original COBOL diskette.
5. Remove all diskettes, making certain to write-protect your new copies by covering the file-protect notch on the right edge of the diskette.	**5.** Type in `A: <CR>` **6.** Remove all original diskettes and put them in a safe place.

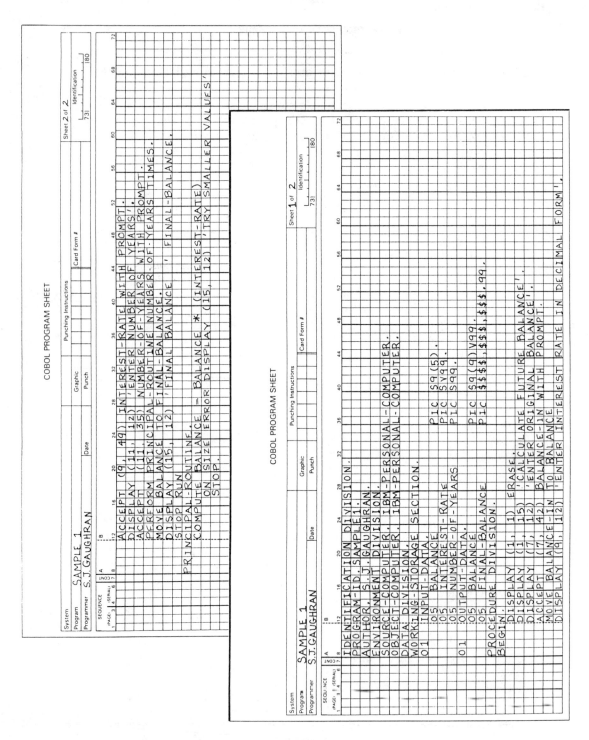

Fig. 1–1. Program SAMPLE1 on coding sheet.

Creating the Source Program

The source program must be created using the text editor EDLIN provided with your DOS operating system or with a word processor. The filename for this program must have the extension .COB; we will use the name SAMPLE1.COB. The COBOL compiler will not process a file that does not have this extension. Later we shall see the extensions .OBJ, .LST, and .EXE for the object file, list, and execute files, respectively.

The program SAMPLE1.COB is available on the supplemental disk, and may be compiled, linked, and executed directly.

Compiling the Program

Following are the steps required to compile the sample COBOL program after it has been typed and saved as SAMPLE1.COB. If you are using an XT or PC equipped with a hard disk, refer to the Appendix at the end of this chapter for details concerning compiling and linking COBOL programs.

1. Change the default drive to B—that is, type in B:. If this is done correctly, the machine should respond with B>.

2. Insert the diskette with your program into drive B. If you have just created the program, it will be in B already.

3. Insert the COBOL diskette into drive A.

4. Type

```
A:COBOL  <CR>
```

5. The compiler responds with a request for the name of the source file as follows:

```
Source filename [.COB]:
```

You respond by typing in the name of the file—in this instance,

```
SAMPLE1 <CR>
```

6. The compiler responds with the prompt

```
Object filename [SAMPLE1.OBJ]:
```

If this is the desired name, then just press <CR>.

7. The final prompt prior to compilation gives us the chance to create a listing of the source program after it has been compiled. The prompt is

```
Source Listing [NUL.LST]:
```

If we enter a filename, for example,

```
SAMPLE1 <CR>
```

then a file (SAMPLE1.LST) will be created on the default drive B containing the source program and compiler messages.

Even if you have copied the program correctly, you will see the warning diagnostic message

```
0031:   /W/ TERMINAL PERIOD ASSUMED ABOVE
   1 Error  or Warning
```

We purposely created this minor error by leaving out the period after the STOP RUN statement in the BEGIN paragraph. This should be corrected, but the program will still execute with a **W** or **Warning** type of message and error.

If you see more error messages than the one shown, it means that you have probably made some errors in entering the source program. This is very easy to do, so if you have more error messages, carefully check not only the spelling of all the entries but also the punctuation and proper column placement. (Remember our earlier comments about column 8 and column 12.)

To correct the warning on line 31 or any other typing errors in the source program requires that you reload your text editor and call in the source program to make the necessary changes. You will in fact be creating an entirely new version of the source program, and unless you change its name, the new version will replace the previous one. After the corrections are made, repeat the compile steps described above. Do not be overly concerned if you still see some diagnostic messages: COBOL is quite specific about correct formatting and punctuation. You will become familiar with these rules as you proceed and create additional programs.

> *This program is available on the supplemental disk as SAMPLE1A.COB.*

Linking the Program

After the source program compiles successfully, you will see the message

```
No Errors or Warnings
```

on the screen. If you were not able to or did not copy both original diskettes onto one DS/DD diskette, and you have two diskettes for the COBOL compiler, then you should remove the COBOL compiler disk from drive A and insert the one labeled LIBRARY into it. If you were able to copy both original disks onto a single DS/DD diskette, then no action is required.

You may now proceed with the linking as follows:

1. Type in

   ```
   A:LINK <CR>
   ```

2. The computer will respond with the prompt

   ```
   Object Modules [OBJ]:
   ```

   You should enter the name that was assigned to the object program—SAMPLE1 in this example:

   ```
   SAMPLE1 <CR>
   ```

3. The computer responds with the prompt

   ```
   Run File [SAMPLE1.EXE]:
   ```

   This will default to a diskette file if you press <CR>.

4. The next prompt is

   ```
   List File [NUL.MAP]:
   ```

   which gives you an opportunity to get a list of the object modules.

We will use the *default option* here and press <CR> so that no list file is created.

5. The final prompt is

   Libraries [LIB]:

which will default to the library programs necessary to complete the link process if you press the <CR> key.

At this point you should see the following prompt for the default drive on the screen, indicating that the link step has been completed:

   B>

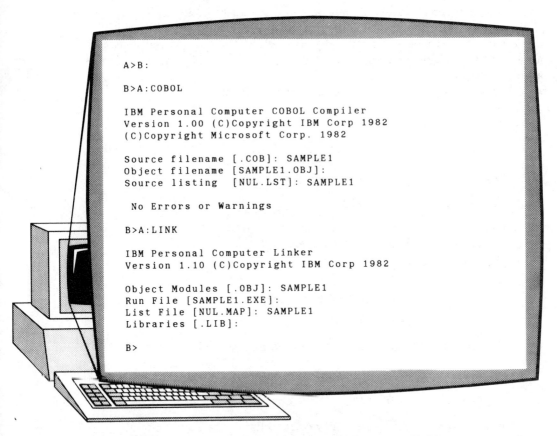

```
A>B:

B>A:COBOL

IBM Personal Computer COBOL Compiler
Version 1.00 (C)Copyright IBM Corp 1982
(C)Copyright Microsoft Corp. 1982

Source filename [.COB]: SAMPLE1
Object filename [SAMPLE1.OBJ]:
Source listing  [NUL.LST]: SAMPLE1

 No Errors or Warnings

B>A:LINK

IBM Personal Computer Linker
Version 1.10 (C)Copyright IBM Corp 1982

Object Modules [.OBJ]: SAMPLE1
Run File [SAMPLE1.EXE]:
List File [NUL.MAP]: SAMPLE1
Libraries [.LIB]:

B>
```

**Fig. 1–2.   Screen entries for compiling and linking
the sample program.**

Type in the name of your .EXE file containing your compiled and linked program—in this case SAMPLE1 (.EXE is not necessary). If for some reason this file cannot be found, the message

```
File Not Found
```

will be displayed. This means the system cannot find your compiled and linked program. You should then type in **DIR** and display the DIRectory of the default drive B to see if SAMPLE1.EXE is present. If it is not, then check back through the previous steps to determine where an error might have occurred. Then repeat the above compilation or linking process until the file SAMPLE1.EXE is produced. Assuming that everything is correct, the program SAMPLE1 will be run.

Figure 1–2 is a summary of all the screen entries up to this point.

When program SAMPLE1.EXE is executed, the screen shown in Fig. 1–3 is displayed, one line at a time. You will enter the original balance, up to five digits; the interest rate, as a decimal fraction; and the number of years, up to 99.

Checking Your Results

When a program is first run, you should have some idea of the expected answer in order to test the correctness of the program's logic

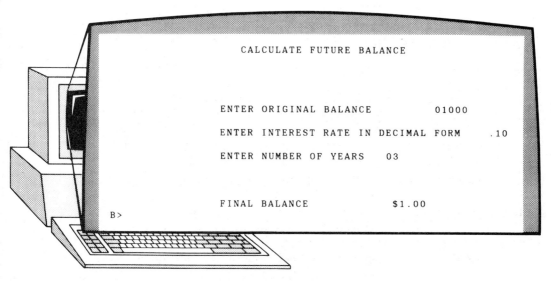

Fig. 1–3. Screen output for sample program.

and the arithmetic computations involved. In response to the prompts shown in Fig. 1–3, enter the data shown in the figure.

We do not need to do very much calculating to know that if you invest $1,000 at 10% for three years, the final balance should not be $1.00 but rather more like $1,331.00. If you check the formula in PRINCIPAL-ROUTINE in Fig. 1–1, you will see that the BALANCE during each repetition of the program is mistakenly a fraction of the previous balance rather than an increased value. The formula should read

```
COMPUTE BALANCE = BALANCE * (1 + INTEREST-RATE) . . .
```

The 1 added to the interest rate ensures that the BALANCE is included every time the calculation is repeated.

We saw earlier, in the warning about a missing period, how **syntax errors,** i.e., violations of COBOL coding rules, are indicated. Here we see the effect of what is called an **execution** or **logic error.** The program runs, but because of an erroneous formula the answer is not correct. Occasionally, an execution or logic error can cause unreconcilable problems that force the system to abort the program.

Make the required change in your source program and execute the compile and link program again. If you then enter the values 1000, .10, and 3, the result will be the correct value of $1,331.

The corrected version of this program is available on the supplemental disk as SAMPLE1B.COB.

You can make another kind of error by entering values that are too large, an error that is particularly likely in a program such as SAMPLE1, which depends on the repetition of a calculation. In SAMPLE1 we have allowed for a final balance of up to 999 million dollars. If your interest rate or the number of years is too high, the final result can exceed this amount. Try it; the message

```
TRY SMALLER VALUES
```

will be displayed by the program. There is really nothing to correct in the program since in its present form it will handle any reasonable dollar amounts. We merely mention this kind of error to illustrate that COBOL is a language that depends on declared field sizes in both numeric and alphanumeric data. Had we not included an out-of-range test in the program and a FINAL-BALANCE beyond the capacity of the field occurred, FINAL-BALANCE would have been truncated with no indication that an error had occurred.

Calculating compound interest once a year is not very common today. What changes to program SAMPLE1 would be required to compound the interest on a quarterly, monthly, or daily basis? To do any of these, you must first multiply the number of years by 4, 12, or 365, as the case may be, outside of the PRINCIPAL-ROUTINE and then change the formula to divide the interest rate by the same value—4, 12, or 365. Try it; the value of $1,000 at 10% for 3 years compounded quarterly will be $1,344.89 rather than $1,331. You might try it for monthly and daily compounding also. Bear in mind, though, that if you do it daily for a number of years, the program may take a little while to run!

The supplemental disk contains the program SAMPLE1C.COB, which you can use to determine your return on an investment for which interest is compounded daily.

COMPACT COMPILATION AND LINKING COMMANDS

As you can see, the process of compiling and linking a COBOL program can require a number of responses from you. In the above procedure, we input each response as it was needed by the compiler or linker. We could, however, have given all the responses to the compiler or linker initially, and it would have referenced and used them as needed. This would have eliminated the need for us to constantly monitor the screen awaiting the request for input. The point at which we can provide all these inputs to the compiler is at the beginning of the compilation and again at the beginning of the linking. All commands discussed here will apply to compiling and executing on the XT, AT, or a PC equipped with a hard disk, except that references to floppy disks must be to the hard disk.

Compact Compilation Commands

Assuming that we have the COBOL compiler in drive A, our source program in drive B, and drive B specified as the default drive, the compact commands for pass one of the compilation of a program are

```
A:COBOL source, object, proglist
```

where **source** is the name of the source program, **object** is the name of the object program, and **proglist** is where we want the source program listing.

No extensions are required for these files, as the default extensions of .COB, .OBJ, and .LST are respectively assumed. If no program listing is desired, it should be assigned to the null device. This is accomplished by placing the word NUL in the relative position occupied by the entry. For example, for the program SAMPLE1B.COB, the entry

```
A:COBOL SAMPLE1B,SAMPLE1B,NUL <CR>
```

would only save the object program in SAMPLE1B.OBJ. If two consecutive commas are used in the relative position occupied by an entry, the default option will be assumed for that entry. The default option for an entry is the source program name followed by the appropriate extension (.OBJ, .LST, and so on).

If one desires the program listing to be displayed on the screen or printed on the printer, the program listing entries that should be used are **CON** and **LPT1,** respectively. That is, the entries

```
A:COBOL SAMPLE1B,,LPT1 <CR>
```

would cause the object program to be saved as SAMPLE1B.OBJ and the program listing to appear on the printer.

Compact Linking Commands

The compact commands for linking the compiled program are

```
A:LINK object, exeprog, objmap, library
```

where **object** is the name of the object program produced by the compilation, **exeprog** is the name of the executable program, **objmap** is the name of the file containing a mapping of the object code, and **library** is the name of the runtime library to be used.

No extensions are required for these files, as the default extensions of .OBJ, .EXE, .MAP, and .LIB are respectively assumed. The object file name must be specified and must be the same as was specified in the previous compilation command. As a .MAP file is not essential, it can be assigned to a NUL device. The other file entries must be specified explicitly or assigned to the default file by placing ',,' in the relative position occupied by the entry. Thus, the entry

```
A:LINK SAMPLE1B,,NUL,, <CR>
```

would effectively create an executable program SAMPLE1B.EXE, eliminate a MAP of the object program, and use the standard default libraries, which must be referenced from drive A.

It is suggested at this time that you run the version of the sample program with all syntax and logical errors removed and use single-line compact commands. Place a copy of your source program in drive B and your COBOL compiler in drive A. For a two-disk drive system with the COBOL compiler and linker on one disk in drive A, the following single-line commands should be typed in:

```
B: <CR>
   (wait for the response B>)
A:COBOL SAMPLE1,,,<CR>
   (wait for compilation to finish)
A:LINK SAMPLE1,,,,<CR>
   (wait for the linker to finish)
SAMPLE1 <CR>
   (the program should begin executing)
```

If your COBOL compiler and library programs are on different diskettes, you will have to make certain that the correct diskette is installed in drive A before compiling or linking.

Making Batch Files

There is one additional thing that we can do to simplify the process of compiling and executing COBOL programs: construct a file of commands containing all the commands we issued above in the order required. This type of file is referred to as a **batch command file**, or simply a **batch file**. The only things that we would have to enter to run any program contained in this book or on the supplemental disk are the names of the source, object, and executable program files.

A batch file is an executable file and must be assigned the extension .BAT. It can be created with the editor or word processor and must contain only one DOS command per line. When the batch file is executed, the system executes the commands as if they were individually typed in from the keyboard. We must make provision for the fact that in a batch file the source, object, and executable program filenames can vary. We do this by placing %n in the file each time a filename or other data will be required from the keyboard. In addition, each % entry is assigned a number so that it can be distinguished from other entries being input. The first entry should be assigned the %n entry %1, the second %2, and so on. You might be wondering, How and when do I communicate to the batch file the values to be used by it? The answer to this is simple: we provide the data as arguments to the name of the batch file at the time we execute it. Simply stated, we provide the names of the required files or arguments immediately after the name of the batch file and separated by commas. For example, the entry

```
COBEX SAMPLE1B,SAMPLE1C <CR>
```

could be used to call the batch file COBEX.BAT and communicate the fact that wherever %1 appears in the batch file SAMPLE1B is to be substituted, and wherever %2 appears SAMPLE1C is to be substituted. SAMPLE1B and SAMPLE1C are the arguments to the batch file in this particular case.

If you have a two-drive system and you have all compiler and linker files on a single DS/DD diskette in drive A, the batch file shown below can be used to compile, link, and execute all programs in this book. If you are using an IBM AT, XT, or a PC equipped with a hard disk, this batch file will work if all references to drive A are changed to drive C and references to drive B are changed to drive A. At this time it is suggested that you use an editor or word processor of your choice to create this file. An appropriate and handy name would be COBEX.BAT.

This batch file is available on the supplemental disk as COBEX.BAT for your use in compiling and linking all programs in this book. If you are using a hard-disk system, use the program HDCOBEX.BAT, which is also on the supplemental disk. To use HDCOBEX.BAT, you must make certain to copy COMMAND.COM and ASSIGN.COM from your DOS diskette into the directory or subdirectory containing the COBOL compiler.

```
REM Batch file to compile and execute program %1
B:
A:COBOL %1,,,
REM   If no errors press any key
PAUSE else press Ctrl-Break
A:LINK %1,,,,
REM   If compilation completed successfully, %1 will execute
PAUSE else press Ctrl-Break
%1
A:
```

This batch file can still be used if your compiler files are on separate disks. All that is required is that you insert the appropriate diskettes at the PAUSE.

The **REM** entries appear on the screen during the execution of the batch file to let you know what is happening. The **PAUSE** command, on the other hand, halts execution of the batch file momentarily in order to allow you to input any keystroke either to resume execution or to break. The PAUSE command in this batch file serves the latter purpose. PAUSE commands can be used to allow you to insert the appropriate compiler and linker diskettes into drive A if you do not have them all on a single diskette. The remaining commands should be familiar: they are the compilation and linking commands we have previously been keying in individually or in single-line compact form.

Execute this program at this time using the command

```
COBEX source
```

where **source** is the name of your COBOL source program. This filename must have the extension .COB. For the sample program, the entry would be COBEX SAMPLE1.

The above batch file is very useful and timesaving if the program has no errors. However, if the program has syntax or logic errors, it may be necessary to remove the COBOL compiler from drive A, install your editor or word processor there, correct the error(s), remove the editor or word processor, return the COBOL disk to drive A, and recompile.

A batch file that will allow you to correct errors in the program and recompile it is:

```
REM Batch file to correct syntax or logic errors in %1.
A:
REM Place disk containing editor or word processor in drive A.
PAUSE Press any key.
REM Correct source program in drive B.
```

```
%2
REM Replace editor or word processor with COBOL disk.
PAUSE Press any key.
B:
REM Calling in batch file COBEX.BAT to execute
       corrected program.
A:COBEX %1
```

It is suggested that you use an editor or word processor of your choice to create this batch file. To simplify its use, the file should be copied onto the diskette containing the source program. The reason for this is that there may be a number of correction steps before your program runs successfully. If the program is called COBFIX.BAT, it can be accessed initially by

```
B:COBFIX source, editor
```

where **source** is the name of the COBOL program to be corrected and **editor** is the command to access the editor or word processor that is to be used to correct the source program. For example, EDLIN could be used to access the editor—or WS to access MicroPro's WordStar, if this is the word processor you have. Entering the above command will cause a message to be printed out telling you to put your editor or word processor disk in drive A and press any key. The system should then access the editor or word processor. Using the commands built into whichever it is you are using, you should be able to correct the program, save the corrected version, and exit the editor or word processor. After that, the current batch file will call the batch file COBEX.BAT and begin compiling and linking the corrected source program. The entire procedure is an example of using one batch file to call another batch file.

The batch file COBFIX.BAT is available on the supplemental disk.

To summarize the above, the steps should be performed as follows:

1. Place the disk containing your COBOL compiler and batch file COBEX.BAT in drive A (the default drive) and the disk containing your source program and the batch file COBFIX.BAT in drive B.

2. Type in the command

```
COBOL source
```

3. If there are no errors in your source program, it should start executing. If there are errors, enter Ctrl-Break and stop compiling or linking. Then invoke the second batch file COBFIX.BAT with the command

```
COBFIX source, editor
```

4. The above command should be repeated each time the program is executed and an error occurs, until all errors are corrected.

5. After all errors have been removed and the program has executed successfully once, it can be executed again and again by simply calling the executable file (the file on drive B which has the source filename and the extension .EXE—it is not necessary to enter the extension .EXE).

EXERCISES

---

1. Describe the major reasons for the introduction and continued use of the COBOL language.

2. What are some of the advantages and disadvantages of the COBOL language?

3. When are problems suitable for a computerized solution? To what kinds of problems is COBOL particularly well-suited?

4. Describe some problems that you believe are not well suited to a COBOL solution.

5. What is the purpose of program documentation? What is entailed?

6. Describe the major aspects of and the need for (a) problem analysis, and (b) program design, coding, testing, and debugging.

7. Describe the kinds of errors (besides coding errors) that can **occur** in a computer program.

8. Enter the program SAMPLE1 included in this chapter. Compile and run the program using the regular COBOL compiling and linking commands.

9. Enter the DOS batch commands, COBEX.BAT. Compile and run SAMPLE1 under control of this batch file.

Solutions to the exercises are provided on the supplemental disk.

APPENDIX:
COMPILING AND LINKING A COBOL PROGRAM ON THE XT OR AT

Compiling the Program

Following are the steps required to compile the sample COBOL program in Fig. 1-1 after it has been typed and saved as SAMPLE1.COB.

1. If your COBOL compiler is in a subdirectory, establish this subdirectory as the current directory; otherwise, type **C:** and proceed directly to step 2. Type

```
C: <CR>
C>

CD\ path <CR>
C>
```

2. Insert the diskette with your program into drive A. If you have just created the program, it will be in A already.

3. Copy your program to the hard disk (drive C) with the command

```
COPY A:SAMPLE1.COB <CR>
```

4. Change the default drive to A. That is, type in A:. If this is done correctly, the machine should respond with A>.

5. Place your DOS diskette in drive A.

6. Type in

```
COPY ASSIGN.COM C: <CR>
```

followed by

```
ASSIGN A=C <CR>
```

7. Type

```
COBOL <CR>
```

8. The compiler responds with a request for the name of the source file as follows:

```
Source filename [.COB]:
```

You respond by typing in the name of the file—in this instance,

```
SAMPLE1 <CR>
```

9. The compiler responds with the prompt

```
Object filename [SAMPLE1.OBJ]:
```

If this is the desired name, then just press <CR>.

10. The final prompt prior to compilation gives us the chance to create a listing of the source program after it has been compiled. The prompt is

```
Source listing [NUL.LST]:
```

If we enter a filename, for example,

```
SAMPLE1 <CR>
```

then a file (in this case, SAMPLE1.LST) containing the source program and compiler messages will be created on the default drive A (which is actually the hard disk because of the assignment made in step 6 above).

Even if you have copied the program correctly, you will see
the warning diagnostic message

```
0031:   /W/ TERMINAL PERIOD ASSUMED ABOVE.
    1  Error or Warning
```

We purposely created this minor error by leaving out the period
after the STOP RUN statement in the BEGIN paragraph. This should
be corrected, but the program will still execute with a **W** or **Warning**
type of message and error.

If you see more error messages than the one shown, it means that
you have probably made some errors in entering the source program.
This is very easy to do, so if you have more error messages, carefully
check not only the spelling of all the entries but also the punctuation
and proper column placement. (Remember our earlier comments about
column 8 and column 12.)

To correct the warning on line 31 or any other typing errors in the
source program requires that you reload your text editor and call in
the source program to make the necessary changes. You will in fact be
creating an entirely new version of the source program, and unless you
change its name, the new version will replace the previous one. After
the corrections are made, repeat the compile steps described above.
Do not be overly concerned if you still see some diagnostic messages:
COBOL is quite specific about correct formatting and punctuation.
You will become familiar with these rules as you proceed and create
additional programs.

---

*This program is available on the supplemental disk as
SAMPLE1A.COB.*

Linking the Program

After the source program compiles successfully, you will see the
message

```
No Errors or Warnings
```

on the screen. You may now proceed with the linking as follows:

1. Type in

   `LINK <CR>`

2. The computer will respond with the prompt

   `Object Modules [OBJ]:`

Enter the name to be assigned to the object program—SAMPLE1 in this example:

   `SAMPLE1 <CR>`

3. The computer responds with the prompt

   `Run File [SAMPLE1.EXE]:`

This will default to C:SAMPLE1.EXE if you press <CR>.

4. The next prompt is

   `List File [NUL.MAP]:`

which gives you an opportunity to get a listing of the object modules. We will use the *default option* here and press <CR> so that no list file is created.

5. The final prompt is

   `Libraries [LIB]:`

while will default to the library programs necessary to complete the link process if you press the <CR> key.

At this point you should see the prompt

   `A>`

for the default drive on the screen, indicating that the link step has been completed. To return control to drive A, it is necessary to change the previous ASSIGNment. This can be accomplished with the statement

   `ASSIGN <CR>`

A second look at Fig. 1–1 will tell you how the compiled and linked program can be executed and verified for correctness.

Compact Linking Commands

The concept of compact linking commands is the same for the hard-disk system as for systems equipped with two diskettes. The only differences are as in the long form: the COBOL original disks and the source program must exist on the hard disk mentioned in the current directory, and all references must be to this drive (generally, drive C). A sequence of compact commands to compile and link the corrected sample program would be:

```
C:
    (Wait for the response C>.)
ASSIGN A=C  <CR>
COBOL SAMPLE1,,,  <CR>
    (Wait for the compilation to complete.)
LINK SAMPLE1,,,,  <CR>
    (Wait for the linker to finish.)
SAMPLE1
    (Program execution will begin.)
ASSIGN  <CR>
```

2

COBOL FUNDAMENTALS

After it has been determined that a problem is suitable for a computerized solution and the particular programming language to be used has been agreed upon, the programmer is ready to proceed with the actual programming of the application. Before the actual COBOL instruction is introduced, there are certain fundamentals that must be understood. Among these are the COBOL character set, COBOL words, constants, rules of punctuation, the general format of COBOL statements, and the organization of a COBOL program.

COBOL CHARACTER SET

The symbols in the character set used by the COBOL language are subdivided into three types of characters:

1. Alphabetic characters

2. Numeric characters

3. Special characters

Figure 2-1 illustrates the complete COBOL character set. Only these characters are acceptable for use in the COBOL language.

Fig. 2–1. COBOL character set

(in ASCII collating sequence beginning with the highest value—*not* the same as the sequence used on larger IBM computer systems)

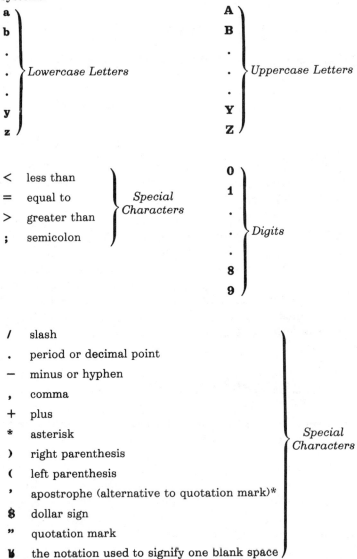

a
b
.
.
.
y
z
} Lowercase Letters

A
B
.
.
.
Y
Z
} Uppercase Letters

< less than
= equal to
> greater than
; semicolon
} Special Characters

0
1
.
.
.
8
9
} Digits

/ slash
. period or decimal point
— minus or hyphen
, comma
+ plus
* asterisk
) right parenthesis
(left parenthesis
' apostrophe (alternative to quotation mark)*
$ dollar sign
" quotation mark
ʙ the notation used to signify one blank space
} Special Characters

*In IBM PC COBOL, either the single (') or double (") quotation mark may be used. In this book we use the single (') quotation mark common to IBM mainframe versions of COBOL.

COBOL WORDS

In the COBOL language only the alphabetic characters, the numeric characters, and one special character—the hyphen (-)—are allowed in the formation of words. Specifically, a COBOL word:

1. Contains from 1 to 30 characters consisting of digits, letters, and/ or the special character, the hyphen (-).

2. Must not begin or end with a hyphen.

3. Must not contain any blanks (spaces).

The blank in COBOL is used as a word separator. A COBOL word is said to be terminated when a blank (space), period, right parenthesis, comma, or semicolon is encountered.

COBOL words consist of two general types:

1. Reserved words

2. Names

Reserved Words

A COBOL **reserved word** is one that has a predefined meaning to the COBOL compiler. For example, the COBOL reserved word ADD means to the COBOL compiler that data items are to be combined under the operation of addition. In general, reserved words are used to identify program units or parts of entries (DATA DIVISION), to indicate specific values or functional meanings (ZEROS, EQUAL), or to indicate a given action (ADD, READ, WRITE). Each reserved word has a unique predefined meaning and must not be substituted for, altered, added to, or used for a purpose other than the specific one for which it was intended. Reserved words are shown in capital letters in this text. A complete list of COBOL reserved words is given in Fig. 2–2.

Fig. 2–2. IBM PC COBOL reserved words

A plus sign (+) indicates additional words required by IBM Personal Computer COBOL for interactive screens, debug extensions, and packed decimal format.

A solid box (■) indicates Standard COBOL reserved words that are not reserved in IBM COBOL. For compatibility, you should avoid using these words as filenames, data-names, and variables in your program.

ACCEPT	BLOCK	COMP-0
ACCESS	BOTTOM	+COMP-3
ADD	BY	CONFIGURATION
ADVANCING		CONTAINS
AFTER	CALL	■ CONTROL(S)
ALL	■ CANCEL	COPY
ALPHABETIC	■ CD	■ CORR(ESPONDING)
■ ALSO	■ CF	COUNT
ALTER	■ CH	CURRENCY
■ ALTERNATE	CHAIN	
AND	CHAINING	DATA
ARE	CHARACTER(S)	DATE
AREA(S)	■ CLOCK-UNITS	DATE-COMPILED
ASCENDING	CLOSE	DATE-WRITTEN
+ASCII	■ COBOL	DAY
ASSIGN	■ CODE	■ DE(TAIL)
AT	CODE-SET	DEBUGGING
AUTHOR	+COL	■ DEBUG-CONTENTS
AUTO	COLLATING	■ DEBUG-ITEM
+AUTO-SKIP	COLUMN	■ DEBUG-NAME
	COMMA	■ DEBUG-SUB-1
+BACKGROUND-COLOR	■ COMMUNICATION	■ DEBUG-SUB-2
+BEEP	COMP	■ DEBUG-SUB-3
BEFORE	COMPUTATIONAL	DECIMAL-POINT
BELL	COMPUTATIONAL-0	DECLARATIVES
BLANK	+COMPUTATIONAL-3	DELETE
BLINK	COMPUTE	DELIMITED

Fig. 2–2. (*continued*)

DELIMITER	EXIT	■ INDICATE
DEPENDING	EXTEND	INITIAL
DESCENDING		■ INITIATE
■ DESTINATION	FD	INPUT
■ DISABLE	FILE	INPUT-OUTPUT
+DISK	FILE-CONTROL	INSPECT
DISPLAY	+FILE-ID	INSTALLATION
DIVIDE	FILLER	INTO
DIVISION	■ FINAL	INVALID
DOWN	FIRST	IS
■ DUPLICATES	FOOTING	I-O
DYNAMIC	FOR	I-O CONTROL
	+FOREGROUND-COLOR	
■ EGI	FROM	JUST(IFIED)
ELSE	+FULL	
■ EMI		KEY
+EMPTY-CHECK	■ GENERATE	
■ ENABLE	GIVING	LABEL
END	GO	■ LAST
END-OF-PAGE	GREATER	LEADING
■ ENTER	■ GROUP	LEFT
ENVIRONMENT		+LEFT-JUSTIFY
EOP	■ HEADING	■ LENGTH
EQUAL	+HIGHLIGHT	+LENGTH-CHECK
+ERASE	HIGH-VALUE(S)	LESS
ERROR		■ LIMIT(S)
ESCAPE	IDENTIFICATION	+LIN
■ ESI	IF	LINAGE
■ EVERY	IN	LINAGE-COUNTER
EXCEPTION	INDEX	LINE(S)
+EXHIBIT	INDEXED	■ LINE-COUNTER

Fig. 2–2. (*continued*)

LINKAGE	OR	REDEFINES
LOCK	ORGANIZATION	■ REEL
LOW-VALUE(S)	OUTPUT	■ REFERENCES
	OVERFLOW	RELATIVE
MEMORY		RELEASE
MERGE	PAGE	■ REMAINDER
■ MESSAGE	■ PAGE-COUNTER	REMOVAL
MODE	PERFORM	■ RENAMES
MODULES	■ PF	REPLACING
MOVE	■ PH	■ REPORT(S)
■ MULTIPLE	PIC(TURE)	■ REPORTING
MULTIPLY	PLUS	+ REQUIRED
	POINTER	RERUN
+ NAMES	■ POSITION	RESERVE
NATIVE	POSITIVE	RESET
NEGATIVE	+ PRINTER	RETURN
NEXT	PROCEDURE(S)	■ REVERSED
■ NO	PROCEED	+ REVERSE-VIDEO
+ NO-ECHO	PROGRAM	■ REWIND
NOT	PROGRAM-ID	REWRITE
NUMBER	+ PROMPT	■ RF
NUMERIC		■ RH
	■ QUEUE	RIGHT
OBJECT-COMPUTER	QUOTE	+ RIGHT-JUSTIFY
OCCURS		ROUNDED
OF	RANDOM	RUN
■ OFF	■ RD	
OMITTED	READ	SAME
ON	+ READY	SCREEN
OPEN	■ RECEIVE	■ SD
■ OPTIONAL	RECORD(S)	SEARCH

Fig. 2–2. (*continued*)

SECTION	+ SWTICH-1	UNSTRING
SECURE	+ SWITCH-2	UNTIL
SECURITY	+ SWITCH-3	UP
■ SEGMENT	+ SWITCH-4	+ UPDATE
■ SEGMENT-LIMIT	+ SWITCH-5	UPON
SELECT	+ SWITCH-6	USAGE
■ SEND	+ SWITCH-7	USE
SENTENCE	+ SWITCH-8	+ USER
SEPARATE	■ SYMBOLIC	USING
SEQUENCE	SYNC(HRONIZED)	
SEQUENTIAL		VALUE(S)
SET	■ TABLE	VARYING
SIGN	TALLYING	
SIZE	■ TAPE	WHEN
SORT	■ TERMINAL	WITH
SORT-MERGE	■ TERMINATE	WORDS
■ SOURCE	■ TEXT	WORKING-STORAGE
SOURCE-COMPUTER	THAN	WRITE
SPACE(S)	THROUGH	
+ SPACE-FILL	THRU	ZERO((E)S)
SPECIAL-NAMES	TIME	+ ZERO-FILL
STANDARD	TIMES	
STANDARD-1	TO	+
START	TOP	−
STATUS	+ TRACE	* ,
STOP	TRAILING	/
STRING	+ TRAILING-SIGN	**
■ SUB-QUEUE-1,2,3,	■ TYPE	>
SUBTRACT		<
■ SUM	+ UNDERLINE	=
■ SUPPRESS	■ UNIT	

Names

We shall initially concern ourselves with four general types of programmer-supplied names used in COBOL programs:

1. Data-names

2. Condition-names

3. Procedure-names

4. Special-names

The rules for the formation of a name in COBOL are:

1. The name must conform to the rules governing the formation of a COBOL word.

2. Except for procedure-names, a name must contain at least one letter of the alphabet.

A **data-name** is a programmer-supplied name or label for any unit of data within a COBOL program. The programmer must assign a distinct data-name to each data item in the program.

Some examples of valid COBOL data-names are:

```
A
BALANCE
A-314
NUMBER-OF-YEARS
YEAR-TO-DATE-GROSS
STOCK-NUMBER-46013
```

It is important to note that the value of the unit of data being stored by the data-name can change, even though the data-name itself remains the same. Thus, GROSS-PAY can have many different values—300, 400, 500, for example—but the data-name of course remains the same.

A **condition-name** is a name given to a specific value, a set of values, or a range of values within a complete set of values that a particular data item may assume. The data item itself is referred to as a **conditional variable.** In the example below, the conditional variable is MARITAL-STATUS. The condition-names SINGLE, MARRIED, SEPARATED, WIDOWED, and DIVORCED refer to possibilities within MARITAL-STATUS and their particular values.

```
05  MARITAL-STATUS PIC 9.
    88  SINGLE     VALUE 1.
    88  MARRIED    VALUE 2.
    88  SEPARATED  VALUE 3.
    88  WIDOWED    VALUE 4.
    88  DIVORCED   VALUE 5.
```

Thus, in a program, one would not have to write

```
IF MARITAL-STATUS = 3 . . .
```

Instead, one could write

```
IF SEPARATED . . .
```

The latter would certainly be clearer to the reader, as he or she would not have to know that SEPARATED is equivalent to a MARITAL-STATUS of 3.

A condition-name must conform to the rules for the formation of a data-name.

A **procedure-name** is a name given to a routine or process within a program. Procedure-names are used to identify paragraphs or sections of a COBOL program. Thus, a procedure-name is classified as either a **paragraph-name** or a **section-name.** The use of procedure-names will be discussed in detail later in the text. For now, it suffices to note that procedure-names must conform to the rules for the formation of COBOL words, except that they may consist solely of numeric characters.

A **special-name** is a user name assigned to one or more names defined within the compiler. It appears in the ENVIRONMENT DIVISION of a COBOL program. For example, the currency symbol may be changed from $ to L by entering CURRENCY SIGN IS 'L' and the decimal changed to a comma by entering DECIMAL-POINT IS COMMA. In the next chapter we shall see the DISPLAY statement used. This statement normally sends its output to the screen. If we wanted the output sent to the printer instead, we would have an entry under SPECIAL-NAMES stating that PRINTER IS LINE-OUT. This would cause the DISPLAY data to appear on the printer.

Special-names must conform to the rules for the formation of data-names.

A list of the types of programmer-supplied names and their uses, together with rules for their formation, is given in Table 2–1. This table will serve as a reference for the reader throughout the text.

Table 2–1. RULES FOR FORMING PROGRAMMER-SUPPLIED NAMES

Type of Name	Use	Number of Characters	Type of Characters	Restrictions
File-name	Name a file		At least one character must be alphabetic, no blanks; cannot begin or end with a hyphen	First eight characters must be unique
Record-name	Name a record			Name must be unique or qualifiable
Data-name	Name a data item			
Condition-name	Name a value of a data item	1 to 30		Name must be unique
Special-name	Name a physical component of the computer system			
Procedure-name	Name a paragraph or section		No alphabetic character required; no blanks; cannot begin or end with a hyphen	
Program-name	Name a program			First eight characters must be unique
Library-name	Name a library entry			

CONSTANTS

A **constant** is a unit of data whose value is not subject to change. Constants are classified into two general types:

1. Literals

2. Figurative constants

Literals

A **literal** is a group of characters whose value is determined by the characters themselves. Literals are of two types:

1. Numeric literals

2. Nonnumeric literals

A **numeric literal** is a constant defined as a string of characters that is used for arithmetic operations. Numeric literals consist of:

1. From 1 to 18 digits.

2. Combinations of the digits 0 through 9, the plus sign (+), the minus sign (−), and the decimal point(.).

3. No more than one decimal point. If present, the decimal point may appear in any position within the literal except the rightmost position. If no decimal point is present, the literal will be treated as an integer.
   Some examples of numeric literals are:

```
-345       3      6.0     -2.0
 +7    47.23    +47.3    +17.4
```

A **nonnumeric literal** is a constant defined as a string of COBOL characters that may be used for any operation other than arithmetic. A nonnumeric literal, or **alphanumeric literal,** as it is commonly called, consists of:

1. From 1 to 120 characters enclosed in quotation marks (") or apostrophes ('). **Note:** The apostrophe is the character (') on the same key as the character (") on the PC keyboard, not the character (`) which is the same key as the tilde (~).

2. Any combination of COBOL characters except the quotation mark or apostrophe. However, an apostrophe may be used within quotation marks and a quotation mark may be used within apostrophes. (See the last two examples below.)

Some examples of alphanumeric literals are:

```
'3'
'34.76'
"ERROR MESSAGE"
'$3000.00'
'1,347.06'
'ADD'
"THE O'BRIEN CO."
'THE ANSWER IS "NO"'
```

In the case of 'ADD' the character string contained within the quotation marks happens to be a reserved word. When used in this manner, the reserved word no longer takes on the meaning for which it was designed, but simply is treated by the COBOL compiler as any other constant.

Figurative Constants

A **figurative constant** is a reserved word with a specific and definite value. It is used to replace a symbol with the same meaning. For example, in the two COBOL statements below, the meanings are identical even though one statement utilizes the symbol 0, while the other utilizes the figurative constant ZERO.

```
MOVE 0 TO AREA-A.
MOVE ZERO TO AREA-A.
```

Examples of figurative constants and the symbols that have equivalent meanings in COBOL are given in Table 2–2.

Table 2–2. COBOL FIGURATIVE CONSTANTS

Symbol	Figurative Constant	Description
b	SPACE or SPACES	One or more blank characters
0	ZERO, ZEROS, or ZEROES	One or more numeric zeros
FF*	HIGH-VALUE or HIGH-VALUES	Highest bit configuration
00*	LOW-VALUE or LOW-VALUES	Lowest bit configuration
"	QUOTE or QUOTES	Double quotation mark(")
none	ALL	One or more occurrences of the stated nonnumeric literal

*Expressed in hexadecimal notation.

The singular and plural forms of a figurative constant are equivalent and may be used interchangeably. Thus, any one of the figurative constants ZERO, ZEROS, or ZEROES on the one hand, and SPACE or SPACES on the other, may be used in a COBOL program for 0 and ' '(a space), respectively, without affecting the meaning of the term.

The **class** of a figurative constant—i.e., its being categorized as al-phabetic, alphanumeric, or numeric—is the same as it would be if the symbol were used. Thus, ZERO is generally numeric (depending, how-ever, on where and how it is used), SPACE(S) is alphabetic or alphanu-meric, and LOW-VALUE(S) and HIGH-VALUE(S) are alphanumeric.

COBOL RULES OF PUNCTUATION

In the COBOL language there are specific standards, or rules, con-cerning the punctuation of sentences and statements. Table 2–3 lists these rules as they apply to the various punctuation characters.

Table 2–3.   COBOL RULES OF PUNCTUATION

Punctuation Character	Associated Punctuation Rules
Ƀ Space	Adjacent COBOL words, parenthetical expressions, and/or literals must be separated by at least one space.
	Except within nonnumeric literals two or more adjacent spaces will be treated as a single space.
(Left parenthesis	A left parenthesis must not be immediately followed by a space.
) Right parenthesis	A right parenthesis must not be immediately preceded by a space.
. Period	A period must not be preceded by a space, but it must be followed by a space.
, Comma	A comma must not be preceded by a space, but it must be followed by a space.
	A comma may be used as a separator between successive operands in a statement.
	A comma may be used to separate a series of clauses.
; Semicolon	A semicolon must not be preceded by a space, but it must be followed by a space.
	A semicolon may be used to separate a series of clauses.
	A semicolon may be used to separate a series of state-ments.

GENERAL FORMAT OF A COBOL STATEMENT

COBOL statements are written in accordance with specific rules that stipulate what words or symbols must be present in a statement, their relative positions in a statement, and what information is to be provided by the programmer. The rules also state how and where this information is to be provided, and whether it is required or optional. The task of understanding and remembering the rules applicable to each type of COBOL statement can be time-consuming. To simplify this task, each COBOL statement will be presented in a general format based on the following conventions:

1. All words printed entirely in capitals are **reserved words.**

2. All reserved words that are underlined are required *unless* contained in a portion of the format that is optional. Reserved words that appear in a format but are not underlined are optional. They may be used, at the discretion of the programmer, to increase the readability of the statement. When used, however, optional reserved words (commonly referred to as **optional words**) must be spelled correctly.

3. Whenever used, special characters (. , ; $+ - <>=$, etc.) other than those described in 5, 6, and 7 below represent the actual occurrence of these characters and are required. Indicated punctuation is *essential* as shown; however, additional punctuation may be inserted according to the rules stated in Table 2–3.

4. Information to be supplied by the programmer is printed in lowercase letters.

5. Brackets ([ ]) are used to indicate that the enclosed item may or may not be used, depending on the particular program. If, however, two or more items are contained within the brackets, *no more than one* of these items may be used in a single statement.

6. Braces { } enclosing vertically stacked items indicate that *one and only one* of the enclosed items must be used.

7. The ellipsis ... indicates that the immediately preceding unit may occur once, or more than once in succession. A **unit** refers to a single lower-case word, or several lowercase words and one or more reserved words enclosed in brackets or braces. If a term

is enclosed in brackets or braces, the entire unit containing the term must be repeated when repetition is required.

8. Required and optional clauses appearing in the general format must appear in the order presented unless otherwise explicitly stated in the accompanying text.

As an example, let us consider the format of the COBOL ADD statement:

GENERAL FORMAT 1

$$\underline{\text{ADD}} \begin{Bmatrix} \text{identifier--1} \\ \text{literal--1} \end{Bmatrix} \begin{bmatrix} \text{identifier--2} \\ \text{literal--2} \end{bmatrix} \dots \underline{\text{TO}} \text{ identifier-m } [\underline{\text{ROUNDED}}]$$

[ON $\underline{\text{SIZE ERROR}}$ imperative-statement]

Without any previous knowledge of this COBOL statement, we can infer the following from its format:

$\underline{\text{ADD}}$	This is a reserved word and must appear in every ADD statement in the position indicated in the format.
$\begin{Bmatrix} \text{identifier-1} \\ \text{literal-1} \end{Bmatrix}$	Because this segment of the format is enclosed in braces ({ }), one and only one of the items contained within the braces must be used. Moreover, since these items are written in lowercase letters, they are to be programmer supplied. A detailed explanation of what is to be supplied by the programmer in each case would be stated in the explanation accompanying the format.
$\begin{bmatrix} \text{identifier-2} \\ \text{literal-2} \end{bmatrix} \dots$	Since this part of the format is enclosed in brackets ([]), it is optional; if it is used, however, only one of the two items shown may be used in a single statement and the item used must be programmer supplied. In addition, the ellipsis following this unit indicates that it may be repeated.
$\underline{\text{TO}}$	The word TO is a required reserved word.
identifier-m	This represents information that must be supplied by the programmer.
[$\underline{\text{ROUNDED}}$]	This is an optional reserved word. If used, it must appear exactly as presented.
[ON $\underline{\text{SIZE ERROR}}$ imperative-statement]	This segment of the format is also optional. If it is used, the reserved words SIZE ERROR must appear as indicated. The reserved word ON is optional. The programmer must supply the item referred to as imperative-statement.

A knowledge of format conventions is required for an understanding of the various COBOL statements. Therefore, it is suggested that these conventions be committed to memory as quickly as possible.

ORGANIZATION OF A COBOL PROGRAM

The COBOL language requires four distinct divisions within each source program. These divisions provide unique information about the programmer, the computer or computers used, and the data and instructions used by and contained within the program. Each of these divisions is required and serves a unique function. The divisions must appear in the following order:

1. The IDENTIFICATION DIVISION

2. The ENVIRONMENT DIVISION

3. The DATA DIVISION

4. The PROCEDURE DIVISION

The IDENTIFICATION DIVISION

The purpose of the IDENTIFICATION DIVISION is to provide a standard method of identifying the particular COBOL program to the computer. Thus, this division includes the name of the program, the name of the programmer, the date the program was written, the purpose of the program, and other relevant information that could be meaningful to anyone reading, cataloging, or analyzing the program. The structure of the IDENTIFICATION DIVISION is given in Fig. 2–3.

IDENTIFICATION DIVISION.

PROGRAM-ID. program-name.

[AUTHOR. comment-entry . . .]

[INSTALLATION. comment-entry . . .]

[DATE-WRITTEN. comment-entry . . .]

[DATE-COMPILED. comment-entry . . .]

[SECURITY. comment-entry . . .]

Fig. 2–3. Structure of the IDENTIFICATION DIVISION.

In the figure, each specific paragraph-name helps to identify the type of information contained within the paragraph it names. For example, the first paragraph, and the *only paragraph required* in this division, is assigned the paragraph-name PROGRAM-ID, which indicates that the information contained therein will identify the program.

The ENVIRONMENT DIVISION

The ENVIRONMENT DIVISION provides information about the computer that translates the COBOL source program (the source computer) and the computer that executes the translated or object program (the object computer). Since this division is concerned with the specifications of the equipment being used to translate and execute the program, its entries are greatly dependent upon the computer system to be used in these operations. The structure of the ENVIRONMENT DIVISION is given in Fig. 2–4.

[ENVIRONMENT DIVISION.

  [CONFIGURATION SECTION.

    SOURCE-COMPUTER. Computer-name [WITH DEBUGGING MODE.]

    OBJECT-COMPUTER. Computer-name

$$\text{[MEMORY SIZE integer} \begin{Bmatrix} \text{WORDS} \\ \text{CHARACTERS} \\ \text{MODULES} \end{Bmatrix} \text{]}$$

    [PROGRAM COLLATING SEQUENCE IS ASCII].

  [SPECIAL-NAMES. [PRINTER IS mnemonic-name]

$$\text{[ASCII IS} \begin{Bmatrix} \text{STANDARD-1} \\ \text{NATIVE} \end{Bmatrix} \text{]}$$

    [CURRENCY SIGN IS literal]

    [DECIMAL-POINT IS COMMA]

$$\text{[SWITCH-n IS comment-id} \begin{Bmatrix} \text{ON} \\ \text{OFF} \end{Bmatrix} \text{IS condition-name]].}$$

  [INPUT-OUTPUT SECTION.

    [FILE-CONTROL. file-control entry . . .].

    [I-O-CONTROL.

      [SAME RECORD AREA FOR file-name . . .] . . .]].

Fig. 2–4.   Structure of the ENVIRONMENT DIVISION.

Because the divisions of a COBOL program are generally concerned with more than one distinct area, they are physically divided into **sections,** each of which relates to a specific area within the division. In the ENVIRONMENT DIVISION, there are two such sections:

1. The CONFIGURATION SECTION

2. The INPUT-OUTPUT SECTION

The CONFIGURATION SECTION   Sections may be further divided into **paragraphs**, each of which relates to a specific area within the section. The CONFIGURATION SECTION of the ENVIRONMENT DIVISION is divided into three paragraphs and covers the general specifications of the computer system(s) used by the program.

The first paragraph is the SOURCE-COMPUTER paragraph. This paragraph specifies the computer on which the program will be compiled. The description of this computer must appear immediately after the paragraph-name SOURCE-COMPUTER. It may appear on the same line as SOURCE-COMPUTER or on the following line.

The second paragraph is the OBJECT-COMPUTER paragraph. As a result of the compilation process, an object program is created that contains the machine-language instructions that are the translated equivalents of the programmer's COBOL instructions. These instructions are then used to execute the program. The object computer is generally the same computer as the source computer; however, it must still be specified in the OBJECT-COMPUTER paragraph of the CONFIGURATION SECTION. The manner of identifying the object computer is exactly the same as that of identifying the source computer.

Both the SOURCE-COMPUTER and OBJECT-COMPUTER paragraphs are treated as comments by the IBM PC COBOL compiler except when the DEBUGGING MODE option is used in the SOURCE-COMPUTER entry. This option will be discussed later.

The third paragraph in the CONFIGURATION SECTION of the ENVIRONMENT DIVISION is the optional SPECIAL-NAMES paragraph. This paragraph associates programmer-supplied **mnemonic-names** (substitute names more easily recognized by a programmer) with **function-names** (names with a fixed meaning defined by the manufacturer of the computer). This will be discussed in greater detail later in the text.

The INPUT-OUTPUT SECTION   The INPUT-OUTPUT SECTION of a COBOL program is concerned with:

1. The name of each data file used with the program.

2. The external storage medium used with each data file required by the program.

3. The assignment of each data file to one or more input or output devices.

4. Additional information needed for the most efficient transmission of data between the file media and the object program.

The DATA DIVISION

The DATA DIVISION describes in detail all the data to be used by the program. This includes a description of data that is to be input and output, a description of data that is defined in the program itself and not externally input, and a description of work areas in storage that will be required during the processing of the data.

The body of the DATA DIVISION, illustrated in Fig. 2–5, is divided into four sections:

1. The FILE SECTION

2. The WORKING-STORAGE SECTION

3. The LINKAGE SECTION

4. The SCREEN SECTION

DATA DIVISION.
   [FILE SECTION.
      [file description entry
      record description entry . . .] . . .]

   [WORKING-STORAGE SECTION.
      [data description entry . . .] . . .]

   [LINKAGE SECTION.
      [data description entry . . .] . . .]

   [SCREEN SECTION.
      [screen description entry . . .] . . .]

Fig. 2–5.   Structure of the DATA DIVISION.

The FILE SECTION The FILE SECTION of the DATA DIVI-
SION describes to the COBOL compiler the format of each file and
each record within each file to be used in the program.

The WORKING-STORAGE SECTION The WORKING-
STORAGE SECTION generally contains descriptions of records not
contained on external files—data records that are created and processed internally during the execution of the object program.

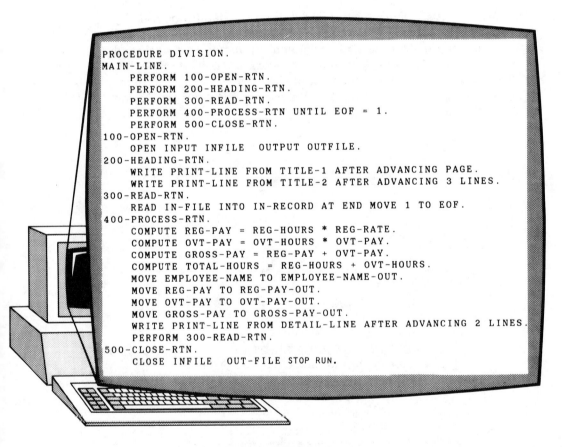

```
PROCEDURE DIVISION.
MAIN-LINE.
    PERFORM 100-OPEN-RTN.
    PERFORM 200-HEADING-RTN.
    PERFORM 300-READ-RTN.
    PERFORM 400-PROCESS-RTN UNTIL EOF = 1.
    PERFORM 500-CLOSE-RTN.
100-OPEN-RTN.
    OPEN INPUT INFILE  OUTPUT OUTFILE.
200-HEADING-RTN.
    WRITE PRINT-LINE FROM TITLE-1 AFTER ADVANCING PAGE.
    WRITE PRINT-LINE FROM TITLE-2 AFTER ADVANCING 3 LINES.
300-READ-RTN.
    READ IN-FILE INTO IN-RECORD AT END MOVE 1 TO EOF.
400-PROCESS-RTN.
    COMPUTE REG-PAY = REG-HOURS * REG-RATE.
    COMPUTE OVT-PAY = OVT-HOURS * OVT-PAY.
    COMPUTE GROSS-PAY = REG-PAY + OVT-PAY.
    COMPUTE TOTAL-HOURS = REG-HOURS + OVT-HOURS.
    MOVE EMPLOYEE-NAME TO EMPLOYEE-NAME-OUT.
    MOVE REG-PAY TO REG-PAY-OUT.
    MOVE OVT-PAY TO OVT-PAY-OUT.
    MOVE GROSS-PAY TO GROSS-PAY-OUT.
    WRITE PRINT-LINE FROM DETAIL-LINE AFTER ADVANCING 2 LINES.
    PERFORM 300-READ-RTN.
500-CLOSE-RTN.
    CLOSE INFILE  OUT-FILE STOP RUN.
```

Fig. 2–6. Sample PROCEDURE DIVISION coding.

The LINKAGE SECTION The LINKAGE SECTION is used to describe data areas that are actually contained in other programs and that will be executed as subprograms to the main program.

The SCREEN SECTION A powerful feature of microcomputer versions of COBOL is the ability to interact with the screen and keyboard for the input and output of data. This is illustrated to some extent by the use of ACCEPT and DISPLAY with position specs mentioned later in this text. The SCREEN SECTION expands this capability by allowing the description of the entire screen rather than line-by-line input and output.

The PROCEDURE DIVISION

The last division to appear in a COBOL program is the PROCE-DURE DIVISION, which contains the instructions in the logical sequence in which they must be executed to create the desired output from the given input data. Essentially, these instructions are written in meaningful English. Figure 2–6, which contains a segment of the PRO-CEDURE DIVISION from a sample program, is illustrative. Figure 2–7 shows the general structure of the PROCEDURE DIVISION. The PROCEDURE DIVISION will be discussed in detail later in the text.

Instructions in the PROCEDURE DIVISION are written in the form of simple statements that can be combined to form sentences. These sentences can in turn be combined or grouped into paragraphs, and the paragraphs can be grouped into sections. Sections are not usually required.

```
PROCEDURE DIVISION. [USING [identifier-1] . . .].

[DECLARATIVES.
  [section-name SECTION. USE sentence.
  [paragraph-name. [sentence . . .] . . .] . . .

  END DECLARATIVES.]
  [[section-name SECTION. [segment number]]
  [paragraph-name. [sentence] . . .] . . .] . . .
```

Fig. 2–7. Structure of the PROCEDURE DIVISION.

The organization of the PROCEDURE DIVISION into sections, paragraphs, and sentences is not required, but it is of great help in a large program because it increases the readability and understanding of the program. In the case of a small program, there is less need for this organization. However, even the minimal PROCEDURE DIVISION given in Fig. 2-6 is made more readable by the paragraph-name 200-HEADING-RTN.

EXERCISES

---

1. Name and describe the principal function of each of the four divisions of a COBOL program.

2. What are the rules for the formation of COBOL data-names?

3. Describe the difference between a data-name and the value described by a data-name.

4. Describe the difference between a data-name and a literal.

5. What are COBOL reserved words? What functions do they perform?

6. Find the errors, if any, in the following literals.

```
TWO                 +6
'10%'               GROSS PAY
.1234               10%
'2.93'              23.4-
1,592.00            125.
```

7. Find the errors, if any, in the following data-names.

```
GRAND TOTAL         FICA-%
9876                567A
ADD                 WRITE-TOTALS
HOURLY-RATE         START
PART-NO.            ZERO
```

8. Analyze the general format of each of the following statements (even though the statements themselves will not be covered until later).

(a) <u>ADD</u> $\begin{Bmatrix} \text{data-name-1} \\ \text{literal-1} \end{Bmatrix}$ <u>TO</u> data-name-2

(b) <u>SUBTRACT</u> $\begin{Bmatrix} \text{data-name-1} \\ \text{literal-1} \end{Bmatrix}$ <u>FROM</u>

data-name-2 [<u>ROUNDED</u>]

(c) <u>DATA</u> $\begin{Bmatrix} \underline{\text{RECORD}} \text{ IS} \\ \underline{\text{RECORDS}} \text{ ARE} \end{Bmatrix}$ [data-name-1]

[data-name-2) . . .

(d) <u>READ</u> filename RECORD [<u>INTO</u> data-name]

$\begin{Bmatrix} \text{AT } \underline{\text{END}} \\ \underline{\text{INVALID}} \text{ KEY} \end{Bmatrix}$ imperative-statement

Solutions to exercises 6, 7, and 8 are provided on the supplemental disk as EXER26.DOC, EXER27.DOC, and EXER28.DOC. Use the DOS command TYPE to display these files.

3

WRITING A SIMPLE COBOL PROGRAM

The first two chapters introduced the fundamentals and basic structure of the COBOL language. With an understanding of these, it is now possible to consider writing an elementary COBOL program.

SAMPLE COBOL PROGRAM

Problem: Write a COBOL program to accept data from the keyboard and prepare a printed report based on that data. Each set of data will consist of an employee's name, hours worked, and hourly rate of pay. The program will calculate the gross pay and print all data in report format. Processing will terminate when a blank set of data is input.

The format for the data is as follows:

NAME	**20 positions**
First Name	10 positions
Middle Initial	1 position
Last Name	10 positions
HOURS WORKED	**3 positions**
	2 integer positions
	1 decimal position
HOURLY RATE	**4 positions**
	2 integer positions
	2 decimal positions

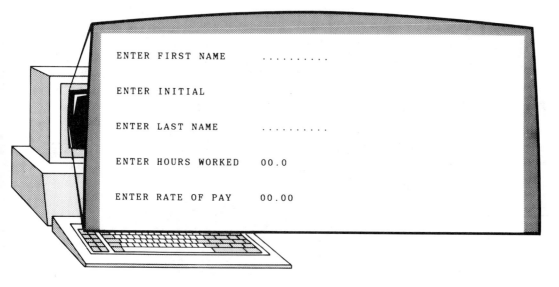

```
ENTER FIRST NAME      . . . . . . . . .

ENTER INITIAL

ENTER LAST NAME       . . . . . . . . .

ENTER HOURS WORKED    00.0

ENTER RATE OF PAY     00.00
```

Fig. 3–1. Screen layout for PROGRAM1.

Figure 3–1 shows how these input specifications will appear on the screen for PROGRAM1, as we shall call our sample program.

Problem Analysis

The first step in the programming process is problem analysis. The size, source, and format of the input data consists of a number of entries, each containing a name, hours worked, and hourly rate. The output from this program is to be a listing of the contents of the input data sets plus the results of the calculation of the gross pay. Since no details were given in the problem description concerning exactly how the output is to appear, we will have to design an output layout for this report. This could be done as shown in Fig. 3–2. The form that was used there for the output layout is referred to as a **printer spacing chart.** Note that the output is represented by X's.

This is the normal convention and means that variable data is to be printed in exactly these spaces.

The processing for this program consists of entering data, calculating gross pay, and printing out a report.

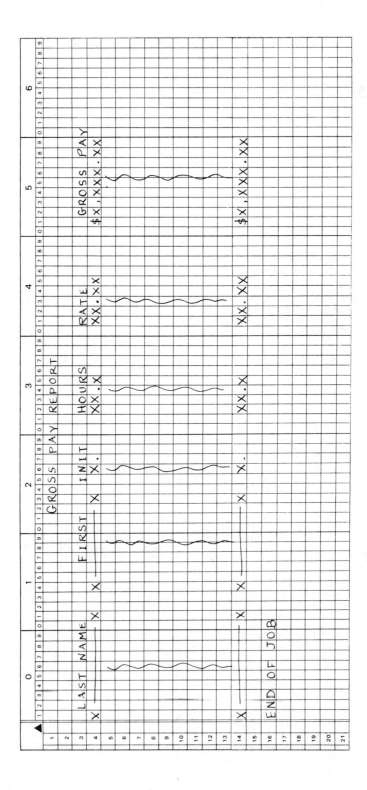

Fig. 3–2. Output layout for report.

Flowcharting

Once the input, processing, and output requirements of the problem are understood, the application can be flowcharted.

The flowchart of the sample problem is a relatively simple one and is shown in Fig. 3-3.

COBOL CODING SHEET

The COBOL coding sheet is the form designed to aid the programmer in writing COBOL instructions for subsequent entry into the computer.

Originally, COBOL was run on batch systems, with punched cards being the principal form of input available. This is the reason for the coding specifications mentioned earlier regarding the placement of entries in column 8 and column 12. We will not be using punched cards, of course, but because of these format requirements, we will use the coding sheet for our illustrations. You may find it worthwhile to use one also, in order to avoid formatting errors. The coding sheet provides for 80 columns, corresponding to the 80 columns available on one line on the display of your IBM PC. The sample coding sheet shown in Fig. 3-4 should be used in conjunction with the following discussion.

Sequence Numbers

Sequence numbers are generally optional with any COBOL compiler, and they are optional for the IBM PC. They were necessary on punched cards to maintain the proper sequence of the source program deck and to facilitate the changes that the programmer would have to make in the program testing process. We shall not use them in this text. The COBOL compiler for the IBM PC generates sequential numbers for each line of code each time the program is compiled, and these are recorded on the .LST file mentioned in Chapter 1.

Continuation

Any sentence or entry that cannot be completed by column 72 may be continued on the next line at column 12 or higher. This may be done with no other action required, provided that the break from one line to the other is at a point in the statement at which one or more spaces occur. If the point at which the line change occurs is in the middle of a word or in the middle of a nonnumeric literal, it is necessary to put a

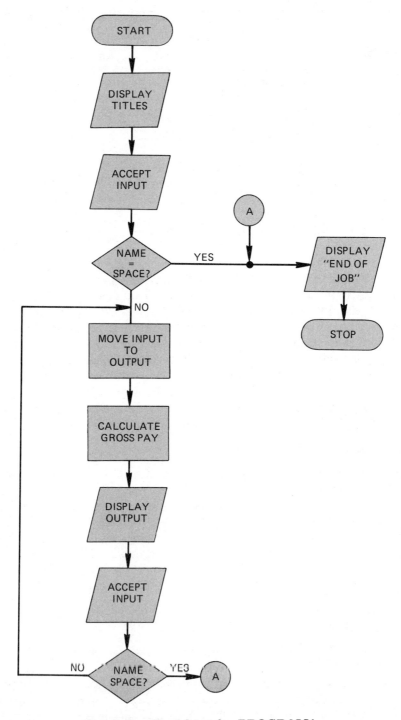

Fig. 3–3. Flowchart for PROGRAM1.

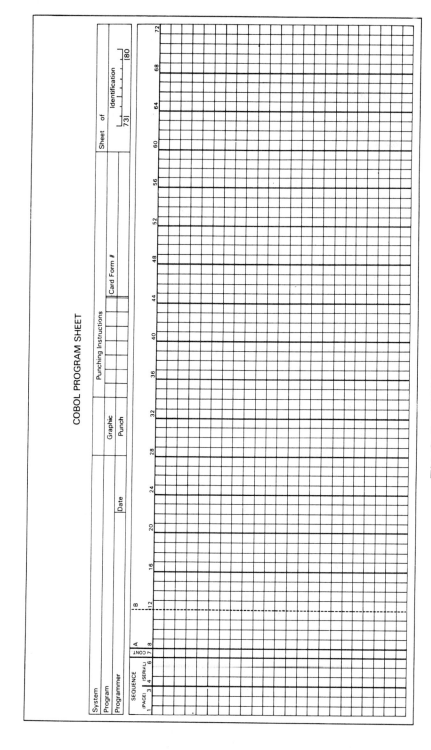

Fig. 3-4. COBOL program sheet.

hyphen (-) in column 7 of the continued line. However, although this kind of line break is permitted in COBOL, it is usually scrupulously avoided and will be avoided in the examples in this text.

A and B Margin Areas

In the COBOL language, certain entries must begin in designated areas. For example, the names of divisions, sections, and paragraphs generally begin in column 8, which is referred to as the A Margin. However, such entries may also begin in column 9, 10, or 11. This field (columns 8 to 11) is referred to as the A Area. Most other entries begin at the B Margin, column 12, but they may also begin at any other column from 13 to 72. This field (columns 12 to 72) is referred to as the B Area.

Identification

Columns 73 through 80 are used by programmers to identify the program or for any other type of identification desired. They are often used in commercial programs to identify the date and source of modifications to individual lines in a program. Anything placed in this optional entry area is ignored by the compiler, remaining just part of the source program. We will not be using this area in this book.

Recording Information on the Coding Sheet

The method of entering data is of great importance when the keying is to be done by someone other than the programmer. This is not usually the case when one is using a personal computer, but the following cautions should be noted anyway: (1) there is only one character to a box on the coding sheet since each corresponds to a position on the screen; (2) care should be taken with those characters that are quite similar, namely:

1 and l

2 and Z

5 and S

0 and O

U and V

In order to make the difference between these characters more pronounced, we shall, for example, record the zero with a slash (∅) and the letter Z with a hyphen (Z̶) in the coding examples in this book.

THE IDENTIFICATION DIVISION

The purpose of the IDENTIFICATION DIVISION is to provide a standard method of identifying the COBOL program to the computer. The number and type of entries in this division will vary from program to program because most of these entries are optional.

Division Heading

The division heading must appear before any entries in the division. As with any division heading, it must begin in the A Area and be immediately followed by a period with no other entries appearing on the line.

Required Entry

The only required entry in the IDENTIFICATION DIVISION is the PROGRAM-ID entry, which identifies the program-name. This entry must appear on the line immediately following the DIVISION heading. The rules governing the formation of program-names are the same as the rules governing the formation of a COBOL word. That is, a program-name must consist of from 1 to 30 characters, each of which is either alphanumeric or a hyphen, must not begin or end with a hyphen, and must not contain any blanks. The first six characters of a program-name are used to identify the object program, so that these characters should be unique in the program-name.

The program-name may follow the PROGRAM-ID entry on the same line, separated by at least one blank, or it may appear on the line immediately following the PROGRAM-ID entry. In either case, it must be immediately followed by a period.

Figure 3–5 shows the completed code for PROGRAM1. Note that the PROGRAM-ID entry begins at the A Margin, while the program-name begins at the B Margin. This is because the PROGRAM-ID is a paragraph-name. A paragraph consists of one or more COBOL statements and is referenced by the paragraph-name that precedes it. Paragraph-names must begin in the A Area, whereas the entries within the paragraph may not begin there and generally begin at the B Margin—although they may begin anywhere in the B Area.

```
        IDENTIFICATION DIVISION.
        PROGRAM-ID.
            PROGRAM1.
        AUTHOR.
            S.J.GAUGHRAN.
        INSTALLATION.
            PERSONAL COMPUTER SYSTEM.
        DATE-WRITTEN.
            01/05/85.
        DATE-COMPILED.
            01/05/85.
        SECURITY.
            NONE.
        ENVIRONMENT DIVISION.
        CONFIGURATION SECTION.
        SOURCE-COMPUTER.
            IBM-PERSONAL-COMPUTER.
        OBJECT-COMPUTER.
            IBM-PERSONAL-COMPUTER.
        SPECIAL-NAMES.
            PRINTER IS LINE-OUT.
        *
        DATA DIVISION.
        WORKING-STORAGE SECTION.
        01   EMPLOYEE-REC-IN.
            05   EMPLOYEE-NAME-IN.
                10   FIRST-NAME-IN    PIC X(10).
                10   INITIAL-IN       PIC X.
                10   LAST-NAME-IN     PIC X(10).
            05   HOURS-IN             PIC S99V9.
            05   RATE-IN              PIC S99V99.
        *
         01   HEADING-OUT.
            05   FILLER               PIC X(10)   VALUE ' LAST NAME'.
            05   FILLER               PIC X(3)    VALUE SPACES.
            05   FILLER               PIC X(5)    VALUE 'FIRST'.
            05   FILLER               PIC X(5)    VALUE SPACES.
            05   FILLER               PIC X(4)    VALUE 'INIT'.
            05   FILLER               PIC X(3)    VALUE SPACES.
            05   FILLER               PIC X(5)    VALUE 'HOURS'.
            05   FILLER               PIC X(4)    VALUE SPACES.
            05   FILLER               PIC X(4)    VALUE 'RATE'.
            05   FILLER               PIC X(6)    VALUE SPACES.
            05   FILLER               PIC X(9)    VALUE 'GROSS PAY'.
        *
         01   EMPLOYEE-REC-OUT.
            05   EMPLOYEE-NAME-OUT.
                10   LAST-NAME-OUT    PIC X(10).
                10   FILLER           PIC X(2)    VALUE SPACES.
                10   FIRST-NAME-OUT   PIC X(10).
                10   FILLER           PIC X(2)    VALUE SPACES.
                10   INITIAL-OUT      PIC X.
                10   FILLER           PIC X       VALUE '.'.
            05   FILLER               PIC X(4)    VALUE SPACES.
            05   HOURS-OUT            PIC ZZ.9.
            05   FILLER               PIC X(5)    VALUE SPACES.
            05   RATE-OUT             PIC ZZ.99.
            05   FILLER               PIC X(5)    VALUE SPACES.
            05   GROSS-PAY-OUT        PIC $Z,ZZZ.99.
        *
        PROCEDURE DIVISION.
        MAIN-ROUTINE.
            DISPLAY (1, 1) ERASE.
            DISPLAY HEADING-OUT UPON LINE-OUT.
            DISPLAY SPACES UPON LINE-OUT.
            PERFORM ACCEPT-ROUTINE.
            PERFORM PROCESS-ROUTINE UNTIL EMPLOYEE-NAME-IN = SPACES.
            DISPLAY SPACES UPON LINE-OUT.
            DISPLAY ' END OF JOB ' UPON LINE-OUT.
            STOP RUN.
```

Fig. 3–5. Compiled code for PROGRAM1.

```
    *
    ACCEPT-ROUTINE.
        DISPLAY (1, 1) ERASE.
        DISPLAY (5, 10) 'ENTER FIRST NAME '.
        ACCEPT  (5, 31) FIRST-NAME-IN WITH PROMPT.
        DISPLAY (8, 10) 'ENTER INITIAL '.
        ACCEPT  (8, 31) INITIAL-IN WITH PROMPT.
        DISPLAY (11, 10) 'ENTER LAST NAME '.
        ACCEPT  (11, 31) LAST-NAME-IN WITH PROMPT.
        DISPLAY (14, 10) 'ENTER HOURS WORKED '.
        ACCEPT  (14, 31) HOURS-IN WITH PROMPT.
        DISPLAY (17, 10) 'ENTER RATE OF PAY '.
        ACCEPT  (17, 31) RATE-IN WITH PROMPT.
    *
    PROCESS-ROUTINE.
        MOVE FIRST-NAME-IN TO FIRST-NAME-OUT.
        MOVE INITIAL-IN TO INITIAL-OUT.
        MOVE LAST-NAME-IN TO LAST-NAME-OUT.
        MOVE RATE-IN TO RATE-OUT.
        MOVE HOURS-IN TO HOURS-OUT.
        MULTIPLY RATE-IN BY HOURS-IN GIVING GROSS-PAY-OUT.
        DISPLAY EMPLOYEE-REC-OUT UPON LINE-OUT.
        PERFORM ACCEPT-ROUTINE.
```

Fig. 3–5.   *(continued)*

Optional Entries

The additional, or optional, entries in the IDENTIFICATION DIVI-
SION serve two major purposes: they further identify the program and
programmer, and they provide more complete documentation. There
are five such optional entries, each of which is identified by a
paragraph-name:

```
AUTHOR.
INSTALLATION.
DATE-WRITTEN.
DATE-COMPILED.
SECURITY.
```

The general format of these entries is as follows:

GENERAL FORMAT 1

[AUTHOR. [comment-entry] . . .]

[INSTALLATION. [comment-entry] . . .]

[DATE-WRITTEN. [comment-entry] . . .]

[DATE-COMPILED. [comment-entry] . . .]

[SECURITY. [comment-entry] . . .]

The **comment-entry** in each of these optional paragraphs is used by the programmer to record program documentary information.

It is also possible for the programmer to insert explanatory comments in this or any other division of a COBOL source program by simply placing an **asterisk** (*) in column 7 of the line. Then, any combination of characters may be included in the A Area and B Area of that line. The asterisk, together with all the characters that follow it on that line, will be produced on the listing of the source program. The comment statement, however, serves no other purpose. It will not become a part of the machine code generated as a result of the compilation. The complete IDENTIFICATION DIVISION containing several explanatory comment lines is shown in Fig. 3–5.

If a **slash** (/) is placed in column 7, then, as with an asterisk placed there, the line will be treated as an explanatory comment. However, the comments contained on the line will now be printed at the *top of a new page* in the compiler listing of the source program.

THE ENVIRONMENT DIVISION

The ENVIRONMENT DIVISION of a COBOL program provides information concerning the equipment, or **hardware,** to be utilized in compiling and executing the program. This means that entries made in this division are heavily *machine dependent,* so that the ENVIRONMENT DIVISION of a COBOL program will vary with the particular hardware or options being used.

The first entry in the ENVIRONMENT DIVISION must be the division heading, which must:

1. Begin in the A Area.

2. Be followed by a period and then one or more blanks.

3. Be the only entry that appears on the line.

The CONFIGURATION SECTION

The CONFIGURATION SECTION of the ENVIRONMENT DIVISION consists of the SOURCE-COMPUTER, OBJECT-COMPUTER, and SPECIAL-NAMES paragraphs and covers the general specifications of the computer system(s) used with the program. On the IBM PC the CONFIGURATION SECTION and its associated paragraphs are optional within a COBOL source program.

The SOURCE-COMPUTER Paragraph   The SOURCE-COM-PUTER paragraph specifies the computer on which the COBOL program is compiled. Each computer capable of compiling a COBOL program can be uniquely identified. For example, an IBM PC is identified by

```
IBM-PERSONAL-COMPUTER
```

The OBJECT-COMPUTER Paragraph   As a result of the compilation process, an object program is created. The manner of identifying the OBJECT-COMPUTER is exactly the same as that of identifying the SOURCE-COMPUTER.

In the case of the sample problem, it will be assumed that the OBJECT-COMPUTER is an IBM PC. Thus, the ENVIRONMENT DIVISION coding would appear as follows:

```
ENVIRONMENT DIVISION.
CONFIGURATION SECTION.
SOURCE-COMPUTER.
    IBM-PERSONAL-COMPUTER.
OBJECT-COMPUTER.
    IBM-PERSONAL-COMPUTER.
```

The SPECIAL-NAMES Paragraph   The SPECIAL-NAMES paragraph associates programmer-supplied mnemonic-names with function-names. We shall illustrate the entire entry for the case of the IBM PC but will discuss only a function-name assigned to the printer at this time.

The general format of the SPECIAL-NAMES paragraph is as follows:

GENERAL FORMAT 2

[SPECIAL-NAMES.

    [PRINTER IS mnemonic-name]

    [ASCII IS $\left\{ \begin{array}{l} \text{STANDARD-1} \\ \text{NATIVE} \end{array} \right\}$]

    [CURRENCY SIGN IS literal]

    [DECIMAL-POINT IS COMMA]

[SWITCH-n IS comment-id $\left\{ \begin{array}{l} \text{ON} \\ \text{OFF} \end{array} \right\}$ IS condition-name]]

In PROGRAM1, we wish to display our output on the printer. This is done with the entry

```
SPECIAL-NAMES.
     PRINTER IS LINE-OUT.
```

Thus, for PROGRAM1, the mnemonic-name LINE-OUT is a synonym for the computer-recognized function-name PRINTER.

It should be noted that only one period may be used within the SPECIAL-NAMES paragraph and that this period must appear immediately after the last entry in the paragraph. We shall encounter this kind of situation, in which a paragraph is permitted to have only one sentence, upon occasion in COBOL.

Since our program does not require any data files, no additional entries are needed in the ENVIRONMENT DIVISION. The complete ENVIRONMENT DIVISION for PROGRAM1 is given in Fig. 3–5.

THE DATA DIVISION

The DATA DIVISION contains the description of all data to be processed by the program. These data consist of two general types:

1. Data stored externally on disk files or entered from the keyboard to be processed by the program.

2. Data created during execution of the program.

The first entry in the DATA DIVISION must be the division heading, which must begin in the A Area, be followed immediately by a period, and be written on a line by itself.

The FILE SECTION

The FILE SECTION describes all data to be used by the program that is stored externally on files. In the sample program, no external data files will be utilized. However, a limited amount of data is to be accepted from the keyboard when requested by the object program during its execution. Similarly, data to be output will not be externally recorded on a file, but will be displayed in edited form (with dollar signs and decimal points inserted where appropriate). Thus, no FILE SECTION is needed in PROGRAM1.

The **WORKING-STORAGE SECTION**

The WORKING-STORAGE SECTION of the DATA DIVISION contains descriptions of records and data items that are created and processed internally during the execution of the object program. Specifically, the section contains data item description entries followed by record description entries as shown in Fig. 3–5.

The Data Item Description Entry   A data item description entry is used to describe a data item that is neither a subdivision of another item nor subdivided itself. The description consists of a level number, a data-name, and an associated description clause.

Level numbers are used to indicate the relationship of data items to one another. A data item description entry is assigned the level number 77, which indicates that the entry (1) is not from an external data file, (2) is not a subdivision of another data item, and (3) is not itself subdivided. Suppose that in our sample problem we had been required to sum up the gross pay calculated for each entry. To do this, we would have to define an area in storage into which this total could be placed. A data item description could be used for this purpose. We would merely have to provide a level number—say, 77—a data-name, and a description clause.

The level number 77 must appear in the A Area (columns 8 through 11) and must be followed by two or more spaces and a data-name that conforms to the rules for the formation of data-names. The data-name must be placed in the B Area (columns 12 through 72), usually beginning in column 12. If the data-name is

```
GROSS-PAY-TOTAL
```

then all that remains for us to do to complete this entry is to choose an appropriate **description** clause for the data item GROSS-PAY-TOTAL. The clause that is used to describe **elementary** data items (items that are not subdivided) is the **PICTURE** clause, which indicates the size of a field, the type of field it is (alphabetic, numeric, or alphanumeric), and whether any editing characters or decimal points are present in the field. The general format of the PICTURE clause is as follows:

GENERAL FORMAT 3

$$\left\{ \begin{array}{l} \text{PICTURE} \\ \text{PIC} \end{array} \right\} \text{ IS character-string}$$

Character-string refers to a limited subset of characters taken from the COBOL character set. The maximum number of characters allowed in a character-string is 30. The specific characters that can be used are:

A X 9 $ Z P * B 0 + – S V , . CR DB

Each of these symbols represents a specific type of data or has a specific meaning. For example, **A** denotes alphabetic data, **X** denotes alphanumeric data (sequences of letters, digits, and certain special characters), and **9** denotes numeric data. (See Table 3–1.)

Table 3–1. PICTURE CHARACTERS

PICTURE Character	Data Type	Specification
X	Alphanumeric	The associated position in the value will contain any character from the COBOL character set.
A	Alphabetic	The associated position in the value will contain an alphabetic character or a blank.
9	Numeric or numeric edited	The associated position in the value will contain any digit.
V	Numeric	The decimal point in the value will be assumed to be at the location of the V. The V does not represent a character position.
.	Numeric edited	The associated position in the value will contain a point or a space. A space will occur if the entire data item is suppressed.
$	Numeric edited	The associated position in the value will contain a dollar sign.
,	Numeric edited	The associated position in the value will contain a comma, blank, or dollar sign.
S	Numeric	A sign (+ or −) will be part of the value of the data item. The S does not represent a character position.
Z	Numeric edited	A leading zero in the associated position will be suppressed and replaced with a blank. No Z may be to the right of a 9.
B	Numeric edited	The associated position in the value will contain a blank.
0	Numeric edited	The associated position in the value will contain a zero.

Table 3–1. (*continued*)

PICTURE Character	Data Type	Specification
−	Numeric edited	A minus sign is inserted into the value when the value is negative; otherwise one blank will appear. The − may appear at either end of the PICTURE.
+	Numeric edited	The appropriate sign (+ or −) will be inserted into the value.
*	Numeric edited	A leading zero in the associated position will be suppressed and replaced with an asterisk.
CR DB	Numeric edited	The negative indicator CR or DB will be inserted when the value is negative; otherwise two blanks will appear.
P	Numeric	Used to scale a quantity up or down by adding a zero in the associated position.
/	Numeric or alphanumeric edited	The associated position will always contain a slash.

The PICTURE characters *, CR, and DB will be treated later in the text.

The size of the data item field is denoted by the number of A's, X's, 9's, or other symbols allowed in a PICTURE clause character-string. For example, the data item description entry

```
77  NUMBER-1  PICTURE IS 999999.
```

indicates that the data item is an elementary one (level 77) whose data-name is NUMBER-1 and which consists of six positions of numeric data (999999). On the other hand, the entry

```
77  VARIABLE  PICTURE AAAA.
```

indicates that the data item is an elementary one whose data-name is VARIABLE and which consists of four alphabetic characters. The PICTURE character-string may contain only one classification type of symbol. That is, the character-string AA999 would be illegal because it refers to two kinds of characters: alphabetic (A) and numeric (9).

To simplify the writing of character-strings associated with PICTURE clauses, a **multiplication factor** may be employed. For example, the character-string 99999 could also be written 9(5), and the character-string ZZZZZ could be written Z(5). The multiplication factor (5) indicates that the 9 and Z are repeated five times, respectively.

In the case of the 77-level data item GROSS-PAY-TOTAL mentioned previously, one additional item must be indicated—the implied decimal point. That is, the computer must be given an indication that the number being stored is a six-digit numerical quantity and that the last two digits are assumed to be decimal places. From Table 3–1, we can see that this can be accomplished by inserting the symbol **V** in the appropriate place in the PICTURE character-string. Thus,

9999V99

indicates a six-digit field with two assumed, or implied, decimal places.

Putting this all together, the data item description entry for an area intended to store the gross pay data would be

77   GROSS-PAY-TOTAL   PICTURE 9999v99.

With this data item description entry, an area is established in the memory of the computer into which the result of the calculation can be placed. It should be noted, however, that we cannot assume anything about the contents of that location at this time: the location contains whatever was left over from the last time it was used. It is best to describe the contents of the said location at this moment to be *unpredictable*. If it were necessary for the location to contain an initial value—zero, for example—one could give it that value by means of the VALUE clause and the figurative constant ZERO, as follows:

77   GROSS-PAY-TOTAL   PICTURE 9(4)V99 VALUE ZERO.

The VALUE clause will be discussed later in this chapter.

It should be noted that a recent trend is to do away with 77-level entries in favor of grouping similar entries under an 01-level entry in the WORKING-STORAGE SECTION. The use of 01-level entries for this purpose will be illustrated later in the text.

The Record Description Entry   The record description entry is used to describe records contained in either the FILE SECTION or the WORKING-STORAGE SECTION. *Every type of record used by a program must have a record description entry*. The general format of this entry is as follows:

GENERAL FORMAT 4

Level Number $\begin{Bmatrix} \text{data-name} \\ \underline{\text{FILLER}} \end{Bmatrix}$

        [PICTURE clause]

        [REDEFINES clause]

        [BLANK WHEN ZERO clause]

        [JUSTIFIED clause]

        [OCCURS clause]

        [SYNCHRONIZED clause]

        [USAGE clause]

        [VALUE clause]

        [SIGN IS $\begin{Bmatrix} \text{TRAILING} \\ \text{LEADING} \end{Bmatrix}$ [SEPARATE CHARACTER]]

Note the occurrence of the level-number entry again. We have seen the use of the level number 77 to indicate an independent elementary data item. Level numbers are also used in record description entries to show numerically the relationship between items within a record. The level number of a particular data item indicates whether that item is to be considered part of another data item or is unrelated to any other data item. The level number **01** indicates that a complete **record** is being described. If the record is to be subdivided, appropriate subsequent level numbers must be used to show the subdivisions of the record.

The sample problem illustrates this concept. The record used there is somewhat simpler than, but representative of, those used in commercial applications. The task of determining an appropriate record description entry for this record might begin with determining an appropriate name for the record. Whenever possible, the name should be descriptive of the contents of the record. One possible choice is

`EMPLOYEE-REC-IN`

Since EMPLOYEE-REC-IN refers to the entire record, it is assigned the level number 01. Each immediate subdivision of this record is assigned a data-name or the name FILLER, and a level number greater than 01 (but less than 50), usually 05. In the case of the record illustrated in Fig. 3–5, there are three 05-level data items or fields: EMPLOYEE-NAME-IN, HOURS-IN, and RATE-IN.

Each of the three 05-level data items that contain data to be referenced by the program must be assigned distinct, unique data-names. As one of these 05-level fields is further subdivided, each subdivision must also be assigned a unique data-name in addition to a level number greater than 05 and less than 50. One appropriate choice is 10. The EMPLOYEE-NAME-IN field, for example, is subdivided into three 10-level fields: FIRST-NAME-IN, LAST-NAME-IN, and INIT-IN. The process would be continued until no fields remained that could be further subdivided. Pictorially, the data structure would appear as follows:

Level Number	01	05	10
	EMPLOYEE-REC-IN	EMPLOYEE-NAME-IN	FIRST-NAME-IN
			LAST-NAME-IN
			INIT-IN
		HOURS-IN	
		RATE-IN	

This graphic view of the structure of the record is the basis for the preparation of the complete record description entry shown in Fig. 3–5.

There is no one numerical sequence that must be employed in assigning level numbers. A data item that is a subdivision of a preceding data item is required only to contain a higher level number than that assigned to the preceding data item. Also, subdivisions of the same grouped data item *must be assigned the same level number.* Level numbers begin with 01 (record level number) and must not exceed 49. There are, however, special-purpose level numbers (77 and 88) that are exceptions to this rule. Successive data description entries are commonly indented according to level number as shown in Fig. 3–5, but this type of arrangement is not a requirement. The only requirements regarding the placement of level numbers are given in Table 3–2.

Once a data-name and level number have been assigned to each grouped (subdivided) data item and to each elementary (not subdivided) data item in the record, an appropriate PICTURE clause can be assigned to each elementary data item. *PICTURE clauses cannot be assigned to grouped data items.* For the input in PROGRAM1, the description entries shown in Fig. 3–5 are a natural reflection of the data structure.

Let us now turn our attention to the descriptions of the output records. You may recall that during problem analysis we created a printer spacing chart showing a possible output layout for our sample problem. (See Fig. 3-2.) Note that in this layout there are two different line formats: the heading line and the data, or detail, line. Each of these line formats represents a record and must be described individually. The same options and constraints apply to these record descriptions as apply to the input record description shown in Fig. 3-5, except that in the case of the output record descriptions we shall make liberal use of the VALUE clause, to be discussed momentarily. The only requirements regarding the placement of level numbers (for input, as well as output, data items) are given in Table 3-2.

Table 3-2. PLACEMENT AND USE OF LEVEL NUMBERS

Level Number	Purpose	Requirements
01	Record description entry	Must begin in the A Area and be followed in the B Area by the associated data-name and appropriate descriptive information
02-49	Subdivisions of 01-level entries that may be group or elementary data items.	May begin in either the A Area or the B Area followed in the B Area by the associated data-name and appropriate descriptive information
77	Independent data item (not a subdivision and not subdivided)	Same requirements that apply to 01-level data items
88	Condition-name (must use VALUE clause)	Same requirements that apply to 02- to 49-level data items

The VALUE clause in the description of an elementary or group data item defined in the WORKING-STORAGE SECTION serves to assign an initial value to the data item at the start of program execution. If the VALUE clause is omitted from the said description, the initial value of the data item is *unpredictable*. The general format of the VALUE clause is:

GENERAL FORMAT 5

<u>VALUE</u> IS literal

The term **literal**, as used in this clause, refers to either a numeric literal, a nonnumeric literal, or a figurative constant. (See Chapter 2 for a detailed explanation of these terms.) Following are some examples of the use of the VALUE clause with a numeric literal or figurative constant.

```
77   ITEM-A              PIC 999      VALUE 345.
77   HOURLY-RATE         PIC 99V999   VALUE 06.350.
77   FICA-RATE           PIC V999     VALUE .070.
01   TOTAL-WS.
     05   TOTAL-GROSS     PIC 9(5)V99  VALUE ZERO.
     05   TOTAL-NET       PIC 9(5)V99  VALUE 0
     05   TOTAL-DEDUCT    PIC 9(4)V99  VALUE 0.00.
```

The initial value given a data item must be consistent with the class or type of data mentioned in the data item's PICTURE clause, but it need not be exactly the same size in terms of the number of integer and decimal positions shown. Care must be taken, however, that no valuable information is truncated. For example, the data item HOURLY-RATE shown above could have been written as

```
77   HOURLY-RATE PICTURE 99V999  VALUE 6.35.
```

without having any significant effect on the values assigned. On the other hand, the statement

```
77   HOURLY-RATE PICTURE 99V999 VALUE 6.3542.
```

would cause the digit 2 to be truncated, so that the actual initial value assigned to HOURLY-RATE would be 6.354. Therefore, it is good programming practice to assign an initial value to a data item that is consistent with the PICTURE description of that data item. Moreover, if a decimal number is assigned as an initial value to a data item containing a V in its PICTURE description, an actual decimal point must be inserted in the number at the position corresponding to the V, unless the value is 0.

Earlier, we stated that the VALUE clause may be used with either elementary or group data items. This statement has one exception: *a VALUE clause may not be used with a group data item if the literal is a numeric literal.* The literal must be a figurative constant or nonnumeric literal to be used in a VALUE clause with a group data item. In addition, when a VALUE clause is used with a group data item, it may *not* be specified at subordinate levels within that group.

Following are some examples of the use of a VALUE clause containing a figurative constant or nonnumeric literal.

```
77  MONTH       PICTURE X(4)      VALUE 'JUNE'.
77  SUM-AREA    PICTURE 9(5)      VALUE ZERO.
01  PRINT-OUT   PICTURE  X(133)   VALUE SPACES.
01  DATE-IN                       VALUE '1014'.
    05  MONTH   PIC XX.
    05  DAY     PIC XX.
```

It is possible to continue a nonnumeric literal from one line of the coding sheet to the next. Many programmers prefer to avoid this by breaking a long literal into several shorter ones. If, however, one wishes to continue a nonnumeric literal onto the next line, the following rules should be applied:

1. Continue the literal to the end of the line (through column 72). No quotation mark (' or ") is placed in column 72.

2. Place a hyphen (-) in column 7 and a quotation mark in the B Area of the continuation line.

3. Continue the literal, beginning in the column immediately to the right of the column containing the quotation mark.

4. The literal must end with a quotation mark followed by a period.

5. The literal may not exceed 120 characters.

Rules concerning the use of the VALUE clause to assign an initial value to a data item in the WORKING-STORAGE SECTION are as follows:

1. The term *literal* in the VALUE clause refers to numeric literals, nonnumeric literals, and figurative constants.

2. The literal used must agree in class and should agree in size with the associated PICTURE clause description.

3. A decimal point **must** be inserted at the appropriate place in the value specified if **a V** is contained in the PICTURE of the data item.

4. When used with a group data item, the literal cannot be a numeric literal.

5. When used with a group data item, the group item is initialized *independently of the USAGE of subordinate elementary or group items.*

6. When used with a group data item, a VALUE clause must not be specified at subordinate levels within that group.

As stated earlier, one of the major uses of the VALUE clause is to develop a report title or heading in WORKING-STORAGE. An example of how this applies to PROGRAM1 is given in Fig. 3–5. In PROGRAM1, there are three record descriptions, or 01-level entries, corresponding to the input records, the heading line, and the output record, respectively. Let us examine these record descriptions more carefully.

The record called EMPLOYEE-REC-IN refers to the input data that will be entered, one item at a time, from the keyboard when the program is executed. Note that the group item EMPLOYEE-NAME-IN does not have a PICTURE clause because it is subdivided into three elementary items, level 10 items that are indented within the B margin. This indentation within the B Margin is not required, but it obviously aids the programmer and reader in understanding how the record is organized. The elementary items in this record do not have VALUE clauses since the values will be supplied through the keyboard.

The record HEADING-OUT is the constant that will supply the necessary column heading shown in Fig. 3–6. We should note that in this record *all* elementary items have VALUE clauses because the record is to be displayed on the printer, and if some of the fields were not assigned values, the contents of those fields would be unpredictable (or would contain garbage, as is said in the profession). All of these elementary items have been given the name FILLER. This is the most convenient way to name these fields, since they will never be addressed individually, but only by the group item name HEADING-OUT. HEADING-OUT could have been defined as PIC X(57) with a single VALUE clause literal, namely,

```
'LAST NAME  FIRST    INIT   HOURS   RATE   GROSS PAY'
```

This is not the usual practice, however, since with longer headings it becomes more difficult to construct the VALUE clause accurately.

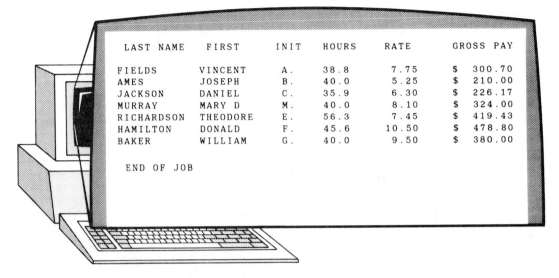

LAST NAME	FIRST	INIT	HOURS	RATE	GROSS PAY
FIELDS	VINCENT	A.	38.8	7.75	$ 300.70
AMES	JOSEPH	B.	40.0	5.25	$ 210.00
JACKSON	DANIEL	C.	35.9	6.30	$ 226.17
MURRAY	MARY D	M.	40.0	8.10	$ 324.00
RICHARDSON	THEODORE	E.	56.3	7.45	$ 419.43
HAMILTON	DONALD	F.	45.6	10.50	$ 478.80
BAKER	WILLIAM	G.	40.0	9.50	$ 380.00

END OF JOB

Fig. 3–6. A constant supplies the column heading.

All that remains is for us to describe the detail line of the output data, also shown in Fig. 3–5. In the figure, the detail line is defined after both the input description and the heading. However, this is not necessary. The order in which these records are described is not essential. What is essential is that a record description be provided for each type of input or output record.

Examination of the description of the record EMPLOYEE-REC-OUT will show its similarity to the descriptions given in the other records. The data names obviously refer to the same data as the input record, but of course the data names are not the same and the order of the data descriptions in EMPLOYEE-REC-OUT corresponds to the order and spacing of the titles in HEADING-OUT.

As with the record HEADING-OUT, FILLER was used to describe the areas that will separate the data fields on the printed report. Each of these fields was assigned an initial value of SPACES. Notice, however, that each was assigned a name different from that in the input record description EMPLOYEE-REC-IN. This is done so that later, when we refer to these areas, the machine will not be confused as to whether we are referring to an input area or an output area. In addition, some of these areas are described differently. For example, the input record description of the two numeric fields was given as S99V9 and S99V99.

In the output record description, however, the PICTURE clauses are ZZ.9, ZZ.99, and $Z,ZZZ.99 for the result field. These differences will allow the program to accept the input as numbers with *assumed* decimal points, a format necessary for processing them as numeric data items, and to print them out with suppression of high-order zeros and insertion of the dollar sign, comma, and decimal point where appropriate. In order to alter the input data in this way, we shall have to carry out some data manipulation in the PROCEDURE DIVISION.

THE PROCEDURE DIVISION

In Chapter 2 we learned that the PROCEDURE DIVISION contains the specific instructions in the logical sequence in which they must be executed to create the desired output from the given input data. In PROGRAM1 the sequence would be as shown in Fig. 3–3.

Since in most programs the PROCEDURE DIVISION will involve several tasks or routines, we generally organize this division into paragraphs in such a way that each paragraph is concerned with only one task or procedure. One can visualize the logical flow through such a structured program as a highway system, such as the one shown in Fig. 3–7.

In the figure, there is a main line or central highway to which several side roads are connected. Along the main line there are procedures (3 and 5) that will be performed without the necessity to branch off the main line. However, there are other procedures (1, 2, and 4) that require that one branch off the main line to perform them, and then return to the main line immediately afterward.

Notice that Procedure 4 is somewhat different from Procedures 1 and 2. The difference is that Procedures 1 and 2 will be performed exactly once, whereas Procedure 4 may be performed from zero to an indefinite number of times depending on when, if ever, the specified exit condition is met. Let us look more closely at how the exit condition affects the number of times Procedure 4 is executed.

If the exit condition is satisfied when control passes to it, Procedure 4 will be passed and not even executed once. If, however, the exit condition is not satisfied when it is encountered, Procedure 4 will be executed over and over until the exit condition is satisfied, at which point control will return to the main line. If the exit condition is never satisfied, an endless loop will result. Care should be taken to make certain that this situation will never occur.

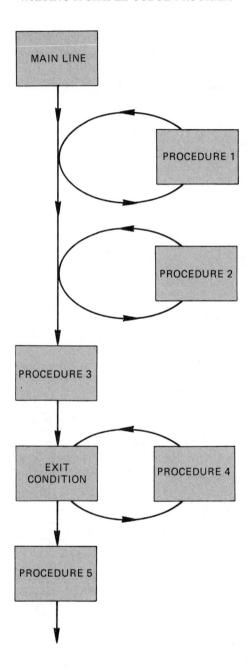

Fig. 3–7. Visual flow through a structured program.

If we were to convert the flowchart shown in Fig. 3–7 to a visual type of presentation, it would appear similar to that shown in Fig. 3–8.

If we follow the visual flow shown in Fig. 3–8, we see that the first thing we must do is to establish a main line. We can do this by creating

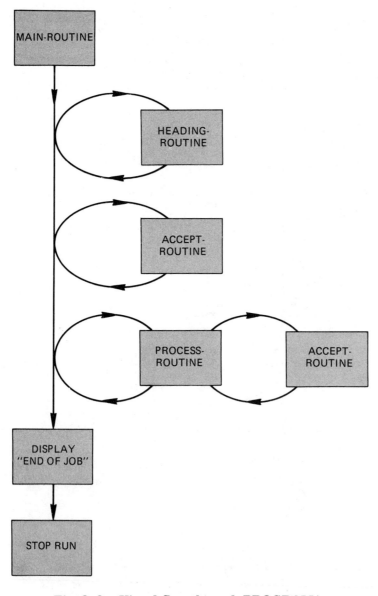

Fig. 3–8.   Visual flow through PROGRAM1.

the paragraph-name MAIN-ROUTINE. Next, we must indicate that we wish to branch off of the main line, execute the HEADING-ROUTINE procedure, and return to the main line. This can be accomplished with the aid of the PERFORM statement.

PERFORM with THRU and TIMES Options

The general format of the PERFORM statement is:

GENERAL FORMAT 6

PERFORM procedure-name-1 $\left\{\begin{array}{l}\text{THRU} \\ \text{THROUGH}\end{array}\right\}$ procedure-name-2]

$[\left\{\begin{array}{l}\text{identifier-1} \\ \text{integer-1}\end{array}\right\}$ TIMES]

Procedure-name-1 and **procedure-name-2** are the names of paragraphs or sections within the PROCEDURE DIVISION.

If the [{THRU/THROUGH} procedure-name-2] and [{identifier-1/ integer-1} TIMES] options are omitted, execution of the PERFORM statement causes control to be transferred to the paragraph or section specified as procedure-name-1. After the last statement in the procedure-name-1 paragraph or section is executed, control returns to the statement following the PERFORM statement, as shown in Fig. 3–9.

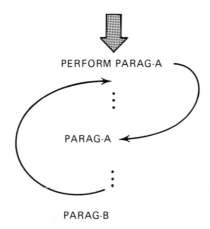

PERFORM PARAG-A

PARAG-A

PARAG-B

Fig. 3–9. PERFORM statement without the THRU or TIMES options.

In the figure, execution of the PERFORM statement causes control
to be transferred to PARAG-A. After the last statement in PARAG-A
is executed, control returns to the statement following the PERFORM
statement.

If the [{identifier-1/integer-1}] TIMES] option were used with the
PERFORM statement shown in Fig. 3–9, the only change would be that
of PARAG-A would have been performed integer-1 times or the number of times specified by the current value of identifier-1, depending on
whether an integer or an identifier was provided. For example, the
PERFORM statement

```
PERFORM PARAG-A 10 TIMES.
```

and the PERFORM statement

```
PERFORM PARAG-A N TIMES.
```

would each PERFORM PARAG-A a number of times. The first statement would clearly PERFORM PARAG-A 10 times since the 10 is explicitly stated. The second statement, however, would PERFORM
PARAG-A the number of times designated by the current value stored
in the data item N. Figure 3–10 illustrates this concept.

The following rules apply to the use of a PERFORM statement with
the TIMES option:

1. If the value of integer-1 or identifier-1 is zero or negative at the
time of execution of the PERFORM statement, the entire statement is skipped.

2. If the value of integer-1 or identifier-1 is positive at the time of
execution of the PERFORM statement, the indicated paragraphs
or sections are executed the specified number of times before
control is returned to the statement immediately following the
PERFORM statement.

3. If the value of identifier-1 is altered after execution of the PER-
FORM statement has commenced but before it has been completed, the number of times the indicated paragraphs or sections
are executed is unaffected.

If the [THRU procedure-name-2] option is specified, execution of
the PERFORM statement causes control to be transferred to the paragraph or section specified as procedure-name-1. Once this transfer has

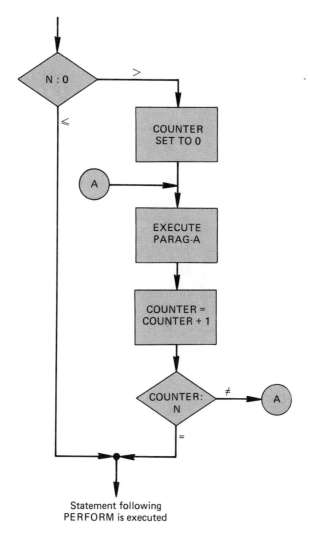

Fig. 3–10. PERFORM statement with the TIMES option.

been made, all paragraphs or sections beginning with procedure-name-1 and ending with procedure-name-2 are executed completely and in sequential order (the order in which they appear). If a TIMES option has been specified also, the process will be repeated the number of times specified. The concept is illustrated by the PERFORM statement shown in Fig. 3–11.

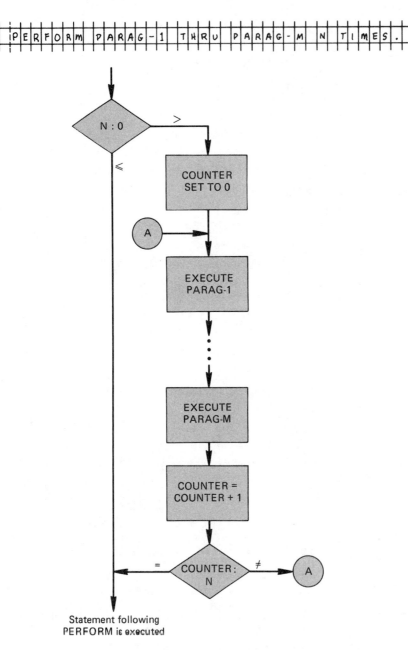

Fig. 3–11. **PERFORM** statement with the **THRU**
and **TIMES** options.

When the PERFORM statement shown in the figure is executed, control is transferred to the PARAG-1 paragraph. After this paragraph has been completely executed, the remaining paragraphs through PARAG-M are executed. Control then returns to the statement following the PERFORM statement.

Note that when the THRU option is used, all paragraphs or sections between procedure-name-1 and procedure-name-2 are executed. If one or more intermediate paragraphs are not to be executed as part of the PERFORM statement, the THRU option should not be used. Such a situation may be handled by using several PERFORM statements.

It may happen that a condition occurring in a given paragraph or section within the range of a PERFORM statement makes it desirable or necessary to skip the remainder of that paragraph or section—and possibly other paragraphs or sections within the range of the statement—and return control to the sentence following the PERFORM statement. Because execution of the PERFORM statement will not be complete until the last paragraph within its range has been executed, a special last paragraph consisting of only one statement—an EXIT statement—must be provided.

The EXIT Statement

The program segment shown in Fig. 3–12 illustrates the purpose and use of the EXIT statement with the PERFORM statement. In this example, execution of the PERFORM statement causes control to be transferred to the PARAG-B paragraph. After this paragraph is executed, execution of the PARAG-C paragraph commences. In this paragraph there is a conditional branching statement that under normal conditions causes continuous execution of the statements in the paragraph but under special conditions skips the remaining instructions in both the PARAG-C and PARAG-D paragraphs. To allow this latter option, the PARAG-EXIT paragraph is added. When executed, this paragraph causes the PERFORM statement to be satisfied and control to be returned to the sentence following the PERFORM statement. If the return to the statement after the PERFORM statement in PARAG-A is accomplished by a GO TO statement in PARAG-C, the PERFORM loop will not be satisfied and the procedures described in these paragraphs may not be executed in normal sequential order at some future point in the program.

It should be noted that execution of the EXIT statement does not satisfy the condition in a PERFORM with a TIMES option or other

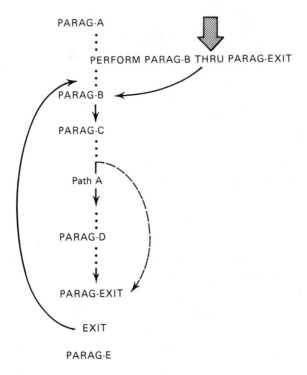

PARAG-A

PERFORM PARAG-B THRU PARAG-EXIT

PARAG-B

PARAG-C

Path A

PARAG-D

PARAG-EXIT

EXIT

PARAG-E

**Fig. 3–12. Use of the EXIT statement with the
PERFORM statement.**

conditional PERFORM. It merely serves as the last statement within
the range of a PERFORM.

Multiple PERFORM Statements

A PERFORM statement may refer to paragraphs contained within
the range of another PERFORM statement or to a PERFORM statement whose range is completely contained within the range of another
PERFORM statement. Such nested PERFORM statements are frequent in COBOL programming and deserve special consideration.

When a PERFORM statement contains another PERFORM statement, the second PERFORM statement must have its range either totally included in or totally excluded from the range of the first
PERFORM statement. That is, the exit point of the first PERFORM
statement must *not* occur before the exit point of the second PER-
FORM statement. (See Fig. 3–13.)

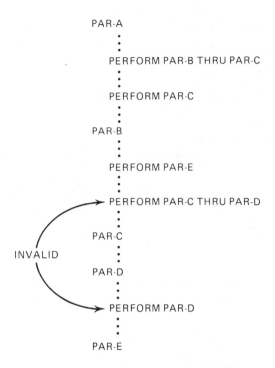

Fig. 3-13. Valid and invalid nested PERFORM statements.

Thus, for PROGRAM1, the statement

```
PERFORM HEADING-ROUTINE.
```

would satisfy our needs. We would then, of course, have to code the routine HEADING-ROUTINE for later use in the PROCEDURE DIVISION. This routine would be concerned with the output of the desired titles and would utilize the DISPLAY statement.

The DISPLAY Statement

The general format of the DISPLAY statement is:

GENERAL FORMAT 7

$$\underline{\text{DISPLAY}} \ [\text{position-spec}] \ \left\{ \begin{matrix} \text{identifier} \\ \text{literal} \\ \underline{\text{ERASE}} \end{matrix} \right\} \ \ldots \ [\underline{\text{UPON}} \ \text{mnemonic-name}]$$

In this format, **identifier** is either a group or elementary data item that is defined in the DATA DIVISION. A DISPLAY statement with an identifier option will cause the current contents of the identifier to be output. If the **literal** option is employed, the literal will be printed out as it appears in the DISPLAY statement. A figurative constant (ZERO, SPACES, etc.) may also be used in a DISPLAY statement.

If the optional clause [UPON mnemonic-name] is utilized, the mnemonic-name must be one specified previously in the SPECIAL-NAMES paragraph of the ENVIRONMENT DIVISION. Had we not done this earlier when we were coding the ENVIRONMENT DIVISION, we would have to do it at this time. If the clause UPON mnemonic-name is not used, the computer will assume that the system output device is used. This is referred to as the default option, which on the IBM PC is the screen.

Thus, to print out a blank line on the printer, identified by the mnemonic-name LINE-OUT in the SPECIAL-NAMES paragraph of the ENVIRONMENT DIVISION, we would use the DISPLAY statement

```
DISPLAY SPACES UPON LINE-OUT.
```

The HEADING-ROUTINE required in our program is

```
HEADING-ROUTINE.
    DISPLAY HEADING-OUT UPON LINE-OUT.
    DISPLAY SPACES UPON LINE-OUT.
```

The position-spec option of this statement refers to the *line* and *column* of the screen at which you want the data to appear. The screen on the IBM PC consists of 25 lines and 80 columns (2000 separate locations). In the position-spec option, the line is specified first, followed by the column. For example, the statement

```
DISPLAY (5, 10) 'ENTER FIRST NAME'.
```

causes the message ENTER FIRST NAME to appear on the fifth line beginning at the tenth space from the left.

When the ERASE option is used with the DISPLAY statement, the entire screen can be cleared prior to displaying some messages. DISPLAY (1, 1) ERASE causes the screen to be cleared, beginning at the upper left position.

The ACCEPT Statement

Two general formats of the ACCEPT STATEMENT are

GENERAL FORMAT 8

ACCEPT identifier

GENERAL FORMAT 9

ACCEPT [position-spec] identifier [WITH PROMPT]

The ACCEPT statement causes a data item to be read from the keyboard and places the appropriate number of characters in the designated area in working storage. Thus, the statement

```
ACCEPT FIRST-NAME-IN.
```

would cause the computer to read from the keyboard a number of characters whose total width does not exceed the field width of FIRST-NAME-IN and store them in the data item called FIRST-NAME-IN. If fewer characters than the number of characters in the field width are entered, the unused spaces at the right in FIRST-NAME-IN will be filled with SPACES. If more characters than the number of characters in the field width of FIRST-NAME-IN are entered, the excess characters will be *truncated*.

Returning to our flow diagram of Fig. 3–8, we see that our next task is to enter the data. This will be accomplished by performing ACCEPT-ROUTINE, which contains a series of DISPLAY and ACCEPT statements. Since we are going to use the keyboard to enter the data, we will use the DISPLAY statement, with default to the screen, to instruct the user regarding how the data is to be entered. We will then use the ACCEPT statement to receive the data from the keyboard.

In order to make the screens more meaningful, rather than having the user merely enter the data in response to an ACCEPT statement, we will use a combination of DISPLAY statements and ACCEPT statements with the PROMPT option to provide for precise entry of the data. Thus, the statements

```
DISPLAY (5, 10) 'ENTER FIRST NAME'.
ACCEPT (5, 31) FIRST-NAME-IN WITH PROMPT.
```

will cause

```
ENTER FIRST NAME ..........
```

to appear on the screen beginning at the fifth line, tenth column. Note that the PROMPT option causes the exact number of periods as corresponds to the size of the PICTURE clause of the fields specified to be shown—in this case 10, in response to the PIC X(10) associated with FIRST-NAME-IN.

The PROMPT option is handled slightly differently with numeric data, in keeping with the nature of that data. Consider the prompt

```
ENTER HOURS WORKED 00.0
```

Initially, the cursor appears at the position immediately to the left of the decimal point. The cursor remains fixed at this position as integer digits are typed in. As each successive digit is typed in, the previously entered digits shift one position to the left. After all integer positions are filled or after a decimal point is entered, the cursor moves to the position immediately to the right of the decimal point and awaits the input of the decimal-place digits. As decimal-place digits are entered, the cursor moves rightward to the next available position. This process continues until all available decimal positions are filled or until the return key is depressed. Note that as integer digits are entered, the cursor remains fixed in place and the previously entered digits move whereas when the decimal places are entered, the cursor moves to the right and the previously entered digits remain fixed in place. Thus, for an entry of 39.6 hours, you would press 39.6 in that order, for correct entry of the data. See Fig. 3–1 for the format of the entire input screen. The ACCEPT-ROUTINE is shown in Fig. 3–5.

If desired, we could have utilized another procedure to specify where the cursor was to appear in the prompt by using the reserved words LIN and COL in the ACCEPT statement. Thus,

```
DISPLAY (5, 10) 'ENTER FIRST NAME   '.
ACCEPT (LIN, COL) FIRST-NAME-IN WITH PROMPT.
```

will cause the same result as when (5, 31) was used as the position spec for the ACCEPT statement. Note that we have left three spaces within the literal so that the cursor will not begin the name immediately after the literal.

The PERFORM with UNTIL Option

At this point in the flow diagram for PROGRAM1, we need a PERFORM statement, but one that is somewhat different from the one we used previously to PERFORM the paragraph HEADING-ROUTINE. Here, we wish to PERFORM PROCESS-ROUTINE a number of times until a certain exit condition is satisfied. The statement that will accomplish this is the PERFORM statement with the UNTIL option, the general format of which is:

GENERAL FORMAT 10

PERFORM procedure-name-1 [THRU procedure-name-2]

UNTIL condition-1

The UNTIL option of the PERFORM statement is very similar in effect to the TIMES option. The UNTIL option, however, provides greater flexibility in controlling the termination of the PERFORM loop. The procedure defined by the range of the PERFORM statement is executed repeatedly until a stipulated condition is satisfied. Note that *first* the condition is tested, and *then* the routine is performed. Thus, if the condition is satisfied when the PERFORM statement is first encountered, the procedure is not even performed once, and control is transferred to the statement immediately following the PERFORM statement. Figure 3–14 illustrates what happens when the computer executes a PERFORM statement with the UNTIL option.

In this format, **condition-1** must be a relational condition or a condition-name condition. As we need not be concerned with a detailed discussion of relational and condition-name conditions at this time, we shall limit our current discussion to one type of relational condition—the equality condition. The form of the equality condition we shall require is

identifier = literal or figurative constant

When a relational condition of this form appears in a PERFORM statement, the paragraphs or sections specified in the statement will be executed until the value contained in the identifier is equal to the literal or figurative constant specified.

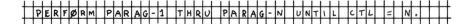

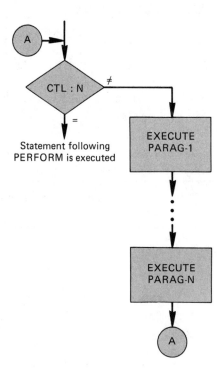

Fig. 3–14.   Execution of a PERFORM statement with the UNTIL option.

In the case of PROGRAM1, data were to be processed until a blank data set was encountered. Thus, we could test any of these fields for blanks and use the results of this test as an exit condition for our PER-FORM statement. This would be a condition that would be true only after the last data set had been entered—for example a condition such as

```
FIRST-NAME-IN = SPACES
```

Alternatively, we could test LAST-NAME-IN or INIT-IN for SPACES.

If FIRST-NAME-IN is tested for SPACES, the PERFORM statement would be

```
PERFORM PROCESS-ROUTINE  UNTIL FIRST-NAME-IN = SPACES.
```

We next must code the routine PROCESS-ROUTINE. The first thing to do is move the data, field by field, from the input area EMPLOYEE-REC-IN to the output area EMPLOYEE-REC-OUT. To do this, we use the MOVE statement.

The MOVE Statement

The general format of the MOVE statement is:

GENERAL FORMAT 11

$\underline{\text{MOVE}}$ $\begin{Bmatrix} \text{identifier-1} \\ \text{literal} \end{Bmatrix}$ $\underline{\text{TO}}$ identifier-2 [identifier-3] . . .

In this format, **identifier-1** and **literal** denote the sending areas and **identifier-2, identifier 3, . . .** denote the receiving areas. Thus, for PROGRAM1, we require five separate MOVE statements, one for each field in the input record EMPLOYEE-REC-IN. Inserting these MOVE statements into PROCESS-ROUTINE, we have

```
PROCESS-ROUTINE.
    MOVE FIRST-NAME-IN TO FIRST-NAME-OUT.
    MOVE INITIAL-IN TO INITIAL-OUT.
    MOVE LAST-NAME-IN TO LAST-NAME-OUT.
    MOVE RATE-IN TO RATE-OUT.
    MOVE HOURS-IN TO HOURS-OUT.
```

The MOVE statement will be discussed in more detail in the next chapter.

Besides the MOVE statements, we have an arithmetic statement in PROCESS-ROUTINE, namely,

```
MULTIPLY RATE-IN BY HOURS-IN GIVING GROSS-PAY-OUT.
```

The meaning of this statement is clear; the statement itself represents the type of arithmetic statements that will be found in Chapter 5.

Referring again to the flowchart for PROGRAM1, we see that two more statements are required to complete the coding of PROCESS-

ROUTINE: a statement to DISPLAY the output line for the processed data, followed by a statement to provide for the entry of new data. The statements in question are the DISPLAY and ACCEPT statements as coded in

```
DISPLAY EMPLOYEE-REC-OUT UPON LINE-OUT.
PERFORM ACCEPT-ROUTINE.
```

PERFORM ACCEPT-ROUTINE will cause the ACCEPT statements to be executed one time.

At this point, the ACCEPT statements will read either another employee's data or, if there are no more, the SPACES entry for FIRST-NAME-IN, which will be the signal for the end of data. Entering SPACES is simple with the ACCEPT statement: merely press the Enter key once for each such statement, and the program will terminate execution of the PERFORM PROCESS-ROUTINE UNTIL FIRST-NAME-IN = SPACES statement.

Returning to the flow diagram for PROGRAM1, we see that all that remains is to DISPLAY the message 'END OF JOB' and STOP program execution. The statements required are:

```
DISPLAY 'END OF JOB' UPON LINE-OUT.
STOP RUN.
```

The STOP Statement

The final statement in the PROCEDURE DIVISION and in PROGRAM1 is the STOP statement, which indicates that processing is completed. The STOP statement causes execution of the program to halt temporarily or permanently, depending on the option chosen. The general format of the statement is:

GENERAL FORMAT 12

$$\underline{STOP} \begin{Bmatrix} \text{literal} \\ \underline{RUN} \end{Bmatrix}$$

If the RUN option is chosen, execution of the object program is permanently terminated, and control is transferred to the operating system. If the literal option is chosen, execution of the program is terminated, and the literal is communicated to the computer operator. At this point, only the operator's intervention can cause execution of the program to be resumed. If the operator does intervene, by pressing the Enter key, program execution will resume with the statement immediately following the STOP statement. The literal option would not be appropriate for the STOP statement of PROGRAM1.

The following are examples of temporary STOP commands that cause the literals 1, 86, INSERT DISK IN A, TYPE IN DATE, and DISK IS FULL, respectively, to be communicated to the computer operator.

```
STOP '1'.
STOP '86'.
STOP 'INSERT DISK IN A'.
STOP 'TYPE IN DATE'.
STOP 'DISK IS FULL'.
```

For PROGRAM1, STOP RUN is the desired form of the STOP statement. This statement and the remainder of the COBOL instructions contained in the PROCEDURE DIVISION complete Fig. 3–5.

On the disk that accompanies this book, the source program PROGRAM1 has the filename CH301.COB. If you have the disk, you may compile and run this program yourself. In fact, why not change the source program (after making a backup copy of it, of course) and run your own version!

EXERCISES

1. Write a program that will ACCEPT a name (20 characters) and an address (35 characters) from two different ACCEPT statements and DISPLAY them on one line of your printer.

2. Write a program to ACCEPT a record for each employee, according to the input layout shown on page 92, and DISPLAY a report as shown on the print layout. The program should continue to ACCEPT data until a Social Security Number of 999999999 is entered.

3. Often, it is necessary to produce more than one copy of output for each set of input data. Write a program to read the name and address shown on page 93 and prepare three mailing labels for each input record. Continue reading data until a blank name is encountered.

Input Layout

Input Record: EMPLOYEE-REC

SOCIAL SECURITY NUMBER	EMPLOYEE NAME		INIT	HOURS	RATE	GROSS
	LAST	FIRST				
1 2 3 4 5 6 7 8 9	1 1 1 1 1 1 1 1 1 1 0 1 2 3 4 5 6 7 8 9	2 2 2 2 2 2 2 2 2 2 0 1 2 3 4 5 6 7 8 9	3 3 0 1	3 3 3 2 3 4	3 3 3 3 5 6 7 8	4 4 4 4 9 0 1 2

Output Layout

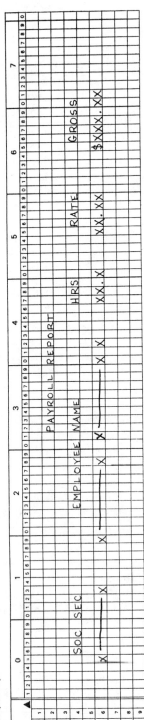

Input Layout

Input Record: LABEL-DATA

NAME	STREET ADDRESS	CITY	STATE	ZIP
1 1 1 1 1 1 1 1 1 1 2 2 2 2 2 2 2 2 2 2	3 3 3 3 3 3 3 3 3 3 4 4 4 4 4 4 4 4 4 4	5 5 5 5 5 5 5 5 5 5	6 6	6 6 6 6 6
1 2 3 4 5 6 7 8 9 0 1 2 3 4 5 6 7 8 9 0	1 2 3 4 5 6 7 8 9 0 1 2 3 4 5 6 7 8 9 0	1 2 3 4 5 6 7 8 9 0	1 2	3 4 5 6 7

Output Layout

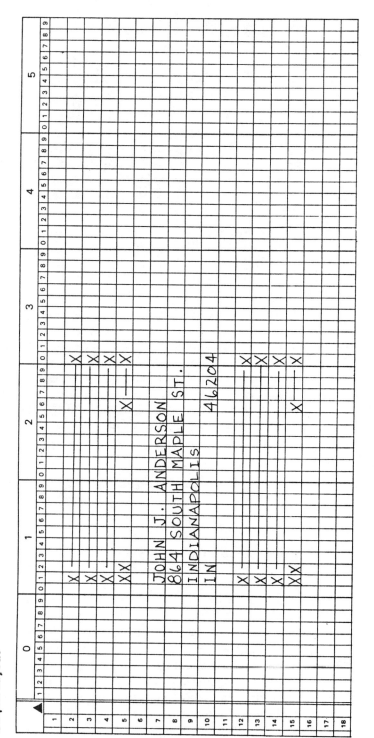

93

4

PROGRAMMING WITH FILES

In Chapter 3, we learned that data can be entered via the ACCEPT statement and printed via the DISPLAY statement. However, these statements are not meant to be used with large volumes of input or output. For such cases, COBOL provides instead the capability of handling related records as files. Accordingly, this chapter discusses the nature, purpose, and use of records and files in COBOL programs. A review of data items, fields, records, and files may be useful.

DATA ITEMS, FIELDS, RECORDS, AND FILES

Before being input to a computer, data must be recorded on an appropriate medium. For example, to add a new employee to the personnel file in a personnel accounting system, the relevant data must be transcribed from an employee's personal data form, such as the one shown in Fig. 4-1, to a medium that a computer will accept. In the past, on mainframe computers, this would have been done via punch cards; today, whether using a mainframe computer or a personal computer, it is normally accomplished by entering the data directly into the computer through a keyboard.

A specific program would be used to accept and edit the data both to ensure the highest possible degree of accuracy and because files are normally created by a program. Some of the programming methods used in computer text editing will be discussed in Chapter 6.

```
                    PERSONAL DATA FORM
NAME    JOHN  JOSCELYN

ADDRESS    24  PARK PL.  SEAFORD  NY  11783
           No    Street    Town    State  ZIP

AGE    49              SEX    MALE

MARITAL STATUS    MARRIED

SOCIAL SECURITY NUMBER    114-36-4972

YEARS EMPLOYED    26

HIGHEST EDUCATION COMPLETED    2 YRS. COLLEGE

EMPLOYEE NUMBER    ØØ234574Ø24Ø5Ø
```

Fig. 4–1.   Typical employee data form.

To illustrate the use of input and output files at this time, we shall use the word processor program or the PC-DOS EDLIN utility program to create our input data. The type of file created in this manner is called a **line sequential** file, a file that is unique to microcomputers.

In the illustration that follows, the same data are contained on both the employee's personal data form and the corresponding personal data record. Both represent *records*, as both are collections of related items of data treated as a unit. Figure 4–1 shows a paper record containing both required data and appropriate descriptive information. Figure 4–2 shows a disk record containing only required data, with *no* descriptive information. The record is subdivided into groups of consecutive columns, or **fields**, into which data items are placed. The programmer, by means of program coding, instructs the computer as to the location and size of each data field in the record and assigns a data-name to each data field. These data-names then serve as labels by means of which the computer can reference each field in future processing.

The data-name assigned to a field by the programmer is generally indicative of the contents of the field. For example, the first field in the record in Fig. 4–2 contains the employee's name and thus might be assigned the data-name EMPLOYEE-NAME. The size of a field is determined by the data to be contained within it. Where possible, data should be coded before it is recorded on the medium to be used. For

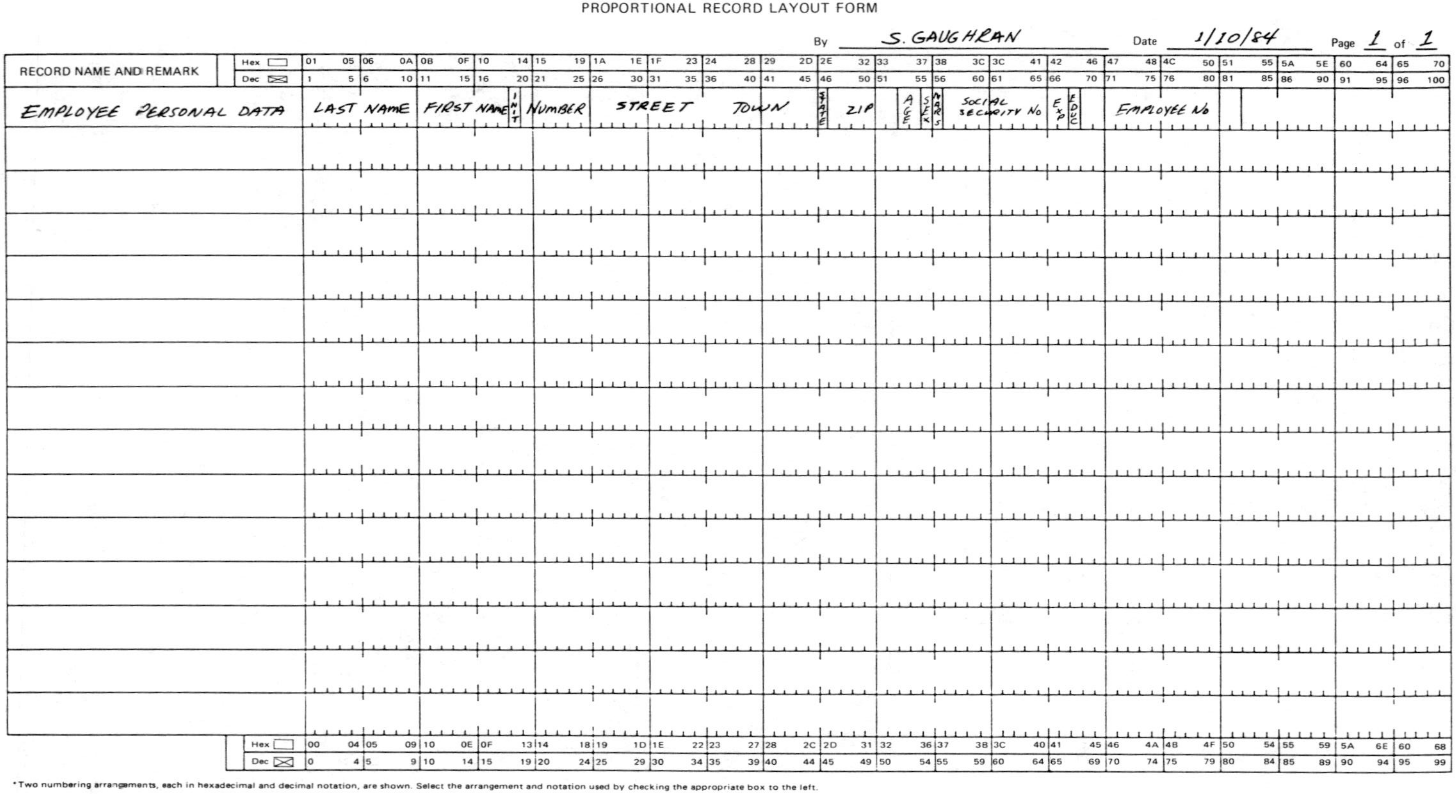

PROPORTIONAL RECORD LAYOUT FORM

By S. GAUGHRAN   Date 1/10/84   Page 1 of 1

RECORD NAME AND REMARK: EMPLOYEE PERSONAL DATA

Hex ☐ Dec ☒

LAST NAME   FIRST NAME   NUMBER   STREET   TOWN   ZIP   STATE ABBREV.   SOCIAL SECURITY No.   EX DZU X 3   EMPLOYEE No.

Fig. 4-2. Employee personal data record format.

*Two numbering arrangements, each in hexadecimal and decimal notation, are shown. Select the arrangement and notation used by checking the appropriate box to the left.

example, for recording an employee's sex in a disk record, one might assign the code 0 to a female employee and the code 1 to a male employee. Or the codes F and M might be used instead. Whatever code is chosen, the information would then be contained in one character position in a form that could be easily decoded by the program.

Fields are classified as either numeric, alphabetic, or alphanumeric according to the type of data they contain. Numeric fields contain only numeric data and are described with or without an implied decimal point. If the field is described without an implied decimal point (no V in its PICTURE clause), the data to be contained in it will be **right-justified**, or placed as far right within the field as possible. If the field is described with an implied decimal point (a V in its PICTURE clause), the data to be contained in it will be justified around the decimal point. Alphabetic fields can contain only alphabetic data, which will be **left-justified**, or placed as far left within the field as possible. Alphanumeric fields can contain both alphabetic and numeric data, as well as special characters such as .*,? and the like; these data are left-justified within the field. Thus, records can be made up of numeric, alphabetic, and alphanumeric fields, as shown in Table 4–1.

Once a record is input to the computer, each data field in the record is assigned a *unique data-name*. These data fields then represent data items that can be used in subsequent processing. Data items are of two types: group data items and elementary data items. A *group data item* is a data item that is subdivided into other data items; an *elementary data item* is a data item that is not subdivided. Suppose that the employee number field in Fig. 4–2 were subdivided as follows:

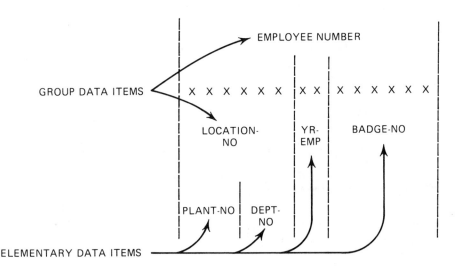

**Table 4–1. EXAMPLES OF DIFFERENT
TYPES OF FIELDS**

Alphabetic	Numeric	Alphanumeric
OUTPUT	47	440 SCREWS
GROSS PAY	394	3,875
OVERTIME	5	4 HARROW DR
CREDIT	143∧ 3876*	ERROR STOP 3

*The symbol ∧ refers to the position of an implied decimal point.

Then EMPLOYEE-NO would be a group data item since it is subdivided into other data items, namely, LOCATION-NO, YR-EMP, and BADGE-NO. Moreover, since LOCATION-NO is subdivided into PLANT-NO and DEPT-NO, it too is a group data item. On the other hand, the data items PLANT-NO, DEPT-NO, YR-EMP, and BADGE-NO are elementary data items since they are not subdivided.

To review, a record is a collection of related items or fields treated as a unit; it generally contains the data pertaining to a single individual or transaction. The availability of all data pertaining to an individual or transaction in one record makes the programmer's task of processing these data relatively simple. This task is further simplified by the fact that related records are stored together in a file. In fact, a file is just that: a collection of related records. In the previous example of the personnel accounting system, the personnel file would be a collection of personnel records, one record for each employee of the company. Such files would be maintained on magnetic disk.

PROGRAMMING WITH FILES

Consider the following problem, which illustrates each of the COBOL divisions.

Problem: Write a program called PROGRAM-LIST to run on an IBM PC. The program is to produce a report, with appropriate descriptive information, that lists the data (Fig. 4–3) contained in the input file, TRANSAC-FILE. The fields contained in this record, together with their descriptions, are shown in Fig. 4–2. The output is to be called TRANSAC-LIST, and its layout is shown in Fig. 4–4. The external names for the input and output files are DISK and PRINTER, respectively. At the completion of the processing of TRANSAC-FILE, the message END OF JOB is to be printed.

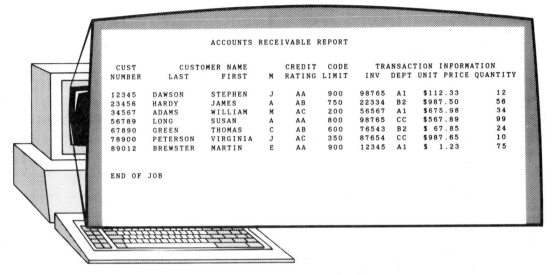

```
                    ACCOUNTS RECEIVABLE REPORT

   CUST          CUSTOMER NAME        CREDIT  CODE      TRANSACTION INFORMATION
  NUMBER      LAST        FIRST    M  RATING LIMIT    INV  DEPT UNIT PRICE QUANTITY

  12345     DAWSON      STEPHEN    J    AA    900    98765  A1   $112.33     12
  23456     HARDY       JAMES      A    AB    750    22334  B2   $987.50     56
  34567     ADAMS       WILLIAM    M    AC    200    56567  A1   $675.98     34
  56789     LONG        SUSAN      A    AA    800    98765  CC   $567.89     99
  67890     GREEN       THOMAS     C    AB    600    76543  B2   $ 67.85     24
  78900     PETERSON    VIRGINIA   J    AC    350    87654  CC   $987.65     10
  89012     BREWSTER    MARTIN     E    AA    900    12345  A1   $  1.23     75


  END OF JOB
```

Fig. 4-3. Output for PROGRAM-LIST.

THE IDENTIFICATION DIVISION

The purpose of this division is to provide a standard method of identifying the particular COBOL program to the computer. For PROGRAM-LIST, the entries in this division would be as follows:

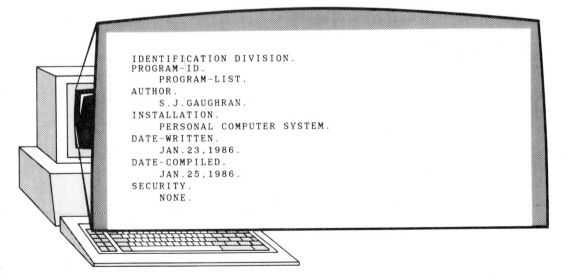

```
IDENTIFICATION DIVISION.
PROGRAM-ID.
     PROGRAM-LIST.
AUTHOR.
     S.J.GAUGHRAN.
INSTALLATION.
     PERSONAL COMPUTER SYSTEM.
DATE-WRITTEN.
     JAN.23,1986.
DATE-COMPILED.
     JAN.25,1986.
SECURITY.
     NONE.
```

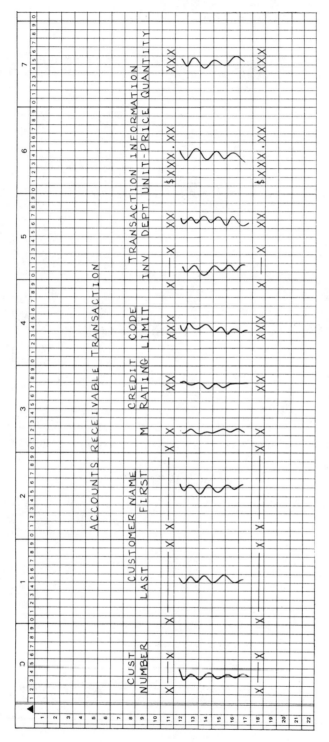

Fig. 4–4. Print layout for TRANSAC-LIST.

Note that only the first three lines—the division header and the PROGRAM-ID entry—are required by COBOL. The other entries are for purposes of documentation only.

THE ENVIRONMENT DIVISION

The ENVIRONMENT DIVISION must provide the information concerning the hardware to be used in compiling and executing the program. Thus, this division is dependent on the devices that will be so used—normally the disk and the printer in the case of the IBM PC. Such information is contained in the INPUT-OUTPUT SECTION of the ENVIRONMENT DIVISION.

The INPUT-OUTPUT SECTION of a COBOL program is concerned with the following:

1. The naming of each file used in the program.

2. The external storage medium (disk or printer) used with each data file.

3. The assignment of each data file to one or more input or output devices.

4. Additional information for the description of the files needed for the efficient transmission of data between the file media and the object program.

The general format of this section is as follows:

GENERAL FORMAT 1

INPUT-OUTPUT SECTION.

FILE CONTROL
    file-control-entry.
    I-O CONTROL.
    input-output-control-entry.

The FILE-CONTROL Paragraph

When a program is concerned with input or output of files, the INPUT-OUTPUT SECTION must contain a FILE-CONTROL paragraph. The primary purpose of this paragraph is to assign these files to the appropriate input and/or output devices. The general format of the FILE-CONTROL paragraph is as follows:

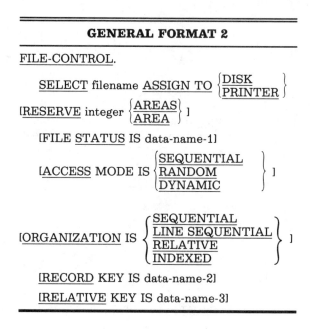

GENERAL FORMAT 2

FILE-CONTROL.

SELECT filename ASSIGN TO $\begin{Bmatrix} \text{DISK} \\ \text{PRINTER} \end{Bmatrix}$

[RESERVE integer $\begin{Bmatrix} \text{AREAS} \\ \text{AREA} \end{Bmatrix}$]

[FILE STATUS IS data-name-1]

[ACCESS MODE IS $\begin{Bmatrix} \text{SEQUENTIAL} \\ \text{RANDOM} \\ \text{DYNAMIC} \end{Bmatrix}$]

[ORGANIZATION IS $\begin{Bmatrix} \text{SEQUENTIAL} \\ \text{LINE SEQUENTIAL} \\ \text{RELATIVE} \\ \text{INDEXED} \end{Bmatrix}$]

[RECORD KEY IS data-name-2]

[RELATIVE KEY IS data-name-3]

The **SELECT clause** assigns a unique name to each file in the program. The filename assigned must conform to the rules that apply to the formation of a data-name and must appear immediately following the word SELECT.

The **ASSIGN clause** indicates to the computer the device(s) that will be used for input and/or output of the file(s) named in the immediately preceding SELECT clause. Allowable entries in the ASSIGN clause in IBM (Microsoft) COBOL are DISK and PRINTER. DISK may refer to input and output files, while the PRINTER entry is, of course, limited to referring to output files.

The **RESERVE clause** is not used in IBM COBOL.

The **FILE STATUS clause** names a two-character alphanumeric data item described by the programmer in the WORKING-STORAGE SECTION that will contain codes placed there by DOS after each input or output operation. The program can then check for successful or unsuccessful completion of the I/O operation and the reason for a failure, if one occurs. This clause plays a more important role in the processing of other than sequential files.

The **ACCESS MODE clause** is not needed for any files that are to be accessed sequentially and the default is SEQUENTIAL. The other modes are RANDOM and DYNAMIC.

In the **ORGANIZATION clause** the default is again SEQUEN-TIAL, but we shall also be using LINE SEQUENTIAL. The other types of organization are RELATIVE and INDEXED.

The **RECORD KEY** and **RELATIVE KEY clauses** are used for other than SEQUENTIAL files.

PROGRAM-LIST will use only three of the above entries in its FILE-CONTROL paragraph: the SELECT clause, the ASSIGN clause, and the ORGANIZATION clause. The entire ENVIRONMENT DIVISION entries for the program are shown in Fig. 4–5.

The I-O CONTROL Paragraph

The I-O-CONTROL paragraph is an optional paragraph that is not directly applicable to our current discussions; therefore, we shall defer consideration of it.

THE DATA DIVISION

We next consider the effect on the DATA DIVISION of utilizing files. Since the DATA DIVISION of a program describes all data used by the program, it is greatly affected by the use of data files. The first section of this division, the FILE SECTION, is devoted exclusively to describing the files used by the program.

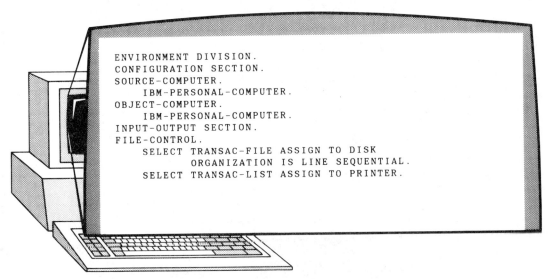

```
ENVIRONMENT DIVISION.
CONFIGURATION SECTION.
SOURCE-COMPUTER.
     IBM-PERSONAL-COMPUTER.
OBJECT-COMPUTER.
     IBM-PERSONAL-COMPUTER.
INPUT-OUTPUT SECTION.
FILE-CONTROL.
     SELECT TRANSAC-FILE ASSIGN TO DISK
          ORGANIZATION IS LINE SEQUENTIAL.
     SELECT TRANSAC-LIST ASSIGN TO PRINTER.
```

Fig. 4–5. ENVIRONMENT DIVISION entries for PROGRAM-LIST.

The FILE SECTION

The FILE SECTION of the DATA DIVISION consists of two types of entries: those describing a data file and those describing the logical record(s) within the file. The general format of the FILE SECTION entry is:

GENERAL FORMAT 3

FILE SECTION.

{file description entry

{record description entry} ... }

The **file description entry** serves to identify a file used in the program. In addition, it provides information concerning the structure of the file and the name(s) of the record(s) contained in the file. When more than one file is used in a program, the file description entries may appear in any order. The general format of the file description entry is as follows:

GENERAL FORMAT 4

FD filename

  LABEL RECORDS clause

  [VALUE OF FILE-ID clause]

  [DATA RECORDS clause]

  [RECORD CONTAINS clause]

  [BLOCK CONTAINS clause]

  [CODE-SET clause]

  [LINAGE clause]

A file description entry must begin with the indicator FD in the A Area and be immediately followed by the filename beginning in the B Area. Filenames must be unique and must not be used for any other purpose in the program. The remaining clauses in a file description entry, with the exception of the LABEL RECORDS clause, are optional and may appear in any order. There must be only one period in a file description entry and it must appear immediately after the last clause in the entry.

The **VALUE OF FILE-ID clause** must appear in any FD that describes a disk file. It must contain the filename (formed according to the rules of DOS) enclosed in quotes, or a data-name that describes a

DATA DIVISION entry that contains the filename. The general format of the VALUE OF FILE-ID clause is:

GENERAL FORMAT 5

VALUE OF FILE-ID IS $\begin{Bmatrix} \text{data-name} \\ \text{literal} \end{Bmatrix}$

The **LABEL RECORDS clause** is required in every file description entry. It indicates to the computer whether labels are located on the file. If the file is labeled, the clause identifies the type of labels. The general format of the LABEL RECORDS clause is:

GENERAL FORMAT 6

LABEL $\begin{Bmatrix} \text{RECORD IS} \\ \text{RECORDS ARE} \end{Bmatrix}$ $\begin{Bmatrix} \text{OMITTED} \\ \text{STANDARD} \end{Bmatrix}$

Labels will be placed on an output file when it is created by a program that includes the LABEL RECORDS clause. The programmer must choose one of the options RECORD, RECORD IS, RECORDS, or RECORDS ARE. The choice has no effect on program execution. Once this choice has been made, the programmer must indicate the **type(s)** of label record(s), if any, that are contained on an input file, and the type(s), if any, that should be placed on an output file.

The OMITTED option indicates, in the case of an input file, that no label record exists, and in the case of an output file, that no label record is to be placed on the file. This option *must* be chosen for a file sent to the printer.

The STANDARD option must be used when processing disk files. When selected, this option causes the computer to check existing standard labels on input files and to create standard labels on output files. No additional statements are required in a COBOL program to perform the label-checking or label-creating functions.

The **DATA RECORDS clause** is an optional clause that identifies the record(s) in the file by name. This clause does not affect the program in any way; it merely serves as additional program documentation. The general format of the DATA RECORDS clause is:

GENERAL FORMAT 7

DATA $\begin{Bmatrix} \text{RECORD IS} \\ \text{RECORDS ARE} \end{Bmatrix}$ data-name-1 [data-name-2] . . .

The **RECORD CONTAINS clause** is an optional clause that identifies the size of the data records in the file. Like the DATA RECORDS clause, it only serves as additional program documentation. The general format of the RECORD CONTAINS clause is:

GENERAL FORMAT 8

<u>RECORD</u> CONTAINS [integer-1 <u>TO</u>] integer-2 CHARACTERS

Incorporating these optional clauses into the file description entries for the files in PROGRAM-LIST yields

```
FD   TRANSAC-FILE
     LABEL RECORDS ARE STANDARD
     VALUE OF FILE-ID IS 'CH401.DAT'.
FD   TRANSAC-LIST
     LABEL RECORDS ARE OMITTED.
```

Notice that only one period is used in each file description entry. More than one period in each entry will be flagged as an error by the compiler.

The **BLOCK CONTAINS clause** is not supported by IBM PC COBOL. If present, it is checked for correct syntax.

The **CODE-SET IS clause** is only for documentation in IBM PC COBOL. It is used to specify files that are not on a diskette and has the following general format:

GENERAL FORMAT 9

<u>CODE</u> <u>SET</u> IS alphabet-name

The general format of the **LINAGE clause** is:

GENERAL FORMAT 10

$$\underline{\text{LINAGE}} \text{ IS } \begin{Bmatrix} \text{data-name-1} \\ \text{integer-1} \end{Bmatrix} \text{ LINES}$$

$$[\text{WITH } \underline{\text{FOOTING}} \text{ AT } \begin{Bmatrix} \text{data-name-2} \\ \text{integer-2} \end{Bmatrix}]$$

$$[\text{LINES AT } \underline{\text{TOP}} \begin{Bmatrix} \text{data-name-3} \\ \text{integer-3} \end{Bmatrix}]$$

$$[\text{LINES AT } \underline{\text{BOTTOM}} \begin{Bmatrix} \text{data-name-4} \\ \text{integer-4} \end{Bmatrix}]$$

This clause creates a counter called LINAGE-COUNTER, which always contains the line number of the current page on the printer. The entry after LINAGE IS allows the programmer to enter the number of lines on the print page; the normal entry might be 66 (for an 11-inch form at 6 lines to the inch). The LINAGE clause also states the number of lines and the top and bottom margin:

```
LINAGE IS 66 LINES TOP 3 BOTTOM 3
```

The counter may be referenced by the program—e.g., IF LINAGE-COUNTER IS GREATER THAN 56 PERFORM HDR-RTN—but it must not be changed by the program. It is automatically reset to 0 by the ADVANCING PAGE option of the WRITE statement and is incremented by the value included in other ADVANCING options.

Each file description entry in the FILE SECTION of the DATA DIVISION must be followed by one or more **record description entries**. In Chapter 3, we saw that the record description entry can be used in the WORKING-STORAGE SECTION. Here, we learn that it can also be used to describe records in the FILE SECTION. It is common practice to describe the record in general terms in the FILE SECTION, and in detail in the WORKING-STORAGE SECTION.

In the FILE SECTION, the description of the record generally consists of an 01-level number, a data-name, and a PICTURE clause describing the length of the record description entry. For PROGRAM-LIST, this would be

```
01   DISK-REC               PIC X(45).
```

and

```
01   PRINT-REC              PIC X(78).
```

The detailed description of these records will appear in the WORKING-STORAGE SECTION.

We can now turn our attention to the file and record description entries for the output file TRANSAC-LIST. These descriptions will be similar to those for the input file TRANSAC-FILE, except that the output file will contain a 78-character record as opposed to the 45-character input record.

The FILE SECTION entries for PROGRAM-LIST are shown in Fig. 4-6.

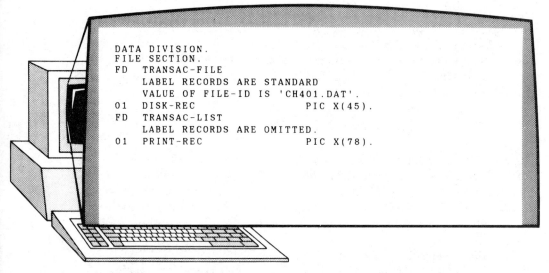

```
DATA DIVISION.
FILE SECTION.
FD   TRANSAC-FILE
     LABEL RECORDS ARE STANDARD
     VALUE OF FILE-ID IS 'CH401.DAT'.
01   DISK-REC                  PIC X(45).
FD   TRANSAC-LIST
     LABEL RECORDS ARE OMITTED.
01   PRINT-REC                 PIC X(78).
```

Fig. 4–6. FILE SECTION entries for the sample problem.

The WORKING-STORAGE SECTION

Among the entries that appear in the WORKING-STORAGE SEC-
TION are the 77-level independent elementary data item description
entries. Earlier, we stated that the current trend is not to use individual 77-level entries, but rather to group these entries under an 01-level
entry. We shall employ this technique in PROGRAM-LIST. Thus, we
begin by setting up the 01-level entries, to which we shall add individual 05-level data item description entries as they are needed.

The two 05-level entries used in the 01-level entry SWITCHES-
MESSAGES-COUNTERS are EOF, which will be used to indicate the
end of our input data file, and a constant called END-MSG, which will
contain the message that is to be printed at the end of the program's
execution. These are shown in Fig. 4–7.

Let us next consider the other 01-level entries in the WORKING-
STORAGE SECTION that are necessary to describe the input and
output records for the program. We begin with the record description
entry for the input file TRANSAC-REC-IN, shown in Fig. 4–8.

Given the pictorial representation shown in Fig. 4–8, the data item
description entry is a relatively simple matter. Figure 4–9 shows the
code.

The file and record description entries for the output file
TRANSAC-LIST can now be considered. As we did with PROGRAM1

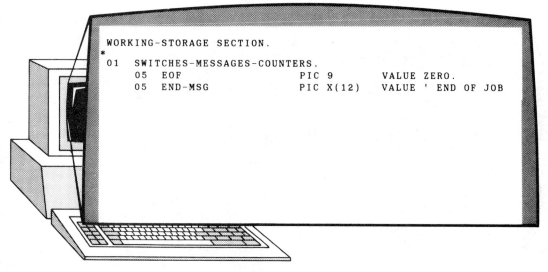

```
WORKING-STORAGE SECTION.
*
 01   SWITCHES-MESSAGES-COUNTERS.
      05   EOF                  PIC 9       VALUE ZERO.
      05   END-MSG              PIC X(12)   VALUE ' END OF JOB
```

Fig. 4-7. WORKING-STORAGE SECTION.

LEVEL NUMBER	01	05	10	15
	TRANSAC-REC-IN	CUSTOMER-NO-IN		
		CUSTOMER-ID-IN	LAST-NAME-IN	
			FIRST-NAME-IN	
			INITIAL-IN	
			CREDIT-CODE-IN	RATING-IN
				LIMIT-AMT-IN
		TRANS-IN	ITEM-NO-IN	INV-NO-IN
				DEPT-NO-IN
			UNIT-PRICE-IN	
			UNITS-IN	

Fig. 4-8. Pictorial view of TRANSAC-REC-IN.

in Chapter 3, we must complete a printer spacing chart before commencing work on the actual output record descriptions. We have already seen this layout in Fig. 4-4.

Once the output layout has been completed, the coding of the individual record descriptions should be straightforward. A comparison

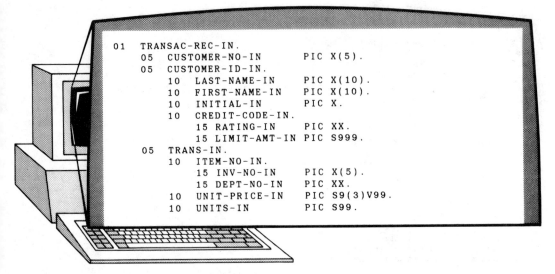

```
01  TRANSAC-REC-IN.
    05  CUSTOMER-NO-IN          PIC X(5).
    05  CUSTOMER-ID-IN.
        10  LAST-NAME-IN        PIC X(10).
        10  FIRST-NAME-IN       PIC X(10).
        10  INITIAL-IN          PIC X.
        10  CREDIT-CODE-IN.
            15 RATING-IN         PIC XX.
            15 LIMIT-AMT-IN PIC S999.
    05  TRANS-IN.
        10  ITEM-NO-IN.
            15 INV-NO-IN        PIC X(5).
            15 DEPT-NO-IN        PIC XX.
        10  UNIT-PRICE-IN       PIC S9(3)V99.
        10  UNITS-IN            PIC S99.
```

Fig. 4–9. Input record description entry for the sample problem.

between these record descriptions and those of PROGRAM1 in Chapter 3 will show great similarity. Basically, only the specific titles, data-names, and spacing considerations will vary. A program listing showing the entries for TRANSAC-REC-OUT is shown in Fig. 4–10.

THE PROCEDURE DIVISION

The organization of the PROCEDURE DIVISION of PROGRAM-LIST is similar to that of PROGRAM1 in Chapter 3. Figure 4–11 shows that several modules have been added to the PROCEDURE DIVISION of the latter, and a READ statement has been substituted for the AC-CEPT statement used there. There are, however, several statements in PROGRAM-LIST that are employed to process files that are not required in PROGRAM1, which does not deal with files. These statements are the OPEN, READ, WRITE, and CLOSE statements.

The OPEN Statement

Before any file can be accessed by the computer, it must be opened. The OPEN statement opens a file for reading or writing as the cover of a book might be opened before it can be read or as a notebook might be

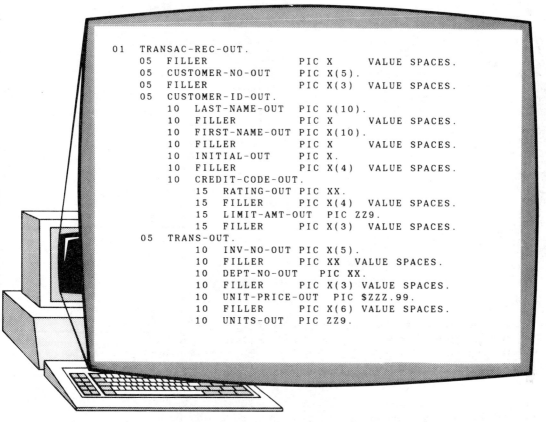

```
01  TRANSAC-REC-OUT.
    05  FILLER                 PIC X     VALUE SPACES.
    05  CUSTOMER-NO-OUT        PIC X(5).
    05  FILLER                 PIC X(3)  VALUE SPACES.
    05  CUSTOMER-ID-OUT.
        10  LAST-NAME-OUT      PIC X(10).
        10  FILLER             PIC X     VALUE SPACES.
        10  FIRST-NAME-OUT     PIC X(10).
        10  FILLER             PIC X     VALUE SPACES.
        10  INITIAL-OUT        PIC X.
        10  FILLER             PIC X(4)  VALUE SPACES.
        10  CREDIT-CODE-OUT.
            15  RATING-OUT PIC XX.
            15  FILLER         PIC X(4)  VALUE SPACES.
            15  LIMIT-AMT-OUT  PIC ZZ9.
            15  FILLER         PIC X(3)  VALUE SPACES.
    05  TRANS-OUT.
        10  INV-NO-OUT PIC X(5).
        10  FILLER             PIC XX    VALUE SPACES.
        10  DEPT-NO-OUT     PIC XX.
        10  FILLER             PIC X(3) VALUE SPACES.
        10  UNIT-PRICE-OUT    PIC $ZZZ.99.
        10  FILLER             PIC X(6) VALUE SPACES.
        10  UNITS-OUT PIC ZZ9.
```

Fig. 4–10. Entries for TRANSAC-REC-OUT.

opened before it can be written in. In COBOL, *no file can be read from or written to before it has been opened.* The general format of the OPEN statement is as follows.

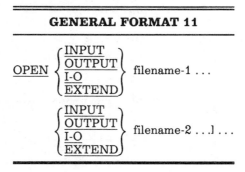

GENERAL FORMAT 11

$$\text{OPEN} \left\{ \begin{array}{l} \text{INPUT} \\ \text{OUTPUT} \\ \text{I-O} \\ \text{EXTEND} \end{array} \right\} \text{filename-1} \ldots$$

$$\left\{ \begin{array}{l} \text{INPUT} \\ \text{OUTPUT} \\ \text{I-O} \\ \text{EXTEND} \end{array} \right\} \text{filename-2} \ldots] \ldots$$

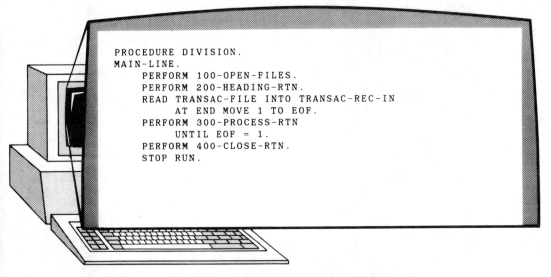

```
PROCEDURE DIVISION.
MAIN-LINE.
    PERFORM 100-OPEN-FILES.
    PERFORM 200-HEADING-RTN.
    READ TRANSAC-FILE INTO TRANSAC-REC-IN
        AT END MOVE 1 TO EOF.
    PERFORM 300-PROCESS-RTN
        UNTIL EOF = 1.
    PERFORM 400-CLOSE-RTN.
    STOP RUN.
```

Fig. 4–11. PROCEDURE DIVISION entry.

In addition to preparing a file for processing, the OPEN statement serves to identify the files as input, output, or both (the last option is for direct access files only); causes the computer to check the device specified in the SELECT clause to determine whether it is available and operational; performs the checking of labels if they are present on an input file; and writes labels if they are desired on an output file. Thus, the OPEN statement *must* appear prior to the first READ and the first WRITE command for that file. A file may be opened more than once in a program, provided that it is closed after each OPEN command. In the discussion that follows, we shall assume that files are opened only once.

Each filename entered in the OPEN statement must be identical to the filename that was assigned to the corresponding file in the file description entries provided by the programmer in the FILE SECTION of the DATA DIVISION.

In the case of PROGRAM-LIST, the procedure 100-OPEN-FILES containing the required OPEN statement would be:

```
100-OPEN-FILES.
    OPEN INPUT  TRANSAC-FILE
         OUTPUT TRANSAC-LIST.
```

This code corresponds to the symbol inscribed "100-OPEN-FILES" in the flow diagram of Fig. 4–12.

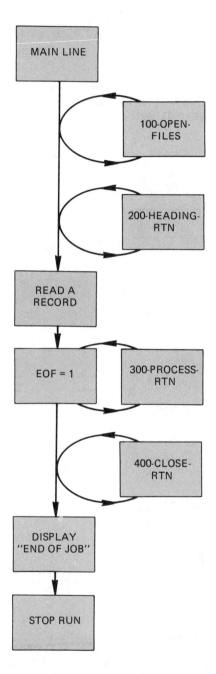

Fig. 4–12. Flowchart diagram for PROGRAM-LIST.

Figure 4–12 indicates that the next step in coding PROGRAM-LIST is to write any required report titles and headings. The printer spacing chart used in laying out those titles and headings (Fig. 4–4) shows that a one-line title and a two-line heading are desired. A WRITE statement is used to output each record, regardless of whether that record is described in the FILE SECTION or the WORKING-STORAGE-SECTION of the DATA DIVISION.

The WRITE Statement

The general format of the WRITE statement is as follows:

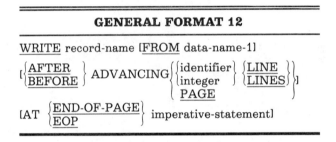

GENERAL FORMAT 12

WRITE record-name [FROM data-name-1]

$$\left[\left\{\begin{matrix}\underline{\text{AFTER}}\\\underline{\text{BEFORE}}\end{matrix}\right\}\ \underline{\text{ADVANCING}}\left\{\begin{matrix}\left\{\begin{matrix}\text{identifier}\\\text{integer}\end{matrix}\right\}\ \left\{\begin{matrix}\underline{\text{LINE}}\\\underline{\text{LINES}}\end{matrix}\right\}\\\underline{\text{PAGE}}\end{matrix}\right\}\right]$$

$$\left[\underline{\text{AT}}\ \left\{\begin{matrix}\underline{\text{END-OF-PAGE}}\\\underline{\text{EOP}}\end{matrix}\right\}\ \text{imperative-statement}\right]$$

Record-name refers to the name of a logical record description in the FILE SECTION of the DATA DIVISION. In the case of PROGRAM-LIST, the record-name is PRINT-REC.

The **FROM identifier-1** option allows the programmer, in one statement, to MOVE identifier-1 (a record defined in working storage or in another file description) to the logical record indicated by the record-name entry, and then to WRITE this record out. For example, the statement

```
WRITE PRINT-REC FROM TITLE-1 AFTER ADVANCING PAGE.
```

would cause the contents of TITLE-1 to be moved, character by character, to TITLE-OUT, which would then be used to print the record. After the WRITE statement is executed, the record is no longer in the logical record denoted by the record-name, but it does remain available in the identifier-1 record.

The **ADVANCING** option of the WRITE statement allows the programmer to control the vertical spacing of a printed report. If this option is omitted, all lines printed will be single spaced. If it is selected, the programmer must explicitly state the number of lines to be spaced over before or after each line is printed.

If the ADVANCING option is chosen, the programmer must code one of the required words BEFORE and AFTER, which stipulate that the output line is to be printed respectively before and after the carriage is advanced a specified number of lines. The number of lines that the carriage is to be advanced before or after printing the output line is specified by one of the following options:

identifier-2 LINE (or LINES)

integer LINE (or LINES)

PAGE

In the **identifier-2 LINE** option, identifier-2 must be a nonnegative numeric elementary data item containing an integer from 0 to 120. When this option is specified, the printed page will be advanced, before or after printing the output line, a number of lines equal to the value of identifier-2. For example, if the elementary data item LINE-COUNT contained the value 5, either of the statements

```
WRITE PRINT-REC BEFORE LINE-COUNT.
WRITE PRINT-REC BEFORE ADVANCING LINE-COUNT LINES.
```

would cause the printing of the record PRINT-REC before the page is advanced five lines. On the other hand, either of the statements

```
WRITE PRINT-REC AFTER LINE-COUNT.
WRITE PRINT-REC AFTER ADVANCING LINE-COUNT LINES.
```

would cause the printing of PRINT-REC after the page is advanced five lines.

In the **integer LINES** option, integer is a nonnegative numeric literal from 0 to 120. When this option is employed, the numeric literal stipulates the number of lines that the printed page will be advanced before or after printing the output line. For example, any of the statements

```
WRITE PRINT-REC BEFORE 3.
WRITE PRINT-REC BEFORE 3 LINES.
WRITE PRINT-REC BEFORE ADVANCING 3 LINES.
```

would cause the printing of the record PRINT-REC before the page is advanced three lines. Similarly, any of the three statements

```
WRITE PRINT-REC AFTER 3.
WRITE PRINT-REC AFTER 3 LINES.
WRITE PRINT-REC AFTER ADVANCING 3 LINES.
```

would cause the printing of PRINT-REC after the printed page is advanced three lines.

As noted in in General Format 12, the number of lines to be advanced may be expressed in the singular or plural (LINE or LINES). Also, if the PAGE option is included in the ADVANCING clause of the WRITE statement, the line is printed after (or before) the paper in the printer is positioned at the top of a new page. Thus, the statement

```
WRITE PRINT-REC FROM TITLE-1 AFTER ADVANCING PAGE.
```

would cause the contents of TITLE-1 to be moved to PRINT-REC, whereupon they would be printed after the paper was moved to the top of a new page.

For PROGRAM-LIST, the procedure 200-HEADING-RTN would be as follows:

```
200-HEADING-RTN.
    WRITE PRINT-REC FROM TITLE-1 AFTER ADVANCING PAGE.
    WRITE PRINT-REC FROM TITLE-2 AFTER ADVANCING 3 LINES.
    WRITE PRINT-REC FROM TITLE 3 AFTER ADVANCING 1 LINE.
    MOVE SPACES TO PRINT-REC.
    WRITE PRINT-REC AFTER ADVANCING 1 LINE.
```

The flow diagram for PROGRAM-LIST (Fig. 4–12) shows that the next step in coding is to input a data record. However, just as the DISPLAY statement was no longer appropriate to output records to a file, the ACCEPT statement is no longer appropriate to input records from a file. Instead, we must use the READ statement.

The READ Statement

The general format of the READ statement is as follows:

GENERAL FORMAT 13

READ filename RECORD [INTO identifier]

   AT END imperative-statement

Execution of a READ statement causes the next logical record in the designated external file to become accessible in the input area described in the corresponding record description entry. If a file contains several record description entries, the records described share the same storage area. A record that is input by means of a READ statement is accessible to the program until it is replaced by the next record accessed from the same file.

The **filename** entry refers to the name assigned to the file in the file description entry in the FILE SECTION.

The **INTO identifier** option allows a record to be read into the area described in the corresponding record description and moves the record into the area specified by **identifier**. (See Fig. 4–13.) Identifier must be the name of a record description entry in the WORKING-STORAGE SECTION or the name of a record in a previously opened output file. Thus, it is possible to read a record into an input area and, with no additional statement, move the record to an output area. The movement of the record will be in accordance with the rules for the MOVE statement (discussed later in this chapter).

The **AT END** option must be specified for all files in sequential access mode. This option provides the computer with instructions to follow after all records in the file have been read. The **imperative-statement** following the required word END describes the specific action to be taken after the file has been completely read.

The flow diagram for PROGRAM-LIST does not indicate specifically what is to be done in the event that there are no data when a READ statement is executed. However, we can reason that if there are no data to be read, there would be no data to be processed in routine 300-PROCESS-RTN. Thus, we would want to indicate that in that case this routine should be skipped. From the flow diagram, we can see that the exit condition for 300-PROCESS-RTN is EOF = 1. Therefore, if we place the value 1 in location EOF upon occurrence of the AT END condition, the exit condition for 300-PROCESS-RTN will be set, and the routine will be skipped. The READ statement that will accomplish this is

```
READ TRANSAC-FILE INTO TRANSAC-REC-IN
     AT END MOVE 1 TO EOF.
```

However, we must make certain that location EOF contains a value other than 1 prior to execution of the READ statement. Otherwise, the routine 300-PROCESS-REC will always be skipped. Therefore, when location EOF is defined in the DATA DIVISION, it must be assigned an initial value not equal to 1—say, 0. We have defined EOF as the

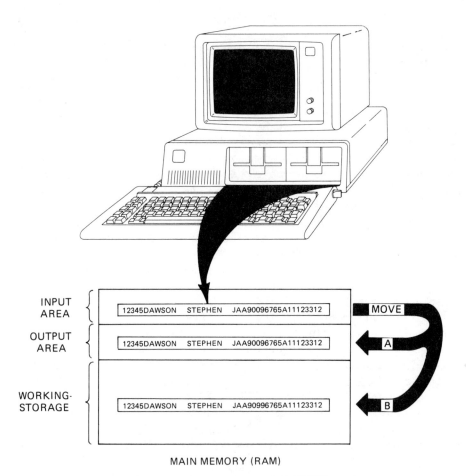

Ⓐ READ TRANSAC-FILE INTO OUTPUT-AREA-RECORD
     AT END MOVE 1 TO EOF.

Ⓑ READ TRANSAC-FILE INTO WORKING-STORAGE-RECORD
     AT END MOVE 1 TO EOF.

INPUT AREA
12345DAWSON   STEPHEN   JAA90096765A11123312

MOVE

OUTPUT AREA
12345DAWSON   STEPHEN   JAA90096765A11123312

Ⓐ

WORKING-STORAGE
12345DAWSON   STEPHEN   JAA90996765A11123312

Ⓑ

MAIN MEMORY (RAM)

Fig. 4–13. READ statement with INTO option.

first data item within the 01-level area SWITCHES-MESSAGES-COUNTERS in the WORKING-STORAGE SECTION of the program. (Soo Fig. 4-7.)

In PROGRAM-LIST, as in the earlier PROGRAM1, once data has been read, we must move it to the appropriate output area, write it out, and read in the next data record. Thus, the first task in routine 300-PROCESS-RTN is to move the data from the input area

TRANSAC-REC-IN to the output area TRANSAC-REC-OUT. This is accomplished with a MOVE statement.

The Simple MOVE Statement

The general format of the simple MOVE statement is as follows:

GENERAL FORMAT 14

MOVE $\begin{Bmatrix} \text{identifier-1} \\ \text{literal} \end{Bmatrix}$ TO identifier-2 [identifier-3] ...

The data designated by **identifier-1** or **literal** are moved to **identifier-2, identifier-3**, etc. It is important to understand that when an item of data is "moved" from one location in primary storage to another, the item is not physically removed from its original storage location. Rather, a copy or image of the data is sent to the new location while the original data item remains unaffected. This process parallels the one that takes place when a person remembers something: the person retrieves the information from his or her memory and uses it without losing—i.e., forgetting—it in the process.

In COBOL, the result of a MOVE operation is dependent on whether the data item moved is an elementary or group data item and what type of data is being moved. The data type is determined by the characters used in the PICTURE clause that describes the elementary data item or subordinate elementary data items. The five basic types of elementary data items and the characters used in their associate PICTURE entries are given in Table 4–2.

Table 4–2. PERMISSIBLE CHARACTERS IN PICTURE ENTRIES

Data Item Type	Permissible Picture Characters
Numeric	9 V P S
Numeric edited	B P V Z 0 9 , . ' + − CR DB $
Alphabetic	A
Alphanumeric	A X 9
Alphanumeric edited	A X 9 B 0 with at least one B or one 0 *or* one 0 and one X *or* one 0 and one A *or* one / and one A *or* one / and one X

Some types of data items cannot be moved to other types. Figure 4–14 illustrates the valid types of MOVE statements. Since the receiving field (i.e., the field receiving the data moved) controls the MOVE operation, the description of the receiving field determines whether or not a MOVE operation, the description of the receiving field determines whether or not a MOVE is valid and controls how much data

SENDING FIELD \ RECEIVING FIELD	Group item	Numeric elementary item	Numeric edited elementary item	Alphabetic elementary item	Alphanumeric elementary item	Alphanumeric edited elementary item
Group item	A			A	A	
Numeric elementary item		N	N		A*	A*
Numeric edited elementary item	A				A	A
Alphabetic elementary item	A			A	A	A
Alphanumeric elementary item	A	N*	N*	A	A	A
Alphanumeric edited elementary item	A			A	A	A
Figurative constants — ZEROS	A	N	N		A	A
Figurative constants — SPACES	A			A	A	A
Literals — Numeric		N	N		A*	A*
Literals — Nonnumeric	A	N	N	A	A	A

A = Alphanumeric MOVE   N = Numeric MOVE

□ – Invalid or unpredictable MOVE

* = Only permissible if the data item is an integer or if the decimal point is at the right of the least significant digit

Fig. 4–14. Permissible MOVE statements.

will be moved. Accordingly, it is necessary to consider, in turn, what happens when the receiving field is equal to, longer than, and shorter than the sending field.

1. If the receiving field is the same size as the sending field (excluding any editing symbols such as $. ,), the contents of the sending field replace the previous contents of the receiving field, character by character. Examples of this type of MOVE are given in Table 4–3.

2. If the receiving field is longer than the sending field, then one of two results occurs. If the MOVE is alphanumeric, data are transferred to the receiving field character by character from left to right, beginning with the leftmost character of the sending field.* Excess positions at the right of the receiving field are then padded or filled with blanks. In addition, if the receiving field is an alphanumeric edited data item, blanks (B) or zeros (0) are inserted as directed by the PICTURE clause associated with the receiving field. Examples of this type of MOVE are given in Table 4–4. When the sending field is numeric, the sign of the data is changed to the equivalent of "no sign." (See Example 4 in Table 4–4.)

   If the MOVE is numeric, the sending and receiving fields are first aligned by the positions of the decimal points as stated or implied in the PICTURE entry for each field. Then the integer and fractional parts of the number are separately treated. The integer portion of the number is moved character by character from right to left, beginning with the character immediately to the left of the stated or implied decimal point. The decimal portion of the number, on the other hand, is moved character by character from left to right, beginning with the character immediately to the right of the stated or implied decimal point. Excess positions at the left of the integer portion of the receiving field are padded with zeros, as are excess positions at the right of the fractional portion of the receiving field.†

---

*It is possible to transfer data character by character into the rightmost position of the receiving field beginning with the rightmost character of the sending field by simply adding the optional words JUSTIFIED RIGHT immediately after the PICTURE specification of the receiving field (02 REC-FIELD PICTURE A(16) JUSTIFIED RIGHT).

†If the receiving field is a numeric edited data item, special characters (. $, + − CR DB) will be inserted as directed in the PICTURE clause associated with the receiving field. If the receiving field PICTURE contains an S, a sign will be generated and stored internally with the number; otherwise bits representing "no sign" will be stored with the number.

Table 4-3. MOVES WITH FIELDS OF EQUAL-SIZE*

	Before				After			
	Sending Field		Receiving Field		Sending Field		Receiving Field	
	Contents	PICTURE	Contents	PICTURE	Contents	PICTURE	Contents	PICTURE
1.	HARRY	X(5)	FREDb	X(5)	HARRY	X(5)	HARRY	X(5)
2.	AC347	X(5)	CABLE	X(5)	AC347	X(5)	AC347	X(5)
3.	4190	9(4)	3478	9(4)	4190	9(4)	4190	9(4)
4.	03142	9(5)	HARRY	X(5)	03142	9(5)	03142	X(5)
5.	36497+	S9(5)	JONES	X(5)	36497+	S9(5)	36497	X(5)
6.	36497+	S9(5)	JONES	9(5)	36497+	S9(5)	36497	9(5)
7.	36497+	S9(5)	JONES	S9(5)	36497+	S9(5)	36497+	S9(5)
8.	76775+	S9(5)	14192−	9(5)+	76775+	S9(5)	76775+	9(5)+
9.	3146	999V9	7522	999V9	3146	999V9	3146	999V9
10.	21446	999V99	412.32	999.99	21446	999V99	214.46	999.99
11.	39147	9999V9	S7,946.2	S9,999.9	39147	999V9	S3,914.7	S9,999.9

*A digit written with a sign over it (7̈) means that the digit and sign are contained in the same byte of storage, with each occupying four bits of the byte.

Table 4-4. MOVES WITH RECEIVING FIELDS LONGER THAN SENDING FIELDS

Type of MOVE	Before				After			
	Sending Field		Receiving Field		Sending Field		Receiving Field	
	Contents	PICTURE	Contents	PICTURE	Contents	PICTURE	Contents	PICTURE
1. Alphanumeric	HARRY	X(5)	FURNITURE	X(9)	HARRY	X(5)	HARRYƀƀƀƀ	X(9)
2. Alphanumeric	AC347	X(5)	TELEVISION	X(10)	AC357	X(5)	AC347ƀƀƀƀƀ	X(10)
3. Alpharumeric	03142	9(5)	TABLES	X(6)	03142	X(5)	03142ƀ	X(6)
4. Alphanumeric	36497⁺	S9(5)	PRODUCT	X(7)	36497⁺	S9(5)	36497ƀƀ	X(7)
5. Alphanumeric	EDIT	X(4)	ƀƀCHARGE	BBX(6)	EDIT	X(4)	ƀƀEDITƀƀ	BBX(6)
6. Alphanumeric	EDIT	X(4)	CHARGEƀƀ	X(6)BB	EDIT	X(4)	EDITƀƀƀƀ	X(6)BB
7. Numeric	4190	9(4)	31468	9(5)	4190	9(4)	04190	9(5)
8. Numeric	76775⁺	S9(5)	3146224	S9(7)	76775⁺	S9(5)	0076775⁺	S9(7)
9. Numeric	3146	999V9	74293	9999V9	3146	999V9	03146	9999V9
10. Numeric	3146	999V9	74293	999V99	3146	999V9	31460	999V99
11. Numeric	3146	999V9	$0742.93	$9999.99	3146	999V9	$0314.60	$9999.99
12. Numeric	3146	999V9	$ƀ742.93	$ZZZZ.99	3146	999V9	$ƀ314.60	$ZZZZ.99
13. Numeric	0000	999V9	$ƀ742.93	$ZZZZ.ZZ	0000	999V9	$ƀƀƀƀƀƀ	$ZZZZ.ZZ
14. Numeric	3146	999V9	$4,972.93	$Z,ZZZ.99	3146	999V9	$ƀƀ314.60	$Z,ZZZ.99
	9999V99	$4,972.93	$Z,ZZZ.99	419537	9999V99	$4,195.37	$Z,ZZZ.99	

123

Table 4-5. MOVES WITH SENDING FIELDS LONGER THAN RECEIVING FIELDS

Type of MOVE	Before				After			
	Sending Field		Receiving Field		Sending Field		Receiving Field	
	Contents	PICTURE	Contents	PICTURE	Contents	PICTURE	Contents	PICTURE
1. Alphanumeric	HARRY	X(5)	JOHN	X(4)	HARRY	X(5)	HARR	X(4)
2. Alphanumeric	AC347	X(5)	BOLT	X(4)	AC347	X(5)	AC34	X(4)
3. Alphanumeric	03142	9(5)	HATS	X(4)	03142	9(5)	0314	X(4)
4. Alphanumeric	36497$\overset{+}{}$	S9(5)	CAPS	X(4)	36497$\overset{+}{}$	S9(5)	3649	X(4)
5. Alphanumeric	1C462A	X(6)	♭PINS	BX(4)	1C462A	X(6)	♭1C46	BX(4)
6. Alphanumeric	1C462A	X(6)	PINS♭	X(4)B	1C462A	X(6)	1C46♭	X(4)B
7. Numeric	41904	9(5)	3162	9(4)	41904$\overset{+}{}$	9(5)	1904	9(4)
8. Numeric	76775$\overset{+}{}$	S9(5)	4975	9(4)	76675$\overset{+}{}$	S9(5)	6775	9(4)
9. Numeric	76775$\overset{-}{}$	S9(5)	+3124	+9(4)	76775$\overset{-}{}$	S9(5)	−6775	+9(4)
10. Numeric	8417	99V99	3	V9	8417	99V99	1	V9
11. Numeric	8417	99V99	3	9V	8417	99V99	4	9V
12. Numeric	38417	999V99	4975	999V9	38417	999V99	3841	999V9
13. Numeric	38417	999V99	4975	99V99	38417	999V99	8417	99V99
14. Numeric	38417	999V99	497	99V9	38417	999V99	841	99V9
15. Numeric	38417	999V99	81465	9999V9	38417	999V99	03841	9999V9
16. Numeric	38417	999V99	46573	99V999	38417	999V99	84170	99V999,

3. If the receiving field is shorter than the sending field in an alphanumeric or numeric MOVE, the operation is terminated by the computer when the receiving field has been filled. Characters not transmitted from the sending field are truncated and do not appear in the receiving field. In the case of a numeric MOVE, the moving of the data into the integer and fractional parts of the receiving field are considered separately by the computer. For example, a numeric MOVE might cause the fractional part of a number in the sending field to be truncated in the receiving field and at the same time cause the integer portion of the same sending field to be padded with zeros in the receiving field. See Table 4–5.

The Literal MOVE Statement

The rules for moving a literal into a given storage area are the same as those for moving data items.

1. The MOVE is controlled by the PICTURE of the receiving field.

2. If the receiving field is a numeric or numeric edited data item, the data are aligned according to the decimal point or are justified if there is no decimal point. Excess areas are filled with zeros or blanks, while excess data are truncated.

3. If the receiving field is an alphabetic, alphanumeric, or alphanumeric edited data item, data are transferred to the receiving field character by character from left to right. Excess areas in the receiving field are padded with blanks, while excess data are truncated.

Table 4–6. EXAMPLES OF LITERAL MOVES

Sending Field	Receiving Field		
	PICTURE	Before	After
'A'	A(5)	XXXXX	Aƀƀƀƀ
'LARRY JOSCELYN'	X(5)	A34B1	Larry
ZEROS	9(5)	31476	00000
SPACES	X(5)	X3412	ƀƀƀƀƀ
136	9(5).99	31452.73	00136.00
2405∧*	9V999	4∧172*	5∧000*

*∧ refers to the position of an assumed decimal point.

Table 4-7. EFFECTS OF DIFFERENT TYPES OF MOVES

Type of MOVE	Receiving Item	Alignment	Padding if Necessary	Truncation if Necessary
Alphanumeric	Group	At left of value	On right with blanks	On right
	Alphabetic or alphanumeric	At left of value	On right with blanks	On right
	Alphanumeric edited	At left of value	On right with blanks or zeros as directed by the receiving field's PICTURE specification	On right
Numeric	Numeric	At decimal point	On left and right with zeros	On left and right
	Numeric edited	At decimal point	On left and right with zeros or special characters as directed by the receiving field's PICTURE specification	On left and right

Figure 4–14 illustrates the valid MOVEs for the various types of literals. Examples of typical literal MOVEs are given in Table 4–6. A summary of the rules pertaining to data alignment, padding, and truncation in the various types of MOVE statements is shown in Table 4–7.

The MOVE statements required for PROGRAM-LIST would be as follows:

```
300-PROCESS-RTN.
      MOVE CUSTOMER-NO-IN TO CUSTOMER-NO-OUT.
      MOVE LAST-NAME-IN   TO LAST-NAME-OUT.
      MOVE FIRST-NAME-IN  TO FIRST-NAME-OUT.
      MOVE INITIAL-IN     TO INITIAL-OUT.
      MOVE RATING-IN      TO RATING-OUT.
      MOVE LIMIT-AMT-IN   TO LIMIT-AMT-OUT.
      MOVE INV-NO-IN      TO INV-NO-OUT.
      MOVE DEPT-NO-IN     TO DEPT-NO-OUT.
      MOVE UNITS-PRICE-IN TO UNIT-PRICE-OUT.
      MOVE UNITS-IN       TO UNITS-OUT.
```

To complete routine 300-PROCESS-RTN, we must WRITE out the record just processed and READ in the next record, as we did in PROGRAM1 in Chapter 3. These can be accomplished with the statements

```
WRITE PRINT-REC FROM TRANSAC-REC-OUT AFTER ADVANCING 1 LINE.
READ TRANSAC-FILE INTO TRANSAC-REC-IN AT END MOVE 1 TO EOF.
```

After processing, all files must be closed. Then termination of program execution can begin.

The CLOSE Statement

The CLOSE statement closes a file much the same as a book is closed after it has been completely read or written. Once a file has been closed, no record in the file can be accessed unless the file is reopened. The general format of the CLOSE statement is:

GENERAL FORMAT 15

CLOSE {filename-1 [WITH LOCK} [, filename-2[WITH LOCK]] ...

There is no designation in the CLOSE statement as to whether the file to be closed is an input or output file, as there was in the OPEN statement. All that is necessary to CLOSE a file is the verb CLOSE followed by the filename(s). **Filename-1, filename-2,** etc. refer to the names of the files being closed and must agree exactly with the names assigned in their respective file description entries.

The optional LOCK pertains to files stored on disk and will be discussed later. In the case of PROGRAM-LIST, the procedure to CLOSE the input file (TRANSAC-FILE) and the output file (TRANSAC-LIST) is:

```
400-CLOSE-RTN.
    MOVE END-MSG TO PRINT-REC.
    WRITE PRINT-REC AFTER ADVANCING 3 LINES.
    CLOSE TRANSAC-FILE
        TRANSAC-LIST.
```

To complete the program, all that is necessary is to provide for printing the message 'END OF JOB' and code STOP RUN. The complete program listing, including these statements, is shown in Fig. 4–15.

The complete source program shown in Fig. 4–15 is available on the supplemental disk under the filename CH401.COB. A sample set of input data is also on the disk, under the name CH401.DAT.

```
          IDENTIFICATION DIVISION.
          PROGRAM-ID.
              PROGRAM-LIST.
          AUTHOR.
              S.J.GAUGHRAN.
          INSTALLATION.
              PERSONAL COMPUTER SYSTEM.
          DATE-WRITTEN.
              JAN.23,1985.
          DATE-COMPILED.
              JAN.25,1985.
          SECURITY.
              NONE.
          ENVIRONMENT DIVISION.
          CONFIGURATION SECTION.
          SOURCE-COMPUTER.
              IBM-PERSONAL-COMPUTER.
          OBJECT-COMPUTER.
              IBM-PERSONAL-COMPUTER.
          INPUT-OUTPUT SECTION.
          FILE-CONTROL.
              SELECT TRANSAC-FILE ASSIGN TO DISK
                     ORGANIZATION IS LINE SEQUENTIAL.
              SELECT TRANSAC-LIST ASSIGN TO PRINTER.
      *
          DATA DIVISION.
          FILE SECTION.
          FD  TRANSAC-FILE
              LABEL RECORDS ARE STANDARD
              VALUE OF FILE-ID IS 'CH401.DAT'.
          01  DISK-REC              PIC X(45).
          FD  TRANSAC-LIST
              LABEL RECORDS ARE OMITTED.
          01  PRINT-REC             PIC X(78).
      *
          WORKING-STORAGE SECTION.
      *
          01  SWITCHES-MESSAGES-COUNTERS.
              05  EOF              PIC 9        VALUE ZERO.
              05  END-MSG          PIC X(12)    VALUE ' END OF JOB '.
      *
          01  TRANSAC-REC-IN.
              05  CUSTOMER-NO-IN   PIC X(5).
              05  CUSTOMER-ID-IN.
                  10  LAST-NAME-IN    PIC X(10).
                  10  FIRST-NAME-IN   PIC X(10).
                  10  INITIAL-IN      PIC X.
                  10  CREDIT-CODE-IN.
                      15  RATING-IN    PIC XX.
                      15  LIMIT-AMT-IN PIC S999.
              05  TRANS-IN.
                  10  ITEM-NO-IN.
                      15  INV-NO-IN    PIC X(5).
                      15  DEPT-NO-IN   PIC XX.
                  10  UNIT-PRICE-IN    PIC S9(3)V99.
                  10  UNITS-IN         PIC S99.
      *
          01  TITLE-1.
              05  FILLER             PIC X(20) VALUE SPACES.
              05  FILLER             PIC X(39) VALUE
                      'ACCOUNTS RECEIVABLE REPORT'.
      *
          01  TITLE-2.
              05  FILLER             PIC XX     VALUE SPACES.
              05  FILLER             PIC X(4)   VALUE 'CUST'.
              05  FILLER             PIC X(8)   VALUE SPACES.
              05  FILLER             PIC X(13)  VALUE 'CUSTOMER NAME'.
              05  FILLER             PIC X(7)   VALUE SPACES.
              05  FILLER             PIC X(6)   VALUE 'CREDIT'.
              05  FILLER             PIC XX     VALUE SPACES.
              05  FILLER             PIC X(4)   VALUE 'CODE'.
              05  FILLER             PIC X(5)   VALUE SPACES.
```

Fig. 4-15. Program listing for the sample problem.

129

```
        05 FILLER              PIC X(23) VALUE
                'TRANSACTION INFORMATION'.
*
    01 TITLE-3.
        05 FILLER              PIC X     VALUE SPACES.
        05 FILLER              PIC X(6)  VALUE 'NUMBER'.
        05 FILLER              PIC X(5)  VALUE SPACES.
        05 FILLER              PIC X(4)  VALUE 'LAST'.
        05 FILLER              PIC X(6)  VALUE SPACES.
        05 FILLER              PIC X(5)  VALUE 'FIRST'.
        05 FILLER              PIC X(4)  VALUE SPACES.
        05 FILLER              PIC X     VALUE 'M'.
        05 FILLER              PIC XX    VALUE SPACES.
        05 FILLER              PIC X(6)  VALUE 'RATING'.
        05 FILLER              PIC X     VALUE SPACES.
        05 FILLER              PIC X(5)  VALUE 'LIMIT'.
        05 FILLER              PIC XXX   VALUE SPACES.
        05 FILLER              PIC XXX   VALUE 'INV'.
        05 FILLER              PIC XX    VALUE SPACES.
        05 FILLER              PIC X(4)  VALUE 'DEPT'.
        05 FILLER              PIC X     VALUE SPACES.
        05 FILLER              PIC X(10) VALUE 'UNIT PRICE'.
        05 FILLER              PIC X     VALUE SPACES.
        05 FILLER              PIC X(8)  VALUE 'QUANTITY'.
*
    01 TRANSAC-REC-OUT.
        05 FILLER              PIC X     VALUE SPACES.
        05 CUSTOMER-NO-OUT     PIC X(5).
        05 FILLER              PIC X(3)  VALUE SPACES.
        05 CUSTOMER-ID-OUT.
            10 LAST-NAME-OUT    PIC X(10).
            10 FILLER           PIC X     VALUE SPACES.
            10 FIRST-NAME-OUT   PIC X(10).
            10 FILLER           PIC X     VALUE SPACES.
            10 INITIAL-OUT      PIC X.
            10 FILLER           PIC X(4)  VALUE SPACES.
            10 CREDIT-CODE-OUT.
                15 RATING-OUT PIC XX.
                15 FILLER      PIC X(4)  VALUE SPACES.
                15 LIMIT-AMT-OUT PIC ZZ9.
                15 FILLER      PIC X(3)  VALUE SPACES.
        05 TRANS-OUT.
            10 INV-NO-OUT PIC X(5).
            10 FILLER     PIC XX   VALUE SPACES.
            10 DEPT-NO-OUT  PIC XX.
            10 FILLER     PIC X(3) VALUE SPACES.
            10 UNIT-PRICE-OUT  PIC $ZZZ.99.
            10 FILLER     PIC X(6) VALUE SPACES.
            10 UNITS-OUT  PIC ZZ9.
*
    PROCEDURE DIVISION.
    MAIN-LINE.
        PERFORM 100-OPEN-FILES.
        PERFORM 200-HEADING-RTN.
        READ TRANSAC-FILE INTO TRANSAC-REC-IN
            AT END MOVE 1 TO EOF.
        PERFORM 300-PROCESS-RTN
            UNTIL EOF = 1.
        PERFORM 400-CLOSE-RTN.
        STOP RUN.

    100-OPEN-FILES.
        OPEN INPUT  TRANSAC-FILE
            OUTPUT TRANSAC-LIST.

    200-HEADING-RTN.
        WRITE PRINT-REC FROM TITLE-1 AFTER ADVANCING PAGE.
        WRITE PRINT-REC FROM TITLE-2 AFTER ADVANCING 3 LINES.
        WRITE PRINT-REC FROM TITLE-3 AFTER ADVANCING 1 LINE.
        MOVE SPACES TO PRINT-REC.
        WRITE PRINT-REC AFTER ADVANCING 1 LINE.

    300-PROCESS-RTN.
        MOVE CUSTOMER-NO-IN TO CUSTOMER-NO-OUT.
```

Fig. 4–15. (*continued*)

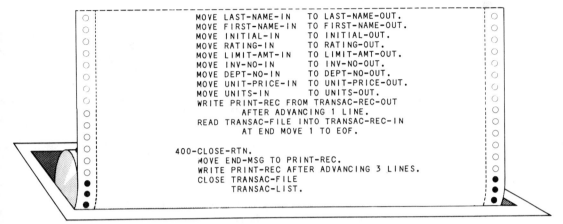

```
          MOVE LAST-NAME-IN    TO LAST-NAME-OUT.
          MOVE FIRST-NAME-IN   TO FIRST-NAME-OUT.
          MOVE INITIAL-IN      TO INITIAL-OUT.
          MOVE RATING-IN       TO RATING-OUT.
          MOVE LIMIT-AMT-IN    TO LIMIT-AMT-OUT.
          MOVE INV-NO-IN       TO INV-NO-OUT.
          MOVE DEPT-NO-IN      TO DEPT-NO-OUT.
          MOVE UNIT-PRICE-IN   TO UNIT-PRICE-OUT.
          MOVE UNITS-IN        TO UNITS-OUT.
          WRITE PRINT-REC FROM TRANSAC-REC-OUT
               AFTER ADVANCING 1 LINE.
          READ TRANSAC-FILE INTO TRANSAC-REC-IN
               AT END MOVE 1 TO EOF.

      400-CLOSE-RTN.
          MOVE END-MSG TO PRINT-REC.
          WRITE PRINT-REC AFTER ADVANCING 3 LINES.
          CLOSE TRANSAC-FILE
                TRANSAC-LIST.
```

Fig. 4-15. (*continued*)

EXERCISES

1. Rewrite Exercise 2 of Chapter 3 (page 91) using the disk for an input file and a regular printer file for output. Remember to change the end-of-data method to conform to the requirements of the READ statement. You may create the input file using EDLIN or your word processor.

2. Rewrite Exercise 3 of Chapter 3, again using a disk for your input file and the printer for the output file.

3. Write a program to READ the Inventory Input File in the input record shown on page 132 and print the Stock Status Report as described in the output layout.

4. An important report for any firm contains information regarding the length of time each customer has owed money. Using the input and output layouts shown on page 133, prepare a report that will illustrate how long each customer has owed the amounts due.

Solutions to the exercises, together with any necessary data files, are provided on the supplemental disk.

Input Layout

Input Record: NVENTORY-REC

WAREHOUSE NUMBER	STOCK NUMBER	DESCRIPTION	UNIT OF MEASURE	QUANT ON HAND	QUANT NO ORDER	UNIT PRICE	LAST VENDOR
123	4567 890	1111111112 1234567890	2222 2345	2222 6789	3333 0123	3333333 4567890	44444444455 12345678901

Output Layout

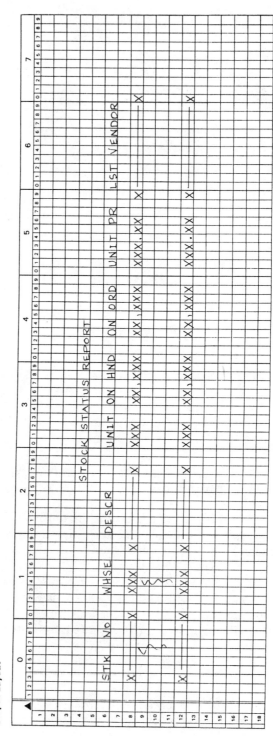

Input Layout

Input Record: CUSTOMER-REC

CUST NUMB	LAST NAME	FIRST NAME	STREET	CITY	STATE	ZIP	CURRENT AMOUNT	30 DAY AMOUNT	60 DAY AMOUNT	90 DAY AMOUNT

Output Layout

ACCOUNTS RECEIVABLE CREDIT REPORT

CUST NO   NAME / ADDRESS   CURRENT   30 DAYS   60 DAYS   90 DAYS

X---X   X---X   X---X   X   X,XXX.XX   X,XXX.XX   X,XXX.XX   X,XXX.XX
         X---X
         X---X
         XX   X---X

6719204 MADISON   STANLEY   483.50   5,293.25   308.75   96.41
         2112 FIRST
         ATLANTA
         GA   12789

8231092 GREY   JOSEPH   12.83
         92 MAPLE ST
         EUGENE
         OR   78901

133

CHAPTER

5

ARITHMETIC OPERATIONS

Up to now, the COBOL programs we have learned to write have been limited in their mathematical capabilities to very simple arithmetic operations that were included for demonstration purposes only. In this chapter we shall discuss more fully the arithmetic capabilities that COBOL has. Its logical or decision-making capabilities will be discussed in Chapter 6.

ARITHMETIC STATEMENTS

Among the most basic statements in COBOL are those that are used for computations. The four basic arithmetic operations of addition, subtraction, multiplication, and division can be specified by the COBOL ADD, SUBTRACT, MULTIPLY, and DIVIDE statements, respectively.

The ADD Statement

The ADD statement denotes the same operation in COBOL that the plus sign (+) does in mathematics—namely, it indicates to the computer that two or more specified numeric values are to be added together. The COBOL ADD statement may be written in either of two formats, the first of which is as follows.

GENERAL FORMAT 1

$$\underline{\text{ADD}} \begin{Bmatrix} \text{identifier-1} \\ \text{literal-1} \end{Bmatrix} \begin{bmatrix} \text{identifier-2} \\ \text{literal-2} \end{bmatrix} \dots \underline{\text{TO}} \text{ identifier-m } [\underline{\text{ROUNDED}}]$$

[ON $\underline{\text{SIZE}}$ $\underline{\text{ERROR}}$ imperative-statement]

The required entries are

$$\underline{\text{ADD}} \begin{matrix} \text{identifier-1} \\ \text{literal-1} \end{matrix} \quad \underline{\text{TO}} \text{ identifier-m}$$

The entries **identifier-1** and **identifier-m** are the names of storage areas containing elementary numeric data items that have been previously defined in the DATA DIVISION. **Literal-1**, on the other hand, is a numeric literal. Identifiers and literals used in arithmetic statements must not exceed 18 digits.

The following example illustrates the ADD statement:

`ADD AMOUNT-A TO AMOUNT-B.`

The data items AMOUNT-A and AMOUNT-B have been previously defined in the DATA DIVISION and have the following PICTURE specifications and contents.

	Picture	Contents
AMOUNT-A	S9999	0347
AMOUNT-B	S9999	0016

When the above ADD statement is executed, two things happen:

1. The contents or **value** of AMOUNT-A is added to the contents or value of AMOUNT-B.

2. The resulting sum is stored in AMOUNT-B.

The process is illustrated in the following diagram:

```
ADD AMOUNT-A TO AMOUNT-B.
```

	AMOUNT-A	AMOUNT-B
Before	0347————————➤ + ————————➤0016	
After	0347	0363

The diagram shows that after the ADD statement has been executed, the previous value of the receiving data item (AMOUNT-B) is replaced by the sum that results from the addition operation.

If it is necessary to store the sum in AMOUNT-A, the statement

```
ADD AMOUNT-B TO AMOUNT-A.
```

would be written instead. In this case the results are as shown in the following diagram:

```
ADD AMOUNT-B TO AMOUNT-A.
```

	AMOUNT-B	AMOUNT-A
Before	0016————————➤ + ————————➤0347	
After	0016	0363

The COBOL ADD statement may be written using the **literal** option, as, for example,

```
ADD 16 TO AMOUNT-A.
```

This statement and the one in the diagram just above are identical in effect when the identifier AMOUNT-B contains the value 16. In most cases, however, the value in the data item is not known at the time the program statement is written. If the value of a data item or constant is known, the literal option may be used; otherwise the identifier option must be used.

It is not permissible to use a literal as the second or receiving field— the field immediately following the reserved word TO. Thus, the following ADD statement is erroneous, as we have indicated by the error flags on both sides of it:

```
****ERROR    ADD AMOUNT-B TO 347.    ERROR****
```

The second or receiving field in an ADD statement serves two purposes: to convey the value of one of the numbers to be added *and* to act as a receiving area for the result of the addition. In the incorrect COBOL statement above, the second field serves only the first purpose; since the literal explicitly states the value of the second number to be added, namely, 347, it cannot also serve as a storage area to contain the result of the addition.

With the addition of the optional entry

$$\begin{bmatrix} \text{identifier-2} \\ \text{literal-2} \end{bmatrix} \ \cdots$$

the ADD statement may be used to add more than two fields. For example, if the data items AMOUNT-1 and AMOUNT-2 were defined in the DATA DIVISION in addition to the data items AMOUNT-A and AMOUNT-B, these four fields could be added together with the following ADD statement:*

```
ADD AMOUNT-A AMOUNT-1 AMOUNT-2 TO AMOUNT-B.
```

When executed, this statement causes the sum of the four values to replace the value previously contained in AMOUNT-B. Thus, if AMOUNT-A and AMOUNT-B are as before, and AMOUNT-1 contains the value 0045 and AMOUNT-2 contains the value 1496, the addition would proceed as shown in the following diagram:

Statement: `ADD AMOUNT-A AMOUNT-1 AMOUNT-2 TO AMOUNT-B.`

	AMOUNT-A	**AMOUNT-1**	**AMOUNT-2**	**AMOUNT-B**
Before	0347	0045	1496	0016
After	0347	0045	1496	1904

If the values of the first three data items are known at the time of programming, the statement may be written (using the literal option) as follows:

```
ADD 347 45 1496 TO AMOUNT-B.
```

---

*Note that commas are optional and may be inserted between operands if desired. The authors have found that there is too little difference between commas and periods on many printers and screens, so to avoid confusion we have chosen to omit commas in the COBOL statements in this book. The comma is optional, *but the period is essential in most COBOL statements.*

Note: In most "mainframe" versions of COBOL, multiple receiving fields after the TO are permitted. However, this feature is not supported in IBM COBOL for the PC or XT.

The second format in which the ADD statement may be written is as follows:

GENERAL FORMAT 2

$$\underline{\text{ADD}} \quad \begin{Bmatrix} \text{identifier-1} \\ \text{literal-1} \end{Bmatrix} \quad \begin{Bmatrix} \text{identifier-2} \\ \text{literal-2} \end{Bmatrix} \quad \begin{bmatrix} \text{identifier-3} \\ \text{literal-3} \end{bmatrix} \dots$$

$\underline{\text{GIVING}}$ identifier-m [$\underline{\text{ROUNDED}}$] [ON $\underline{\text{SIZE}}$ $\underline{\text{ERROR}}$ imperative-statement]

The basic difference between this format and General Format 1 is the removal of the reserved word TO and the addition of the reserved word GIVING. This version of the ADD statement causes the values of the two or more operands preceding the word GIVING to be added together and the sum to be stored as the *new value* of identifier-m. Thus, none of the items being added are lost since a distinct area (identifier-m) is set aside exclusively to receive the sum. Note that the previous value of identifier-m is of no concern to us since this field serves only as a receiving field for the results of the addition. Thus, identifier-m does not have to contain valid numeric data even if it is defined as numeric. Identifier-m may also be defined as a numeric edited item (a data item whose PICTURE clause contains editing symbols such as . $, etc.).

An example of the use of the ADD statement with the GIVING option is the statement

```
ADD REGULAR-PAY OVERTIME-PAY GIVING GROSS-PAY.
```

where the data items REGULAR-PAY and OVERTIME-PAY are to be added and the result is to be stored in GROSS-PAY. Note that the reserved word TO is not used—indeed, it cannot be used with the GIVING option.

The SUBTRACT Statement

Like the ADD statement, the SUBTRACT statement is available in two formats, the first of which is:

GENERAL FORMAT 3

SUBTRACT $\begin{Bmatrix} \text{identifier-1} \\ \text{literal-1} \end{Bmatrix}$ $\begin{bmatrix} \text{identifier-2} \\ \text{literal-2} \end{bmatrix}$ ... <u>FROM</u> identifier-m [<u>ROUNDED</u>]

[ON <u>SIZE</u> <u>ERROR</u> imperative-statement]

In this format, the sum of the current values of the identifiers (or literals) listed prior to the reserved word FROM is subtracted from the current value of identifier-m and the resulting difference will replace the value currently in identifier-m. Identifiers used in this format of the SUBTRACT statement must be numeric items only; in particular, they must not be numeric edited items.

Following is an illustration of the SUBTRACT statement:

```
SUBTRACT ST-TAX FED-TAX FICA FROM GROSS-PAY.
```

The execution of this statement can be thought of as taking place in three steps:

1. The values in ST-TAX, FED-TAX, and FICA are added together.

2. The sum obtained in step 1 is subtracted from the current value in GROSS-PAY.

3. The difference obtained in step 2 is stored as the new value of GROSS-PAY.

This format of the SUBTRACT statement is similar to the first format of the ADD statement in that the result of the operation replaces the previous value of a data item. In the above example, the previous value of GROSS-PAY is replaced by the computed difference.

Suppose that the original values of ST-TAX, FED-TAX, FICA, and GROSS-PAY are as given in the Before column of the table below. Then the results of execution of this SUBTRACT statement

```
SUBTRACT ST-TAX FED-TAX FICA FROM GROSS-PAY.
```

are as shown in the After column of the table.

	ST-TAX	FED-TAX	FICA	GROSS-PAY
Before	26.10	90.00	21.40	468.60
After	26.10	90.00	21.40	331.10

Although strictly correct, the above statement might be inappropriate for a particular computer application because:

1. The previous value of GROSS-PAY is lost.

2. The name assigned to the resulting data item (GROSS-PAY) no longer represents its contents. A more appropriate name would be NET-PAY.

A SUBTRACT statement that would eliminate these problems would be

```
SUBTRACT ST-TAX FED-TAX FICA FROM GROSS-PAY GIVING NET-PAY.
```

This statement is an example of the second format of the SUBTRACT statement, namely,

---

GENERAL FORMAT 4

SUBTRACT {identifier-1 / literal-1} [identifier-2 / literal-2] [identifier-3 / literal-3] ...

FROM identifier-m GIVING identifier-n [ROUNDED]

[ON SIZE ERROR imperative-statement]

In this format, the sum of the current values of the identifiers (or literals) preceding the required word FROM is subtracted from the current value of identifier-m (or literal-m), and the difference is stored in identifier-n, which may be either an elementary numeric item or a numeric edited item. Again, the receiving field must not be a literal.

The execution of the SUBTRACT statement

```
SUBTRACT ST-TAX FED-TAX FICA FROM GROSS-PAY GIVING NET-PAY.
```

takes place in three steps:

1. The values in ST-TAX, FED-TAX, and FICA are added together.

2. The sum obtained in step 1 is subtracted from the value in GROSS-PAY.

3. The difference obtained in step 2 is stored in NET-PAY.

The following table shows the values of the variables before and after execution.

	ST-TAX	FED-TAX	FICA	GROSS-PAY	NET-PAY
Before	26.10	90.00	21.40	468.60	999.99
After	26.10	90.00	21.40	468.60	331.10

Thus, the only difference between the execution of this SUBTRACT statement and the corresponding General Format 3 type of SUBTRACT statement (one exactly the same, except without the GIVING option) is that here the result is stored in NET-PAY and the value previously in GROSS-PAY is not replaced.

The MULTIPLY Statement

The MULTIPLY statement is used to find the product of two data items. It has the following two formats:

GENERAL FORMAT 5

MULTIPLY $\begin{Bmatrix} \text{identifier-1} \\ \text{literal-1} \end{Bmatrix}$ BY identifier-2 [ROUNDED]

[ON SIZE ERROR imperative-statement]

GENERAL FORMAT 6

MULTIPLY $\begin{Bmatrix} \text{identifier-1} \\ \text{literal-1} \end{Bmatrix}$ BY $\begin{Bmatrix} \text{identifier-2} \\ \text{literal-2} \end{Bmatrix}$ GIVING identifier-3 [ROUNDED]

[ON SIZE ERROR imperative-statement]

In the first format, the value of identifier-1 or literal-1 is multiplied by the value identifier-2 and the product replaces the old value of identifier-2. In the second format, the value of identifier-1 or literal-1 is multiplied by the value of identifier-2 or literal-2, and the product replaces the old value of identifier-3. Thus, the values of all the operands are maintained, and only the value of the receiving field is altered.

In either format, the receiving field cannot be a literal. Moreover, all identifiers must be elementary numeric items except identifier 3 in General Format 6, which may be a numeric edited item. In all cases, literals must be numeric.

Suppose that four data items have been previously defined and have the following values and PICTURE:

Data Item	Value	PICTURE
QUANTITY	012	S999
LIST-PRICE	008	S999
COST-PRICE	015	S999
TOTAL-PRICE	???	S999

Then the following four tables show the values of the variables listed before and after execution of the MULTIPLY statement directly above them.

MULTIPLY QUANTITY BY LIST-PRICE.

	QUANTITY	LIST-PRICE
Before	012	008
After	012	096

MULTIPLY 7 BY LIST-PRICE.

	LIST-PRICE
Before	008
After	056

MULTIPLY LIST-PRICE BY 19 GIVING TOTAL-PRICE.

	LIST-PRICE	TOTAL-PRICE
Before	008	???
After	008	152

MULTIPLY QUANTITY BY COST-PRICE GIVING TOTAL-PRICE.

	QUANTITY	COST-PRICE	TOTAL-PRICE
Before	012	015	???
After	012	015	180

The DIVIDE Statement

The DIVIDE statement is used to determine the quotient of the division of one data item by another. It has the following two formats.

GENERAL FORMAT 7

DIVIDE $\left\{ \begin{array}{l} \text{identifier-1} \\ \text{literal-1} \end{array} \right\}$ INTO identifier-2 [ROUNDED]

[ON SIZE ERROR imperative-statement]

GENERAL FORMAT 8

DIVIDE $\left\{ \begin{array}{l} \text{identifier-1} \\ \text{literal-1} \end{array} \right\}$ $\left\{ \begin{array}{l} \text{INTO} \\ \text{BY} \end{array} \right\}$ $\left\{ \begin{array}{l} \text{identifier-2} \\ \text{literal-2} \end{array} \right\}$ GIVING identifier-3 [ROUNDED]

[ON SIZE ERROR imperative-statement]

In the first format, the value of identifier-1 (or literal-1) is divided into the value of identifier-2 and the quotient replaces the old value of identifier-2. In the second format, the value of identifier-1 (or literal-1) is divided **INTO** or **BY** the value of identifier-2 (or literal-2) and the quotient is stored in identifier-3.

In examining some typical DIVIDE statements, suppose that five data items have been previously defined and have the following values and PICTUREs:

Data Item	Value	PICTURE
TOTAL-COST	017.00	S999V99
ITEM-COST	05.00	S99V99
TOTAL-ITEMS	??.??	S99V99
INTEGER-ITEMS	??	S99
FRACT-ITEMS	?.??	S9V99

Then the following four tables show the values of the variables listed before and after execution of the DIVIDE statements directly above them.

```
DIVIDE 5 INTO TOTAL-COST.
```

	TOTAL-COST
Before	017.00
After	003.40

```
DIVIDE ITEM-COST INTO TOTAL-COST.
```

	ITEM-COST	TOTAL-COST
Before	05.00	017.00
After	05.00	003.40

```
DIVIDE ITEM-COST INTO TOTAL-COST GIVING TOTAL-ITEMS.
```

	TOTAL-COST	ITEM-COST	TOTAL-ITEMS
Before	05.00	017.00	??.??
After	05.00	017.00	03.40

DIVIDE TOTAL-COST BY ITEM-COST GIVING TOTAL-ITEMS.

	TOTAL-COST	ITEM-COST	TOTAL-ITEMS
Before	017.00	05.00	??.??
After	017.00	05.00	03.40

The COMPUTE Statement

Arithmetic operations may also be expressed by the COMPUTE statement. The principal advantage of this statement is that it allows the coding of complex arithmetic instructions that are not capable of being coded with only the ADD, SUBTRACT, MULTIPLY, and DIVIDE statements. The following table lists the six basic symbols used to denote arithmetic operations in IBM PC COBOL.

Symbol	Operation
=	equals; assignment or replacement
* *	exponentiation
*	multiplication
/	division
+	addition
−	subtraction

The general format of the COMPUTE statement is as follows:

GENERAL FORMAT 9

COMPUTE identifier-1 [ROUNDED] [identifier-2] [ROUNDED] ...=
arithmetic-expression [ON SIZE ERROR imperative-statement]

Execution of this statement causes the arithmetic expression to the right of the equals sign to be evaluated. The result replaces the previous contents of identifier-1. An arithmetic expression in COBOL may consist of any of the following:

1. An identifier described as a numeric elementary item.

2. A numeric literal.

3. Identifiers and/or literals, as defined in 1 and 2 above, separated by arithmetic operators.

4. Two or more arithmetic expressions, as defined in 1, 2, and 3 above, separated by arithmetic operators.

5. An arithmetic expression, as defined in 1, 2, 3, and 4 above, enclosed in parentheses.

6. Any arithmetic expression preceded by a minus sign ($-$).

Identifier-1, identifier-2 (if stated), etc., may be either elementary numeric items or numeric edited items. Of course, since they represent the receiving fields, they *must not* be literals.

To illustrate the COMPUTE statement, suppose that an average must be determined from three examination grades given by the following previously defined data-names and values:

```
GRD-1 = 87
GRD-2 = 88
GRD-3 = 80
```

Then the statement

```
COMPUTE AVERAGE = (GRD-1 + GRD-2 + GRD-3) / 3.
```

will give the desired result, and the table following shows the values of the variables before and after execution.

	GRD-1	GRD-2	GRD-3	AVERAGE
Before	87	88	80	??
After	87	88	80	85

In the statement, the equals sign means that the result of carrying out the arithmetic operations *to the right* of the sign is placed in the storage location named *on the left* of the sign, replacing the value that was previously in that location.

In some cases it becomes necessary to update the contents of a location that is used to accumulate a sum or that serves as a counter. For example, suppose that a count is kept of the number of times the record OUT-REC is printed. A sequence of PROCEDURE DIVISION statements that accomplishes this is the following:

```
WRITE-RTN.
    WRITE OUT-REC.
    COMPUTE LINE-COUNT = LINE-COUNT + 1.
```

Now, from a purely mathematical standpoint, the statement COMPUTE LINE-COUNT = LINE-COUNT + 1 is incorrect because a number cannot be equal to one more than itself. However, in COBOL, the interpretation of the equals sign in a COMPUTE statement makes the statement meaningful. In COBOL, the statement is taken to mean that *the present value of LINE-COUNT is replaced by the present value of LINE-COUNT, plus 1*. That is, the numeric literal 1 is added to the present value of LINE-COUNT, and the resulting sum is stored as the new value of LINE-COUNT. This technique can be used in any procedure that requires replacing current values with updated ones.

At least one blank must precede and follow any arithmetic symbol, including the equals sign. This requirement serves to distinguish between a minus sign and a hyphen: a blank must precede and follow a minus sign (A − B), but never a hyphen (GROSS-PAY).

The programmer must always make certain that all data items (other than literals) used in a COMPUTE statement are defined (described in the DATA DIVISION) and that storage locations with these data-names contain the correct values. Thus, it would make little sense to write the COMPUTE statement

```
COMPUTE A = (B + C) / D.
```

if B, C, and/or D had never been defined or assigned a value.

A summary of the COBOL arithmetic statements and their options is given in Fig. 5–1.

Hierarchy of Arithmetic Operations   Arithmetic operations in a COMPUTE statement can be written with the symbols appearing in any order. However, the order in which the computer performs these operations is predefined. It is essential that this order be understood

Arithmetic statements	GIVING variable-name	variable-name ROUNDED	SIZE ERROR statement
ADD { identifier-1 / numeric-literal-1 } [identifier-2 / numeric-literal-2] ... TO identifier-m	X	X	X
SUBTRACT { identifier-1 / numeric-literal-1 } [identifier-2 / numeric-literal-2] ... FROM identifier-m	X	X	X
MULTIPLY { identifier-1 / numeric-literal-1 } BY identifier-2	X	X	X
DIVIDE { identifier-1 / numeric-literal-1 } INTO identifier-2	X	X	X
COMPUTE identifier-1 = { identifier-2 / numeric-literal-1 / arithmetic-expression }		X	X
*The reserved word TO is omitted when the GIVING option is specified.			

Allowable Options

Fig. 5–1. Arithmetic statements and their options.

so that no confusion or errors will result. Accordingly, consider the following statement:

```
COMPUTE X = A + B * C
```

Without the ordering of arithmetic operations, this statement could mean two entirely different things mathematically, namely,

$$X = (A + B) * C$$

or

$$X = A + (B * C)$$

To avoid this ambiguity, the computer assigns a priority, or **hierarchy**, to arithmetic operations and these operations are executed accordingly. The following table presents the hierarchy of arithmetical operations, beginning with the highest priority at the top of the table and proceeding through to the lowest priority at the bottom.

Operation	Description
$+, -$	Unary plus and minus
$**$	Exponentiation
$*, /$	Multiplication and division, in the order of their occurrence in the statement
$+, -$	Addition and subtraction, in the order of their occurrence in the statement

Thus, the computer always interprets the above COMPUTE statement as

$$X = A + (B * C)$$

since multiplication is an operation of higher priority than addition and is completed first. Operations of equal priority are evaluated in the order in which they appear, from left to right.

In COBOL, as in mathematics, expressions in parentheses are evaluated before expressions that are not contained in parentheses. In the case of nested parentheses (parentheses within parentheses), the innermost parenthetical expression is evaluated first, then successive outer ones. The remaining expressions that are not enclosed in parentheses are then evaluated in the order dictated by the operations involved. For example, in the expression

$$Y * (Z - K)$$

the parenthetical expression $Z - K$ is evaluated first. *Then* the resulting difference is multiplied by Y. Similarly, in the expression

$$(Y * (Z - K)) **4$$

the innermost parenthetical expression $(Z - K)$ is evaluated first, the next innermost parenthetical expression (Y times the result of the previous evaluation) is evaluated next, and finally the product is raised to the fourth power.

Some examples of COBOL statements and their mathematical interpretations are given in Table 5-1.

Table 5–1. SOME COBOL EXPRESSIONS AND THEIR MATHEMATICAL INTERPRETATIONS

Expression	Interpretation
A − B/C * D ** 2	$A - (B/C)D^2$
P * (+ R/N) ** (N * Y)	$P \times (1 + R/N)^{N \times Y}$
2 * B/C ** A− K/3	$\dfrac{2 \times B}{C^A} - \dfrac{K}{3}$
A/B * C−E + F	$\dfrac{A \times C}{B} - E + F$

Rounded and Size Error Options

Special consideration must be given to a sum, difference, product, or quotient that is larger than the field reserved for the result. Suppose that the statement

```
ADD AMOUNT-1 AMOUNT-2 TO AMOUNT-3.
```

is used to add the following data items, with PICTUREs and values indicated:

```
AMOUNT-1    PIC  S999V99      038.477
AMOUNT-2    PIC  S9999V999    0419.369
AMOUNT-3    PIC  S9999V99     1426.48
```

Suppose also that these values are unknown to the programmer and that the sum must be stored in AMOUNT-3. Then the statement might fail to perform the task required of it by the programmer because the area specified to receive the sum is not large enough to contain the number of decimal places in the sum. That is, the sum (1884.326) contains three decimal places, while the PICTURE clause for AMOUNT-3 provides space for only two decimal places. In such a case the computer would *truncate* the sum (i.e., cut off the *rightmost or least significant* decimal places for which there is no room in the receiving field (AMOUNT-3)) and store the truncated sum (1884.32) in AMOUNT-3. However, the result the programmer might have wanted might have been to *round off* the sum to two decimal places (1884.33) and store the rounded sum in AMOUNT-3. Fortunately, this option can be indicated to the computer merely by inserting the reserved word **ROUNDED** following a blank space after the identifier AMOUNT-3, resulting in the following ADD statement:

```
ADD AMOUNT-1 AMOUNT-2 TO AMOUNT-3 ROUNDED.
```

Additional examples of arithmetic statements containing the ROUNDED option are:

```
ADD REG-PAY OVT-PAY TO GROSS-PAY ROUNDED.
ADD ST-TAX FED-TAX FICA GIVING DEDUCTNS ROUNDED.
SUBTRACT AMOUNT-1 AMOUNT-2 FROM TOTAL-AMT ROUNDED.
MULTIPLY HOURS BY RATE GIVING PAY ROUNDED.
DIVIDE AMOUNT-1 INTO AMOUNT-2 ROUNDED.
DIVIDE TOTAL-PRICE BY QUANT GIVING UNIT-PRC ROUNDED.
COMPUTE GROSS-PAY ROUNDED = REG-HRS * RATE + OVRTM-HRS *
    (RATE *1.5).
```

In each of these examples, the result obtained from performing the indicated operation will be rounded to the number of decimal places indicated in the PICTURE clause of the *result field*.

A type of truncation of a far more serious nature occurs when the sum, difference, product, or quotient of two or more items exceeds the number of integer positions allocated for the result. In such cases, the *leftmost or most significant* digits are truncated. Consider, for example, the statement

```
ADD AMOUNT-1 TO AMOUNT-2 ROUNDED.
```

If the data-items have the PICTUREs and contents given by

```
AMOUNT-1    PIC S9(5)V999    13476.277
AMOUNT-2    PIC S9(4)V99      8412.76
```

the sum 21889.037 undergoes two alterations. First, its least significant digit (7) is rounded off as specified by the ROUNDED option; second, its most significant digit (2) is truncated. After execution of the statement, the data-item AMOUNT-2 contains the rounded and truncated sum 1889.04, an obvious *size error*. It is important to note that when this kind of error occurs, *no indication is given by the computer that it has occurred.*

If, however, the size error occurs when the SIZE ERROR option has been specified, the identifier affected by the SIZE ERROR option *is not altered.* Instead, after the addition is completed, the imperative-statement specified in the SIZE ERROR option will be executed. An imperative-statement is any COBOL statement that gives an unconditional command—that is, a command that is not subject to any conditions. IBM PC COBOL allows the imperative-statement to be made up of several commands; all such commands following the words SIZE ERROR and preceding the first period are considered by the computer as part of the imperative-statement. The following code is illustrative.

```
ADD AMOUNT-1 TO AMOUNT-2 ROUNDED
    ON SIZE ERROR
        DISPLAY AMOUNT-1 AMOUNT-2
        COMPUTE COUNTR = COUNTR + 1
        PERFORM WRITE-RTN.
PERFORM WRAP-UP-RTN.
```

If a SIZE ERROR occurs after AMOUNT-2 is calculated and ROUNDED, the three statements contained in the SIZE ERROR clause will be executed.

Sample statements containing the SIZE ERROR option are:

```
ADD COMMISSION TO PAY ON SIZE ERROR PERFORM ERR-RTN.
ADD ST-TAX FED-TAX FICA GIVING DEDUCTIONS
    ON SIZE ERROR PERFORM ERR-RTN.
SUBTRACT ST-TAX FED-TAX FICA FROM GROSS-PAY GIVING NET-PAY
    ON SIZE ERROR PERFORM ERR-RTN.
MULTIPLY HOURS BY RATE GIVING PAY ROUNDED
    SIZE ERROR STOP RUN.
DIVIDE GRADE-TOTAL BY NO-GRADES GIVING AVEAGE ROUNDED
    ON SIZE ERROR STOP 'DIVIDE SIZE ERROR'.
COMPUTE GROSS-PAY ROUNDED = REG-HRS * RATE + OVT-HRS *
    (RATE * 1.5) ON SIZE ERROR PERFORM CLOSE-RTN STOP RUN.
```

Note that in a DIVIDE statement, *division by zero always results in a SIZE ERROR.*

SIGNED FIELDS

A numeric item used in an arithmetic operation may contain a negative value. It is then the programmer's responsibility to make certain that the computer retains the minus sign. The programmer instructs the computer to do so in the DATA DIVISION by including the letter *S* (for Sign) in the PICTURE clause for the data item—for example,

```
02 ITEM    PIC S99.
```

As the example indicates, the S is similar to the assumed decimal point character (V) used in PICTURE clauses in that no area in the DATA DIVISION is reserved for the position of the sign (except when the specification SEPARATE is used in the SIGN clause—see General Format 10 below). Instead, the character S instructs the compiler to generate the necessary code to retain the sign of the result field after each arithmetic operation. This code consists of certain bits (binary digits) being set in the rightmost or low-order positions of that field to indicate the sign, either negative or positive. If an S is not included in the PICTURE specification of a data item and a negative value results, *the negative sign will be lost* and the data item will be treated as an absolute value, i.e., a positive number. Signs, therefore, must be taken into consideration when data are input, moved, tested, or output.

GENERAL FORMAT 10

[SIGN IS] $\begin{Bmatrix} \text{LEADING} \\ \text{TRAILING} \end{Bmatrix}$ [SEPARATE CHARACTER]

When data are input or output from disk or are manipulated internally, the above provision of the S in the PICTURE specification will provide correct results. However, when data are input from the keyboard, it is convenient to enter the sign as a separate character and to have it stored either before or after the numeric value, as desired. General Format 10 shows the format of the SIGN IS clause, which is included in the specification of the data item and which states whether the SIGN is to be

LEADING SEPARATE   (i.e., before the numeric value—e.g., +123 or −123)

TRAILING SEPARATE   (i.e., after the numeric value—e.g., 123+ or 123−)

LEADING   (e.g., A23 or J23)

TRAILING   (e.g., 12C or 12L)

The LEADING SEPARATE and TRAILING SEPARATE options have the sign as a separate character, and the *size* of the data item is *automatically increased* accordingly. The LEADING and TRAILING options (without the word SEPARATE) have the sign *embedded* in the leftmost or rightmost digit position, respectively. The characters A through I represent +1 through +9, respectively, whereas the characters J through R represent the characters −1 through −9, respectively. If the SIGN IS clause is omitted, the default is to the TRAILING option. This default option is a carryover from the days when most original input of data was via punch cards. It was common usage to include the size as a zone punch (row 11 for − and row 12 for +) over the units (rightmost) digit in a field. The practice is continued internally for the sign of numeric data items in COBOL.

It is necessary to coordinate the specification of the SIGN IS clause with the description of the data to be input by means of the ACCEPT statement. If the data item is described with the clause SIGN IS LEADING SEPARATE, then no special entry is required in the ACCEPT statement since its default is to the LEADING SEPARATE usage. If the data item is described with the clause SIGN IS TRAILING SEPARATE, then the ACCEPT statement must have a note to this effect, for example:

```
ACCEPT (10, 15) AMOUNT-IN WITH PROMPT TRAILING-SIGN
```

(plus any other options used with the ACCEPT).

Note that when numeric data are entered in response to an ACCEPT statement with a prompt, the sign is entered *after* the numeric value no matter which of the options is used.

ARITHMETIC INSTRUCTIONS IN A SIMPLE PROGRAM

Consider a program to reconcile a checkbook, a task we all find necessary to accomplish periodically. Suppose that you have received your statement from the bank. In order to determine the correct current balance, you must reconcile the difference between those transactions performed up to the time the bank printed the statement and those you have recorded in your checkbook up to the present. This involves adding additional deposits to the statement balance and subtracting the checks that you have written but that are not reflected in the statement. Also, there may be transactions (service charges, error corrections, etc.) that are recorded on the statement but not in your checkbook. These must be added or subtracted from your checkbook balance, as well. (For example, a service charge would be subtracted from your checkbook balance.)

The program to balance the checkbook is presented in Fig. 5–2 (page 156). There is no FILE SECTION needed in the DATA DIVISION since all input and output will be by means of ACCEPT and DISPLAY statements. Also, since the program uses the DISPLAY statement for both the screen (the default) and the printer, we have made the following entry in the SPECIAL-NAMES paragraph of the CONFIGURATION SECTION:

```
SPECIAL-NAMES.
    PRINTER IS LINE-OUT.
```

This statement will cause output to be directed to the printer when the statement DISPLAY . . . UPON LINE-OUT is executed.

Some of the working storage entries specify that the sign is to be treated as a separate leading character. A sign is necessary for the input to this program since some of the entries (STATEMENT-BALANCE, BOOK-BALANCE, and ADJUSTMENT) may denote either positive or negative values. No sign is necessary for the DEPOSIT and CHECK data items, since they are always treated as denoting positive values, which will be added or subtracted by the program logic.

Figure 5–3 (page 158) shows the screen during execution of the program assuming the following test data:

Statement balance	$450.00
Checkbook balance	$225.25
Deposits not on statement	$100.00
Checks not on statement	$119.55
	75.00
	25.40
	65.00
	35.05
Adjustments	+4.75

It is recommended that you copy or enter, compile, and run this program as you did with the programs in previous chapters.

```
        IDENTIFICATION DIVISION.
        PROGRAM-ID.
            CH501.
        AUTHOR.
            S.J.GAUGHRAN.
        INSTALLATION.
            PERSONAL COMPUTER SYSTEM.
        DATE-WRITTEN.
            01/12/85.
        DATE-COMPILED.
            01/12/85.
        SECURITY.
            NONE.
        ENVIRONMENT DIVISION.
        CONFIGURATION SECTION.
        SOURCE-COMPUTER.
            IBM-PERSONAL-COMPUTER.
        OBJECT-COMPUTER.
            IBM-PERSONAL-COMPUTER.
        SPECIAL-NAMES.
            PRINTER IS LINE-OUT.
       *
        DATA DIVISION.
       *
        WORKING-STORAGE SECTION.
        01  INPUT-AND-WORKAREAS.
            05   STATEMENT-BALANCE    PIC S9(5)V99
                     SIGN IS LEADING SEPARATE.
            05   STATEMENT-OUT        PIC $ZZ,ZZZ.99-.
            05   BOOK-BALANCE         PIC S9(5)V99
                     SIGN IS LEADING SEPARATE.
            05   BOOK-OUT             PIC $ZZ,ZZZ.99-.
            05   ADJUSTMENT           PIC S9(5)V99 VALUE 1
                     SIGN IS LEADING SEPARATE.
            05   ADJUSTMENT-OUT       PIC ZZ,ZZZ.99-.
            05   DEPOSIT              PIC S9(5)V99 VALUE 1.
            05   DEPOSIT-OUT          PIC ZZ,ZZZ.99-.
            05   CHECK                PIC S9(5)V99 VALUE 1.
            05   CHECK-OUT            PIC ZZ,ZZZ.99-.
            05   DIFFERENCE           PIC ZZ,ZZZ.99+.
            05   NEW-BALANCE          PIC ZZ,ZZZ.99-.
       *
        PROCEDURE DIVISION.
        MAIN-MODULE.
            PERFORM INITIAL-RTN.
            DISPLAY (9, 11) 'ENTER DEPOSITS NOT ON STATEMENT '.
            DISPLAY (10, 17) 'IF NO DEPOSITS OR IF ALL ENTERED TYPE 0'.
            DISPLAY '    DEPOSITS   ' UPON LINE-OUT.
            PERFORM DEPOSIT-RTN UNTIL DEPOSIT = 0.
            DISPLAY (12, 11) 'ENTER CHECKS NOT ON STATEMENT (NO SIGN)'.
            DISPLAY (13, 17) 'IF NO CHECKS OR IF ALL ENTERED TYPE 0'.
            DISPLAY '    CHECKS    ' UPON LINE-OUT.
            PERFORM CHECK-RTN   UNTIL CHECK  = 0.
            DISPLAY (15, 11) 'ENTER ADJUSTMENTS NOT IN CHECK BOOK'.
            DISPLAY (16, 17) 'WITH LEADING + OR - SIGN AS APPROPRIATE'.
            DISPLAY '    ADJ.     ' UPON LINE-OUT.
            PERFORM ADJUST-RTN  UNTIL ADJUSTMENT = 0.
            PERFORM CLOSING-RTN.
            STOP RUN.
       *
        INITIAL-RTN.
            DISPLAY (1, 1) ERASE.
            DISPLAY (1, 26) 'CHECK RECONCILIATION PROGRAM'.
            DISPLAY (3, 11) 'ENTER BALANCE FROM STATEMENT WITH'.
            DISPLAY (4, 17) 'LEADING SIGN (- FOR NEGATIVE BALANCE)'.
            DISPLAY (5, 11) 'STATEMENT BALANCE:'.
            ACCEPT (5, 30) STATEMENT-BALANCE WITH PROMPT.
            MOVE STATEMENT-BALANCE TO STATEMENT-OUT.
            DISPLAY 'STATEMENT BALANCE: ' STATEMENT-OUT UPON LINE-OUT.
            DISPLAY (6, 11) 'ENTER BALANCE FROM CHECK BOOK WITH'.
            DISPLAY (7, 17) 'LEADING SIGN (- FOR NEGATIVE BALANCE'.
            DISPLAY (8, 11) 'CHECK BOOK BALANCE:'
```

Fig. 5–2. Sample COBOL program.

```
      ACCEPT  (8, 29) BOOK-BALANCE WITH PROMPT.
      MOVE BOOK-BALANCE TO BOOK-OUT.
      DISPLAY 'CHECK BOOK BALANCE:' BOOK-OUT UPON LINE-OUT.
DEPOSIT-RTN.
      DISPLAY (11, 11) 'DEPOSIT:'.
      ACCEPT  (11, 24) DEPOSIT WITH PROMPT.
      MOVE DEPOSIT TO DEPOSIT-OUT.
      DISPLAY DEPOSIT-OUT UPON LINE-OUT.
      ADD DEPOSIT TO STATEMENT-BALANCE.
*
CHECK-RTN.
      DISPLAY (14, 11) 'CHECK:'.
      ACCEPT  (14, 20) CHECK WITH PROMPT.
      MOVE CHECK TO CHECK-OUT.
      DISPLAY CHECK-OUT UPON LINE-OUT.
      SUBTRACT CHECK FROM STATEMENT-BALANCE.
*
ADJUST-RTN.
      DISPLAY (17, 11) 'ADJUSTMENT:'.
      ACCEPT  (17, 23) ADJUSTMENT WITH PROMPT.
      MOVE ADJUSTMENT TO ADJUSTMENT-OUT.
      DISPLAY ADJUSTMENT-OUT UPON LINE-OUT.
      ADD ADJUSTMENT TO BOOK-BALANCE.
*
CLOSING-RTN.
      MOVE STATEMENT-BALANCE TO NEW-BALANCE.
      DISPLAY (19, 11) ' RECONCILED BALANCE IS: ' NEW-BALANCE.
      DISPLAY 'NEW BALANCE: ' NEW-BALANCE UPON LINE-OUT.
      SUBTRACT BOOK-BALANCE FROM STATEMENT-BALANCE
                     GIVING DIFFERENCE.
      DISPLAY (21, 11) 'THE DIFFERENCE BETWEEN STATEMENT'.
      DISPLAY 'DIFFERENCE:   ' DIFFERENCE UPON LINE-OUT.
      DISPLAY (22, 17) 'CHECK BOOK IS: ' DIFFERENCE.
      DISPLAY (23, 11) 'IF + THEN STATEMENT IS HIGHER'.
      DISPLAY (24, 11) 'IF NOT ZERO RE-CHECK ENTRIES'.
```

Fig. 5–2. (*continued*)

This program is available on the supplemental disk as CH501.COB.

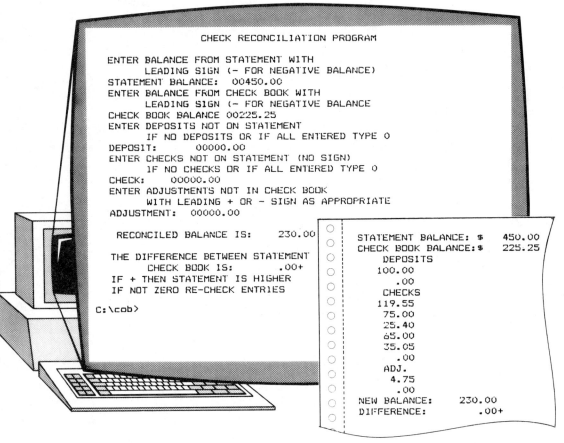

```
                    CHECK RECONCILIATION PROGRAM

  ENTER BALANCE FROM STATEMENT WITH
          LEADING SIGN (- FOR NEGATIVE BALANCE)
  STATEMENT BALANCE:   00450.00
  ENTER BALANCE FROM CHECK BOOK WITH
          LEADING SIGN (- FOR NEGATIVE BALANCE
  CHECK BOOK BALANCE 00225.25
  ENTER DEPOSITS NOT ON STATEMENT
          IF NO DEPOSITS OR IF ALL ENTERED TYPE 0
  DEPOSIT:       00000.00
  ENTER CHECKS NOT ON STATEMENT (NO SIGN)
          IF NO CHECKS OR IF ALL ENTERED TYPE 0
  CHECK:     00000.00
  ENTER ADJUSTMENTS NOT IN CHECK BOOK
          WITH LEADING + OR - SIGN AS APPROPRIATE
  ADJUSTMENT:   00000.00

   RECONCILED BALANCE IS:      230.00

  THE DIFFERENCE BETWEEN STATEMENT
        CHECK BOOK IS:           .00+
  IF + THEN STATEMENT IS HIGHER
  IF NOT ZERO RE-CHECK ENTRIES

  C:\cob>
```

```
  STATEMENT BALANCE: $    450.00
  CHECK BOOK BALANCE:$    225.25
      DEPOSITS
  100.00
     .00
      CHECKS
  119.55
   75.00
   25.40
   65.00
   35.05
     .00
  ADJ.
    4.75
     .00
  NEW BALANCE:     230.00
  DIFFERENCE:        .00+
```

Fig. 5-3.   Screen and printed output for sample problem.

EXERCISES

1. Write a program to read the Inventory Input file shown in the input layout on the opposite page and print the Stock Status Report as specified in the output layout. This report requires that the value of each item on hand be calculated and printed. In addition, the total value of all the items on hand and on order is to be printed at the end of the data.

Input Layout

Input Record: INVENTORY-REC

UNUSED	STOCK NUMBER	DESCRIPTION	UNIT OF MEASURE	QUANT ON HAND	QUANT ON ORDER	UNIT PRICE

Output Layout

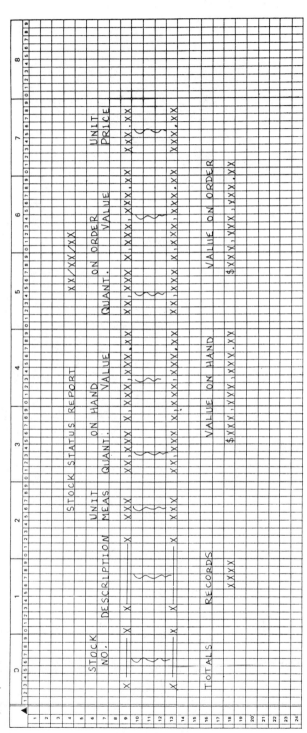

Input Layout

Input Record: SALES-REC-ONE

SALESPERSON NUMBER	SALESPERSON NAME	BRANCH	COMM RATE V999
1 2 3 4 5	6 7 8 9 0 1 2 3 4 5 6 7 8 9 0	1 1 1 1 1 1 1 1 1 1	2 2 2 2 2 2 2 2 2
		1 2 3 4 5 6 7 8 9 0	1 2 3 4 5 6 7 8

Input Record: SALES-REC-TWO

SALESPERSON NUMBER	SALES	RETURNS
1 2 3 4 5	6 7 8 9 0 1 2 3 4 5	1 1 1 1 1 1 1 1 1
		6 7 8 9

Output Layout

MONTHLY COMMISSION REPORT

NUMBER	NAME	SALES	RETURNS	NET	RATE	COMMISSION

2. Write a program to read a Sales Commission file that contains the two types of records shown in the input layout on the opposite page. Each line of the report requires that the two records for each salesperson be read in order. Compute the net sales and commission for each salesperson, and total all sales, returns, net sales, and commissions. Then print out these totals after the last record has been processed.

Use the following formulas in your program:

Net Sales = Sales − Returns (sales should be greater than returns) Commission = Rate × Net Sales

3. A program is needed to print out the monthly payments for individual auto loans. The input data and the report are described, respectively, in the input layout and output layout shown on page 162. The output is to be triple spaced, and the LINAGE clause should be used to skip to the top of a new page when necessary. Write the program.

4. The report described on page 163 is to be used to record the fuel usage and cost for a fleet of vehicles. The input record will provide identifying data about the vehicle, the odometer reading at the beginning and ending of the period, the amount of fuel used, and the cost per gallon. The program is to calculate the number of miles traveled, cost of fuel, miles per gallon, and cost per mile for each vehicle. In addition, at the end of data, totals are needed for the number of vehicles, number of miles traveled, amount of fuel used, and cost of the fuel. Also, averages for cost per mile, cost per gallon, and miles per gallon are required. Use the input and output layouts shown, and write the program.

Solutions to the exercises, together with any necessary data files, are provided on the supplemental disk.

Input Layout

Input Record: LOAN-DATA

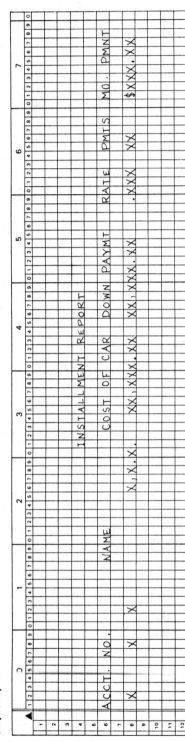

Output Layout

162

Input Layout

Input Record: M LEAGE-DATA

VEHICLE NUMBER	MAKE	YEAR	ODOMETER INITIAL READING	ODOMETER FINAL READING	GAL USED	COST PER GAL
1 2 3 4 5 6 7	8 9 0 1 2 3 4 5 6	7 8	9 0 1 2 3 4 5	6 7 8 9 0 1 2	3 4 5 6 7 8	9 0 1 2 3

Output Layout

VEHICLE FUEL REPORT

VEH NO	MAKE	YR	BEG MILES	END MILES	MILES	GAL USED	COST/ GAL	FUEL COST	MPG	COST/ MILE
XXXX	X	XX	XXX,XXX	XXX,XXX	X,XXX	XXX.X	$X.XXX	$X,XXX.XX	XX.X	$XX.XX
XXXX	X	XX	XXX,XXX	XXX,XXX	X,XXX	XXX.X	$X.XXX	$X,XXX.XX	XX.X	$XX.XX
XXXX	X	XX	XXX,XXX	XXX,XXX	X,XXX	XXX.X	$X.XXX	$X,XXX.XX	XX.X	$XX.XX

TOTALS	VEHICLES	MILES	FUEL USED	COST/GAL	FUEL COST	MPG	COST/ MILE
	XXX,XXX	XX,XXX	XX,XXX.XX	$X.XXX	$X,XXX.XX	XX.X	$X.XXX

C H A P T E R

6

BRANCHING STATEMENTS

The PROCEDURE DIVISION describes the operations performed by a program in a series of statements that are combined into sentences and that are executed *sequentially*—that is, in the order in which they appear in the program. Thus, the first statement to appear is executed first, the second statement to appear is executed next, and so on, until all the statements in the PROCEDURE DIVISION have been executed.

At times it is necessary to interrupt the sequential order in which COBOL statements are executed and branch to other statements. This change in the order of statement execution is called **branching**. Branching can be accomplished with the following two types of instructions:

1. **Unconditional branching statements** cause a program to branch or deviate from the sequential processing of statements unconditionally, i.e., without being subject to any conditions. The programmer should make minimal use of such statements.

2. **Conditional branching statements** cause a program to branch from the sequential processing of statements upon satisfaction of a predetermined condition at the time the statement is executed. A programmer often uses a conditional branch to leave a program loop so that processing can end.

Statements that perform unconditional or conditional branching functions have been discussed in previous chapters. For example, the STOP RUN command is an unconditional branching statement that transfers control from the application program back to the supervisory control program of the computer operating system. Similarly, the AT END option used with the READ statement forms a conditional branching statement that branches—i.e., executes the command(s) following the words AT END—if all data records have been read. Otherwise, a data record is read and sequential processing continues.

Some statements can be classified as either conditional or unconditional branching statements, depending on the options selected.

THE GO TO STATEMENT

The GO TO statement causes the unconditional transfer from one paragraph to another in the PROCEDURE DIVISION of a COBOL program. Some programmers believe that statements that unconditionally transfer control within a program should never be used. Others believe that an internal transfer of control may be used, but only *within* a PERFORM loop with a THRU option to transfer control to the exit paragraph. Since some programmers still use the GO TO statement, even if only on a limited basis, it is necessary, in studying the COBOL language, to become familiar with this statement.

The general format of the GO TO statement is as follows:

GENERAL FORMAT 1

GO TO [procedure-name-1 [[procedure-name-2] ... DEPENDING ON data-name]]

The **procedure-name-1** option is used when it is desirable to branch to the routine identified by the paragraph-name or section-name indicated by procedure-name-1. Each time the GO TO statement is executed, control is transferred to that paragraph. (See Fig. 6–1.)

As stated earlier, the GO TO statement is sometimes used to transfer control to the exit paragraph in a PERFORM...THRU loop. Figure 6–1 illustrates this situation, in which the GO TO statement is an unconditional branching statement. Although not recommended, the GO

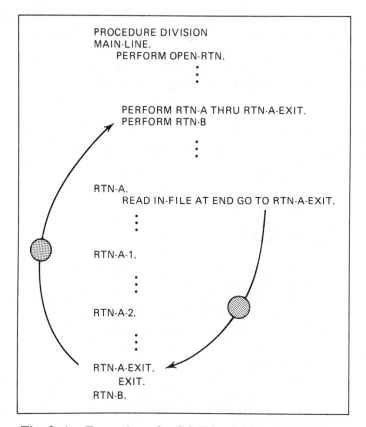

```
PROCEDURE DIVISION
MAIN-LINE.
     PERFORM OPEN-RTN.
                .
                .
                .

     PERFORM RTN-A THRU RTN-A-EXIT.
     PERFORM RTN-B
                .
                .
                .

RTN-A.
     READ IN-FILE AT END GO TO RTN-A-EXIT.
                .
                .
RTN-A-1.
                .
                .
RTN-A-2.
                .
                .
RTN-A-EXIT.
     EXIT.
RTN-B.
```

Fig. 6–1. Execution of a GO TO within a PERFORM.

TO statement can also serve as a conditional branching statement, if the DEPENDING ON option is employed.

In the DEPENDING ON option, control is transferred to one of a series of PROCEDURE DIVISION paragraphs *depending on the value of the identifier at the time the statement is executed.* For example, if the value of the identifier is 1, control is transferred to the paragraph indicated by procedure-name-1; if the value of the identifier is 2, control is transferred to the paragraph indicated by procedure-name-2, and so on; if the value of the identifier is n, control is transferred to the paragraph indicated by procedure-name-n. There is a correspondence between the values that the identifier may assume and the list of procedure names. Also, these values must be only positive or unsigned integers (i.e., 1,2,3...,n).

The following rules govern the DEPENDING ON option of the GO TO statement:

1. If the value of the identifier is other than an integer from 1 to n, the GO TO statement will be ignored.

2. The identifier must be an elementary numeric data item that is described as an integer (contains no decimal places) with a PICTURE description of no more than four digits.

An example of a GO TO statement with the DEPENDING ON option in a case structure is shown in Fig. 6–2.

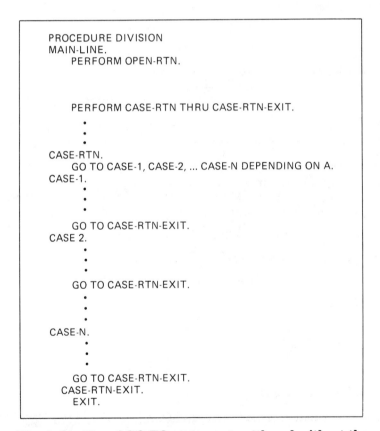

```
PROCEDURE DIVISION
MAIN-LINE.
      PERFORM OPEN-RTN.


      PERFORM CASE-RTN THRU CASE-RTN-EXIT.
      •
      •
      •
CASE-RTN.
      GO TO CASE-1, CASE-2, ... CASE-N DEPENDING ON A.
CASE-1.
      •
      •
      •
      GO TO CASE-RTN-EXIT.
CASE 2.
      •
      •
      •
      GO TO CASE-RTN-EXIT.
      •
      •
      •
CASE-N.
      •
      •
      •
      GO TO CASE-RTN-EXIT.
CASE-RTN-EXIT.
      EXIT.
```

Fig. 6–2. Use of GO TO statements with and without the DEPENDING ON option.

THE IF STATEMENT

The IF statement provides the capability of testing a condition and taking appropriate action depending on whether the condition tested is true or false. There are four types of conditions:

1. Relational

2. Class

3. Sign

4. Condition-name

The general format of the IF statement is as follows:

GENERAL FORMAT 2

$\underline{\text{IF}}$ condition $\left\{ \begin{array}{l} \text{statement-1} \\ \underline{\text{NEXT}}\ \underline{\text{SENTENCE}} \end{array} \right\}$ [$\underline{\text{ELSE}}$ $\left\{ \begin{array}{l} \text{statement-2} \\ \underline{\text{NEXT}}\ \underline{\text{SENTENCE}} \end{array} \right\}$]

The sequence of events that occurs when an IF statement is executed depends greatly on the form of the IF statement and the nature of the condition being tested at the time of execution of the statement. The simplest version of the IF statement is

$\underline{\text{IF}}$ condition $\left\{ \begin{array}{l} \text{statement-1} \\ \underline{\text{NEXT}}\ \underline{\text{SENTENCE}} \end{array} \right\}$

When an IF statement of this type is executed, the following events take place:

1. The **condition** is tested.

2. If the condition is *true*, the statement(s) immediately following the condition is executed.

    a. If the **statement-1** option is indicated, then all imperative statements immediately following the condition and preceding the sentence period are executed.

b. If the NEXT SENTENCE option is specified, then the statement immediately following the period at the end of the IF statement is executed. (This option is used only in conjunction with the ELSE option.)

3. If the condition is *false*, the statement immediately following the IF statement sentence is executed.

An example of an IF statement, together with a flowchart segment indicating the procedure followed in the execution of the statement, is given in Fig. 6–3.

A more explicit version of the IF statement contains the ELSE option. In this version, the program is explicitly directed to execute one statement if the condition is true, and another statement if the condi-

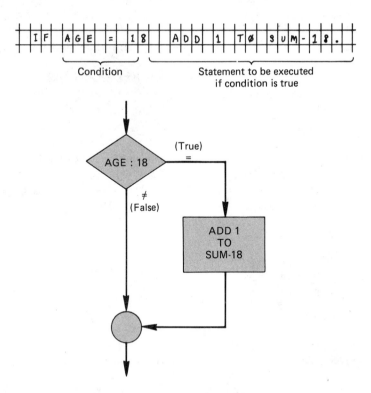

Fig. 6–3. Simple IF statement.

tion is false. When an IF statement of this type is executed, the following sequence of events takes place:

1. The **condition** is tested.

2. If the condition is *true*, the statement immediately following the condition (statement-1 or NEXT SENTENCE) is executed.

3. If the condition is *false*, the statement following the reserved word ELSE (statement-2 or NEXT SENTENCE) is executed.

In no case should the entry NEXT SENTENCE be used both before and after the reserved word ELSE. The result of such usage is a purposeless statement because, whether the statement is true or false, control is transferred to the statement immediately following the period in the IF statement. Note that if NEXT SENTENCE is not explicitly stated in an IF statement with the ELSE option, then after statement-1 or statement-2 has been executed (depending on whether the condition being tested is true or false), the statement immediately following the period at the end of the IF statement is executed.

Figure 6–4 illustrates the IF statement with the ELSE option.

An imperative statement contained in an IF statement may include several PERFORM statements. When this occurs, it is important that one understand that execution of the imperative statement will cause each PERFORM to be executed in the order listed. As one PERFORM is executed, control will be transferred to the next PERFORM in sequence in the imperative statement until all statements that comprise the imperative statement have been executed. Then control will be transferred to the next sentence—the sentence following the IF statement sentence. For example, in the statement

```
IF A > B
        PERFORM PAR-A
        PERFORM PAR-B
        PERFORM PAR-C
ELSE
        PERFORM PAR-D
        ADD 1 TO TOTAL-AMT
        PERFORM PAR-E.
PERFORM PAR-F.
```

if the condition is satisfied (A is greater than B), PAR-A will be PERFORMed, then PAR-B will be PERFORMed, and then PAR-C will be PERFORMed. Execution of the imperative statement will then be com-

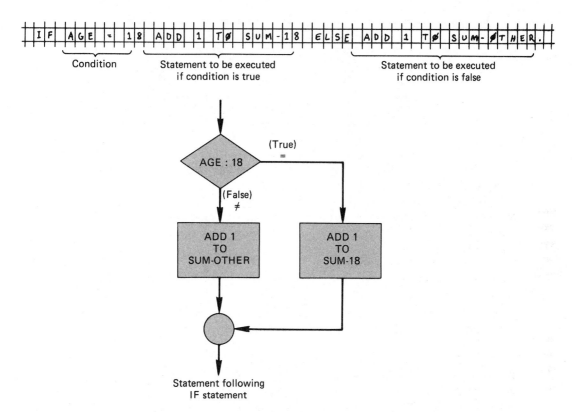

Fig. 6–4. IF statement with ELSE option.

pleted for this condition, and control will be transferred to the next sentence (PERFORM PAR-F). If, on the other hand, the condition is not satisfied (A is not greater than B), PAR-D will be PERFORMed, 1 will be added to TOTAL-AMT, and PAR-E will be PERFORMed. Execution of the imperative statement will then be completed for the ELSE condition, and, as before, the next sentence (PERFORM PAR-F) is executed.

With the above as background, we can now examine how the four types of conditions mentioned earlier are used to perform tests with the IF statement.

The Relational Condition

A relational test determines the relationship between two data items that may be identifiers or literals. The general format of the relational condition used with the IF statement is:

GENERAL FORMAT 3

$$\text{IF } \begin{Bmatrix} \text{identifier-1} \\ \text{literal-1} \end{Bmatrix} \text{ relational-operator } \begin{Bmatrix} \text{identifier-2} \\ \text{literal-2} \end{Bmatrix}$$

$$\begin{Bmatrix} \text{statement-1} \\ \underline{\text{NEXT SENTENCE}} \end{Bmatrix} \quad [\underline{\text{ELSE}} \begin{Bmatrix} \text{statement-2} \\ \underline{\text{NEXT SENTENCE}} \end{Bmatrix}]$$

The first operand is generally referred to as the *subject* of the condition, the second as the *object* of the condition. Either of these may be an *identifier* or a *literal*. Note that a literal used in a relational condition may be a figurative constant (ZERO, SPACES, etc.). The following restrictions apply to the type of operand used with the subject and object of the condition:

1. The subject and object of the condition may *not both* be literals.

2. When the subject and object are not both numeric operands, and neither is a literal, their USAGE must be the same.

Restriction 2 mentions a term we have not yet seen: USAGE. Most computers are capable of storing data in more than one form, e.g., ASCII, packed decimal, binary, etc. The specification of the appropriate form of storage for each data item used in a program can affect the efficiency of the resulting object program. Thus, COBOL provides us with a means by which we can specify the form in which a data item is to be stored—the USAGE clause. If this clause is not used in the description of a data item, the computer assumes USAGE DISPLAY, which means that the computer stores the data in zoned decimal format. If we wish any other storage format, binary for example, we must instruct the computer accordingly. At this time we are not overly concerned with program efficiency, so we have not specified any USAGE in our examples. USAGE will be discussed in more detail in the next chapter.

The relation tested in an IF statement that contains a relational condition is denoted by the **relational operator**. The formats of the possible relational operators, together with their meanings, are given in Table 6–1.

When a relational operator is used with an IF statement, it must be both preceded and followed by a space. Following are some examples of valid relational comparisons.

```
IF AMOUNT > 75.00 NEXT SENTENCE
ELSE PERFORM ERROR-RTN-1.

IF SALARY IS GREATER THAN MINIMUM-SAL
    PERFORM TAX-ROUTINE.

IF BALANCE IS EQUAL TO ZERO
        PERFORM NEXT-CUST-RTN
ELSE PERFORM UPDATE-BAL-RTN.
```

Table 6–1. RELATIONAL OPERATORS USABLE WITH THE IF STATEMENT

Relational Operator	Relation Being Tested
IS [NOT] GREATER THAN IS [NOT] >	The subject is GREATER THAN or NOT GREATER THAN the object of the condition
IS [NOT] LESS THAN IS NOT <	The subject is LESS THAN or NOT LESS THAN the object of the condition
IS [NOT] EQUAL TO IS [NOT] =	The subject is EQUAL TO or NOT EQUAL TO the object of the condition

Note: The symbols >, <, and = can be substituted for GREATER THAN, LESS THAN, and EQUAL TO, respectively, with no change in effect.

When **numeric** items are compared, the following procedure is carried out in the order listed:

1. The decimal points are aligned in the subject and object.

2. High- and low-order positions in each operand are filled with zeros to make certain that both operands are the same size.

3. The subject and object of the condition are compared with respect to their algebraic values. In an algebraic comparison:

    a. Unsigned numeric operands are considered positive.
    b. 0, +0, and −0 are considered equal.
    c. A positive numeric quantity is considered greater than 0.
    d. 0 is considered greater than a negative numeric quantity.

Numeric items may be compared even if their USAGE is different. However, appropriate USAGE assignments for numeric quantities substantially reduce the time taken to convert the usage of numeric display items between DISPLAY and COMPUTATIONAL-3 so that items may be compared.

In a *nonnumeric* comparison, one or both of the operands are nonnumeric. If one of the operands is described as a numeric data item, it is compared as if it were moved to an alphanumeric data item of the same size and the contents of this alphanumeric receiving field were then compared with the nonnumeric operand. In nonnumeric comparisons, the determination of whether the subject is greater than, less than, or equal to the object is made on the basis of the ASCII (American Standard Code for Information Interchange) collating sequence. This sequence, used on the IBM PC and most microcomputers, is shown in Fig. 6–5.

Fig. 6–5. ASCII Collating Sequence

(in ASCII collating sequence beginning with the highest value— *not* the same as the sequence used on larger IBM computer systems)

a
b
.
.   } *Lowercase Letters*
.
y
z

A
B
.
.   } *Uppercase Letters*
.
Y
Z

<   less than
=   equal to   } *Special Characters*
>   greater than
;   semicolon

Fig. 6-5. (*continued*)

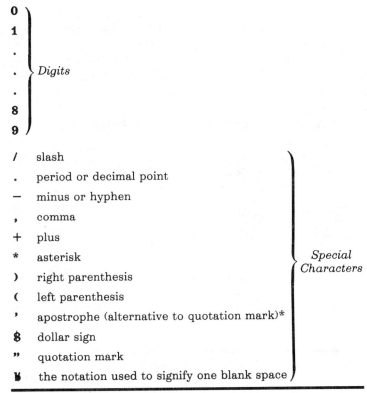

0	
1	
.	
.	*Digits*
.	
8	
9	

/   slash

.   period or decimal point

—   minus or hyphen

,   comma

+   plus

*   asterisk

)   right parenthesis   *Special Characters*

(left parenthesis

'   apostrophe (alternative to quotation mark)*

$ dollar sign

"   quotation mark

Ƀ   the notation used to signify one blank space

*In IBM PC COBOL, either the single (') or double (") quotation mark may be used. In this book we use the single (') quotation mark common to IBM mainframe versions of COBOL.

If the operands being compared are of *equal* length, the comparison is made character by character, beginning with the leftmost or high-order character in each operand and continuing rightward until all characters have been compared or until a pair of unlike characters have been encountered. In this case, the operand containing the larger character according to the collating sequence is considered the larger; otherwise, the operands are considered equal.

If the operands being compared are of *unequal* lengths, the comparison proceeds as if the operands are equal in length until all characters in the shorter operand have been compared against the corresponding characters in the longer operand or until a pair of unlike characters is encountered. If such a pair is encountered, the result for comparison of operands of equal length prevails. If no such pair is encountered, the longer operand is considered the larger *provided that the additional characters in the longer operand are not all blanks.* If the additional characters in the longer operand are blanks, the two operands are considered equal. Thus, on an IBM PC computer, "JOHN" would be considered less than "JOHNSON" but equal to "JOHN". Table 6–2 shows the results of several other relational comparisons.

Table 6–2. **EXAMPLES OF RELATIONAL COMPARISONS**

Value of Subject	Value of Object	Result of Comparison*
AAAA	7	>(greater than)
HARRY	JOHN	<(less than)
114	JOHN	<
47	36	>
SMITH	SMITHSONIAN	<
COST	COSTѢѢѢ	=(equal to)
ABCD	abcd	<
ѢѢѢCOST	COSTѢѢѢ	<

*The results assume the ASCII collating sequence.

Not all relational comparisons are valid in ANS COBOL. Those that are are shown in Fig. 6–6.

The Class Condition

When used with an IF statement, the class condition enables the programmer to test whether a given data item is numeric or alphabetic and to transfer control in accordance with the results of the test. Class condition tests are commonly used to verify that data input to a computer program is of the intended class: numeric or alphabetic. Performed early in a program, this type of test can save much time that would otherwise have been wasted in processing incorrect input data. For example, it is sometimes necessary to know that a data item is numeric before attempting to use it in an arithmetic expression. In such a case, it makes sense to test the value of the data item to determine its class prior to attempting to use it in the expression.

FIRST OPERAND (Subject) \ SECOND OPERAND (Object)	Group Item	Alphanumeric Elementary Item	Alphabetic Elementary Item	Alphanumeric Edited Elementary Item	Numeric Elementary Item	Numeric Edited Elementary Item	Figurative Constant*	ZERO	Nonnumeric Literal	Numeric Literal
Group Item	A	A	A	A	A**	A	A	A	A	A
Alphabetic Elementary Item	A	A	A	A	A**	A	A	A	A	A
Alphanumeric Elementary Item	A	A	A	A	A**	A	A	A	A	A
Alphanumeric Edited Elementary Item	A	A	A	A	A**	A	A	A	A	A
Numeric Elementary Item	A**	A**	A**	A**	A**	A**	A**	N	A**	N
Numeric Edited Elementary Item	A	A	A	A	A**	A	A	A	A	A
Figurative Constant	A	A	A	A	A**	A				
ZERO	A	A	A	A	N	A				
Nonnumeric Literal	A	A	A	A	A**	A				
Numeric Literal	A	A	A	A	N	A				

N = Numeric comparison (Numeric values are compared algebraically)

A = Nonnumeric comparison (One character at a time according to the collating sequence)

□ = Invalid comparison

* = Includes all figurative constants *except* ZERO

** = Permissible only if the item's USAGE is DISPLAY

Fig. 6-6. Valid comparisons.

The general format of the class condition used with the IF statement is as follows:

GENERAL FORMAT 4

IF identifier IS [NOT] $\left\{ \begin{matrix} \text{NUMERIC} \\ \text{ALPHABETIC} \end{matrix} \right\}$

$\left\{ \begin{matrix} \text{statement-1} \\ \text{NEXT SENTENCE} \end{matrix} \right\}$ [ELSE $\left\{ \begin{matrix} \text{statement-2} \\ \text{NEXT SENTENCE} \end{matrix} \right\}$]

When a class condition is being tested, the identifier must be described as USAGE DISPLAY, either implicitly (i.e., without any USAGE specification) or explicitly. We shall discuss the USAGE clause in greater detail in Chapter 7.

Suppose now that we wish to test the data item TOTAL to make certain that it is NUMERIC before attempting to subtract the field AMOUNT from it and produce the difference BALANCE. The following statement accomplishes the task:

```
IF TOTAL NUMERIC
    SUBTRACT AMOUNT FROM TOTAL GIVING BALANCE
ELSE
    MOVE 'INVALID INPUT DATA' TO ERROR-REC
    WRITE ERROR-RECORD FROM ERROR-REC.
```

A data item is NUMERIC if it contains only any of the digits 0 through 9, with or without a sign. If the PICTURE clause has an S for the sign, the data item must contain a valid sign to pass the class test for NUMERIC. If the PICTURE clause does not have an S, the data item must not contain a sign in order to pass the NUMERIC test. The NUMERIC and NOT NUMERIC condition tests can be performed *only* on data items described as numeric, numeric edited, alphanumeric, or alphanumeric edited; they cannot be performed on data items described as alphabetic.

A data item is ALPHABETIC if it contains only any of the characters **A through Z and/or blank(s)**. Note that only *uppercase* or capital letters are considered to be alphabetic. Thus, "john" is not alphabetic, whereas "JOHN" is. An ALPHABETIC condition test can be performed *only* on data items described as alphabetic, numeric edited, alphanumeric, or alphanumeric edited; it cannot be performed on data items described as numeric.

Some examples of valid and invalid class condition tests are shown in Table 6–3.

Table 6–3. EXAMPLES OF VALID AND INVALID CLASS CONDITION TESTS

Identifier	PICTURE	Contents	Class Test	Test Result
AMOUNT	99V99	3472	IF AMOUNT IS NUMERIC ...	T
AMOUNT	99V99	3472	IF AMOUNT IS NOT NUMERIC ...	F
AMOUNT	99V99	3472	IF AMOUNT IS ALPHABETIC ...	I
AMOUNT	99V99	3472	IF AMOUNT IS NOT ALPHABETIC ...	I
AMOUNT	S99V99	3472	IF AMOUNT IS NUMERIC ...	T
AMOUNT	$ZZZ.99	$ƀƀ2.47	IF AMOUNT IS NUMERIC ...	F
AMOUNT	$ZZZ.99	$ƀƀ2.47	IF AMOUNT IS ALPHABETIC ...	F
NAME	A(5)	HARRY	IF NAME IS NOT NUMERIC ...	I
NAME	A(5)	HARRY	IF NAME IS ALPHABETIC ...	T
NAME	A(5)	HARRY	IF NAME IS NOT ALPHABETIC ...	F
NAME	A(5)	JOEƀƀ	IF NAME IS ALPHABETIC ...	T
ITEM-A	X(5)	HARRY	IF ITEM A IS NUMERIC ...	F
ITEM-A	X(5)	HARRY	IF ITEM A IS ALPHABETIC ...	T
ITEM-A	X(5)	00384	IF ITEM A IS NUMERIC ...	T
ITEM-A	X(5)	00384	IF ITEM A IS ALPHABETIC ...	F
ITEM-A	BBX(5)	ƀƀHARRY	IF ITEM A IS NUMERIC ...	F
ITEM-A	BBX5	ƀƀHARRY	IF ITEM A IS NOT ALPHABETIC ...	F

T = Class condition test is TRUE.
F = Class condition test is FALSE.
I = Class condition test is INVALID.

The Sign Condition

The purpose of a sign condition test is to determine whether a given numeric data item or arithmetic expression is *positive* (greater than zero), *negative* (less than zero), *zero* (equal to zero), *not positive* (less than or equal to zero), *not negative* (greater than or equal to zero), or *not zero* (greater than or less than zero). An unsigned field is always either positive or zero.

The general format of a sign condition used with the IF statement is as follows:

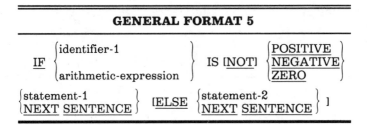

GENERAL FORMAT 5

IF $\left\{ \begin{array}{l} \text{identifier-1} \\ \text{arithmetic-expression} \end{array} \right\}$ IS [NOT] $\left\{ \begin{array}{l} \text{POSITIVE} \\ \text{NEGATIVE} \\ \text{ZERO} \end{array} \right\}$

$\left\{ \begin{array}{l} \text{statement-1} \\ \text{NEXT SENTENCE} \end{array} \right\}$ [ELSE $\left\{ \begin{array}{l} \text{statement-2} \\ \text{NEXT SENTENCE} \end{array} \right\}$]

As with the class condition test, the sign condition test is frequently used to determine the appropriateness of data. For example, if the expression

$$X = \frac{3*A - B**2}{C}$$

is to be evaluated, it would be advisable first to make certain that C is not zero (because it is mathematically invalid to divide by zero). An IF statement that would test the data for this condition is the following:

```
IF C IS ZERO
    PERFORM ERROR-RTN-1
ELSE
    COMPUTE X = (3 * A - B ** 2) / C.
```

The Condition-Name Condition

The VALUE Clause in Condition-Name Entries We have seen that the VALUE clause may be used in the DATA DIVISION to establish the initial values of data items defined in the WORKING-STORAGE SECTION. It may also be used to equate a condition-name to a single value or a range of values that an elementary data item may assume. When used in this context, the VALUE clause may appear in the FILE SECTION also.

The general format of the VALUE clause that assigns a single value to a condition-name is:

GENERAL FORMAT 6

88 condition-name VALUE IS literal

A condition-name is a name assigned by the programmer to the *values that a given data item may assume* during program execution.

Condition-names are formed according to the rules for the formation of data-names.

A condition-name entry allows a descriptive condition-name to be assigned to a value, set of values, or range of values that may appear in a data item. These condition-names can then be utilized in PROCE-DURE DIVISION statements to determine the presence of the value or values. However, the type of the literal appearing in a condition-name entry must be consistent with the data type of the conditional variable. For example, consider the following DATA DIVISION segment:

```
03   COUNTY-CITY-DATA.
            88   BRONX              VALUE '01NYC'.
            88   BROOKLYN           VALUE '04NYC'.
            88   MANHATTAN          VALUE '07NYC'.
            88   QUEENS             VALUE '13NYC'.
            88   STATEN-ISLAND      VALUE '15NYC'.
       04   COUNTY   PICTURE   99.
            88   DUCHESS            VALUE 03.
            88   KINGS              VALUE 04.
            88   NEW-YORK           VALUE 07.
            88   RICHMOND           VALUE 15.
       04   CITY      PICTURE X(3).
            88   BUFFALO            VALUE 'BUF'.
            88   NEW-YORK-CITY      VALUE 'NYC'.
            88   POUGHKEEPSIE       VALUE 'POK'.
03   POPULATION.
            .
            .
            .
```

In the above code, COUNTY-CITY-DATA, COUNTY, and CITY are all conditional variables with their associated condition-names immediately following the level number 88. The PICTURE assigned to COUN-TY restricts the value of the condition-name to a two-digit numeric literal. Similarly, the PICTURE assigned to CITY restricts the value of the condition-name to a three-character nonnumeric literal. Thus, any values of the condition-names associated with the group item COUNTY-CITY-DATA cannot exceed five characters, and the literal must be nonnumeric.

The following rules apply to the use of condition-name entries:

1. The VALUE clause is required and is the only clause allowed in a condition-name entry.

2. The condition-name entries are for a given conditional variable or another 88-level entry.

It is possible to assign a set or range of values, or a series of ranges, to a condition-name. (However, it is not possible in IBM PC COBOL to assign a list *and* a range in the same VALUE clause.) The general format of the VALUE clause with the THRU option that provides the capability of assigning ranges or series of ranges is as follows:

GENERAL FORMAT 7

$\left\{ \begin{array}{l} \underline{\text{VALUE}} \text{ is} \\ \underline{\text{VALUES}} \underline{\text{ARE}} \end{array} \right\}$ literal-1[THRU]literal-2][literal-3[THRU]literal-4]] . . .

Whenever the THRU option is employed, the value of literal-1 must be less than that of literal-2, the value of literal-3 must be less than that of literal-4, and so on.

As an example, if condition-names are assigned to the possible final grades that a student may receive in a course, the entries can be written as follows:

```
02   FINAL-GRADE   PICTURE 99V9.
     88   A         VALUES ARE 89.5 THRU 100.0.
     88   B         VALUES ARE 79.5 THRU 89.4.
     88   C         VALUES ARE 69.5 THRU 79.4.
     88   D         VALUES ARE 59.5 THRU 69.4.
     88   F         VALUES ARE  0.0 THRU 59.4.
     88   HONORS    VALUES ARE 85.0 THRU 100.0.
```

As with General Format 6 of the VALUE statement, literals must agree in SIZE and TYPE with the associated PICTURE specification.

Use of the Condition-Name Entry in Conditional Statements

Once a condition-name has been defined and equated to a value or set of values in the DATA DIVISION, it may be used in a condition-name condition appearing in the PROCEDURE DIVISION.

The general format of the condition-name condition used with the IF statement is as follows:

GENERAL FORMAT 8

$\underline{\text{IF}}$ condition-name $\left\{ \begin{array}{l} \text{statement-1} \\ \underline{\text{NEXT}} \underline{\text{SENTENCE}} \end{array} \right\}$ [$\underline{\text{ELSE}}$ $\left\{ \begin{array}{l} \text{statement-2} \\ \underline{\text{NEXT}} \underline{\text{SENTENCE}} \end{array} \right\}$]

Thus, if the DATA DIVISION contained the entries

```
02  SEX-CODE    PICTURE 9.
    88  MALE        VALUE 1.
    88  FEMALE      VALUE 2.
    88  VALID       VALUE 1 THRU 2.
```

SEX-CODE can be tested in the PROCEDURE DIVISION with the statement

```
IF SEX-CODE = 0 OR SEX-CODE > 2
    PERFORM ERROR-RTN.
IF SEX-CODE = 1
    PERFORM PROC-A
IF SEX-CODE = 2
    PERFORM PROC-B.
```

or with the statement

```
IF NOT VALID
    PERFORM ERROR-RTN.
IF MALE
    PERFORM PROC-A
ELSE
    PERFORM PROC-B.
```

Both statements have the same effect, but the latter is easier to read and understand. Therefore, it is more meaningful as self-documentation in a COBOL program.

COMPOUND CONDITIONALS

The flexibility of the IF statement may be increased by employing the COBOL **logical operators** AND, OR, and NOT. Logical operators apply to one or more individual conditional expressions to form a new, often multiconditional (compound conditional) expression. For example, in the statement

```
IF A = B AND A < C GO TO WRAP-UP.
```

the logical operator AND applies to the separate expressions $A = B$ and $A < C$ to form the multiconditional expression $A = B$ AND $A < C$, and the entire statement is called a **compound conditional statement**.

The general format of a compound conditional statement containing two conditions is as follows:

GENERAL FORMAT 9

IF condition-1 $\left\{\begin{matrix} \underline{AND} \\ OR \end{matrix}\right\}$ condition-2 $\left\{\begin{matrix} \text{statement-1} \\ \underline{NEXT}\ \underline{SENTENCE} \end{matrix}\right\}$

[$\underline{ELSE}$ $\left\{\begin{matrix} \text{statement-2} \\ \underline{NEXT}\ \underline{SENTENCE} \end{matrix}\right\}$]

The truth or falsity of the compound conditional expression depends on the truth or falsity of each of the individual expressions. Tables 6–4 and 6–5 illustrate this relationship for the AND and OR logical operators, respectively.

Let us flesh out the table with a couple of examples. For the statement

```
IF  A  =  B  AND  A  <  C
      PERFORM  WRAP - UP.
```

Table 6–4 indicates that both of the individual conditions A = B and A < C must be true for the compound condition to be true. Any other combination of true and false values for these conditions results in a false value for the compound condition A = B AND A < C. Similarly, consider the statement

```
IF  A  =  B  OR  A  <  K
      PERFORM  WRAP - UP.
```

Table 6–5 indicates that at least one of the individual conditions A = B and A < K must be true for the compound condition to be true. In other words, for the combined condition to be true, the individual conditions must not both be false.

Table 6–4.   TRUTH VALUES FOR *AND* COMPOUND CONDITIONAL

Condition-1	Condition-2	Condition-1 AND Condition-2
TRUE	TRUE	TRUE
TRUE	FALSE	FALSE
FALSE	TRUE	FALSE
FALSE	FALSE	FALSE

**Table 6–5.   TRUTH VALUES FOR *OR*
COMPOUND CONDITIONAL**

Condition-1	Condition-2	Condition-1 OR Condition-2
TRUE	TRUE	TRUE
TRUE	FALSE	TRUE
FALSE	TRUE	TRUE
FALSE	FALSE	FALSE

It is possible for a compound conditional statement to contain more than two conditions and one logical operator. For example, it may be necessary to determine the value of a compound condition that would be true if A = B and A < C or if A > B and A = C. The following statement contains the required compound condition:

```
IF (A = B AND A < C) or (A > B AND A = C)
    PERFORM RTN-A
ELSE
    PERFORM RTN-B.
```

An examination of Tables 6–4 and 6–5 confirms that this statement does what it is intended to do. Since the main logical operator (the one that binds the two pairs of conditions in parentheses) is OR, we look to Table 6–5 first. Table 6–5 indicates that for the compound condition (A = B AND A < C) or (A > B AND A = C) to be true, at least one of the conditions (A = B AND A < C) and (A > B AND A = C) must be true. Since the main (and only) logical operator in each of these conditions is AND, we next check Table 6–4. Table 6–4 indicates that for the former condition to be true, both A = B and A < C must be true; and for the latter condition to be true, both A > B and A = C must be true. Accordingly, for the compound condition to be true, either A = B and A < C must both be true or A > B and A = C must both be true. But this is just the intent of the statement.

Much thought goes into determining an appropriate compound conditional statement for a given problem because first thoughts are often misleading, if not altogether incorrect. For example, suppose that ROUTINE-A is to be executed if the data item ITEM-A is between 1 and 5 inclusive. A first thought might suggest the following statement:

```
IF ITEM-A = 1 OR ITEM-A = 2 OR ITEM-A = 3 OR ITEM-A = 4
    OR ITEM-A = 5
    PERFORM ROUTINE-A.
```

However, this statement handles only integer values between 1 and 5 inclusive; it does not consider all values in the range. For example, the value 3.59 is in the range but would not result in a true condition if assigned to ITEM-A. Rather, a statement is needed that branches to ROUTINE-A under the following three conditions:

```
ITEM-A = 1
ITEM-A > 1 AND ITEM-A < 5
ITEM-A = 5
```

This results in the compound conditional statement

```
IF ITEM-A = 1 OR ITEM-A > 1 AND ITEM-A < 5 OR ITEM-A = 5
    PERFORM ROUTINE-A.
```

Since this statement does not contain any parentheses to indicate the order of execution of the AND and OR logical operators, the order in which they are actually executed could change the entire meaning of the statement. Let us investigate this possibility.

The Hierarchy Rule

The order of execution of operators in COBOL is as follows:

1. Arithmetic operators.

2. Relational operators.

3. NOT operators.

4. All AND operators, starting with the leftmost condition and proceeding to the rightmost.

5. All OR operators, starting with the leftmost condition and proceeding to the rightmost.

Parentheses can be used as in mathematics to alter this hierarchical order of evaluation. In such cases, parenthetical expressions are evaluated from the innermost to the outermost set of parentheses.

Applying the above rules to the IF statement discussed above, namely,

```
IF ITEM-A = 1 OR ITEM-A > 1 AND ITEM-A < 5 OR ITEM-A = 5
   PERFORM ROUTINE-A.
```

the order of execution of the operators is as follows:

1. The relational operators ($=$, $>$, and $<$) are executed, causing the associated conditions (ITEM-A $= 1$, ITEM-A > 1, ITEM-A < 5) to be evaluated to determine whether they are true or false.

2. The logical operator AND is then executed to determine the truth value (true or false) of the condition ITEM-A > 1 AND ITEM-A < 5.

3. The truth value from step 2 is then combined with the truth value of ITEM-A $= 1$ under the rules pertaining to the logical operator OR to determine the truth value for the compound condition ITEM-A $= 1$ OR ITEM-A > 1 AND ITEM-A < 5.

4. The truth value from step 3 is combined with the truth value of ITEM-A $= 5$ under the rules pertaining to the logical operator OR to determine the truth value for the entire compound condition.

5. The truth value obtained in step 4 is then used to determine whether control will be transferred to ROUTINE-A.

Thus, if ITEM-A has the noninteger value 3.59, as before, the results of a step-by-step analysis as above are as follows:

1. ITEM-A $= 1$ is FALSE.
   ITEM-A > 1 is TRUE.
   ITEM-A < 5 is TRUE.
   ITEM-A $= 5$ is FALSE.

2. ITEM-A > 1 AND ITEM-A < 5 is TRUE.

3. ITEM-A $= 1$ OR ITEM-A > 1 AND ITEM-A < 5 is TRUE.

4. ITEM-A $= 1$ OR ITEM-A > 1 AND ITEM-A < 5 OR ITEM-A $= 5$ is TRUE.

5. Control will be transferred to paragraph ROUTINE-A.

Implied Subjects and Operators

A feature of IBM COBOL that can be used to simplify the writing of compound conditional statements is the ability to handle an implied subject. In the previous example, the subject of each of the conditions was the same: ITEM-A. With the implied-subject capability, it is necessary to state the subject only once. Thus, the statement

```
IF ITEM-A = 1 OR ITEM-A > 1 AND ITEM-A < 5 OR ITEM-A = 5
    PERFORM ROUTINE-A.
```

could have been written

```
IF ITEM-A = 1 OR > 1 AND < 5 OR = 5
    PERFORM ROUTINE-A.
```

or even

```
IF ITEM-A NOT < 1 AND NOT > 5
    PERFORM ROUTINE-A.
```

using an implied subject. In general, when a series of relational conditions specifies the same subject or the same subject and relational operator, the said subject and/or operator may be omitted from those relational conditions that immediately follow the initial relational condition. Other examples of the use of conditional statements with implied subjects are given in Table 6–6. Note that the implied subject and operator is permitted *only* in relational tests, *not* with the class or the sign test.

Table 6–6.   EXAMPLES OF IMPLIED SUBJECT AND RELATIONAL OPERATOR CONDITIONALS

Conditional with Explicitly Stated Subject and Operators	Conditional with Implied Subject and Operators
A = B OR A NOT < C	A = B OR NOT < C
A > 10 OR A = 10	A > 10 OR = 10
A = B AND A = C	A = B AND C
A NOT = B AND A NOT = C	A NOT = B AND C
A = 3 OR A = 4 OR A = 5	A = 3 OR 4 OR 5
A < B AND NOT A > C AND A > D	A < B AND NOT > C AND D

NESTED IF STATEMENTS

In the format of the IF statement presented earlier, namely,

IF condition $\begin{Bmatrix} \text{statement-1} \\ \text{NEXT SENTENCE} \end{Bmatrix}$ [ELSE $\begin{Bmatrix} \text{statement-2} \\ \text{NEXT SENTENCE} \end{Bmatrix}$]

statement-1 and statement-2 denoted imperative statements. It is possible, however, in IBM COBOL to replace these statements with other IF statements—that is, IF statements may be **nested**.

Nested IF statements consist of vertically paired IF and ELSE statements that proceed from left to right. To interpret these statements correctly, the first or leftmost ELSE must be located. The rule is that it always pertains to the immediately preceding unmatched IF. Proceeding to the right, the next ELSE statement pertains to the next IF statement to the right of the previous one and so on. Schematically, the relationship can be portrayed as

```
IF...
    IF...
        IF...
         .
         .    ...
         .
        ELSE...
    ELSE...
ELSE...
```

The flowchart sequence shown in Fig. 6–7 exemplifies this relationship.

Coding the sequence of Fig. 6–7 by means of *sequential* IF statements with compound conditions yields the following.

```
IF MAR-ST = 1 AND AGE < 21
    PERFORM RTN-B.
IF MAR-ST = 1 AND AGE = 21
    PERFORM RTN-C.
PERFORM RTN-A.
```

As you can see, there are numerous ways in which routines involving IF statements can be coded. The method chosen should be the one that is the *least error prone* and the *clearest* for another programmer or user to read.

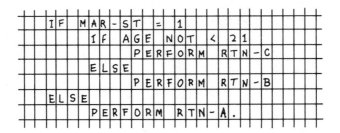

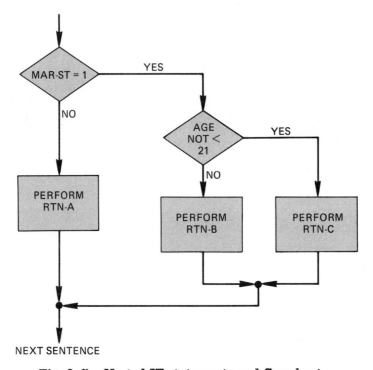

Fig. 6–7. Nested IF statements and flowchart.

SPECIAL APPLICATIONS OF THE IF STATEMENT

Two applications that require the use of the IF statement and that appear in many programs in the field are concerned with checking input data prior to processing and providing control breaks within a program.

Input Data Validation

In any COBOL program it is important to make every effort to verify that data input is valid before attempting to process it. There are few things that can frustrate a programmer or end user more than having a program hang up due to bad data. You can be certain that if such a thing is going to happen, it is going to happen at the most inappropriate time. Thus, most programmers make provision for the possibility that an input data error could slip through the preprocessing checking procedures, regardless of how carefully planned they are. Some of the things that a programmer can check before processing external data are that alphabetic and numeric fields contain only alphabetic and numeric data, respectively, that a data item that is supposed to be within a certain range is truly within that range, and so on.

Checking for valid numeric data is automatically built into the ACCEPT statement with the PROMPT option. This is a great help when handling data interactively—i.e., through the terminal. If data have been defined as numeric, for example, S9(5)V99, the prompt appears as follows on the screen:

```
STATEMENT BALANCE: 00000.00
```

If, in response to this prompt, you try to enter data that are not valid numeric data or a valid sign, the IBM PC sounds a tone and refuses to accept the data.

If the data that are being processed are being read from disk, such automatic error checking does not occur. However, the program shown in Fig. 6-8 illustrates how we can check for invalid numeric data that are read from a file. The input data to be checked in this program include RATING-IN, an alphanumeric field that is being checked for the presence of valid ratings. We have decided that the valid ratings are A, AA, B, BB, and C; note that we have used a condition-name (88 level) for this purpose. The program also checks for valid numeric data in the fields called LIMIT-AMT-IN, UNIT-PRICE-IN, and UNITS-IN. We have redefined both the input data items and the output data items for these numeric fields. Note the use of the IF...ELSE statements in the PROCEDURE DIVISION for proper processing of these items. If any of the input data, rating or numeric, are not valid, the program prints out both the message BAD to the right of the data and the actual data for inspection (see Fig. 6-9). Note also that there are a number of ways that these data checks can be implemented. We have merely chosen the method that best illustrates the concepts involved.

```
        IDENTIFICATION DIVISION.
        PROGRAM-ID.
            PROGRAM-LIST.
        AUTHOR.
            S.J.GAUGHRAN.
        INSTALLATION.
            PERSONAL COMPUTER SYSTEM.
        DATE-WRITTEN.
            JAN.23,1985.
        DATE-COMPILED.
            JAN.25,1985.
        SECURITY.
            NONE.
        ENVIRONMENT DIVISION.
        CONFIGURATION SECTION.
        SOURCE-COMPUTER.
            IBM-PERSONAL-COMPUTER.
        OBJECT-COMPUTER.
            IBM-PERSONAL-COMPUTER.
        INPUT-OUTPUT SECTION.
        FILE-CONTROL.
            SELECT TRANSAC-FILE ASSIGN TO DISK
                    ORGANIZATION IS LINE SEQUENTIAL.
            SELECT TRANSAC-LIST ASSIGN TO PRINTER.
       *
        DATA DIVISION.
        FILE SECTION.
        FD  TRANSAC-FILE
            LABEL RECORDS ARE STANDARD
            VALUE OF FILE-ID IS 'CH601.DAT'.
        01  DISK-REC               PIC X(45).
        FD  TRANSAC-LIST
            LABEL RECORDS ARE OMITTED.
        01  PRINT-REC              PIC X(78).
       *
        WORKING-STORAGE SECTION.
       *
        01  SWITCHES-MESSAGES-COUNTERS.
            05  EOF               PIC 9         VALUE ZERO.
            05  ERROR-MSG         PIC X(4)      VALUE ' BAD'.
            05  END-MSG           PIC X(12)     VALUE ' END OF JOB '.
       *
        01  TRANSAC-REC-IN.
            05  CUSTOMER-NO-IN     PIC X(5).
            05  CUSTOMER-ID-IN.
                10  LAST-NAME-IN   PIC X(10).
                10  FIRST-NAME-IN  PIC X(10).
                10  INITIAL-IN     PIC X.
                10  CREDIT-CODE-IN.
                    15  RATING-IN   PIC XX.
                        88 VALID-RATING    VALUE 'A' 'AA' 'B' 'BB' 'C'.
                    15  LIMIT-AMT-IN PIC S999.
**** NEW LINE INSERTED BELOW ******************************
                    15  LIMIT-AMT-IN-X  REDEFINES LIMIT-AMT-IN
                                       PIC X(3).
            05  TRANS-IN.
                10  ITEM-NO-IN.
                    15  INV-NO-IN   PIC X(5).
                    15  DEPT-NO-IN  PIC XX.
                10  UNIT-PRICE-IN  PIC S9(3)V99.
**** NEW STATEMENTS INSERTED BELOW *************************
                10  UNIT-PRICE-IN-X  REDEFINES UNIT-PRICE-IN
                                       PIC X(5).
                10  UNITS-IN       PIC S99.
                10  UNITS-IN-X  REDEFINES  UNITS-IN
                                       PIC X(2).
       *
        01  TITLE-1.
            05  FILLER            PIC X(20) VALUE SPACES.
            05  FILLER            PIC X(39) VALUE
                   'ACCOUNTS RECEIVABLE REPORT'.
```

Fig. 6–8. Validity check program.

```
*
01   TITLE-2.
     05  FILLER            PIC XX     VALUE SPACES.
     05  FILLER            PIC X(4)   VALUE 'CUST'.
     05  FILLER            PIC X(8)   VALUE SPACES.
     05  FILLER            PIC X(13)  VALUE 'CUSTOMER NAME'.
     05  FILLER            PIC X(7)   VALUE SPACES.
     05  FILLER            PIC X(6)   VALUE 'CREDIT'.
     05  FILLER            PIC XX     VALUE SPACES.
     05  FILLER            PIC X(4)   VALUE 'CODE'.
     05  FILLER            PIC X(5)   VALUE SPACES.
     05  FILLER            PIC X(23)  VALUE
             'TRANSACTION INFORMATION'.
*
01   TITLE-3.
     05  FILLER            PIC X      VALUE SPACES.
     05  FILLER            PIC X(6)   VALUE 'NUMBER'.
     05  FILLER            PIC X(5)   VALUE SPACES.
     05  FILLER            PIC X(4)   VALUE 'LAST'.
     05  FILLER            PIC X(6)   VALUE SPACES.
     05  FILLER            PIC X(5)   VALUE 'FIRST'.
     05  FILLER            PIC X(4)   VALUE SPACES.
     05  FILLER            PIC X      VALUE 'M'.
     05  FILLER            PIC XX     VALUE SPACES.
     05  FILLER            PIC X(6)   VALUE 'RATING'.
     05  FILLER            PIC X      VALUE SPACES.
     05  FILLER            PIC X(5)   VALUE 'LIMIT'.
     05  FILLER            PIC XXX    VALUE SPACES.
     05  FILLER            PIC XXX    VALUE 'INV'.
     05  FILLER            PIC XX     VALUE SPACES.
     05  FILLER            PIC X(4)   VALUE 'DEPT'.
     05  FILLER            PIC X      VALUE SPACES.
     05  FILLER            PIC X(10)  VALUE 'UNIT PRICE'.
     05  FILLER            PIC X      VALUE SPACES.
     05  FILLER            PIC X(8)   VALUE 'QUANTITY'.
*
01   TRANSAC-REC-OUT.
     05  FILLER            PIC X      VALUE SPACES.
     05  CUSTOMER-NO-OUT   PIC X(5).
     05  FILLER            PIC X(3)   VALUE SPACES.
     05  CUSTOMER-ID-OUT.
         10  LAST-NAME-OUT  PIC X(10).
         10  FILLER.        PIC X      VALUE SPACES.
         10  FIRST-NAME-OUT PIC X(10).
         10  FILLER         PIC X      VALUE SPACES.
         10  INITIAL-OUT    PIC X.
         10  FILLER         PIC X(4)   VALUE SPACES.
         10  CREDIT-CODE-OUT.
             15  RATING-OUT PIC XX.
             15  FILLER     PIC X(4)   VALUE SPACES.
             15  LIMIT-AMT-OUT PIC ZZ9.
**** NEW LINE INSERTED BELOW ********************************
             15  LIMIT-AMT-OUT-X REDEFINES LIMIT-AMT-OUT
                               PIC X(3).
             15  FILLER     PIC X(3)   VALUE SPACES.
     05  TRANS-OUT.
         10  INV-NO-OUT PIC X(5).
         10  FILLER         PIC XX     VALUE SPACES.
         10  DEPT-NO-OUT    PIC XX.
         10  FILLER         PIC X(3)   VALUE SPACES.
         10  UNIT-PRICE-OUT PIC $ZZZ.99.
**** NEW LINE INSERTED BELOW ********************************
         10  UNIT-PRICE-OUT-X  REDEFINES UNIT-PRICE-OUT
                               PIC X(7).
         10  FILLER         PIC X(3)   VALUE SPACES.
         10  UNITS-OUT PIC Z9.
**** NEW LINE INSERTED BELOW ********************************
         10  UNITS-OUT-X  REDEFINES UNITS-OUT
                               PIC X(2).
         10  MSG-OUT       PIC X(4)   VALUE SPACES.
*
PROCEDURE DIVISION.
```

Fig. 6–8. (*continued*)

```
    MAIN-LINE.
        PERFORM 100-OPEN-FILES.
        PERFORM 200-HEADING-RTN.
        READ TRANSAC-FILE INTO TRANSAC-REC-IN
            AT END MOVE 1 TO EOF.
        PERFORM 300-PROCESS-RTN
            UNTIL EOF = 1.
        PERFORM 400-CLOSE-RTN.
        STOP RUN.

    100-OPEN-FILES.
        OPEN INPUT   TRANSAC-FILE
             OUTPUT  TRANSAC-LIST.

    200-HEADING-RTN.
        WRITE PRINT-REC FROM TITLE-1 AFTER ADVANCING PAGE.
        WRITE PRINT-REC FROM TITLE-2 AFTER ADVANCING 3 LINES.
        WRITE PRINT-REC FROM TITLE-3 AFTER ADVANCING 1 LINE.
        MOVE SPACES TO PRINT-REC.
        WRITE PRINT-REC AFTER ADVANCING 1 LINE.

    300-PROCESS-RTN.
        MOVE CUSTOMER-NO-IN TO CUSTOMER-NO-OUT.
        MOVE LAST-NAME-IN   TO LAST-NAME-OUT.
        MOVE FIRST-NAME-IN  TO FIRST-NAME-OUT.
        MOVE INITIAL-IN     TO INITIAL-OUT.
        MOVE RATING-IN      TO RATING-OUT.
**** NEW STATEMENTS INSERTED BELOW ***************************
        IF VALID-RATING     NEXT SENTENCE
        ELSE                MOVE ERROR-MSG TO MSG-OUT.
        IF LIMIT-AMT-IN NUMERIC
                            MOVE LIMIT-AMT-IN   TO LIMIT-AMT-OUT
        ELSE                MOVE LIMIT-AMT-IN-X TO LIMIT-AMT-OUT-X
                            MOVE ERROR-MSG      TO MSG-OUT.
        MOVE INV-NO-IN      TO INV-NO-OUT.
        MOVE DEPT-NO-IN     TO DEPT-NO-OUT.
**** NEW STATEMENTS INSERTED BELOW ***************************
        IF UNIT-PRICE-IN NUMERIC
                            MOVE UNIT-PRICE-IN   TO UNIT-PRICE-OUT
        ELSE                MOVE UNIT-PRICE-IN-X TO UNIT-PRICE-OUT-X
                            MOVE ERROR-MSG       TO MSG-OUT.
        IF UNITS-IN NUMERIC
                            MOVE UNITS-IN        TO UNITS-OUT
        ELSE                MOVE UNITS-IN-X      TO UNITS-OUT-X
                            MOVE ERROR-MSG       TO MSG-OUT.
        WRITE PRINT-REC FROM TRANSAC-REC-OUT
            AFTER ADVANCING 1 LINE.
**** NEW LINE INSERTED BELOW *********************************
        MOVE SPACES         TO MSG-OUT.
        READ TRANSAC-FILE INTO TRANSAC-REC-IN
            AT END MOVE 1 TO EOF.

    400-CLOSE-RTN.
        MOVE END-MSG TO PRINT-REC.
        WRITE PRINT-REC AFTER ADVANCING 3 LINES.
        CLOSE TRANSAC-FILE
              TRANSAC-LIST.
```

Fig. 6–8. (*continued*)

You may have noticed in the figure that a new clause has been used in the input and output record descriptions TRANSAC-REC-IN and TRANSAC-REC-OUT in the WORKING-STORAGE SECTION. This clause, called the REDEFINES clause, allows us to define the same

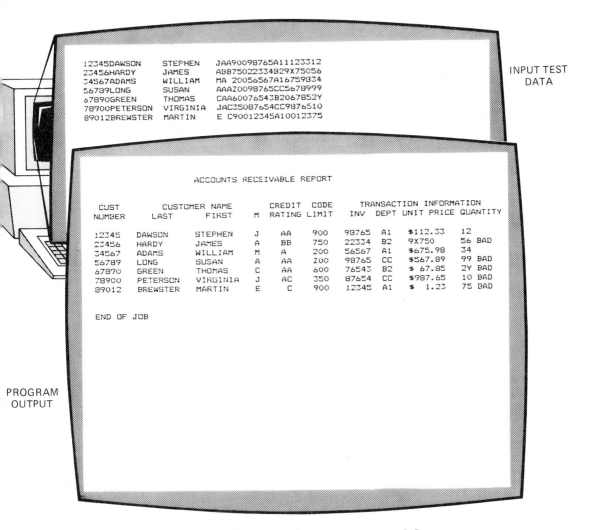

INPUT TEST DATA

PROGRAM OUTPUT

Fig. 6-9. **Program output shows message and data.**

storage area with two different names and two different PICTURE clauses. The reason that this is needed is that two different types of data can exist in the designated location. Thus, if LIMIT-AMT-IN is numeric, the data in it can be moved to a numeric receiving area (LIMIT-AMT-OUT), but if it is not numeric, the data in it must be moved to a nonnumeric receiving area. Accordingly, the receiving area is defined in two different ways: LIMIT-AMT-OUT is defined with PIC

Z99 to receive the good data, and LIMIT-AMT-OUT-X is defined with PIC X(3) to receive nonnumeric data. Keep in mind, however, that LIMIT-AMT-OUT and LIMIT-AMT-OUT-X are two different names, with two different associated descriptions, for the same storage area.

Compilers differ in their requirements regarding the sending field description when a data item is moved to a redefined field. For example, some compilers require that when data from a sending field described as numeric with an implied decimal point are moved to a redefined alphanumeric field, the sending field must also be redefined. In such cases, if the data test out valid, they are moved from the input data field to the corresponding output field. However, if the data test out invalid, they are moved from the redefined input field to the redefined output field. It will be safest to REDEFINE both the sending and receiving fields, as this will work in all cases.

Before proceeding any further with the program, let us examine the REDEFINES clause more carefully.

This program is available on the supplemental disk as CH601.COB. Appropriate test data go under the name CH601.DAT.

The REDEFINES Clause   As mentioned, the REDEFINES clause is used when it is desirable to refer to the same storage area by multiple data-names, or when there is a need to describe a data storage area in more than one manner. That is, it redefines the *storage area*, not the contents of the area. The general format of the REDEFINES clause is as follows:

GENERAL FORMAT 10

---

level-number data-name-1 <u>REDEFINES</u> data-name-2

Data-name-2 is the data-name associated with a previous data item description entry, while **data-name-1** is an alternative name for the same area. The level numbers of both data-names must be identical, and there must be no entries having numerically lower level numbers

Table 6-7. A/R BILLING PROGRAM RECORDS

Record	Columns	Contents	PICTURE
1	1	Credit code	X
	2-65	Customer identification	X(64)
	66-73	Credit amount	$ZZZZ.99
	74-80	Blank field	X(7)
2	1	Balance code	X
	2-65	Customer identification	X(64)
	66-73	Balance due	$ZZZZ.99
	74-80	Minimum payment	$ZZZ.99

between the data item description entries of these items. The following simplistic, but useful, application explains the nature and uses of the REDEFINES clause.

Suppose that an accounts receivable (A/R) billing program is required to output a customer billing file containing two input records with similar, but not identical, formats. The formats are shown in Table 6-7. Then the REDEFINES clause may be used in the following way.

```
01  ACCTS-REC-BILLING.
    02  CODE-OUT                        PIC X.
    02  CUST-ID                         PIC X(64).
    02  AMOUNT                          PIC $Z,ZZZ.99.
    02  BLK-FLD                         PIC X(7).
    02  MIN-PAYMENT REDEFINES BLK-FLD PIC $ZZZ.99.
```

With the REDEFINES clause used thus, two output record formats are described with only one record description entry. Note that the REDEFINES clause is used with a PICTURE clause that differs from the PICTURE clause of the preceding item that it redefines. Also, the REDEFINES clause precedes the PICTURE clause. In general, when the REDEFINES clause is used in conjunction with other clauses, it must precede all of them; that is, it must be the first entry after the level number and data-name. The following restrictions apply to the REDEFINES clause:

1. It must not be used with 88-level items.

2. It must not be used at the 01 level in the FILE SECTION.

3. A VALUE must not be assigned to a storage area that is redefined.

4. It must contain a PICTURE clause when it redefines an elementary data item.

5. When a group data item is redefined, each subordinate elementary data item must contain a PICTURE clause.

Another example of the use of the REDEFINES clause is given in Fig. 6–10. In this example, the storage area is totally changed in the redefinition.

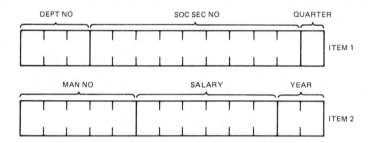

Fig. 6–10. Example of REDEFINES clause usage.

Control Breaks

A **control break** occurs when the value in a given data field of a sequential file changes from the value previously read to a new value. Figure 6–11 presents some examples.

Note that a control break occurs each time the customer number changes. Thus, since the customer number field is being used to determine when a control break occurs, it is referred to as the **control field**. The data file being tested for control breaks must have its control field data arranged sequentially.

The purpose of the control break is to determine when to perform some unique type of processing, such as computing the total of all transactions for the customer just processed. It is possible for a pro-

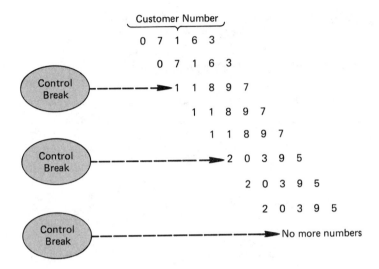

Fig. 6–11. Example of control breaks.

gram to contain multiple control breaks. For example, a program could total sales by salesperson, by district, and by region. To accomplish this, the input file would be in sequence according to three control fields: region number, district number, and salesperson number. That is, the input records must be in region number sequence, in district number sequence within each region number, and in salesperson number sequence within each district number. Figure 6–12 shows just such a series of sequences.

Suppose we wish to write a program to produce the report of Fig. 6–12—that is, a program that totals sales by region, by district, and finally by salesperson. In the program, each transaction must be read in and processed. When a change in salesperson number occurs, a control break routine must be performed that will cause the printing of the total sales for the particular salesperson. When a change in district number occurs, two control breaks are performed:

1. A minor control break that prints the salesperson's total.

2. An intermediate control break that prints the total sales for the district.

When a change in region number occurs, three control breaks are performed:

1. A minor control break that prints the salesperson's total.

2. An intermediate control break that prints the total sales for the district.

3. A major control break that prints the total sales for the region.

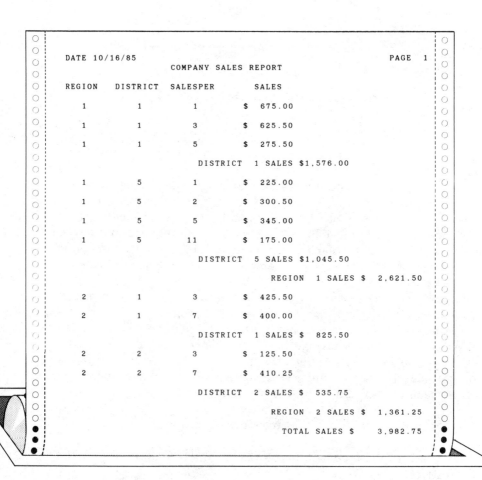

```
DATE 10/16/85                                                PAGE  1
                         COMPANY SALES REPORT

  REGION     DISTRICT   SALESPER        SALES

     1          1          1        $   675.00

     1          1          3        $   625.50

     1          1          5        $   275.50

                       DISTRICT  1 SALES $1,576.00

     1          5          1        $   225.00

     1          5          2        $   300.50

     1          5          5        $   345.00

     1          5         11        $   175.00

                       DISTRICT  5 SALES $1,045.50

                                REGION   1 SALES $  2,621.50

     2          1          3        $   425.50

     2          1          7        $   400.00

                       DISTRICT  1 SALES $   825.50

     2          2          3        $   125.50

     2          2          7        $   410.25

                       DISTRICT  2 SALES $   535.75

                                REGION   2 SALES $  1,361.25

                                   TOTAL SALES $   3,982.75
```

Fig. 6–12. Output from control break program.

A program to produce the desired report is shown in Fig. 6–13. Note that in BREAK-TEST-RTN a test for a major control break is performed first. This is done simply because when a major control break occurs, an intermediate and a minor break must also occur. That is, when a change in district number occurs, a change in region number and salesperson number must also occur. Thus, the major or region break routine will initiate the district break routine, which in turn will initiate the salesperson break routine—a "domino effect." If a major or region break *has not occurred*, an intermediate or district break is tested for. The process is then repeated until a break is detected or until it has been determined that no break has occurred. If no break has occurred, control passes to routine NO-BREAK, where the individual sales for the transaction in question are simply added to the total sales for the salesperson being processed.

The method that is used to determine whether or not a break has occurred is the same regardless of the level of the break being tested. This method consists of a few simple steps:

1. The value of the control field contained on the first record is stored in a holding area (SLSPR-STORE, DIST-STORE, or REG-STORE in our program).

2. The value of the control field in each subsequent record is compared with the stored value.

3. If the current value of the control field differs from the stored value, a control break is performed. Otherwise, processing continues and no control break is performed for this level.

One final point: note in Fig. 6–13 that the MAIN-LINE routine contains the statement PERFORM REGION-BREAK. This is simply because after the last record has been read and an AT END condition occurs, the break test routine will not be performed. Thus, to cause the total sales for the last salesperson in the last district in the last region to be printed out, we must directly invoke the statement PERFORM REGION-BREAK.

The control break program is available on the supplemental disk as CH602.COB, with its test data as CH602.DAT.

```
IDENTIFICATION DIVISION.
PROGRAM-ID.
    CONTROL-BREAK.
AUTHOR.
    S.J.GAUGHRAN.
INSTALLATION.
    PERSONAL COMPUTER SYSTEM.
DATE-WRITTEN.
    FEB. 21,1985.
DATE-COMPILED.
    FEB. 25,1985.
SECURITY.
    NONE.
ENVIRONMENT DIVISION.
CONFIGURATION SECTION.
SOURCE-COMPUTER.
    IBM-PERSONAL-COMPUTER.
OBJECT-COMPUTER.
    IBM-PERSONAL-COMPUTER.
SPECIAL-NAMES.
    PRINTER IS LINE-OUT.
INPUT-OUTPUT SECTION.
FILE-CONTROL.
    SELECT IN-FILE  ASSIGN TO DISK
        ORGANIZATION IS LINE SEQUENTIAL.
    SELECT OUT-FILE ASSIGN TO PRINTER.
DATA DIVISION.
FILE SECTION.
FD  IN-FILE
    LABEL RECORDS ARE STANDARD
    VALUE OF FILE-ID IS 'CH602.DAT'
    RECORD CONTAINS 11 CHARACTERS.
01  IN-REC              PIC X(11).
FD  OUT-FILE
    LABEL RECORDS ARE OMITTED
    RECORD CONTAINS 133 CHARACTERS.
01  OUT-REC             PIC X(133).
WORKING-STORAGE SECTION.
01  IN-REC-WS.
    05  REG-NO-IN       PIC 99.
    05  DIST-NO-IN      PIC 99.
    05  SLSPR-NO-IN     PIC 99.
    05  SALES-IN        PIC 999V99.
01  TITLE-ONE.
    05  FILLER          PIC X(6)  VALUE ' DATE '.
    05  DATE-OUT.
        10  MONTH-OUT   PIC Z9.
        10  FILLER      PIC X      VALUE '/'.
        10  DAY-OUT     PIC Z9.
        10  FILLER      PIC X      VALUE '/'.
        10  YEAR-OUT    PIC 99.
    05  FILLER          PIC X(45) VALUE SPACES.
    05  FILLER          PIC X(5)  VALUE 'PAGE '.
    05  PAGE-OUT        PIC Z9.
01  TITLE-TWO.
    05  FILLER          PIC X(20) VALUE SPACES.
    05  FILLER          PIC X(20) VALUE 'COMPANY SALES REPORT'.
01  TITLE-THREE.
    05  FILLER          PIC X      VALUE SPACES.
    05  FILLER          PIC X(6)  VALUE 'REGION'.
    05  FILLER          PIC X(3)  VALUE SPACES.
    05  FILLER          PIC X(8)  VALUE 'DISTRICT'.
    05  FILLER          PIC X(2)  VALUE SPACES.
    05  FILLER          PIC X(8)  VALUE 'SALESPER'.
    05  FILLER          PIC X(7)  VALUE SPACES.
    05  FILLER          PIC X(5)  VALUE 'SALES'.
01  TOTAL-LINE-1.
    05  FILLER          PIC X(3)  VALUE SPACES.
    05  REG-NO-OUT      PIC Z9.
    05  FILLER          PIC X(8)  VALUE SPACES.
    05  DIST-NO-OUT     PIC Z9.
    05  FILLER          PIC X(8)  VALUE SPACES.
```

Fig. 6-13. Control break program.

```
        05  SLSPR-NO-OUT      PIC Z9.
        05  FILLER            PIC X(8)  VALUE SPACES.
        05  SALES-OUT         PIC $Z,ZZ9.99.
    01  TOTAL-LINE-2.
        05  FILLER            PIC X(25) VALUE SPACES.
        05  FILLER            PIC X(9)  VALUE 'DISTRICT '.
        05  DIST-NO-O         PIC Z9.
        05  FILLER            PIC X(7)  VALUE ' SALES '.
        05  DIST-TOT-O        PIC $Z,ZZ9.99.
    01  TOTAL-LINE-3.
        05  FILLER            PIC X(38) VALUE SPACES.
        05  FILLER            PIC X(7)  VALUE 'REGION '.
        05  REG-NO-O          PIC Z9.
        05  FILLER            PIC X(7)  VALUE ' SALES '.
        05  REG-TOT-O         PIC $ZZZ,ZZ9.99.
    01  TOTAL-LINE-4.
        05  FILLER            PIC X(40) VALUE SPACES.
        05  FILLER            PIC X(12) VALUE 'TOTAL SALES '.
        05  FINAL-TOT-O       PIC $Z,ZZZ,ZZ9.99.
    01  INDICATORS-WORKAREAS.
        05  EOF               PIC 9      VALUE ZERO.
        05  DATE-IN.
            10  YEAR-IN       PIC 99.
            10  MONTH-IN      PIC 99.
            10  DAY-IN        PIC 99.
        05  SLSPR-STORE       PIC 99.
        05  DIST-STORE        PIC 99.
        05  REG-STORE         PIC 99.
        05  LINE-NO-CTR       PIC 99     VALUE ZERO.
        05  PAGE-NO-CTR       PIC 99     VALUE ZERO.
        05  SLSPR-TOT         PIC 9(4)V99  VALUE ZERO.
        05  DIST-TOT          PIC 9(5)V99  VALUE ZERO.
        05  REG-TOT           PIC 9(6)V99  VALUE ZERO.
        05  FINAL-TOT         PIC 9(7)V99  VALUE ZERO.
*
    PROCEDURE DIVISION.
    MAIN-LINE.
        PERFORM OPEN-RTN.
        PERFORM HEADING-RTN.
        PERFORM READ-HOLD-RTN.
        PERFORM BREAK-TEST-RTN UNTIL EOF = 1.
        PERFORM REGION-BREAK.
        PERFORM FINAL-TOT-RTN.
        PERFORM CLOSE-RTN.
        STOP RUN.
    OPEN-RTN.
        OPEN INPUT  IN-FILE
             OUTPUT OUT-FILE.
    HEADING-RTN.
        ADD 1 TO PAGE-NO-CTR.
*****************************************************************
* The date is brought in through the ACCEPT ... FROM DATE *
* feature of IBM PC COBOL in the form of a six digit      *
* numeric value - YYMMDD, e.g. Feb. 29, 1984 is 840229.   *
* The field must be manipulated to be printed in the      *
* conventional form of MM/DD/YY.                          *
*****************************************************************
        ACCEPT DATE-IN FROM DATE.
        MOVE MONTH-IN        TO MONTH-OUT.
        MOVE DAY-IN          TO DAY-OUT.
        MOVE YEAR-IN         TO YEAR-OUT.
        MOVE PAGE-NO-CTR     TO PAGE-OUT.
        WRITE OUT-REC FROM TITLE-ONE AFTER ADVANCING PAGE.
        WRITE OUT-REC FROM TITLE-TWO AFTER ADVANCING 1 LINE.
        WRITE OUT-REC FROM TITLE-THREE AFTER ADVANCING 2 LINES.
        MOVE ZERO            TO LINE-NO-CTR.
    READ-HOLD-RTN.
        READ IN-FILE INTO IN-REC-WS AT END MOVE 1 TO EOF.
        IF EOF = ZERO
            MOVE REG-NO-IN     TO REG-STORE
            MOVE DIST-NO-IN    TO DIST-STORE
            MOVE SLSPR-NO-IN   TO SLSPR-STORE.
    BREAK-TEST-RTN.
```

Fig. 6–13. (*continued*)

```
***************************************************************
*  Note: A test for a major control break is done first.     *
***************************************************************
      IF REG-NO-IN  NOT = REG-STORE
          PERFORM REGION-BREAK.
***************************************************************
*  Note: A test for an intermediate break is done next.      *
***************************************************************
      IF DIST-NO-IN  NOT = DIST-STORE
          PERFORM DIST-BREAK.
***************************************************************
*  Note: A test for a minor break is done last.              *
***************************************************************
      IF SLSPR-NO-IN  NOT = SLSPR-STORE
          PERFORM SLSPR-BREAK.
      PERFORM NO-BREAK.
      READ IN-FILE INTO IN-REC-WS AT END MOVE 1 TO EOF.
  REGION-BREAK.
      PERFORM DIST-BREAK.
      MOVE REG-STORE      TO REG-NO-O.
      MOVE REG-TOT        TO REG-TOT-O.
      WRITE OUT-REC FROM TOTAL-LINE-3
              AFTER ADVANCING 2 LINES.
      IF LINE-NO-CTR > 24
              PERFORM HEADING-RTN.
      ADD 1               TO LINE-NO-CTR.
      MOVE REG-NO-IN      TO REG-STORE.
      MOVE ZEROS          TO REG-TOT.
  DIST-BREAK.
      PERFORM SLSPR-BREAK.
      MOVE DIST-STORE     TO DIST-NO-O.
      MOVE DIST-TOT       TO DIST-TOT-O.
      WRITE OUT-REC FROM TOTAL-LINE-2
              AFTER ADVANCING 2 LINES.
      IF LINE-NO-CTR > 24
              PERFORM HEADING-RTN.
      ADD 1               TO LINE-NO-CTR.
      MOVE DIST-NO-IN     TO DIST-STORE.
      MOVE ZEROS          TO DIST-TOT.
  SLSPR-BREAK.
      MOVE REG-STORE      TO REG-NO-OUT.
      MOVE DIST-STORE     TO DIST-NO-OUT.
      MOVE SLSPR-STORE    TO SLSPR-NO-OUT.
      MOVE SLSPR-TOT      TO SALES-OUT.
      WRITE OUT-REC FROM TOTAL-LINE-1
              AFTER ADVANCING 2 LINES.
      IF LINE-NO-CTR  > 24
              PERFORM HEADING-RTN.
      ADD 1               TO LINE-NO-CTR.
      MOVE SLSPR-NO-IN    TO SLSPR-STORE.
      MOVE ZEROS          TO SLSPR-TOT.
***************************************************************
* LINE-NO-CTR is used to count lines so that a page break*
* can be initiated at the proper time. This program      *
* assumes 24 lines - double spaced to a page.            *
***************************************************************
      IF LINE-NO-CTR  > 24
              PERFORM HEADING-RTN.
  NO-BREAK.
      ADD SALES-IN        TO SLSPR-TOT.
      ADD SALES-IN        TO REG-TOT.
      ADD SALES-IN        TO DIST-TOT.
      ADD SALES-IN        TO FINAL-TOT.
  FINAL-TOT-RTN.
      MOVE FINAL-TOT      TO FINAL-TOT-O.
      WRITE OUT-REC FROM TOTAL-LINE-4
              AFTER ADVANCING 2 LINES.
  CLOSE-RTN.
      CLOSE IN-FILE
              OUT-FILE.
```

Fig. 6-13. (*continued*)

EXERCISES

1. A routine that appears in every payroll program is the FICA deduction routine. Assume that the deduction is 6.7% on the first $37,500 of income or a maximum of $2,512.50 for the year. Write a program that will calculate the amount of contribution for a specific payroll period, given the year-to-date FICA contribution and the current gross salary as described in the input layout below. Prepare a report showing what the salary will be after this one deduction. Include totals as indicated on the output layout shown on page 206.

2. Write a program that will select the highest and lowest value from a list of numbers. The numbers in the list will not be in any specific sequence. Enter the numbers using either an ACCEPT or a READ statement, and describe the one line of output on the screen or the printer. (See page 207.)

3. A program is needed to prepare a listing of student grades in the format described in the output layout on page 208. The input records are in sequence by course number *within* student number. There may be *one or several records* for each student. The control break is to be taken on student number. Credits are given for all the courses listed, except those in which a passing grade was not achieved. Totals are required for the number of students, credits attempted, and credits earned.

4. The National Computer Stores chain needs a program to summarize their sales for all stores. There is one input record for each type of product sold in each store. The records are *in sequence* by product number, within store, within state. The output is to appear as shown in the output layout on page 209, with a total printed for each store and each state, and a grand total.

Solutions to the exercises, together with any necessary data files, are provided on the supplemental disk.

Input Layout

Input Record: PAYROLL-DATA

EMP. NO.	NAME	YEAR TO DATE FICA	BI-WEEKLY SALARY

```
          1111 111111222222222233333333
1234567 8901234567890123456789012345678
```

Output Layout

PAYROLL REPORT

EMP NO   NAME   YTD FICA   SALARY   FICA   NET SALARY

XXXXXXX   X   X,XXX.XX   X,XXX.XX   X,XXX.XX   X,XXX.XX

TOTALS   XX,XXX.XX XX,XXX.XX XX,XXX.XX XX,XXX.XX

Output Layout

A print spacing chart with the following printed on line 3:

```
LOWEST VALUE IS XXXXX    HIGHEST VALUE IS XXXXXX
```

Input Layout

Input Record: STUDENT-REC

STUDENT NUMBER	STUDENT NAME	COURSE NUMBER		COURSE TITLE	CREDIT	GRADE
		DEPT	NUMB			
1234567	89011111111112222222222	2222	333	33333333444444444455555	5555	555
	0123456	7890	123	45678901234567890123456		

Output Layout

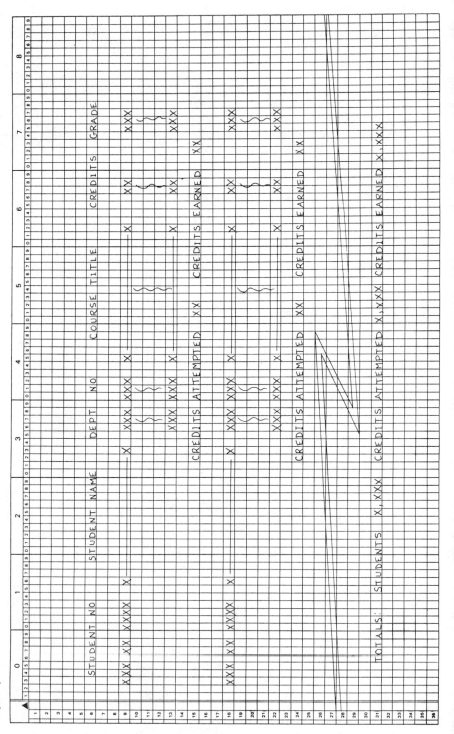

Input Layout

Input Record: SALES-REC

STORE NUMBER	STATE	PRODUCT NUMBER	PRODUCT DESCRIPTION	QUANT SOLD	AMOUNT SOLD ($)

(column positions)
1 2 3 4 5 6 7 | 8 9 0 1 2 3 4 5 | 6 7 8 9 0 1 2 3 4 5 | 6 7 8 9 0 1 2 3 | 0 1 2 3

Output Layout

NATIONAL COMPUTER STORE

STATE   STORE   PROD NO   PRODUCT DESCRIPTION   QUANTITY   AMOUNT

XXXX   X—X   X—X   XX,XXX   XXX,XXX.XX

XXXX   X—X   X—X   XX,XXX   XXX,XXX.XX

STORE TOTAL $X,XXX,XXX.XX*

XXXX   X—X   X—X   XX,XXX   XXX,XXX.XX

STORE TOTAL $X,XXX,XXX.XX*

STATE TOTAL $XX,XXX,XXX.XX**

GRAND TOTAL $XXX,XXX,XXX.XX***

7

ADVANCED TOPICS

Chapter 7 introduces some of the more advanced concepts of COBOL as contrasted with material covered in previous chapters. Many of the statements and clauses presented are relatively sophisticated; however, using them judiciously can simplify the programming of problems and result in shorter compile times and more efficient programs.

THE USAGE CLAUSE

The USAGE clause is an optional clause that allows the programmer to specify the form in which a data item is to be stored. Most modern computers are capable of storing data in more than one form. Specification of the appropriate form of storage for each data item used in the program can affect the efficiency of the resulting object program. The USAGE clause specifies only the principal purpose of the data and thus in no way restricts how the data may be used. This clause may be used with both elementary and group data items. However, if used with a group data item, it applies to each elementary item within the group. The general format of the USAGE clause is as follows:

GENERAL FORMAT 1

USAGE IS
$$\left\{ \begin{array}{l} \text{DISPLAY} \\ \left\{ \begin{array}{l} \text{COMPUTATIONAL} \\ \text{COMP} \end{array} \right\} \\ \left\{ \begin{array}{l} \text{COMPUTATIONAL-0} \\ \text{COMP-0} \end{array} \right\} \\ \left\{ \begin{array}{l} \text{COMPUTATIONAL-3} \\ \text{COMP-3} \end{array} \right\} \\ \text{INDEX} \end{array} \right\}$$

The **DISPLAY** option specifies that the data item is stored in character form, with each character occupying one byte of storage (eight bits, four for the zone and four for the digit portions). This option is required for data items that are input from keyboards, data that are to be displayed on the CRT, and data items that are to be printed, where the data items in each case are described as either alphabetic, alphanumeric, numeric, or numeric edited. It is also required for data that are contained in disk files that are described as LINE SEQUENTIAL; other types of disk files may have the types of usage described below. Omission of the USAGE clause has the same effect as specifying the clause with the DISPLAY option.

The *COMPUTATIONAL* (or *COMP*) option is *identical to the DISPLAY option in IBM PC COBOL*. It is included in this version of COBOL to be compatible with other versions, but it is treated as a comment entry. It should be noted here that the USAGE clause is concerned with the internal bit configuration of data and is therefore quite machine dependent. (Some readers may know that the COMPUTATIONAL clause on mainframe IBM computers refers to numeric values stored in binary format.)

The **COMPUTATIONAL-3** (or **COMP-3**) option may be specified only for numeric data items. Specifying an item as COMP-3 means that the item is stored as an internal decimal item in packed decimal format. That is, two decimal digits are stored in one byte (eight bits), with the sign contained in the low-order or rightmost four bits of the low-order or rightmost byte. Thus, the decimal number -38471 would require five bytes of storage in DISPLAY format but only three bytes of storage in COMP-3 format. Since a data item is stored in a whole or integer number of bytes, and since in COMP-3 one half byte (four bits) is used for the algebraic sign of the number, room is always left for an odd number of decimal digits. Thus, the PICTURE of a data item described as COMP-3 should contain an odd number of 9s. For example, if a COMP-3 data item is described with the PICTURE S99V99, the computer allocates three bytes of storage. But the computer can store five decimal digits in three bytes with USAGE COMP-3. Therefore, it is better for the programmer to describe the data item as PICTURE S999V99.

As noted above, USAGE may be specified at any level in the data description, but if it is specified at the group level, it applies to all elementary items in the group. Accordingly, the entries

```
01   ACCUMULATORS.
     05   OPENING-BALANCE     PIC  S9(5)V99     COMP-3.
     05   BALANCE             PIC  S9(5)V99     COMP-3.
     05   CHECK-AMOUNT-WS     PIC  S9(5)V99     COMP-3.
     05   CHECK-N-WS          PIC  S9(5)       COMP-3.
```

and

```
01   ACCUMULATORS    COMP-3.
     05   OPENING-BALANCE     PIC  S9(5)V99.
     05   BALANCE             PIC  S9(5)V99.
     05   CHECK-AMOUNT-WS     PIC  S9(5)V99.
     05   CHECK-NO-WS         PIC  S9(5).
```

would cause the same results.

The **COMPUTATIONAL-0** (or **COMP-0**) option is similar to the COMP option for mainframe computers in that it describes data that are to be stored in binary format. However, where mainframe computers usually refer to COMP data as being contained in four bytes, the COMP-0 option refers to binary data contained in two bytes of storage. This option would be used to store numeric *integer* data in the range −32767 through 32767, the largest value that can be stored in 16 bits, i.e., two 8-bit bytes. The advantage of using this somewhat restricted format is the speed at which arithmetic can take place on binary integer values.

THE SYNCHRONIZED CLAUSE

When a data item is stated to be COMPUTATIONAL (or COMP) on, for example, an IBM mainframe computer, it must be stored beginning in certain numbered bytes before it can be operated upon. For example, a four-byte COMPUTATIONAL field must begin in a stored address that is a multiple of 4. Such a situation, or one similar to it, exists on most computer systems. On the IBM PC, however, *the SYNCHRONIZED clause is treated as a comment* since there is no boundary alignment problem in that system because all data items are automatically aligned on word boundaries.

The general format of the SYNCHRONIZED clause is:

GENERAL FORMAT 2

$$\left\{ \begin{array}{l} \text{SYNC} \\ \text{SYNCHRONIZED} \end{array} \right\} \quad \left[\begin{array}{l} \text{LEFT} \\ \text{RIGHT} \end{array} \right]$$

THE JUSTIFIED CLAUSE

When alphabetic or alphanumeric data are moved from one storage area to another, the leftmost character of the sending field is moved to the leftmost position in the receiving field. Each successive character to the right in the sending field is then moved to the corresponding position in the receiving field until there are no more characters in the sending field or until the receiving field has been completely filled. In the former case, the remainder of the receiving field is filled with blanks; in the latter, any remaining characters in the sending field are truncated or lost to the receiving field. If, conversely, the data must be aligned and moved from *right to left*, the JUSTIFIED clause is used, the general format of which is:

GENERAL FORMAT 3

JUSTIFIED RIGHT

If this clause is specified and the sending field is longer than the receiving field, the leftmost characters in the sending field are truncated. If the sending field is shorter than the receiving field, the leftmost positions in the receiving field are filled with spaces. The following rules apply to the use of the JUSTIFIED clause:

1. It may only be specified for elementary data items.

2. It may only be used for positioning data with an alphanumeric receiving field.

THE BLANK WHEN ZERO CLAUSE

When used with a given data item in a record description entry, the BLANK WHEN ZERO clause causes any numeric edited data item that contains all zeros to be filled with blanks. The general format of this statement is as follows:

GENERAL FORMAT 4

BLANK WHEN ZERO

The BLANK WHEN ZERO clause may only be used with elementary numeric or numeric edited data items. As an example, the statement

```
05   FIELD-A   PIC $Z,ZZZ.99   BLANK WHEN ZERO.
```

will cause blanks to be printed out when a value of zero is moved to FIELD-A. Similarly, the statement

```
05   FIELD-A   PIC $Z,ZZZ.99.
```

will cause $ßßßßßß.00 to be printed out when a value of zero is moved to FIELD-A. (ß denotes a blank space.)

ADDITIONAL PICTURE ENTRIES

The basic PICTURE character strings may include several additional, very useful edit characters and character strings. Some represent more advanced uses of previously discussed edit characters, while others are completely new edit characters. A complete list of these characters, including their types and specifications, is given in Table 7–1.

Table 7–1.   ADDITIONAL EDIT CHARACTERS

PICTURE Character	Data Type	Specification
$	Numeric edited	The associated position in the value will contain a dollar sign, a digit, or a blank. The leftmost $ in the floating string does not represent a digit position. If the string of $'s is specified only to the left of a decimal point, the rightmost $ in the PICTURE corresponding to a position that precedes the leading nonzero digit in the value will be printed. A string of $'s that extends to the right of a decimal point will have the same effect as a string that extends to the left of the point unless the value is zero, in which case blanks will appear. All positions corresponding to $ positions to the right of the printed $ will contain digits; all to the left will contain blanks.
*	Numeric edited	A leading zero in the associated position will be suppressed and replaced with an asterisk.
B	Numeric edited	The associated position in the value will contain a blank, $, or *. When a B is included in a string of $'s, *s, or Z's, a zero, $, or * may appear in its position.
0	Numeric edited	The associated position in the value will contain a blank, $, or *. When a B is included in a string of $'s, *s, or Zs, a zero, $, or * may appear in its position.
CR	Numeric edited	· A negative indicator will be inserted into the value when the value is negative; otherwise, two blanks will appear. These symbols must appear at the right end of the PICTURE.
—	Numeric edited	A minus sign is inserted into the value when the value is negative; one blank will appear. Otherwise, a — may be "floated" with the rules given for $.
+	Numeric edited	The appropriate sign (+ or −) will be inserted into the value. A + may be "floated" with the rules given for $.

The first editing character shown in the table is the **floating dollar sign**. That the dollar sign is *floating* means that only the rightmost $ in the PICTURE of a data item corresponding to a position that precedes the leading nonzero digit in the value of the data item will be printed.

Thus, if a data item with the PICTURE

S9(4)V99

and containing the value

001475

is moved to a data item with the PICTURE

$$,$$$.99

the edited result is

ƀƀƀ$14.75

where ƀ represents a blank space.

It could be said that the dollar sign floats rightward in the field until it encounters a nonzero digit or until it reaches the position occupied by the rightmost $ in the PICTURE specification. Each leading zero suppressed and any comma adjacent to a suppressed zero are replaced by a blank that is inserted at the left of the printed field.

The second editing character in Table 7–1, the **check protection asterisk**, functions in a manner similar to that of the floating dollar sign, except that an asterisk is placed in the edited data item corresponding to *each* nonsignificant or leading zero suppressed and, if necessary, to any commas adjacent to a suppressed zero. Thus, if a sending field with the PICTURE

S9(5)V99

and containing the value

0001475

is moved to a data item with the PICTURE

$**,***.99

the edited result is

$****14.75

Notice that all leading zeros and the unused comma are replaced with asterisks. In general, any commas within a string of zero-suppression characters are replaced if they are to the left of the first nonzero digit. This is also true for any *B's or 0's* within a string of suppression characters. (See third and fourth entries of Table 7–1.) But a B, 0, or fixed insertion symbol ($,−, or +) to the left of the string of suppression characters will not be replaced. That is, if a sending field with the PICTURE

S9(5)

and containing the value

00347

is moved to a data item with the PICTURE

$ZZ,ZZZ,000

the edited result is

$ɓɓɓ347,000

But if the sending field with the PICTURE

S9(5)

and containing the value

12345

is moved to a data item with the PICTURE

$00,ZZZ,ZZZ

the edited result is

$00,ɓ12,345

Examples of the use of the above editing characters are given in Table 7–2.

Table 7-2.   EXAMPLES OF THE USE OF FLOATING AND INSERTION EDIT CHARACTERS

Sending Field		Receiving Field	
PICTURE	Data	PICTURE	Edited Result
1. S9(4)V99	134725	$$$$$.99	$1347.25
2. S9(4)V99	134725̄	$$$$$.99	$1347.25̄
3. S9(4)V99	000725	$$$$$.99	ƀƀƀ$7.25
4. S9(4)V99	000005	$$$$$.99	ƀƀƀƀ$.05
5. S9(4)V99	134725	$*,***.99	$1,347.25
6. S9(4)V99	134725̄	$*,***.99	$1,347.25
7. S9(4)V99	004725	$*,***.99	$***47.25
8. S9(4)V99	000005	$*,***.99	$*****.05
9. S9(4)V99	134725	**,***.99	*1,347.25
10. S9(5)	58068	Z,ZZZ,Z00	5,806,800
11. S9(5)	58068̄	Z,ZZZ,Z00	5,806,800
12. S9(5)	58068̄	−Z,ZZZ,Z00	−5,806.800
13. S9(5)	08068	Z,ZZZ,Z00	ƀƀ806,800
14. S9(5)	00008	Z,ZZZ,Z00	ƀƀƀƀƀƀ800
15. S9(4)V99	147935	$B*,***.99	$ƀ1,479.35
16. S9(4)V99	007935	$B*,***.99	$ƀ***79.35
17. S9(4)	0035̄	ZZZZB-	ƀƀ35ƀ-
18. S9(4)	0000	ZZZZB-	blank
19. S9(4)V99	147935̄	$B*,***,***,**B-	$ƀ****1,479.35ƀ-

The last four edit characters of Table 7-1, commonly referred to as **sign characters**, are concerned with the placement of an algebraic sign (+ or −) or sign indicator (CR for *credit* or DB for *debit*) in an edited data item. These edit characters are useless in the receiving field unless the sending field has provisions for maintaining an algebraic sign (an S in its PICTURE clause). The rules concerning the placement and effect of using these symbols in PICTURE specifications are given in Table 7-3.

From the table, we can see that the characters CR and DB are printed only if the data item being edited is negative; otherwise, two blanks

Table 7-3.   SIGN SYMBOL PLACEMENT AND EFFECT

Edit Symbol	Placement in PICTURE Specification	Receiving Field	
		For a Positive or 0 Sending Field	For a Negative Sending Field
CR	Rightmost character in PICTURE Clause	ƀƀ (two blanks)	CR
DB	Rightmost character in PICTURE Clause	ƀƀ (two blanks)	DB
+	Rightmost or leftmost character in PICTURE Clause	+	−
−	Rightmost or leftmost character in PICTURE Clause	ƀ (one blank)	−

will be printed. In the case of the + and − symbols, however, the sign of the sending field is inserted in the result unless the − character is used and the sending field is positive or zero, in which case a blank is inserted in the edited data item. The + and − characters may also be used in floating format in much the same manner as the floating $ was employed. Examples of the use of the sign characters are given in Table 7-4.

THE INSPECT STATEMENT

The INSPECT statement serves three general purposes:

1. To replace certain occurrences of a given character or series of characters in a data item with another character or series of characters.

2. To count the number of occurrences of a given character or series of characters in a data item.

3. To count and replace certain occurrences of a given character or series of characters in a data item with another character or series of characters.

Table 7–4. EXAMPLES OF THE USE OF SIGN CHARACTERS

Sending Field		Receiving Field	
PICTURE	Data	PICTURE	Edited Result
1. S999V99	03847	999.99+	038.47+
2. S999V99	03847	+999.99	+038.47
3. S999V99	03847	999.99−	038.47ƀ
4. S999V99	0384$\overline{7}$	+999.99	−038.47
5. S999V99	0384$\overline{7}$	−999.99	−038.47
6. S999V99	13847	+99.99	+38.47
7. S999V99	0384$\overline{7}$	−$999.99	−$038.47
8. S9(5)	03847	ZZ,ZZZCR	ƀ3,847ƀƀ
9. S9(5)	0384$\overline{7}$	ZZ,ZZZCR	ƀ3,847CR
10. S9(5)	03847	ZZ,ZZZDC	ƀ3,847ƀƀ
11. S9(5)	0384$\overline{7}$	ZZ,ZZZDB	ƀ3,847DB
12. S9(4)V99	00384$\overline{7}$	Z,ZZZ.99CR	ƀƀƀ38.47CR
13. S9(4)V99	11384$\overline{7}$	$$,$$$.99CR	$1,138.47CR
14. S9(4)V99	113847	$$,$$$.99CR	$1,138.47ƀƀ
15. S9(4)	384$\overline{7}$	Z,ZZZ,000CR	3,847,000CR
16. S9(4)	384$\overline{7}$	Z,ZZZBCR	3,347ƀCR
17. S9(4)	3847	Z,ZZZBCR	3,847ƀƀƀ
18. S9(4)V99	113847	++,+++.99	+1,138.47
19. S9(4)V99	11384$\overline{7}$	++,+++.99	−1,138.47
20. S9(4)V99	003847	++,+++.99	ƀƀƀ+38.47
21. S9(4)V99	00384$\overline{7}$	++,+++.99	ƀƀƀ−38.47
22. S9(4)V99	000007	++,+++.99	ƀƀƀƀƀ+.07
23. S9(4)V99	00000$\overline{7}$	++,+++.99	ƀƀƀƀƀ−.07
24. S9(4)V99	113847	−−,−−−.99	ƀ,1,138.47
25. S9(4)V99	11384$\overline{7}$	−−,−−−.99	−1,138.47
26. S9(4)V99	003847	−−,−−−.99	ƀƀƀƀ38.47
27. S9(4)V99	003847	−−,−−−.99	ƀƀƀ−38.47
28. S9(4)V99	000007	−−,−−−.99	ƀƀƀƀƀƀ.07
29. S9(4)V99	00000$\overline{7}$	−−,−−−.99	ƀƀƀƀƀ−.07

The general format of the INSPECT statement is:

GENERAL FORMAT 5

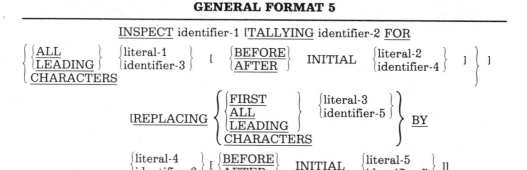

The REPLACING Option

The most common use of the INSPECT statement is given in the first purpose mentioned above: to replace certain specified characters with other specified characters. This is accomplished with the RE-PLACING option. For example, one usually wishes to replace blanks with zeros in numeric fields. In general, blanks should not be present in a numeric field. However, it sometimes happens that leading zeros in a numeric field are keyed in at a terminal as blanks, or that when a field contains a value of zero, it is filled with blanks. Before such data items are used in an arithmetic operation or moved to an edited output field, the program should INSPECT the data item, REPLACING any blanks with zeros.

In General Format 5, **identifier-1** may be defined as numeric or nonnumeric, but **identifier-2** must be defined as nonnumeric; **literal** refers to a *one-character* nonnumeric literal or any figurative constant except ALL; and **identifier-3** through **identifier-7** refer to data-names of items of data whose length is one.

The following points should be remembered:

1. When identifier-1 contains an S in its PICTURE clause to indicate the presence of an algebraic sign, the sign will not be considered by the INSPECT statement.

2. When identifier-1 is described as nonnumeric, inspection begins with the leftmost character in the field and proceeds rightward until all characters have been inspected.

3. When identifier-1 is described as numeric, it must consist of only numeric characters, but it may contain an algebraic sign. Inspection of a numeric identifier will begin with the leftmost characters in the field and proceed rightward until all characters have been inspected.

4. Identifier-1 must be specified implicitly or explicitly as USAGE IS DISPLAY.

The CHARACTERS BY Clause

The CHARACTERS BY clause causes no comparison to take place. Instead, the characters in identifier-1 are simply replaced by the characters specified in literal-4 or identifier-6. If the INITIAL option is not specified, all characters in identifier-1 are replaced. If it is specified, only the characters BEFORE or AFTER the INITIAL occurrence of literal-5 or identifier-7 will be replaced. For example, suppose that IDENT contained the characters ABCBA. Then the statements

```
INSPECT IDENT REPLACING CHARACTERS BY 'X'.
INSPECT IDENT REPLACING CHARACTERS BY 'X' BEFORE INITIAL 'C'.
INSPECT IDENT REPLACING CHARACTERS BY 'X' AFTER INITIAL 'C'.
```

would cause the contents of IDENT to be changed to XXXXX,XXCBA, and ABCXX, respectively. Similarly, if the location CHAR contained the character X, the statements

```
INSPECT IDENT REPLACING CHARACTERS BY CHAR.
INSPECT IDENT REPLACING CHARACTERS BY CHAR BEFORE INITIAL 'C'.
INSPECT IDENT REPLACING CHARACTERS BY CHAR AFTER INITIAL 'C'.
```

would cause the same results as the three previous statements. Table 7–5 presents several examples of the use of the CHARACTERS BY clause in the INSPECT statement.

The ALL, LEADING, and FIRST Clauses

The ALL, LEADING, and FIRST clauses of the INSPECT statement with the REPLACING option allow us to replace all occurrences, leading occurrences, and the first occurrence, respectively, of a specific character (literal-3 or identifier-5) by a specific character (literal-4 or

Table 7–5. EXAMPLES OF THE USE OF THE INSPECT STATEMENT

IDENT before Execution	INSPECT Statement	IDENT after Execution
38476	INSPECT IDENT REPLACING CHARACTERS BY '0'.	00000
38476̄	INSPECT IDENT REPLACING CHARACTERS BY '0'.	00000
00476	INSPECT IDENT REPLACING CHARACTERS BY 'ƀ' BEFORE '4'.	ƀƀ476
00476	INSPECT IDENT REPLACING CHARACTERS BY 'ƀ' AFTER '4'.	004ƀƀ
ƀƀ476	INSPECT IDENT REPLACING ALL 'ƀ' BY '0'.	00476
ƀƀ476	INSPECT IDENT REPLACING ALL 'ƀ' BY '0'.	00470
ƀƀ476	INSPECT IDENT REPLACING ALL 'ƀ' BY '0' AFTER INITIAL '4'.	ƀƀ470
ƀƀ476	INSPECT IDENT REPLACING ALL '0' BY 'ƀ' BEFORE 'ƀ'.	ƀƀ476
ƀƀ047	INSPECT IDENT REPLACING ALL 'ƀ' BY '0' BEFORE INITIAL '0'.	00047
XYX-X	INSPECT IDENT REPLACING ALL 'X' BY 'Z' BEFORE '—'.	ZYZ-X
ƀƀ476	INSPECT IDENT REPLACING FIRST 'ƀ' BY '0'.	0ƀ476
C0476	INSPECT IDENT REPLACING FIRST '0' BY 'ƀ'.	ƀ0476
***47	INSPECT IDENT REPLACING FIRST '*' BY '$'.	$**47
00476	INSPECT IDENT REPLACING FIRST '0' BY 'ƀ' AFTER '0'.	0ƀ476
ƀƀ676	INSPECT IDENT REPLACING LEADING 'ƀ' BY '*'.	***76
ƀƀ476	INSPECT IDENT REPLACING LEADING 'ƀ' BY '0'.	00476
A347A	INSPECT IDENT REPLACING LEADING 'A' BY 'X'.	X347A
+4753	INSPECT IDENT REPLACING LEADING '+' BY '0'.	04753
ABCX4Z	INSPECT IDENT REPLACING LEADING 'X' BY 'Z' AFTER 'C'.	ABCZ4Z

identifier-6). If the INITIAL option is not chosen, the following rules apply to the use of ALL, LEADING, and FIRST, respectively:

1. In the ALL option, all occurrences of the character described by literal-3 or identifier-5 are replaced by the character described by literal-4 or identifier-6.

2. In the LEADING OPTION, all occurrences of the character described by literal-3 or identifier-5 are replaced by the character described by literal-4 or identifier-6 until a character other than that specified by literal-3 or identifier-5 is encountered.

3. In the FIRST option, only the first occurrence of the character described by literal-3 or identifier-5 is replaced by the character described by literal-4 or identifier-6.

To illustrate the use of these clauses, suppose that the identifier IDENT contains the characters AABCABCABD. Then the statements

```
INSPECT IDENT REPLACING ALL 'A' BY '0'.
INSPECT IDENT REPLACING ALL 'B' BY '0'.
INSPECT IDENT REPLACING LEADING 'A' BY '0'.
INSPECT IDENT REPLACING FIRST 'A' BY '0'.
```

would cause the contents of IDENT to be changed to 00BC0BC0BD, AA0CA0CA0D, 00BCABCABD, and 0ABCABCABD, respectively. Additional examples of the use of the INSPECT statement with the ALL, LEADING, and FIRST clauses are shown in Table 7–5.

The TALLYING Option

In the TALLYING option of the INSPECT statement, **identifier-2** is a counter that tallies the number of occurrences of a character in a specified data item. Identifier-2 must be a numeric field defined in the WORKING-STORAGE SECTION implicitly or explicitly with USAGE IS DISPLAY, and the programmer must make certain to initialize the field to zero before it is used. In all cases the word FOR is required.

If the CHARACTERS option is chosen and the INITIAL option is not, the counter will be incremented by 1 for each character in identifier-1. Thus, at the end of the operation, identifier-2 will contain a count of the number of characters in identifier-1. If both the CHAR-

ACTERS and INITIAL options are chosen, identifier-2 will maintain a count of the number of characters contained in identifier-1 BEFORE or AFTER the first occurrence of literal-2 or identifier-4. The ALL and LEADING options function in the same manner as they did in the RE-PLACING clause, except that the occurrence of literal-1 or identifier-3 is not replaced with anything, but is simply tallied in identifier-2. Table 7–6 gives some examples of the use of the INSPECT statement with the TALLYING option.

The TALLYING-and-REPLACING Option

In addition to their separate usage, the TALLYING and REPLAC-ING options may be used together as a unit in the same INSPECT statement. In such case the TALLYING clause executes as if there were two separate and distinct INSPECT statements. Some examples of the INSPECT statement with the TALLYING-and-REPLACING option are shown in Table 7–7.

THE STRING STATEMENT

The STRING statement facilitates the joining together of two or more fields to form one field, a process generally referred to as **concatenation**. The general format of the STRING statement is as follows:

GENERAL FORMAT 6

$$\text{STRING} \begin{Bmatrix} \text{literal-1} \\ \text{identifier-1} \end{Bmatrix} \begin{bmatrix} \text{literal-2} \\ \text{identifier-2} \end{bmatrix} \cdots$$

$$\text{DELIMITED BY} \begin{Bmatrix} \text{literal-3} \\ \text{identifier-3} \\ \text{SIZE} \end{Bmatrix} \cdots$$

INTO identifier-4 [WITH POINTER identifier-5]
[ON OVERFLOW imperative-statement]

All literals must be either nonnumeric or any figurative constant except ALL. All identifiers except identifier-5 must be implicitly or explicitly described as USAGE IS DISPLAY.

Table 7–6. EXAMPLES OF THE INSPECT STATEMENT WITH THE TALLYING OPTION

IDENT before Execution	INSPECT Statement	CTR1*
349699	INSPECT IDENT TALLYING CTR1 FOR CHARACTERS.	0006
349699	INSPECT IDENT TALLYING CTR1 FOR CHARACTERS.	0006
143.75	INSPECT IDENT TALLYING CTR1 FOR CHARACTERS BEFORE '.'.	0003
000452	INSPECT IDENT TALLYING CTR1 FOR CHARACTERS AFTER '0'.	0005
349699	INSPECT IDENT TALLYING CTR1 FOR ALL '9'.	0003
A3B47A	INSPECT IDENT TALLYING CTR1 FOR ALL 'A'.	0002
000075	INSPECT IDENT TALLYING CTR1 FOR ALL '0'.	0004
A3B47A	INSPECT IDENT TALLYING CTR1 FOR ALL 'A'.	0002
000075	INSPECT IDENT TALLYING CTR1 FOR LEADING '0'.	0004
bbb375	INSPECT IDENT TALLYING CTR1 FOR LEADING ' '.	0003
$*1.50	INSPECT IDENT TALLYING CTR1 FOR '*' AFTER '$'.	0001
BABBCB	INSPECT IDENT TALLYING CTR1 FOR LEADING 'A' AFTER 'B'.	0004

*It is assumed that CTR1 is described as PIC 9999 VALUE ZERO.

Table 7–7. **EXAMPLES OF THE INSPECT STATEMENT WITH THE TALLYING-AND-REPLACING OPTION***

IDENT before Execution	INSPECT Statement	IDENT after Execution	CTR1	CTR2
ƀƀƀ699	INSPECT IDENT TALLYING CTR1 FOR LEADING " " REPLACING LEADING " " BY '*'.	***699	0003	N/A
04-15-84	INSPECT IDENT TALLYING CTR1 FOR ALL '-' REPLACING ALL '-' BY '/'.	04/15/84	0002	N/A
T'TFTFFTF	INSPECT IDENT TALLYING CTR1 FOR ALL 'T' REPLACING ALL 'T' BY '1'.	11F1FF1F	0004	0000
	INSPECT IDENT TALLYING CTR2 FOR ALL 'F' REPLACING ALL 'F' BY '0'	11010010	0004	0004
ƀƀƀƀ86.45	INSPECT IDENT TALLYING CTR1 FOR LEADING " " AFTER INITIAL " " REPLACING ALL " " BY '*' AFTER " "	ƀ***86.45	0003	N/A
	INSPECT IDENT TALLYING CTR1 FOR LEADING " " REPLACING FIRST " " BY '$'.	$***86.45	0004	N/A

*It is assumed that CTR1 and CTR2 are described as PIC 9999 VALUE ZERO; N/A = not applicable.

The identifiers or literals listed in front of the word DELIMITED represent the sending fields that are being concatenated. Identifier-4 represents the field into which the result of the concatenation is sent and stored. If the SIZE option is selected, all characters in the sending fields are concatenated in the receiving field. If the literal-3 or identifier-3 option is chosen, all characters in the sending field are sent until the character or characters specified in literal-3 or identifier-3 are encountered. Thus, literal-3 or identifier-3 marks the boundary of, or *delimits*, the characters sent. If the POINTER option is used, identifier-5 must be an elementary numeric integer data item containing an integer greater than or equal to 1. Then, when the characters are moved from the sending fields to the receiving field, they will be moved beginning with the character position specified by the current value of identifier-5. As characters are thus moved, the value of identifier-5 will automatically be incremented to reflect the relative position to which the next character will be moved.

To illustrate the concatenation process, as invoked by the STRING statement, suppose that the five fields A, B, C, D, and E are defined as follows:

```
A PIC X(5)  VALUE 'ABC**'.
B PIC X(5)  VALUE 'DEF*A'.
C PIC X(5)  VALUE 'GHIJ*'.
D PIC X(15) VALUE  '123456778012345'.
E PIC 99 VALUE 5.
```

Then the statement

```
STRING A B C DELIMITED BY SIZE INTO D.
```

will place the value 'ABC**DEF*AGHIJ*' in D. However, the statement

```
STRING A B C DELIMITED BY '*' INTO D.
```

will place the value 'ABCDEFGHIJ12345' in D.

If we employ the POINTER option, the statement

```
STRING A B C DELIMITED BY '*' INTO D WITH POINTER E.
```

will place the value '1234ABCDEFGHIJ5' in D. In addition, the value of

E will now be 15, its initial value 5 plus 10 for the number of characters sent.

The following points are worth remembering:

1. At the completion of execution of the STRING statement, only the portion of identifier-4 replaced by characters sent will be changed. All other portions of identifier-4 will be as they were before execution of the STRING statement commenced.

2. If, at some point in the execution of the STRING statement, the value of identifier-5 becomes less than 1 or greater than the number of character positions in identifier-4, no further characters will be transferred to identifier-4, and the imperative statement in the ON OVERFLOW clause will be executed if specified.

3. If no ON OVERFLOW clause is specified and one of the conditions mentioned in (2) occurs, control will be transferred to the next executable statement.

Other examples of the use of the STRING statement are shown in Table 7–8.

THE UNSTRING STATEMENT

The UNSTRING statement performs the reverse function of the STRING statement. That is, it causes the contiguous data in a sending field to be separated and placed into two or more receiving fields. The general format of the UNSTRING statement is as follows:

GENERAL FORMAT 7

UNSTRING identifier-1 [DELIMITED BY [ALL] $\begin{Bmatrix} \text{literal-1} \\ \text{identifier-2} \end{Bmatrix}$

[OR [ALL] $\begin{Bmatrix} \text{literal-2} \\ \text{identifier-3} \end{Bmatrix}$] ...]

INTO [identifier-4 [DELIMITER IN identifier-5]
      [COUNT IN identifier-6]] ...
      [WITH POINTER identifier-7]
      [TALLYING IN identifier-8]
      [ON OVERFLOW imperative-statement]

Table 7–8. EXAMPLES OF THE USE OF THE STRING STATEMENT

STRING STATEMENT	ITM-A PIC X(5)	ITM-B PIC X(5)	ITM-C PIC X(5)	REC-FIELD[a] PIC X(15)	PT-FIELD[b] Before	After
STRING ITM-A ITM-B ITM-C DELIMITED BY SIZE INTO REC-FIELD.	JAN.*	ƀƀ4,*	ƀ1984	JAN.*ƀƀ4,*ƀ1984	N/A	N/A
STRING ITM-A ITM-B ITM-C DELIMITED BY '*' INTO REC-FIELD.	JAN.*	ƀƀ4,*	ƀ1984	JAN.ƀƀ4,ƀ1984ƀƀ	N/A	N/A
STRING ITM-A ITM-B ITM-C DELIMITED BY '*' INTO REC-FIELD WITH POINTER PT-FIELD.	JAN.*	ƀƀ4,*	ƀ1984	JAN.ƀƀ4,ƀ1984ƀƀ	0001	0014
STRING ITM-A ITM-B ITM-C DELIMITED BY '*' INTO REC-FIELD WITH POINTER PT-FIELD.	JOEƀ*	S.ƀ**	LEE**	JOEƀS.ƀLEEƀƀƀƀ	0001	0011

[a] It is assumed that the field REC-FIELD contained blanks before execution of the STRING statement.
[b] N/A = not applicable.

In the UNSTRING statement, the delimiter in the sending field indicates where the sending field is to be separated. For example, if the fields A, B, C, and D are respectively defined as

```
A PIC X(5) VALUE 'ABCDE'.
B PIC X(5) VALUE 'FGHIJ'.
C PIC X(5) VALUE 'KLMNO'.
D PIC C(15) VALUE '1234*5678*9012'.
```

then the statement

```
UNSTRING D DELIMITED BY '*' INTO A B C.
```

places the values '1234ⱕ', '5678ⱕ', and '9012ⱕ', in A, B, and C, respectively. Notice that the last position in the receiving fields was replaced with a blank space. This is because any positions not filled with transmitted characters will be filled with blanks, as in an alphanumeric MOVE. Notice also that the delimiter itself was not moved to any receiving field. If D contained the value '1234**567**890*' and the ALL option were used—that is, if the UNSTRING statement were

```
UNSTRING D DELIMITED BY ALL '*' INTO A B C.
```

then the resulting values of A, B, and C would have been '1234ⱕ', '567ⱕⱕ', and '890ⱕⱕ', respectively.

If the DELIMITED BY clause is not specified, characters will be transferred until the receiving fields are filled, one by one, until there are no more characters to be transferred. If the DELIMITED BY clause is specified, characters will be transferred until the delimiter is reached or until a receiving field is filled. If a receiving field becomes filled before a delimiter is reached, an overflow condition occurs and the imperative statement following ON OVERFLOW will be executed if this option is stated. If ON OVERFLOW is not stated, the next statement will be executed.

The DELIMITER IN and COUNT IN clauses may be specified only if the DELIMITED BY clause is specified. The DELIMITER IN clause is used to store the delimiter, if desired. If in addition, it is desired to keep track of how many characters were sent to a particular receiving field, the COUNT IN clause is specified. Thus, together, these options allow the programmer to keep track of the actual delimiters used (several can be specified with the OR option) and the number of characters transferred.

In addition to the above-mentioned options, one can choose the POINTER and TALLYING options. The POINTER option adds 1 to the initial value of identifier-7 for each character examined in identifier-1, including delimiters. The TALLYING option adds 1 to the initial value of identifier-8 for each receiving field to which characters are actually transferred.

Further examples of the use of the UNSTRING statement are shown in Table 7–9.

THE COPY STATEMENT

A programmer often uses a common sequence of instructions over and over again. For example, many programs in a payroll system require both access to the master file and a file description entry together with one or more record description entries for the file. To eliminate the necessity for this duplication of coding, the overlapping entries can be placed in another file that is accessible to the programmer. The source program may then call in the desired routine from the other file at the appropriate time.

Another advantage of including commonly used entries and routines in other files is that if, for some reason, an entry or routine is modified or updated, all programs that access it will be using the same updated version.

In order to access a file, routine, or procedure contained in another file at compile time, a COPY statement is used. The COPY statement permits the user to include prewritten ENVIRONMENT, DATA, and PROCEDURE DIVISION entries in the program at the time the program is compiled. Its general format is as follows:

GENERAL FORMAT 8

COPY text-name

Text-name refers to the name by which the file, record, procedure, etc., is identified. It must conform to the rules for the formation of a filename and must be on a disk accessible during compilation. In a floppy disk system the latter would normally be the same disk as your

Table 7–9. EXAMPLES OF THE USE OF THE UNSTRING STATEMENT*

UNSTRING Statement	SEND-FIELD PIC X(15)	ITM-A PIC X(5)	ITM-B PIC X(5)	ITM-C PIC X(5)	COUNT FLDS			PT-FLD		TAL-FLD
					CT1	CT2	CT3	Before	After	
UNSTRING SEND-FIELD INTO ITM-A ITM-B ITM-C.	JAN.*ɓɓ4,*1984*	JAN.*	ɓɓ4,*	1984*	N/A	N/A	N/A	N/A	N/A	N/A
UNSTRING SEND-FIELD DELIMITED BY '*' INTO ITM-A ITM-B ITM-C.	JAN.*ɓɓ4,*1984*	JAN.ɓ	ɓɓ4,ɓ	1984ɓ	N/A	N/A	N/A	N/A	N/A	N/A
UNSTRING SEND-FIELD DELIMITED BY '*' INTO ITM-A COUNT IN CT1 ITM-B COUNT IN CT2 ITM-C COUNT IN CT3 WITH POINTER PT-FIELD TALLYING IN TAL-FLD.	JAN.*ɓɓ4,*1984*	JAN.ɓ	ɓɓ4,ɓ	1984ɓ	4	4	4	0001	0016	3
UNSTRING SEND-FIELD DELIMITED BY '*' or '/' INTO ITM-A ITM-B ITM-C.	JAN.*ɓɓ4,/1984/	JAN.ɓ	ɓɓ4,ɓ	1984ɓ	N/A	N/A	N/A	N/A	N/A	N/A
UNSTRING SEND-FIELD DELIMITED BY ALL '*' INTO ITM-A ITM-B ITM-C.	JAN.**ɓɓ4,*1984*	JAN.ɓ	ɓ4,ɓɓ	1984ɓ	N/A	N/A	N/A	N/A	N/A	N/A

*N/A = not applicable.

source program. Suppose, accordingly, that the following record description was stored on the B disk drive under the text-name (filename) REORDREC.DAT:

```
01  REORDER.
    05  ITEM-DESC   PIC X(20).
    05  INV-NO      PIC 9(7).
    05  ON-HAND     PIC 9(3).
    05  REORD-PT    PIC 9(4).
    05  ORD-QUANT   PIC 9(4).
    05  UNIT-PRC    PIC 999V99.
    05  VENDOR-NO   PIC 9(6).
    05  FILLER      PIC X(31).
```

Then the programmer would no longer be required to repeat these entries in the DATA DIVISION of subsequent programs. Instead, the COPY statement

```
COPY B:REORDREC.DAT.
```

could be inserted in these source programs beginning in whatever column the description is to be copied to—in this case anywhere after column 8. Then, just before the program is compiled, the entries contained on the disk in the B drive under the filename REORDREC.DAT will be included in the source program. And after compilation, they will appear in the .LST file as follows:

```
COPY B:REORDREC.DAT.
01  REORDER.
    05  ITEM-DESC    PIC X(20).
    05  INV-NO      PIC 9(7).
    05  ON-HAND     PIC 9(3).
    05  REORD-PT    PIC 9(4).
    05  ORD-QUANT   PIC 9(4).
    05  UNIT-PRC    PIC 999V99.
    05  VENDOR-NO   PIC 9(6).
    05  FILLER      PIC X(31).
```

The following rules apply to the use of the COPY statement:

1. The filename must be a DOS filename that is *not* enclosed in quotes.

2. The COPY statement should be the last statement on a line.

3. After the requested information has been copied from the file specified, compilation proceeds as if the statements copied had originally been written in the source program.

4. Execution of the COPY statement is terminated when the last entry stored under the filename referenced has been copied into the source program.

5. No COPY statement may be included in the statements copied.

When the COPY statement was originally included in mainframe versions of COBOL, it was normal for the programmer to work from a hardcopy listing of the program after the first compile. On those versions of COBOL, the lines copied were indicated by a C printed to the left of each line. The text copied, therefore, was readily visible to the programmer. IBM PC COBOL also shows the lines copied, but on the compiled .LST file (without the letter C indicator), not in the source program. However, since programmers using the IBM PC will be using a text editor or word processor to create their source programs, they can use the same to copy the needed statements into the source program, bypassing the COPY statement entirely.

The Accept Statement Revisited

Earlier, we discussed several features of the ACCEPT statement. We shall now review those features and consider some new ones.

The purpose of the ACCEPT statement is to provide access to data that exist outside the program without the necessity of creating and reading a file. One form of the statement allows access to DOS to obtain the date and time and also allows control codes to be entered from the keyboard. Its general format is as follows:

GENERAL FORMAT 9

$$\text{ACCEPT identifier-1 } \left[\underline{\text{FROM}} \left\{ \begin{array}{l} \underline{\text{DATE}} \\ \underline{\text{DAY}} \\ \underline{\text{TIME}} \\ \underline{\text{ESCAPE KEY}} \end{array} \right\} \right]$$

In the **DATE** option, identifier-1 should be a six-digit numeric field defined in the DATA DIVISION. The current date will be transferred from DOS (if you provided the date when you booted the system) in the format YYMMDD. That is, March 31, 1984 (03/31/84) will appear as 840331. This format is the ANS standard for the DATE, and some manipulation is normally required to make use of it. For example, if the field DATE-IN were described as

```
05   DATE-IN.
     10 YR-IN   PIC 99.
     10 MO-IN   PIC 99.
     10 DAY-IN PIC 99.
```

and DATE-OUT as

```
05   DATE-OUT.
     10 MO-OUT   PIC 99.
     10 FILLER   PIC X VALUE '/'.
     10 DAY-OUT PIC 99.
     10 FILLER   PIC X VALUE '/'.
     10 YR-OUT   PIC 99.
```

then the following code would produce the date in an acceptable form:

```
ACCEPT DATE-IN FROM DATE.
MOVE YR-IN        TO YR-OUT.
MOVE MO-IN        TO MO-OUT.
MOVE DAY-IN       TO DAY-OUT.
```

The **DAY** option provides the Julian date, which is most convenient to use when arithmetic operations involving the date need to be carried out. Thus, the statement

```
ACCEPT DAY-IN FROM DAY.
```

will provide the current date from DOS, where it will have been manipulated into the form YYNNN, in which YY is the year and NNN is the number of days that have elapsed since the beginning of the year. According to this format, March 31, 1984 will appear as 84096. (1984 was a leap year).

The TIME option returns the time of day in the form HHMMSSFF, where HH is the current hour on a 24-hour-clock basis, MM the minutes, SS the seconds, and FF the hundredths of a second. Identifier-1 should be an eight-digit numeric field. Here again, it is assumed that the correct time was entered when the system was booted.

Using Function Keys and the Escape Key

The last option of the ACCEPT statement in General Format 9 is used as a convenient way to enter special codes such as end-of-job signals and special status codes. You could use it, for example, to transmit codes to your COBOL program via some of the ten function keys on your PC. Thus, the statement

```
ACCEPT STATUS-CODE FROM ESCAPE KEY.
```

will place the values shown in the second column of the table below in the two-digit field STATUS-CODE when the corresponding keys listed in the first column are pressed. (STATUS-CODE will of course have previously been defined by the programmer in the DATA DIVISION.)

Keyboard Character	Value
Backtab key	99
Esc key	01
<CR> or tab key	00
Function key (01–10)	02–11

If the FROM option is omitted altogether from the ACCEPT statement, the string of characters entered from the keyboard (up to the number described in the identifier) will be placed in the storage location in the WORKING-STORAGE SECTION of the program that is named in the ACCEPT statement. The data are entered from wherever the cursor is located prior to entering the ACCEPT statement, and after the characters are typed the <CR> key is pressed. The format of the data entered must conform to that indicated in the PICTURE clause of the named field, or else a beep is sounded by the IBM PC and the cursor does not move.

Another form of the ACCEPT statement, shown in General Format 10 below, is an expansion of the one used in Chapter 3, in which position specifications and the PROMPT option were used.

GENERAL FORMAT 10

ACCEPT position-spec identifier WITH $\left\{\begin{array}{l}\text{SPACE-FILL}\\\text{ZERO-FILL}\\\text{LEFT-JUSTIFY}\\\text{RIGHT-JUSTIFY}\\\text{TRAILING-SIGN}\\\text{PROMPT}\\\text{UPDATE}\\\text{LENGTH-CHECK}\\\text{AUTO-SKIP}\\\text{BEEP}\\\text{NO-ECHO}\\\text{EMPTY-CHECK}\end{array}\right\}$

In the example

```
05   ADDRESS-OUT     PIC X(20).
                  .
                  .
                  .
ACCEPT (7, 24) ADDRESS-OUT WITH PROMPT.
```

20 periods (...................) will appear on the screen beginning at line 7, column 24 when the ACCEPT statement is executed. As the data are entered, the periods are replaced by the characters entered. The maximum number of characters entered in this case will be 20 because of the PICTURE clause. In a similar manner, the code

```
05 CHECK-NO-WS      PIC S9(5).
                  .
                  .
                  .
ACCEPT (LIN, COL) CHECK-NO-WS WITH PROMPT.
```

will result in five zeros (00000) appearing on the screen beginning at whatever position the cursor happens to be when the ACCEPT statement is executed. In this case, of course, only digits (with a sign, if applicable) will be accepted by the computer. **LIN** and **COL** are special COBOL registers that contain the present coordinates of the cursor. Entries may be made relative with their use, e.g., LIN + 6 and COL − 4.

Many of the options shown in General Format 10 may be used in the same ACCEPT statement. As we proceed through the list in our discussion below, exceptions will be noted.

The **ZERO-FILL** and **SPACE-FILL** options must not be used together in the same statement. The ZERO-FILL option causes unkeyed positions of an alphanumeric or alphanumeric edited field to be filled with ASCII zeros, and unkeyed positions of a numeric or numeric edited field to be filled with numeric zeros. Similarly, the SPACE-FILL option causes unkeyed positions of an alphanumeric or alphanumeric edited field to be filled with spaces. If used with a numeric field, it causes the screen to show spaces.

In any case, the above two options only affect the data *as they appear on the screen*. In the receiving field, numeric data items always have unused positions filled with zeros and alphanumeric data items are always filled with spaces.

The **LEFT-JUSTIFY** option for alphanumeric fields, and both the **LEFT-** and **RIGHT-JUSTIFY** options for numeric fields, are treated as comments. When used with an alphanumeric field, the RIGHT-JUSTIFY option causes the data input field (the appropriate portion of the screen) to have its data appear right justified instead of left justified, as is the usual case. There is no corresponding change to the receiving field unless it contains the JUSTIFIED RIGHT clause. The LEFT-JUSTIFY and RIGHT-JUSTIFY options must not appear in the same statement.

The **UPDATE** option causes the data that appear in the receiving field *before execution of the ACCEPT statement* to appear on the screen. The operator may then change the data by keying in new data and pressing the <CR> key, or he or she may leave the data unchanged by merely pressing the <CR> key.

The **LENGTH-CHECK** option causes the <CR> key to be ignored unless *the entire field is full*. In numeric fields, this requires the appropriate number of both integer and decimal positions to be keyed. Following is an example.

```
05   STATE-WS        PIC XX.
05   ZIP-WS          PIC X(5).
             .
             .
             .
ACCEPT (9, 24) STATE-WS WITH PROMPT LENGTH-CHECK.
ACCEPT (9, 28) ZIP-WS   WITH PROMPT LENGTH-CHECK.
```

The above ACCEPT statements are used for input of two fields that, if correct, should always be the same size. STATE-WS must contain two characters (the standard two-letter abbreviation), and ZIP-WS (the zip code) should be five characters long.

The **EMPTY-CHECK** option requires that *at least one character* has been entered for the designated field. It would not be logical to use the LENGTH-CHECK and EMPTY-CHECK in the same statement. An example of an ACCEPT statement with EMPTY-CHECK option is

```
ACCEPT (13, 15) OPENING-BALANCE WITH PROMPT EMPTY-CHECK.
```

Upon execution of the statement, an entry must be made in the OPENING-BALANCE field, or the program will not continue.

The **AUTO-SKIP** option causes various kinds of termination of acceptance of data without use of the <CR> key. Acceptance of data is terminated for an alphanumeric data item when all positions have been filled; for the integer part of a numeric data item when all integer positions have been filled; and for an entire ACCEPT statement when all positions are filled. The examples used above with the LENGTH-CHECK option could also include the AUTO-SKIP option.

```
ACCEPT (9, 24) STATE-WS WITH PROMPT LENGTH-CHECK AUTO-SKIP.
ACCEPT (9, 28) ZIP-WS  WITH PROMPT LENGTH-CHECK AUTO-SKIP.
```

This would save the operator from pressing the <CR> key since, as noted above, the STATE-WS and ZIP-WS fields will be completely filled if the entry is correct.

The **BEEP** option causes the IBM PC speaker to sound once when execution of the ACCEPT statement begins in order to draw the operator's attention.

NO-ECHO is used when one does not want the characters typed to appear on the screen. Instead of the usual prompt of periods or zeros, a series of asterisks (*) is displayed according to the size of the data item. When the entry is keyed, the asterisks are *not* replaced, so that the keyed characters are not visible. Those familiar with time-sharing systems will have seen this option used in conjunction with passwords and other confidential data. When using this option, the operator is denied visual verification of the data entered, so it should be used sparingly. The following series of entries could be used for checking a password:

```
DISPLAY (2, 1) 'ENTER PASSWORD'.
ACCEPT  (LIN, COL) PASSWORD WITH NO-ECHO.
IF PASSWORD NOT = VALID-PASSWORD
    DISPLAY (3, 1) 'NOT AUTHORIZED USER '
    STOP RUN.
```

The **TRAILING-SIGN** option causes the sign of a numeric entry to be ACCEPTed from the rightmost position entered on the screen, rather than the leftmost position (the default). This has no effect on the position of the sign in the receiving field.

The last format of the ACCEPT statement is:

GENERAL FORMAT 11

ACCEPT screen-name ON ESCAPE imperative-statement

In this format, the capabilities of the ACCEPT statement greatly increased when used with the SCREEN SECTION and the appropriate format of the DISPLAY statement. The SCREEN SECTION will be covered in Chapter 8.

Figure 7–1 shows a program that uses a number of the statements explained in this chapter—particularly the variations of the ACCEPT statement. The program is an interactive check-writing program. It, or a variation of it, could be used to prepare checks for business or personal use. In addition to preparing the checks, the program keeps track of the balance and has a simple method for allocating expenditures to several categories. A sample of the screen during initialization of the CHECKWRITE program is shown in Fig. 7–2.

The first item to appear on the screen is a request to enter the correct password. In the sample program we have used the five-character password STEVO; you can change that to any password you desire. The ACCEPT statement associated with the password uses the NO-ECHO option mentioned above, which causes a prompt of asterisks to appear on the screen before and after the entry. When the password is entered, it is compared to VALID-PASSWORD, which has a VALUE in working storage. If the password is not correct, a message that the user is unauthorized is DISPLAYed, and the program stops.

The next entry requested is the check number to be printed on the first check, which is increased as each check is printed. After entry of the check number, the program executes the ACCEPT ... FROM DATE statement, obtaining the current date from DOS, a technique also described above. Finally, OPENING-BALANCE is entered, and initialization of the program is complete. Note that the ACCEPT statement for OPENING-BALANCE includes the EMPTY-CHECK option, which causes the program to require that an entry be made in response to the prompt. A <CR> will thus not be allowed unless some number is keyed in first. (The value 0 is of course acceptable.)

```
       IDENTIFICATION DIVISION.
       PROGRAM-ID.
           CHECKWRITE.
       AUTHOR.
           S.J.GAUGHRAN.
       INSTALLATION.
           PERSONAL COMPUTER SYSTEM.
       DATE-WRITTEN.
           JULY 11, 1984.
       SECURITY.
           PASSWORD PROTECTED.
      ************************************************************
      * This program writes checks, keeps a running balance and allows *
      * the user to allocate the expenditures to several categories.   *
      * It includes automatic date insertion and incrementing of check *
      * numbers. At the end totals are printed for the account balance,*
      * and the allocated categories. Data entry to the program is     *
      * through the keyboard with output to both the screen and the    *
      * printer.                                                        *
      ************************************************************
       ENVIRONMENT DIVISION.
       CONFIGURATION SECTION.
       SOURCE-COMPUTER.
           IBM-PERSONAL-COMPUTER.
       OBJECT-COMPUTER.
           IBM-PERSONAL-COMPUTER.
       INPUT-OUTPUT SECTION.
       FILE-CONTROL.
           SELECT PRINTFILE ASSIGN TO PRINTER.
      ************************************************************
       DATA DIVISION.
       FILE SECTION.
       FD  PRINTFILE
           LABEL RECORDS ARE OMITTED.
       01  PRINT-REC           PIC X(133).
      ************************************************************
       WORKING-STORAGE SECTION.
       01  WORKAREAS.
           05   STATUS-CODE      PIC 99.
           05   CITY-WS          PIC X(20).
           05   STATE-WS         PIC XX.
           05   ZIP-WS           PIC X(5).
           05   PASSWORD         PIC X(5).
           05   VALID-PASSWORD   PIC X(5)   VALUE 'STEVO'.
           05   F-KEY            PIC X.
           05   DATE-IN.
               10  YR-IN   PIC 99.
               10  MO-IN   PIC 99.
               10  DAY-IN  PIC 99.
       01  ACCUMULATORS    COMP-3.
           05   OPENING-BALANCE  PIC S9(5)V99.
           05   BALANCE          PIC S9(5)V99.
           05   CHECK-AMOUNT-WS  PIC S9(5)V99.
           05   CHECK-NO-WS      PIC S9(5).
           05   NUM-CHKS-WS      PIC S9(5)      VALUE ZERO.
           05   REG-TOT-WS       PIC S9(5)V99 VALUE ZERO.
           05   MED-TOT-WS       PIC S9(5)V99 VALUE ZERO.
           05   BUS-TOT-WS       PIC S9(5)V99 VALUE ZERO.
           05   TAX-TOT-WS       PIC S9(5)V99 VALUE ZERO.
           05   OTHER-TOT-WS     PIC S9(5)V99 VALUE ZERO.
           05   UNALL-TOT-WS     PIC S9(5)V99 VALUE ZERO.
       01  HDR-1.
           05   FILLER           PIC X(28) VALUE SPACES.
           05   FILLER           PIC X(17) VALUE 'THE F & G COMPANY'.
       01  HDR-2.
           05   FILLER           PIC X(20) VALUE SPACES.
           05   FILLER           PIC X(16) VALUE 'GARDEN CITY, NY'.
       01  LINE-1.
           05   FILLER           PIC X(05) VALUE SPACES.
           05   FILLER           PIC X(10) VALUE 'CHECK NO. '.
           05   CHECK-NO-OUT     PIC Z(06).
           05   FILLER           PIC X(44) VALUE SPACES.
```

Fig. 7-1. Listing of CHECKWRITE program.

242

```
         05  FILLER            PIC X(06) VALUE 'DATE '.
         05  DATE-OUT.
             10  MO-OUT    PIC 99.
             10  FILLER    PIC X    VALUE '/'.
             10  DAY-OUT   PIC 99.
             10  FILLER    PIC X    VALUE '/'.
             10  YR-OUT    PIC 99.
     01  LINE-2.
         05  FILLER            PIC X(05) VALUE SPACES.
         05  FILLER            PIC X(20) VALUE
                          'PAY TO THE ORDER OF '.
         05  NAME-OUT          PIC X(20).
         05  FILLER            PIC X(17) VALUE SPACES.
         05  FILLER            PIC X(09) VALUE 'EXACTLY  '.
         05  CHECK-AMOUNT-OUT  PIC **,***.99.
     01  LINE-3.
         05  FILLER            PIC X(25) VALUE SPACES.
         05  ADDRESS-OUT       PIC X(20).
     01  LINE-4.
         05  FILLER            PIC X(25) VALUE SPACES.
         05  CITY-STATE-ZIP    PIC X(30).
     01  LINE-5.
         05  FILLER            PIC X(05) VALUE SPACES.
         05  FILLER            PIC X(18) VALUE
                          'LAST NATIONAL BANK'.
     01  LINE-6.
         05  FILLER            PIC X(05) VALUE SPACES.
         05  FILLER            PIC X(16) VALUE
                          'SEAFORD,NY 11783'.
     01  DASHES.
         05  FILLER            PIC X(79) VALUE ALL '_'.
     01  TOTAL-LINE-1.
         05  FILLER            PIC X(03) VALUE SPACES.
         05  FILLER            PIC X(09) VALUE 'REG. EXP.'.
         05  FILLER            PIC X(04) VALUE SPACES.
         05  FILLER            PIC X(07) VALUE 'MEDICAL'.
         05  FILLER            PIC X(04) VALUE SPACES.
         05  FILLER            PIC X(08) VALUE 'BUSINESS'.
         05  FILLER            PIC X(05) VALUE SPACES.
         05  FILLER            PIC X(05) VALUE 'TAXES'.
         05  FILLER            PIC X(08) VALUE SPACES.
         05  FILLER            PIC X(05) VALUE 'OTHER'.
         05  FILLER            PIC X(03) VALUE SPACES.
         05  FILLER            PIC X(11) VALUE 'UNALLOCATED'.
     01  TOTAL-LINE-2.
         05  FILLER            PIC X(02) VALUE SPACES.
         05  REG-TOT-OUT       PIC Z,ZZZ.99.
         05  FILLER            PIC X(04) VALUE SPACES.
         05  MED-TOT-OUT       PIC Z,ZZZ.99.
         05  FILLER            PIC X(04) VALUE SPACES.
         05  BUS-TOT-OUT       PIC Z,ZZZ.99.
         05  FILLER            PIC X(04) VALUE SPACES.
         05  TAX-TOT-OUT       PIC Z,ZZZ.99.
         05  FILLER            PIC X(04) VALUE SPACES.
         05  OTHER-TOT-OUT     PIC Z,ZZZ.99.
         05  FILLER            PIC X(04) VALUE SPACES.
         05  UNALL-TOT-OUT     PIC Z,ZZZ.99.
     01  TOTAL-LINE-3.
         05  FILLER            PIC X(14) VALUE SPACES.
         05  FILLER            PIC X(16) VALUE 'OPENING BALANCE'.
         05  FILLER            PIC X(08) VALUE SPACES.
         05  FILLER            PIC X(13) VALUE 'TOTAL WRITTEN'.
         05  FILLER            PIC X(06) VALUE SPACES.
         05  FILLER            PIC X(15) VALUE 'CLOSING BALANCE'.
     01  TOTAL-LINE-4.
         05  FILLER            PIC X(16) VALUE SPACES.
         05  OPEN-BAL-OUT      PIC $Z,ZZZ.99-.
         05  FILLER            PIC X(13) VALUE SPACES.
         05  TOT-WRITTEN-OUT   PIC $Z,ZZZ.99.
         05  FILLER            PIC X(13) VALUE SPACES.
         05  CLOSE-BAL-OUT     PIC $Z,ZZZ.99-.
     01  TOTAL-LINE-5.
         05  FILLER            PIC X(14) VALUE SPACES.
         05  FILLER            PIC X(16) VALUE 'NUMBER OF CHECKS'.
```

Fig. 7–1. (*continued*)

```
        05  FILLER              PIC X(14) VALUE SPACES.
        05  FILLER              PIC X(18) VALUE 'NEXT CHECK NUMBER '.
    01  TOTAL-LINE-6.
        05  FILLER              PIC X(17) VALUE SPACES.
        05  NUM-CHKS-OUT        PIC Z,ZZ9.
        05  FILLER              PIC X(26) VALUE SPACES.
        05  NEXT-CHK-NO-OUT PIC ZZZZZ.
    ****************************************************************
    PROCEDURE DIVISION.
    BEGIN.
        OPEN OUTPUT PRINTFILE.
        MOVE SPACES TO PRINT-REC.
        WRITE PRINT-REC AFTER ADVANCING PAGE.
        PERFORM INITIAL-ACCEPT.
        PERFORM CHECK-ACCEPT THRU CHECK-ACCEPT-EXIT.
        PERFORM LOOP-RTN UNTIL STATUS-CODE = 01.
        PERFORM TOTAL-RTN.
        CLOSE PRINTFILE.
        STOP RUN.
    ****************************************************************
    LOOP-RTN.
        WRITE PRINT-REC FROM HDR-1
            AFTER ADVANCING 5 LINES.
        WRITE PRINT-REC FROM HDR-2
            AFTER ADVANCING 1 LINE.
        WRITE PRINT-REC FROM LINE-1
            AFTER ADVANCING 1 LINE.
        WRITE PRINT-REC FROM LINE-2
            AFTER ADVANCING 2 LINES.
        WRITE PRINT-REC FROM LINE-3
            AFTER ADVANCING 2 LINES.
        WRITE PRINT-REC FROM LINE-4
            AFTER ADVANCING 2 LINES.
        WRITE PRINT-REC FROM LINE-5
            AFTER ADVANCING 2 LINES.
        WRITE PRINT-REC FROM LINE-6
            AFTER ADVANCING 3 LINES.
        ADD   1      TO CHECK-NO-WS.
        WRITE PRINT-REC FROM DASHES
            AFTER ADVANCING 2 LINES.
        MOVE SPACES TO LINE-3
                       LINE-4.
        PERFORM CHECK-ACCEPT THRU CHECK-ACCEPT-EXIT.
    ****************************************************************
    INITIAL-ACCEPT.
        DISPLAY (1, 1) ERASE.
        DISPLAY (1, 25) 'CHECK WRITING PROGRAM'
        DISPLAY (2, 1) ' ENTER PASSWORD '.
        ACCEPT (LIN, COL) PASSWORD WITH NO-ECHO.
        IF PASSWORD NOT = VALID-PASSWORD
            DISPLAY (3, 1) ' NOT AUTHORIZED USER OF CHECKWRITE '
            STOP RUN.
        DISPLAY (7, 1) 'ENTER THE BEGINNING CHECK NUMBER  '.
        ACCEPT (LIN, COL) CHECK-NO-WS WITH PROMPT.
        ACCEPT DATE-IN FROM DATE.
            MOVE YR-IN         TO YR-OUT.
            MOVE MO-IN         TO MO-OUT.
            MOVE DAY-IN        TO DAY-OUT.
        DISPLAY (11, 1) 'ENTER THE OPENING BALANCE WITH '.
        DISPLAY (12, 3) 'TRAILING SIGN IF NEGATIVE '.
        ACCEPT (14, 15) OPENING-BALANCE WITH PROMPT EMPTY-CHECK
                                        TRAILING-SIGN.
        MOVE OPENING-BALANCE TO BALANCE.
        DISPLAY (1, 1) ERASE.
        DISPLAY (1, 1) 'F1 REG. EXP.// F2  MEDICAL // F3  BUSINESS '.
        DISPLAY (LIN, COL) '// F4  TAXES // F5  OTHER DEDUCTIBLE '.
    ****************************************************************
    CHECK-ACCEPT.
        DISPLAY (2, 1) ERASE.
        DISPLAY (2, 26) ' PRESS ESC TO END JOB '.
        DISPLAY (4, 1) ' ENTER NAME OF PAYEE  '.
        ACCEPT (LIN, COL) NAME-OUT WITH PROMPT BEEP.
        DISPLAY (2, 26) '                      '.
        ACCEPT STATUS-CODE FROM ESCAPE KEY.
```

Fig. 7-1. (*continued*)

```
           IF STATUS-CODE = 01 GO TO CHECK-ACCEPT-EXIT.
           DISPLAY (7, 1) ' ENTER STREET ADDRESS '
           DISPLAY (6, 1) ' IF NO ADDRESS PRESS F6 '.
           ACCEPT (7, 24) ADDRESS-OUT WITH PROMPT.
           ACCEPT STATUS-CODE FROM ESCAPE KEY.
           IF STATUS-CODE = 07 NEXT SENTENCE
           ELSE
               DISPLAY (8, 1) ' ENTER CITY '
               ACCEPT (8, 24) CITY-WS WITH PROMPT
               DISPLAY (9, 1) ' ENTER STATE & ZIP '
               ACCEPT (9, 24) STATE-WS WITH PROMPT LENGTH-CHECK
                                                 AUTO-SKIP
               ACCEPT (9, 28) ZIP-WS WITH PROMPT LENGTH-CHECK
                                                 AUTO-SKIP
               STRING CITY-WS   DELIMITED BY ' '
                      ' '        DELIMITED BY SIZE
                      STATE-WS DELIMITED BY SIZE
                      ' '        DELIMITED BY SIZE
                      ZIP-WS    DELIMITED BY SIZE
                               INTO CITY-STATE-ZIP.
           DISPLAY (11, 1) ' ENTER CHECK AMOUNT '.
           ACCEPT  (LIN, COL) CHECK-AMOUNT-WS WITH PROMPT EMPTY-CHECK.
           DISPLAY (13, 1) ' PRESS FUNCTION KEY FOR ALLOCATION '.
           DISPLAY (14, 1) ' IF UNALLOCATED PRESS ENTER '.
           ACCEPT (15, 1) F-KEY WITH PROMPT.
           ACCEPT STATUS-CODE FROM ESCAPE KEY.
           PERFORM ALLOCATION-CHECK.
           MOVE CHECK-NO-WS      TO CHECK-NO-OUT.
           ADD 1                 TO NUM-CHKS-WS.
           SUBTRACT CHECK-AMOUNT-WS FROM BALANCE.
           MOVE CHECK-AMOUNT-WS TO CHECK-AMOUNT-OUT.
       CHECK-ACCEPT-EXIT.
           EXIT.
   ****************************************************************
       ALLOCATION-CHECK.
           IF STATUS-CODE  = 02
                               ADD CHECK-AMOUNT-WS TO REG-TOT-WS
           ELSE  IF STATUS-CODE = 03
                               ADD CHECK-AMOUNT-WS TO MED-TOT-WS
                 ELSE IF STATUS-CODE  = 04
                               ADD CHECK-AMOUNT-WS TO BUS-TOT-WS
                     ELSE IF STATUS-CODE  = 05
                               ADD CHECK-AMOUNT-WS TO TAX-TOT-WS
                         ELSE IF STATUS-CODE  = 06
                               ADD CHECK-AMOUNT-WS TO OTHER-TOT-WS
                             ELSE
                               ADD CHECK-AMOUNT-WS TO UNALL-TOT-WS.
   ****************************************************************
       TOTAL-RTN.
           MOVE REG-TOT-WS       TO REG-TOT-OUT.
           MOVE MED-TOT-WS       TO MED-TOT-OUT.
           MOVE BUS-TOT-WS       TO BUS-TOT-OUT.
           MOVE TAX-TOT-WS       TO TAX-TOT-OUT.
           MOVE OTHER-TOT-WS     TO OTHER-TOT-OUT.
           MOVE UNALL-TOT-WS     TO UNALL-TOT-OUT.
           MOVE NUM-CHKS-WS      TO NUM-CHKS-OUT.
           MOVE CHECK-NO-WS      TO NEXT-CHK-NO-OUT.
           SUBTRACT BALANCE      FROM OPENING-BALANCE
                                 GIVING TOT-WRITTEN-OUT.
           MOVE OPENING-BALANCE TO OPEN-BAL-OUT.
           MOVE BALANCE          TO CLOSE-BAL-OUT.
           DISPLAY (1, 1) ERASE.
           DISPLAY (2, 1) TOTAL-LINE-1.
           DISPLAY (4, 1) TOTAL-LINE-2.
           IF BALANCE IS NEGATIVE
               DISPLAY (18, 10) ' GET TO THE BANK, QUICKLY !! '
               DISPLAY (20, 10) ' YOUR BALANCE IS   ' CLOSE-BAL-OUT.
           DISPLAY (6, 1) TOTAL-LINE-3.
           DISPLAY (8, 1) TOTAL-LINE-4.
           DISPLAY (10, 1) TOTAL-LINE-5.
           DISPLAY (12, 1) TOTAL-LINE-6.
   ****************************************************************
```

Fig. 7–1. (*continued*)

245

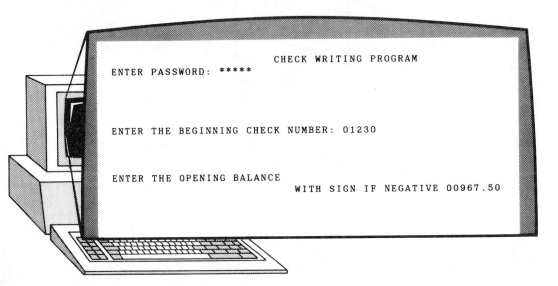

```
                         CHECK  WRITING  PROGRAM
ENTER  PASSWORD:  *****




ENTER  THE  BEGINNING  CHECK  NUMBER:  01230




ENTER  THE  OPENING  BALANCE
                         WITH  SIGN  IF  NEGATIVE  00967.50
```

**Fig. 7–2.   Screen from CHECKWRITE program
during program initialization.**

During execution of CHECKWRITE, the data are entered for each
individual check that is to be written. The operator must key in the
name of the payee in response to the appropriate prompt. You will
note in executing the program that at the same time that the prompt
for the name appears on the screen, the message 'PRESS ESC TO
END JOB' appears above it. Using the same logic as in previous programs, we shall signal the end of data by having some special code appear in place of a normal input set of data. As shown earlier, FROM
ESCAPE KEY is one of the options available with General Format 9 of
the ACCEPT statement. With this option, if ESC is pressed instead of
entering the payee's name, a code of 01 is placed in the field called
STATUS-CODE, which is tested by the program and is used to signal
that there are no more data to be processed.

After the name is entered, the operator is given the option as to
whether an address is to be entered. If no address is required on the
current check, the function key F0 is pressed in response to a message
prompt, and, using the statement ACCEPT STATUS-CODE FROM
ESCAPE KEY again, the program tests whether the address entry

routine is to be bypassed. Note that when the function keys F1 through F10 are used, the code returned by each key is offset by one digit. For example, pressing F6 returns a code of 07 in STATUS-CODE, pressing F3 returns 04, etc.

Input of address data to program CHECKWRITE uses several features covered in this chapter. The statement used to accept the street ADDRESS is similar to those used to accept the check number and payee's name above. However, the statements used to accept STATE and ZIP make use of additional options. Since STATE will always contain a two-letter code and ZIP will always contain five digits, we have included the LENGTH-CHECK option. The EMPTY-CHECK option used above with OPENING-BALANCE required that at least one character be entered; here, the LENGTH-CHECK option requires that the *exact* number of characters be entered. In addition, since the same number of characters will always be entered for these two data items, we have included the AUTO-SKIP option, which will relieve the operator of the need to press <CR> after typing in the data: when the field is full, the cursor will skip to the next field.

Since the number of characters in the name of each CITY may vary within the 20 characters allowed in the program, we have included the STRING statement to concatenate the CITY, STATE, and ZIP fields. Thus, instead of having data like

```
    LIMA               , OH 98765
```

or

```
    PORTLAND           , OR 12345
```

print on the checks, we were able to have them appear as

```
        LIMA, OH 98765
```

and

```
        PORTLAND, OR 12345
```

Finally, CHECK-AMOUNT is entered. Here again, the EMPTY-CHECK option is used to ensure that an amount is entered. After CHECK-AMOUNT is keyed in, a message appears to 'PRESS FUNCTION KEY FOR ALLOCATION.' This message has been included not only to allow the operator to keep track of the balance of the checking account, but also to allocate each check to some category of expense. The function keys F1 through F5 are used, and the message

`F1 REG. EXP.// F2 MEDICAL // F3 BUSINESS // F4 TAXES //F5 OTHER`

appears at the top of the screen throughout the check-writing phase. As each function key is pressed, the program will add the amount of that check to the total for the appropriate category. If no key is pressed, the amount will be added to an unallocated category.

```
     F1 REG. EXP. // F2 MEDICAL // F3 BUSINESS // F4 TAXES // F5 OTHER DEDUCTIBLE

                      PRESS ESC TO END JOB

              ENTER NAME OF PAYEE     ....................

              ENTER STREET ADDRESS ....................

              ENTER CITY             ....................

              ENTER STATE & ZIP      ..    .....

              ENTER CHECK AMOUNT     ........


              PRESS FUNCTION KEY FOR ALLOCATION
                 IF UNALLOCATED PRESS F6
```

Fig. 7–3. Screen from CHECKWRITE program during program execution.

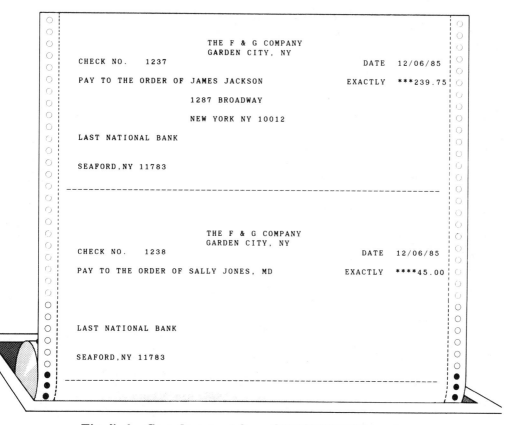

Fig. 7–4. Sample output from CHECKWRITE program.

When this last entry has been made, the check will print and the program will loop back to request the name of the payee, to cause another check to be prepared, or to end the job.

Figure 7–3 shows a sample screen from the CHECKWRITE program during program execution, and Fig. 7–4 shows the printed output of two sample checks.

After an end-of-data signal occurs (pressing the ESC key instead of entering a payee name), the program displays some totals on the screen. (You can alter the program to print these totals on paper, if desired.) Shown are the totals from the various categories, the opening balance, the total for the checks written, and the closing balance. Try

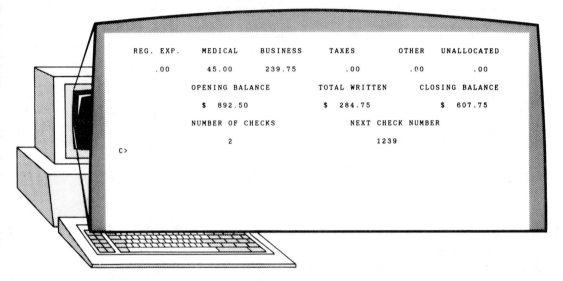

```
    REG. EXP.     MEDICAL    BUSINESS      TAXES         OTHER     UNALLOCATED
         .00       45.00      239.75         .00          .00          .00

                 OPENING BALANCE        TOTAL WRITTEN      CLOSING BALANCE

                  $  892.50             $  284.75          $  607.75

                 NUMBER OF CHECKS             NEXT CHECK NUMBER

                       2                         1239
    C>
```

Fig. 7–5.   Screen from CHECKWRITE showing end-of-job totals.

running the program so that there is a negative balance, and see what happens! Finally, the total number of checks written and the number of the next check are displayed. Figure 7–5 shows the screen that displays the end-of-job totals.

> *This program is available on the supplemental disk under the filename CH701.COB.*

Why not copy program CHECKWRITE from the text or the disk, alter it, and run it with titles and allocations suitable to your own use.

EXERCISES

1. Prepare a sales register as described in the output layout on page 252. The input file is to contain blank characters in the product sales field if there are no sales for that product. Do not print any-

thing in the field for a product that has no sales. Totals are to be calculated and printed for each product.

2. The report described on page 253 is a combined cash journal showing both debits and credits to the cash account. Credits will have a minus sign as part of the amount field. Print out the letters CR, using editing, for the credit (minus) items, which should also be subtracted from the balance that is to appear at the end of the report. Use the floating $ in the cash balance field.

3. Print out the "dunning" notice shown on page 254. The input is a two-record "set" that should always be in the file in the order code (1 or 2) within customer number. Using the REDEFINES clause, create *one* input record in the FILE SECTION. The numeric fields should be checked to make sure that they contain valid numeric data, particularly high-order zeros, before any processing takes place.

Solutions to the exercises, together with any necessary data files, are provided on the supplemental disk.

Input Layout

Input Record: SALES-REC

SALES PERSON NUMBER	BRANCH	SALES PERSON NAME	INIT FM	SALES PRODUCT A	SALES PRODUCT B	SALES PRODUCT C

Output Layout

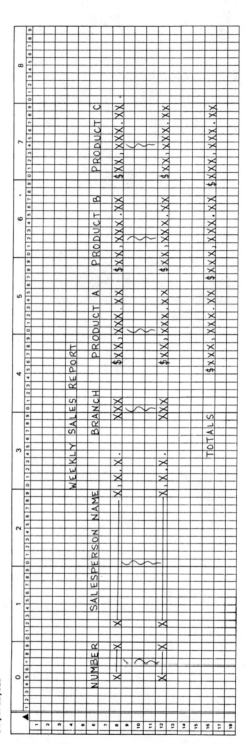

WEEKLY SALES REPORT

NUMBER   SALESPERSON NAME   BRANCH   PRODUCT A   PRODUCT B   PRODUCT C

TOTALS

Input Layout

Input Record: JOURNAL-REC

ITEM IDENT.	DESCRIPTION	UNUSED	AMOUNT
1 2 3 4 5	6 7 8 9 0 1 2 3 4 5 6 7	8 9 0 1 2 3 4 5 6 7 8 9 0	1 2 3 4 5 6 7

Output Layout

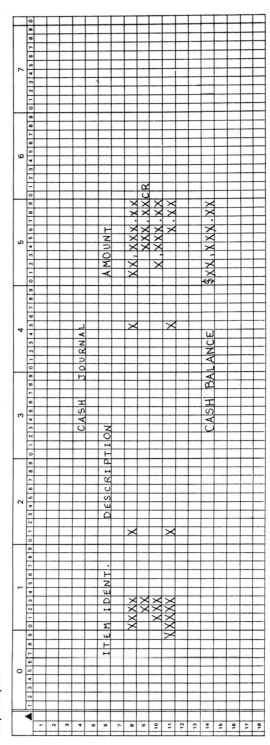

Input Record: CUSTOMER-REC-1

CODE 1	CUSTOMER NUMBER	CUSTOMER NAME	STREET ADDRESS	BALANCED OWED.	NO. OF DAYS

Input Record: CUSTOMER-F EC-2

CODE 2	CUSTOMER NUMBER	CITY	STATE	ZIP	UNUSED

Output Layout

```
AJAX DEPARTMENT STORES
ANY ADDRESS
YOUR CITY, STATE 12345

                                    (CUST. NO)
(NAME)
X                                   XXXXXX
'STREET ADDR)
X                          X        OUR RECORDS INDICATE THAT YOU
               (STATE) (ZIP)        HAVE AN OUTSTANDING BALANCE OF
XX             XX XXXXX             (BALANCE OWED)      (NO. OF DAYS)
X      X                           $X,XXX.XX FOR OVER XXXX DAYS.

                                    PLEASE REMIT.
```

8

COBOL DEBUGGING AIDS AND INTERACTIVE I/O

In the previous chapters you have learned how to write, enter, compile, link, execute, and debug simple COBOL programs using the IBM (Microsoft) version of American National Standard COBOL.

Now we will concentrate on some of the more advanced features of the COBOL language, particularly the areas involving table handling and methods of file organization and access. We have included a chapter on the COBOL SORT and MERGE, although this is an optional feature in IBM COBOL for the PC, XT, and AT.

Let's begin by examining some of the more useful program debugging aids available to us in IBM COBOL. These will prove extremely helpful in removing troublesome and elusive programming errors or bugs.

DEBUGGING COBOL PROGRAMS

The COBOL language contains several features that are quite useful in debugging programs. Before we examine these features in detail, let's review some of the types of errors that you are likely to encounter.

TYPES OF COBOL ERRORS

Syntax Errors

Syntax errors are the result of entering COBOL statements that are not in the correct form or that are used incorrectly. You should now be familiar with the diagnostic messages that the COBOL compiler generates after the COBOL phase of the compile operation in response to syntax errors. These messages include the line number in the source program that includes the error or the file occurrence if it is associated with a file. Messages preceded by /W/ or /F/ are warnings and will not prevent you from linking and executing the program—all other messages represent errors that are serious enough to prevent the successful linking and running of the program. Thus, they must be corrected and the program recompiled. This is illustrated in Fig. 8–1.

Linker Errors

This type of error is rare. Usually errors of this type result from situations such as an object program that is too large or the inability of

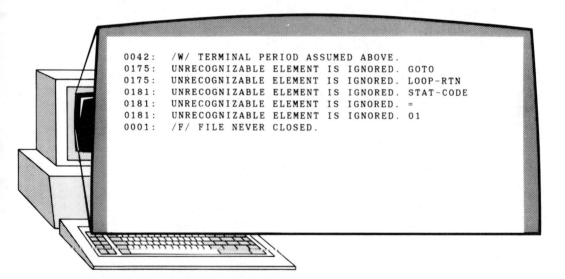

```
0042:   /W/ TERMINAL PERIOD ASSUMED ABOVE.
0175:   UNRECOGNIZABLE ELEMENT IS IGNORED. GOTO
0175:   UNRECOGNIZABLE ELEMENT IS IGNORED. LOOP-RTN
0181:   UNRECOGNIZABLE ELEMENT IS IGNORED. STAT-CODE
0181:   UNRECOGNIZABLE ELEMENT IS IGNORED. =
0181:   UNRECOGNIZABLE ELEMENT IS IGNORED. 01
0001:   /F/ FILE NEVER CLOSED.
```

Fig. 8–1. Sample compile time diagnostics.

the linker to locate a module called as an external subroutine. Two examples of this type of error follow:

```
FATAL ERROR:
Invalid Object Module
Input File: SYNTAX.OBJ pos: 00003 Record Type: 00
```

This message indicates that there is a problem at link time with the .OBJ file. This error resulted from an interruption during the compile.

The message

```
Unresolved Externals:

JOB-TUB in file(s):
            CH13-2.OBJ(CH13-2)
```

results from the inability of the linker to find an external subroutine (subprogram). The correct name is JOB-TAB. Subprograms will be covered later in the book.

Runtime Errors

When a program has successfully compiled and linked it is still possible to have execution or runtime errors. Two of the most common type of execution or runtime errors are input/output errors and data exception errors.

Input/Output Error

```
** RUN-TIME ERR:
INPUT/OUTPUT
CREATE
00041
```

This error was caused because the .EXE program was not able to find a data set called CREATE.DAT. The reference to this data set was made on line 00041 of the source program. Errors of this type typically are caused because the disk containing the file was not available or because the file was named incorrectly. In the case above, we deliberately misnamed the file as CRATE.DAT rather than the correct name—CREATE.DAT.

Data Exception Error   As we have noted earlier, valid numeric data must be provided for the computer to perform a numeric operation. The failure to provide this data (due to not initializing numeric fields, misdefining input records, or entering bad data) *is the most common cause of runtime errors.* An example of the screen display for one such error follows:

```
** RUN-TIME ERR:
NON-NUMERIC DATA
PAYROLL
00143
```

The message tells us that the program called PAYROLL halted at line 00143 in the source program because invalid (nonnumeric) data was encountered while attempting to execute an arithmetic operation. The corrective action for this error would include reviewing the record description to ensure that the numeric field had been correctly described; checking the appropriate data item in WORKING-STORAGE to ensure that accumulators have been properly initialized; and checking the contents of any input data item to verify they do in fact contain numeric data.

Logic Errors   All the errors shown above resulted in a message at compile time, link time, or runtime. They are sometimes troublesome but most often the error message gives a clear indication, or at least a clue, as to the cause of the error. Logic errors, however, are less obvious. There are no built-in error messages for logic errors. Usually the only indication is that the program abnormally terminates (hangs up) or the output from the program is incorrect.

DEBUGGING AIDS

COBOL offers some aid in diagnosing logic errors. These are the TRACE, DISPLAY, and EXHIBIT statements.

TRACE Statement

The purpose of the TRACE is to display a list of the paragraphs in the order in which they are run. With this version of IBM COBOL the output from the TRACE is *always* directed to the screen—to get a printed copy of this listing you will have to use the PRTSC feature. If you were to include the TRACE feature in the program CH801, detailed later in this chapter, the output on the screen would appear as follows:

```
100-OPEN-FILES
200-HEADING-RTN
300-PROCESS-RTN
300-PROCESS-RTN
300-PROCESS-RTN
300-PROCESS-RTN
300-PROCESS-RTN
300-PROCESS-RTN
400-CLOSE-RTN
```

This is a useful method to verify the path taken by the program logic.

GENERAL FORMAT 1

$\begin{Bmatrix} \text{READY} \\ \text{RESET} \end{Bmatrix}$ TRACE

The READY TRACE statement is included in the PROCEDURE DIVISION at the point that the trace is to be started. It should be noted that the listing on the screen will NOT include the name of the paragraph that contains the READY TRACE. The example above does not include the paragraph name MAIN-LINE, which is the paragraph containing the READY TRACE in program CH801.

The READY TRACE can be turned off by the command RESET TRACE. In a long program or in a situation in which you want to trace only a portion of the program logic, you would insert the READY TRACE and RESET TRACE in the program. They may be included as many times as necessary. An important feature, *which is not documented in the IBM COBOL manual*, is the ability to include the READY and RESET TRACE commands in conditional statements:

```
IF ACCOUNT-BALANCE IS NEGATIVE
            READY TRACE
            PERFORM NEGATIVE-BALANCE-RTN
            RESET TRACE.
```

This would cause the TRACE to be active for that portion of the program connected with a negative balance. The RESET TRACE would be included at the end of the statement to turn the feature off.

DISPLAY Statement

The DISPLAY statement is also available to be inserted at any point in the program to direct to the screen or the printer the contents of any data in the WORKING-STORAGE SECTION.

GENERAL FORMAT 2

$$\underline{\text{DISPLAY}} \text{ [position-spec]} \begin{Bmatrix} \text{identifier} \\ \text{literal} \\ \underline{\text{ERASE}} \end{Bmatrix} \text{ UPON mnemonic-name}$$

The statement

```
DISPLAY AMOUNT-1.
```

causes the contents of that field to be displayed on the screen. To cause the data to appear on the printer, the statement

```
DISPLAY AMOUNT-1 UPON LINE-PRINTER.
```

can be used where LINE-PRINTER has been described in the SPECIAL-NAMES paragraph:

```
SPECIAL-NAMES.
    PRINTER IS LINE-PRINTER.
```

The DISPLAY does not automatically identify the field unless we do so in the statement, that is:

```
DISPLAY 'AMOUNT-1 = ' AMOUNT-1 UPON LINE-PRINTER.
```

EXHIBIT Statement

Another method more frequently indentified with debugging is the EXHIBIT statement. This statement also displays data on the screen or the printer. But in doing so, it automatically displays the name of the field.

GENERAL FORMAT 3

EXHIBIT NAMED [position-spec] $\left\{\begin{array}{l}\text{identifier}\\\text{literal}\\\text{ERASE}\end{array}\right\}$ ... [UPON mnemonic-name]

The statement

```
EXHIBIT AMOUNT-1.
```

will cause the following to appear when this statement is executed:

```
AMOUNT-1 = 001234
```

This assumes that the contents of AMOUNT-1 is an unsigned value of 001234 even if the picture clause specifies 9(4)V99. This is because the EXHIBIT shows values in their internal form, ignoring the decimal position and retaining leading zeros. If a sign were present this would appear as:

```
AMOUNT-1 = 00123D  if the sign is plus, and
AMOUNT-1 = 00123M  if the sign is negative.
```

This follows the internal sign convention, which carries the sign as the rightmost position in the field:

Positive: A through I (for $+1$ through $+9$)

Negative: J through R (for -1 through -9)

(A plus zero will be a { and a negative zero a }.)

The word **NAMED** is optional, and the name of the data item will be displayed in any case. The rest of the format for the EXHIBIT is identical to that for the DISPLAY (with the exception of the screen option of the DISPLAY, which is covered later in this chapter).

DEBUGGING MODE Clause

It may be desirable to include debugging statements in your program (such as the TRACE, EXHIBIT, DISPLAY, or any other statement) **that are** not to be executed every time the program is compiled.

This may be accomplished by including the WITH DEBUGGING MODE clause in the SOURCE-COMPUTER paragraph of the ENVIRONMENT DIVISION's CONFIGURATION SECTION.

GENERAL FORMAT 4

SOURCE-COMPUTER. Computer-name
[with DEBUGGING MODE].

When this statement is included and the program is compiled, all statements in the PROCEDURE DIVISION that have the letter D in column 7 will be included in the compilation and executed. To ignore these statements, you must remove the WITH DEBUGGING MODE clause and recompile the program. These statements may remain as part of the source program indefinitely and included as needed during the testing process.

The program CH801.COB shown in Fig. 8–2 includes these options.

Program CH801.COB is available on the supplemental disk.

INTERACTIVE INPUT/OUTPUT

The ACCEPT and DISPLAY statements were discussed in detail in Chapter 3. The emphasis at that time was on entering data or displaying data on a line-by-line basis. The formatting of the data on the screen was done principally in the PROCEDURE DIVISION by executing such statements as

```
DISPLAY (5, 10) 'ENTER FIRST NAME'.
ACCEPT (5, 31) FIRST-NAME-IN WITH PROMPT.
```

Execution of these statements cause the following to appear on line 5, column 10:

```
ENTER FIRST NAME           . . . . . . . . . .
```

```
**************************************************************
IDENTIFICATION DIVISION.
**************************************************************
PROGRAM-ID.
    PROGRAM-LIST-REV.
AUTHOR.
    S.J.GAUGHRAN.
INSTALLATION.
    PERSONAL COMPUTER SYSTEM.
DATE-WRITTEN.
    AUG. 2,1984.
DATE-COMPILED.
    AUG. 2,1984.
SECURITY.
    NONE.
**************************************************************
ENVIRONMENT DIVISION.
**************************************************************
CONFIGURATION SECTION.
SOURCE-COMPUTER.
    IBM-PERSONAL-COMPUTER
                    WITH DEBUGGING MODE.
OBJECT-COMPUTER.
    IBM-PERSONAL-COMPUTER.
SPECIAL-NAMES.
    PRINTER IS LINE-OUT.
INPUT-OUTPUT SECTION.
FILE-CONTROL.
    SELECT TRANSAC-FILE ASSIGN TO DISK
        ORGANIZATION IS LINE SEQUENTIAL.
    SELECT TRANSAC-LIST ASSIGN TO PRINTER.
**************************************************************
DATA DIVISION.
**************************************************************
FILE SECTION.
FD  TRANSAC-FILE
    LABEL RECORDS ARE STANDARD
    VALUE OF FILE-ID IS 'CH601.DAT'.
01  DISK-REC                PIC X(45).
FD  TRANSAC-LIST
    LABEL RECORDS ARE OMITTED.
01  PRINT-REC               PIC X(78).
**************************************************************
WORKING-STORAGE SECTION.
**************************************************************
01  SWITCHES-MESSAGES-COUNTERS.
    05  EOF                 PIC 9       VALUE ZERO.
    05  ERROR-MSG           PIC X(4)    VALUE ' BAD'.
    05  END-MSG             PIC X(12)   VALUE ' END OF JOB '.
    05  LINE-CTR            PIC 99      VALUE ZERO.
**************************************************************
01  TRANSAC-REC-IN.
    05  CUSTOMER-NO-IN      PIC X(5).
    05  CUSTOMER-ID-IN.
        10  LAST-NAME-IN    PIC X(10).
        10  FIRST-NAME-IN   PIC X(10).
        10  INITIAL-IN      PIC X.
        10  CREDIT-CODE-IN.
            15  RATING-IN   PIC XX.
                88 VALID-RATING    VALUE 'A' 'AA' 'B' 'BB' 'C'.
            15  LIMIT-AMT-IN PIC S999.
            15  LIMIT-AMT-IN-X  REDEFINES LIMIT-AMT-IN
                            PIC X(3).
    05  TRANS-IN.
        10  ITEM-NO-IN.
            15  INV-NO-IN   PIC X(5).
            15  DEPT-NO-IN  PIC XX.
        10  UNIT-PRICE-IN   PIC S9(3)V99.
        10  UNIT-PRICE-IN-X REDEFINES UNIT-PRICE-IN
                            PIC X(5).
        10  UNITS-IN        PIC S99.
```

Fig. 8–2. Program CH801.COB debugging statements.

263

```
            10   UNITS-IN-X  REDEFINES  UNITS-IN
                 PIC X(2).
************************************************************
01   TITLE-1.
     05  FILLER            PIC X(20) VALUE SPACES.
     05  FILLER            PIC X(39) VALUE
             'ACCOUNTS RECEIVABLE REPORT'.
************************************************************
01   TITLE-2.
     05  FILLER            PIC XX    VALUE SPACES.
     05  FILLER            PIC X(4)  VALUE 'CUST'.
     05  FILLER            PIC X(8)  VALUE SPACES.
     05  FILLER            PIC X(13) VALUE 'CUSTOMER NAME'.
     05  FILLER            PIC X(7)  VALUE SPACES.
     05  FILLER            PIC X(6)  VALUE 'CREDIT'.
     05  FILLER            PIC XX    VALUE SPACES.
     05  FILLER            PIC X(4)  VALUE 'CODE'.
     05  FILLER            PIC X(5)  VALUE SPACES.
     05  FILLER            PIC X(23) VALUE
             'TRANSACTION INFORMATION'.
************************************************************
01   TITLE-3.
     05  FILLER            PIC X     VALUE SPACES.
     05  FILLER            PIC X(6)  VALUE 'NUMBER'.
     05  FILLER            PIC X(5)  VALUE SPACES.
     05  FILLER            PIC X(4)  VALUE 'LAST'.
     05  FILLER            PIC X(6)  VALUE SPACES.
     05  FILLER            PIC X(5)  VALUE 'FIRST'.
     05  FILLER            PIC X(4)  VALUE SPACES.
     05  FILLER            PIC X     VALUE 'M'.
     05  FILLER            PIC XX    VALUE SPACES.
     05  FILLER            PIC X(6)  VALUE 'RATING'.
     05  FILLER            PIC X     VALUE SPACES.
     05  FILLER            PIC X(5)  VALUE 'LIMIT'.
     05  FILLER            PIC XXX   VALUE SPACES.
     05  FILLER            PIC XXX   VALUE 'INV'.
     05  FILLER            PIC XX    VALUE SPACES.
     05  FILLER            PIC X(4)  VALUE 'DEPT'.
     05  FILLER            PIC X     VALUE SPACES.
     05  FILLER            PIC X(10) VALUE 'UNIT PRICE'.
     05  FILLER            PIC X     VALUE SPACES.
     05  FILLER            PIC X(8)  VALUE 'QUANTITY'.
************************************************************
01   TRANSAC-REC-OUT.
     05  FILLER            PIC X     VALUE SPACES.
     05  CUSTOMER-NO-OUT   PIC X(5).
     05  FILLER            PIC X(3)  VALUE SPACES.
     05  CUSTOMER-ID-OUT.
         10  LAST-NAME-OUT  PIC X(10).
         10  FILLER         PIC X     VALUE SPACES.
         10  FIRST-NAME-OUT PIC X(10).
         10  FILLER         PIC X     VALUE SPACES.
         10  INITIAL-OUT    PIC X.
         10  FILLER         PIC X(4)  VALUE SPACES.
         10  CREDIT-CODE-OUT.
             15  RATING-OUT PIC XX.
             15  FILLER     PIC X(4)  VALUE SPACES.
             15  LIMIT-AMT-OUT  PIC ZZ9.
             15  LIMIT-AMT-OUT-X REDEFINES LIMIT-AMT-OUT
                      PIC X(3).
             15  FILLER     PIC X(3)  VALUE SPACES.
     05  TRANS-OUT.
         10  INV-NO-OUT PIC X(5).
         10  FILLER     PIC XX  VALUE SPACES.
         10  DEPT-NO-OUT   PIC XX.
         10  FILLER     PIC X(3) VALUE SPACES.
         10  UNIT-PRICE-OUT  PIC $ZZZ.99.
         10  UNIT-PRICE-OUT-X  REDEFINES UNIT-PRICE-OUT
                  PIC X(7).
         10  FILLER     PIC X(3) VALUE SPACES.
         10  UNITS-OUT  PIC Z9.
         10  UNITS-OUT-X  REDEFINES  UNITS-OUT
                  PIC X(2).
         10  MSG-OUT    PIC X(4) VALUE SPACES.
```

Fig. 8–2. (*continued*)

```
     ***********************************************************
      PROCEDURE DIVISION.
     ***********************************************************
      MAIN-LINE.
D         READY TRACE.
          PERFORM 100-OPEN-FILES.
          PERFORM 200-HEADING-RTN.
          READ TRANSAC-FILE INTO TRANSAC-REC-IN
               AT END MOVE 1 TO EOF.
          PERFORM 300-PROCESS-RTN
               UNTIL EOF = 1.
          PERFORM 400-CLOSE-RTN.
          STOP RUN.
     ***********************************************************
      100-OPEN-FILES.
          OPEN INPUT  TRANSAC-FILE
               OUTPUT TRANSAC-LIST.
     ***********************************************************
      200-HEADING-RTN.
          WRITE PRINT-REC FROM TITLE-1 AFTER ADVANCING PAGE.
          WRITE PRINT-REC FROM TITLE-2 AFTER ADVANCING 3 LINES.
          WRITE PRINT-REC FROM TITLE-3 AFTER ADVANCING 1 LINE.
          MOVE SPACES TO PRINT-REC.
          WRITE PRINT-REC AFTER ADVANCING 1 LINE.
          MOVE ZEROS  TO LINE-CTR.
     ***********************************************************
      300-PROCESS-RTN.
          MOVE CUSTOMER-NO-IN TO CUSTOMER-NO-OUT.
          MOVE LAST-NAME-IN   TO LAST-NAME-OUT.
          MOVE FIRST-NAME-IN  TO FIRST-NAME-OUT.
          MOVE INITIAL-IN     TO INITIAL-OUT.
          MOVE RATING-IN      TO RATING-OUT.
          IF VALID-RATING     NEXT SENTENCE
          ELSE                MOVE ERROR-MSG TO MSG-OUT.
          IF LIMIT-AMT-IN NUMERIC
                              MOVE LIMIT-AMT-IN   TO LIMIT-AMT-OUT
          ELSE                MOVE LIMIT-AMT-IN-X TO LIMIT-AMT-OUT-X
                              MOVE ERROR-MSG        TO MSG-OUT.
          MOVE INV-NO-IN      TO INV-NO-OUT.
          MOVE DEPT-NO-IN     TO DEPT-NO-OUT.
          IF UNIT-PRICE-IN NUMERIC
                              MOVE UNIT-PRICE-IN TO UNIT-PRICE-OUT
          ELSE                MOVE UNIT-PRICE-IN-X TO UNIT-PRICE-OUT-X
                              MOVE ERROR-MSG        TO MSG-OUT.
D         EXHIBIT UNIT-PRICE-IN UPON LINE-OUT.
          IF UNITS-IN NUMERIC
                              MOVE UNITS-IN       TO UNITS-OUT
          ELSE                MOVE UNITS-IN-X     TO UNITS-OUT-X
                              MOVE ERROR-MSG        TO MSG-OUT.
D         EXHIBIT NAMED UNITS-IN UPON LINE-OUT.
          WRITE PRINT-REC FROM TRANSAC-REC-OUT
               AFTER ADVANCING 1 LINE.
          ADD 1               TO LINE-CTR.
          IF LINE-CTR > 45  READY TRACE
                            PERFORM 200-HEADING-RTN
                            RESET TRACE.
          MOVE SPACES        TO MSG-OUT.
          READ TRANSAC-FILE INTO TRANSAC-REC-IN
               AT END MOVE 1 TO EOF.
D         IF EOF = 1 RESET TRACE.
     ***********************************************************
      400-CLOSE-RTN.
          MOVE END-MSG TO PRINT-REC.
          WRITE PRINT-REC AFTER ADVANCING 3 LINES.
          CLOSE TRANSAC-FILE
               TRANSAC-LIST.
     ***********************************************************
```

Fig. 8–2. (continued)

Execution of these statements also causes the data entered in response to this prompt to be placed in working-storage at:

```
10 FIRST-NAME-IN  PIC X(10).
```

GENERAL FORMAT 5

ACCEPT position-spec   identifier [WITH {

[SPACE-FILL]

[ZERO-FILL]

[LEFT-JUSTIFY]

[RIGHT-JUSTIFY]

[TRAILING-SIGN]

[PROMPT]

[UPDATE]

[LENGTH-CHECK]

[EMPTY-CHECK]

[AUTO-SKIP]

[BEEP]

[NO-ECHO]

THE SCREEN SECTION

The SCREEN SECTION is the last of the four possible sections in the DATA DIVISION. The FILE SECTION, WORKING-STORAGE SECTION, and the LINKAGE SECTION (if used) will precede it. The LINKAGE SECTION is used with subprograms and will be discussed later in the book.

The purpose of the SCREEN SECTION is to describe the format of an *entire* screen rather than each individual line, as we have previously discussed. The entries in the SCREEN SECTION are similar to those used in other DATA DIVISION sections. As with group and elementary data items described in the FILE and WORKING-STORAGE SECTIONs, SCREEN SECTION entries describe the relative position of each subordinate data item within a group item and specify the character makeup of an elementary data item. However, SCREEN SECTION entries also include other characteristics, such as the exact position on the screen of any prompts, the location of the cursor for data entry, and specifications regarding the appearance of the screen in terms of colors, blinking and reverse video, etc.

GENERAL FORMAT 6

level-number   screen-name [AUTO] [SECURE] [REQUIRED] [FULL].

GENERAL FORMAT 7

level-number [screen-name]   [BLANK SCREEN]

[LINE NUMBER IS [PLUS] integer-1]

[COLUMN NUMBER IS [PLUS] integer-2]

[BLANK LINE]

[BELL]

[UNDERLINE]

[REVERSE-VIDEO]

[HIGHLIGHT]

[BLINK]

[FOREGROUND-COLOR integer-3]

[BACKGROUND-COLOR integer-4]

[VALUE IS literal-1]

$\left[\begin{Bmatrix} \text{PICTURE} \\ \text{PIC} \end{Bmatrix} \text{ IS picture-string} \right]$

$\begin{Bmatrix} \text{[FROM literal-2} \\ \text{identifier-1]} \\ \text{[TO identifier-2]} \\ \text{[USING identifier-3]} \end{Bmatrix}$

[BLANK WHEN ZERO]

$\left[\begin{Bmatrix} \text{JUSTIFIED} \\ \text{JUST} \end{Bmatrix} \text{ RIGHT} \right]$

[AUTO]

[SECURE]

[REQUIRED]

[FULL]

Interaction with ACCEPT and DISPLAY Statements

Let's begin our discussion of SCREEN SECTION entries by describing how they are used in conjunction with PROCEDURE DIVISION entries to accept data entered interactively and display it in a specified format on the screen. This is accomplished using the versions of the ACCEPT and DISPLAY shown below.

GENERAL FORMAT 8

ACCEPT screen-name

DISPLAY screen-name

These PROCEDURE DIVISION entries are much simpler than those previously used because they contain no positional and feature specifications. These specifications are provided in the SCREEN SECTION.

In an interactive data entry environment, a combination of a DISPLAY screen-name followed by an ACCEPT screen-name would be used. The single entry

```
DISPLAY screen-name
```

causes the constants and prompts for an entire screen to be displayed. Execution of the subsequent

```
ACCEPT screen-name
```

statement causes

1. the cursor to be positioned at the first item to be entered

2. data to be accepted according to the specifications described in the SCREEN SECTION

3. the data entered and accepted to be displayed

4. the cursor to be positioned at the next item to be entered

5. steps 2, 3, and 4 to be repeated until all entries have been accepted

6. program execution to continue with the next sequential instruction

```
*****************************************************************
  SCREEN SECTION.
*****************************************************************
  01  INITIAL-SCREEN.
      05  BLANK SCREEN.
      05  LINE 1 COLUMN 25 VALUE 'CHECK WRITING PROGRAM' BLINK.
      05  LINE 2 COLUMN 1  VALUE 'ENTER PASSWORD: ' HIGHLIGHT.
      05  PIC X(5)         TO PASSWORD SECURE .
      05  LINE 7 COLUMN 1
                         VALUE 'ENTER THE BEGINNING CHECK NUMBER: '.
      05  PIC 9(5)          TO CHECK-NO-WS .
      05  LINE 11 COLUMN 1 VALUE  'ENTER THE OPENING BALANCE '.
      05  LINE 12 COLUMN 27 VALUE ' WITH SIGN IF NEGATIVE '.
      05  PIC   99999.99-  TO OPENING-BALANCE.
*****************************************************************
  01  CHECK-SCREEN.
      05  BLANK SCREEN.
      05  LINE 1   COLUMN 1  REVERSE-VIDEO
                             VALUE 'F1 REG. EXP. // F2 MEDICAL //'.
      05  LINE 1   COLUMN 30 REVERSE-VIDEO
                             VALUE ' F3 BUSINESS // F4 TAXES // '.
      05  LINE 1   COLUMN 58 REVERSE-VIDEO
                             VALUE 'F5 OTHER DEDUCTIBLE '.
      05  LINE 3   COLUMN 27 REVERSE-VIDEO
                             VALUE ' PRESS ESC TO END JOB '.
      05  LINE 6   COLUMN 21 VALUE ' ENTER NAME OF PAYEE '
                             UNDERLINE.
      05  LINE 6   COLUMN 43 PIC X(20) TO NAME-OUT BELL.
      05  LINE 9   COLUMN 21 VALUE ' ENTER STREET ADDRESS '.
      05  LINE 9   COLUMN 43 PIC X(20) TO ADDRESS-OUT.
      05  LINE 12  COLUMN 21 VALUE ' ENTER CITY '.
      05  LINE 12  COLUMN 43 PIC X(20) TO CITY-OUT.
      05  LINE 15  COLUMN 21 VALUE ' ENTER STATE & ZIP'.
      05  LINE 15  COLUMN 43 PIC XX     TO STATE-OUT AUTO FULL.
      05  LINE 15  COLUMN 49 PIC X(5) TO ZIP-OUT AUTO FULL.
      05  LINE 18  COLUMN 21 VALUE ' ENTER CHECK AMOUNT '.
      05  LINE 18  COLUMN 43 PIC 9(5)V99 TO CHECK-AMOUNT-WS
                                         REQUIRED.
      05  LINE 22 COLUMN 22 REVERSE-VIDEO VALUE
                               'PRESS FUNCTION KEY FOR ALLOCATION'.
      05  LINE 23 COLUMN 27 REVERSE-VIDEO VALUE
                               'IF UNALLOCATED PRESS F6 '.
*****************************************************************
  01  TOTAL-SCREEN.
      05  BLANK SCREEN.
      05  LINE 2 COLUMN 4   REVERSE-VIDEO
                            VALUE 'REG. EXP.     MEDICAL      '.
      05  REVERSE-VIDEO
                    VALUE 'BUSINESS     TAXES        OTHER      '.
      05  REVERSE-VIDEO       VALUE  'UNALLOCATED'.
      05  LINE 4 COLUMN 3   PIC Z,ZZZ.99 FROM REG-TOT-WS.
      05          COLUMN 15  PIC Z,ZZZ.99 FROM MED-TOT-WS.
      05          COLUMN 27  PIC Z,ZZZ.99 FROM BUS-TOT-WS.
      05          COLUMN 39  PIC Z,ZZZ.99 FROM TAX-TOT-WS.
      05          COLUMN 51  PIC Z,ZZZ.99 FROM OTHER-TOT-WS.
      05          COLUMN 63  PIC Z,ZZZ.99 FROM UNALL-TOT-WS.
      05  LINE 6 COLUMN 15 REVERSE-VIDEO VALUE 'OPENING BALANCE'.
      05          COLUMN 39 REVERSE-VIDEO VALUE 'TOTAL WRITTEN'.
      05          COLUMN 58 REVERSE-VIDEO VALUE 'CLOSING BALANCE'.
      05  LINE 8 COLUMN 17  PIC $Z,ZZZ.99- FROM OPENING-BALANCE.
      05          COLUMN 40  PIC $Z,ZZZ.99  FROM TOT-WRITTEN-OUT.
      05          COLUMN 62  PIC $Z,ZZZ.99- FROM BALANCE.
      05  LINE 10 COLUMN 15 REVERSE-VIDEO VALUE 'NUMBER OF CHECKS'.
      05          COLUMN 45 REVERSE-VIDEO
                            VALUE 'NEXT CHECK NUMBER'.
      05  LINE 12 COLUMN 18 PIC Z,ZZZ FROM NUM-CHKS-WS.
      05          COLUMN 49 PIC ZZZZZ FROM CHECK-NO-WS.
*****************************************************************
```

**Fig. 8–3. Sample SCREEN SECTION from
program CH802M.COB.**

269

The SCREEN SECTION shown in Fig. 8–3 is used to initialize the program CH802M.COB, which is a check-writing program (a variation of a program introduced earlier). The PROCEDURE DIVISION entries for processing this data are shown in Fig. 8–4. These entries assume a computer system equipped with a monochrome screen.

The statement

```
DISPLAY INITIAL-SCREEN
```

causes the entire screen to be displayed as shown in Fig. 8–5.

The user follows the displayed instructions and the automatic positioning of the cursor to enter the data. After all the data has been entered as shown in Fig. 8–6, the remaining instructions in the paragraph INITIAL-ACCEPT will be executed.

The first entry of INITIAL-SCREEN is

```
05 BLANK SCREEN.
```

This entry is optional but is generally the first elementary item in a screen description, as it causes the previous contents of the screen to

```
***********************************************************************
INITIAL-ACCEPT.
     DISPLAY INITIAL-SCREEN.
     ACCEPT  INITIAL-SCREEN.
     IF PASSWORD NOT = VALID-PASSWORD
         DISPLAY (3, 1) ' NOT AUTHORIZED USER OF CHECKWRITE '
         STOP RUN.
     ACCEPT DATE-IN FROM DATE.
         MOVE YR-IN       TO YR-OUT.
         MOVE MO-IN       TO MO-OUT.
         MOVE DAY-IN      TO DAY-OUT.
     MOVE OPENING-BALANCE TO BALANCE.
***********************************************************************
CHECK-ACCEPT.
     DISPLAY CHECK-SCREEN.
     ACCEPT  CHECK-SCREEN ON ESCAPE  MOVE 01 TO STATUS-CODE
                                     GO TO CHECK-ACCEPT-EXIT.
     ACCEPT (15, 1) F-KEY WITH PROMPT.
     ACCEPT STATUS-CODE FROM ESCAPE KEY.
     PERFORM ALLOCATION-CHECK.
     MOVE CHECK-NO-WS       TO CHECK-NO-OUT.
     ADD 1                  TO NUM-CHKS-WS.
     SUBTRACT CHECK-AMOUNT-WS FROM BALANCE.
     MOVE CHECK-AMOUNT-WS TO CHECK-AMOUNT-OUT.
CHECK-ACCEPT-EXIT.
     EXIT.
***********************************************************************
```

Fig. 8–4. Sample DISPLAY and ACCEPT entries.

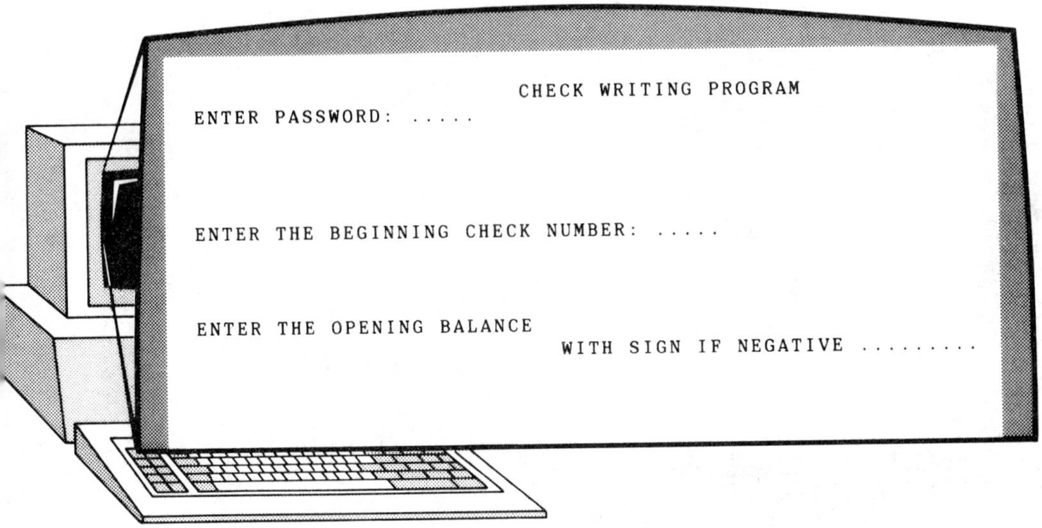

Fig. 8–5. Sample screen *before* any data entry.

be erased. Notice that this entry differs from the ERASE clause of the DISPLAY statement used previously. You should be prepared for these differences, since they occur quite often in the specifications for the SCREEN SECTION entries. These differences will be summarized in Fig. 8–7.

The second elementary item

```
05 LINE 1 COLUMN 25 VALUE 'CHECK WRITING PROGRAM'.
```

causes the title of the program to be displayed on the first line 25 spaces from the left, exactly where specified. Similarly, the entry

```
05 LINE 2 COLUMN 1 VALUE 'ENTER PASSWORD: '.
```

causes the prompt

```
ENTER PASSWORD: .....
```

to be displayed.

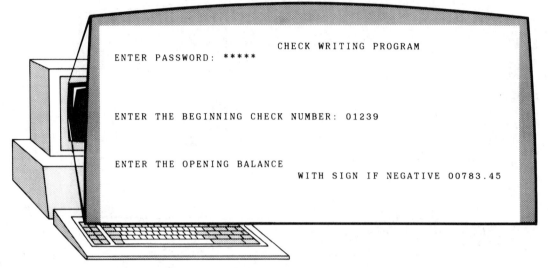

Fig. 8–6. Sample screen *after* data entry.

The entry

    05 PIC X(5)   TO PASSWORD SECURE.

causes the cursor to hold its position immediately after the previous
display, awaiting the entry of a five-position alphanumeric password
[PIC X(5)]. Once received, this data will be moved to the location specified (PASSWORD). However, in response to the specification SE-
CURE, five asterisks will be displayed. That is, after the password is
entered, the screen will show

    ENTER PASSWORD: *****

The next two entries execute similar operations for the beginning
check number and the opening balance. In both cases, however, the
data is echoed on the screen because no SECURE option was included
in either entry. The remainder of the paragraph INITIAL-ACCEPT
checks the validity of the password—if correct, the remaining initialization steps are executed; otherwise, the message

    NOT AUTHORIZED USER OF CHECKWRITE

is displayed and program execution halts.

SCREEN SECTION	ACCEPT ... DISPLAY
AUTO	AUTO-SKIP
BELL	BEEP
REQUIRED	EMPTY-CHECK
FULL	LENGTH-CHECK
SECURE	NO-ECHO
Not necessary—always on	PROMPT
JUSTIFIED	RIGHT-JUSTIFY
USING	UPDATE
	DISPLAY
BLANK SCREEN	ERASE

Fig. 8–7. Differences between SCREEN SECTION and ACCEPT ... DISPLAY.

Group Screen Description

As with other records, an 01 level is required for each screen that is to be defined. The name used in the DISPLAY screen-name and AC-CEPT screen-name must be the name of the 01 level.

```
01 INITIAL-SCREEN.
```

The group description can also have the entries AUTO, SECURE, REQUIRED, and FULL. These options will be described later. Their use in the group item ensures that the option specified will be effective for all elementary items in that group.

```
01 INPUT-AMOUNTS AUTO REQUIRED.
```

Elementary Screen Description

All elementary items must have level numbers corresponding to the same rules for the other sections of the DATA DIVISION.

The individual specifications are presented here in the same order as the general format.

The BLANK SCREEN Clause   The entire screen is erased when the DISPLAY screen-name is executed. This specification also causes the cursor to be positioned at the first line, first column—the home position. Nothing happens regarding this specification in an ACCEPT screen-name statement. If the FOREGROUND-COLOR or BACKGROUND-COLOR has been used previously, the color is returned to the default color.

```
05 BLANK SCREEN.
```

The LINE and LINE PLUS Clauses   This specification positions the cursor at a specific line on the screen. This specification is active only during an ACCEPT screen-name. If no LINE option is included, the cursor remains at the current line. This option will normally be used when entering data so that the screen may be appropriately formatted. If the LINE PLUS option is used, the cursor will be positioned at the appropriate number of lines from the current cursor position.

```
05 LINE 25.
05 LINE PLUS 5.
```

This will usually appear along with other entries.

The COLUMN Clause   If the LINE option is used without the COLUMN option, the cursor will be positioned at the first column on a line; if the COLUMN option is used alone, the cursor will be positioned at the appropriate column on the current line. After positioning by the LINE and COLUMN specifications, the cursor moves from left to right depending on the length of the data item. In the example shown here the word ENTER will begin at line 7, column 1; after the text is displayed, the cursor will be sitting at line 7, column 41.

```
05 LINE 7 COLUMN 1 VALUE 'ENTER THE BEGINNING CHECK NUMBER:
```

The COLUMN PLUS integer option may also be used here to move the cursor a specific number of positions to the right.

The BLANK LINE Clause   This causes the current line to be erased from the cursor position to the end of the line. This does *not* cause the cursor to be repositioned.

```
05 BLANK LINE.
```

The BELL Clause The speaker sounds during an ACCEPT screen-name when an elementary item is ready to accept data. Nothing happens during a DISPLAY screen-name for this option. The purpose of this feature is to get the user's attention when the program requires data input.

```
05 LINE 6 COLUMN 43 PIC X(20) TO NAME-OUT BELL.
```

The HIGHLIGHT Clause During the DISPLAY an elementary item containing this option will be shown in high intensity.

```
05 LINE 7 COLUMN 10 VALUE 'ENTER PASSWORD: ' HIGHLIGHT.
```

The BLINK Clause A DISPLAY item blinks on the screen when this option is specified.

```
05 LINE 1 COLUMN 25 VALUE 'CHECK WRITING PROGRAM ' BLINK.
```

The REVERSE-VIDEO Clause On a color monitor this option causes the foreground and background colors to be reversed. On a monochrome monitor the background and foreground are also reversed.

```
05 LINE 2 COLUMN 27 REVERSE-VIDEO
                    VALUE 'PRESS ESC TO END JOB '.
```

The UNDERLINE Clause This option works *only* on a mono-chrome monitor. It causes the data item to be underlined. It will be ignored on a color monitor.

```
05 LINE 6 COLUMN 21 VALUE ' ENTER NAME OF PAYEE '
                    UNDERLINE.
```

The FOREGROUND-COLOR Clause This option (and the BACKGROUND-COLOR option that follows) are available only on color monitors. The entry is followed by an integer in the range 0 to 15, according to the following table:

Range/Color	Range/Color
0 black	8 gray
1 blue	9 light blue
2 green	10 light green
3 cyan (greenish blue)	11 light cyan
4 red	12 light red
5 magenta (purplish red)	13 light magenta
6 brown	14 yellow
7 white	15 high-intensity white

The following entry will cause the background color to be white and the foreground (printing on the screen) to be red:

```
05 BLANK SCREEN BACKGROUND-COLOR 7 FOREGROUND-COLOR 4.
```

The BACKGROUND-COLOR Clause   This option, which specifies the color of the background, requires an integer in the range 0–7. If this option is not stated, the default is black. If the integers 8–15 are specified, they will cause the colors 0–7 to blink.

```
05 BLANK SCREEN BACKGROUND-COLOR 1 FOREGROUND-COLOR 14.
```

This entry would cause yellow letters to be displayed on a blue background. Note that this entry should be put on a line with some other entry in order for it to work.

In our sample program (CH802C.COB), which is also on the supplemental disk, we have provided for those options that are unique to color screens. The following entries have been changed in order to provide color:

```
01   INITIAL-SCREEN.
     05   BLANK SCREEN   BACKGROUND-COLOR 1 FOREGROUND-COLOR 14.
                      .
                      .
                      .

01   CHECK SCREEN.
     05   BLANK SCREEN   BACKGROUND-COLOR 1 FOREGROUND-COLOR 14.
                      .
                      .
                      .
```

```
01   TOTAL-SCREEN.
     05   BLANK SCREEN   BACKGROUND-COLOR 7 FOREGROUND-COLOR 4.
                              .
                              .
                              .

01   OVERDRAW-SCREEN.
     05   BLANK SCREEN   BACKGROUND-COLOR 4 FOREGROUND-COLOR 15.
                              .
                              .
                              .
```

> *A color version of this program is CH802C.COB on the supplemental disk.*

The VALUE IS Clause   The literal following this specification will be displayed on the screen when referenced by a DISPLAY screen-name. The literal is treated as alphanumeric and must be enclosed in quotes. A PICTURE clause cannot be associated with this statement. This screen item is ignored by the ACCEPT statement.

```
05 LINE 9 COLUMN 21 VALUE ' ENTER STREET ADDRESS '.
```

The PICTURE Clause   This entry specifies the format in which data are to be shown on the screen. The rules for this PICTURE are the same as those for any PICTURE clause in working storage. When used in conjunction with a DISPLAY and the attributes FROM or USING are added, the data take on the pattern indicated by the PICTURE before being displayed on the screen.
   The entries:

```
05 LINE 9 COLUMN 21 VALUE ' ENTER STREET ADDRESS '.
05 LINE 9 COLUMN 43 PIC X(20) TO ADDRESS-OUT.
```

cause the following to appear on the screen:

```
ENTER STREET ADDRESS ....................
```

When used with the ACCEPT, the contents of the field being entered are shown on the screen conforming to the PICTURE of the screen item. In this case 20 periods are shown on the screen in accordance with the PIC X(20).

The FROM, TO, and USING Clauses

When these are added to the description of a screen item, they implicitly provide the necessary moves to or from the named areas in the FILE, WORKING-STORAGE, or LINKAGE SECTIONs. During a DISPLAY the data contained in the field specified by a FROM or USING are moved to the screen item and displayed on the screen.

The TO specification identifies the data item to which data that has been entered during an ACCEPT screen-name are to be moved. The TO is effective only during an ACCEPT, the USING during both the DISPLAY and ACCEPT, and the FROM effective only during a DISPLAY screen-name.

The clause TO ADDRESS-OUT causes the data entered in response to the prompt to be moved to that location.

The statements

```
05   LINE 6 COLUMN 15 REVERSE-VIDEO VALUE 'OPENING BALANCE'.
05           COLUMN 39 REVERSE-VIDEO VALUE 'TOTAL WRITTEN'.
05           COLUMN 58 REVERSE-VIDEO VALUE 'CLOSING BALANCE'.
05   LINE 8 COLUMN 17 PIC $Z,ZZZ.99- FROM OPENING-BALANCE.
05           COLUMN 40 PIC $Z,ZZZ.99 FROM TOT-WRITTEN-OUT.
05           COLUMN 62 PIC $Z,ZZZ.99- FROM BALANCE.
```

cause the following to appear:

```
OPENING BALANCE    TOTAL WRITTEN      CLOSING BALANCE

    $1,125.50        $   225.00         $   900.50
```

The value from the opening balance, total dollar amount of the checks written, and the closing balance are all taken from the working storage areas and displayed on the screen according to the PICs specified.

The USING is provided in place of the UPDATE specification in the Format 3 ACCEPT. Its purpose is to provide the ability to first display the data during the DISPLAY operation, then to allow for changes in the data and have it returned to the original location by the ACCEPT screen-name statement.

The BLANK WHEN ZERO Clause

This option has the same effect as it does when used to format printed output. If the contents of the screen item is zeros, the screen will show spaces.

The JUSTIFIED or JUST Clause   The contents of the entered screen item will be placed at the right side of the area specified on the screen. When moved to a data item in another area of storage, however, the data are left justified as in a normal MOVE.

The AUTO Clause   When this option is used, the cursor automatically skips to the next item when the field is filled. This entry saves the operator from pressing the return key. It is normally used with fields that are always full, such as zip code, date, etc. It is functional only during an ACCEPT.

```
05  LINE 15 COLUMN 43 PIC XX    TO STATE-OUT AUTO FULL.
```

In this case there is a required two-letter state abbreviation called for. Since the two letters will always be present, there is no need for the operator to press the enter key; the AUTO specification causes the entry to be accepted automatically after the second letter is entered.

The SECURE Clause   During an ACCEPT this option causes the data being entered to be echoed by an asterisk (*) rather than having the actual data visible. In the sample program for writing checks (CH802M.COB and CH802C.COB), we have used this option to protect the password from being viewed by someone watching the user.

```
05 PIC X(5)          TO PASSWORD SECURE  .
```

The REQUIRED Clause   This option specifies that at least one character must be entered before the return or other terminator is accepted. It does not ensure the accuracy of data, but ensures only that some data has been entered.

```
05  LINE 18 COLUMN 43 PIC 9(5)V99 TO CHECK-AMOUNT-WS
                                  REQUIRED.
```

In this case the check amount must be present in a check-writing program, and this entry ensures that it is.

The FULL Clause   The previous option required at least one character; this option requires that the screen item be completely filled with data before the return is accepted. Items like the zip code or date mentioned above would be likely candidates for this option.

```
05  LINE 15 COLUMN 49  PIC X(5) TO ZIP-OUT AUTO FULL.
```

This entry makes sure that the zip code field is completely filled, since a zip of less than five characters would not be correct.

Customizing Screens

While COBOL is admittedly not a language suitable to executing graphics, it is possible to use some of its features to enhance the appearance of the screens.

One method is to combine the features of the SCREEN SECTION with those of the other uses of DISPLAY to draw some lines around the screen entries. We have done this in our sample program by adding several statements and routines so that the CHECK-SCREEN will appear as shown in Fig. 8–8:

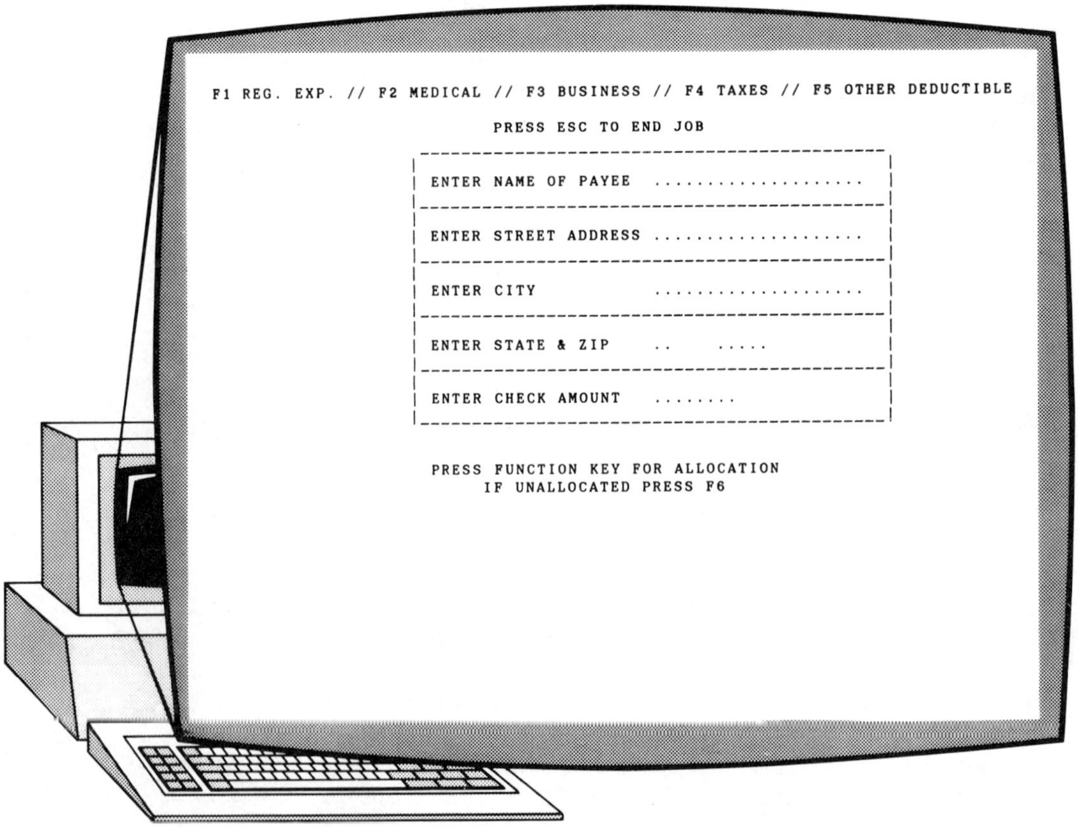

```
F1 REG. EXP. // F2 MEDICAL // F3 BUSINESS // F4 TAXES // F5 OTHER DEDUCTIBLE

                          PRESS ESC TO END JOB

       --------------------------------------------------------
       |                                                      |
       | ENTER NAME OF PAYEE    ...................           |
       |                                                      |
       --------------------------------------------------------
       |                                                      |
       | ENTER STREET ADDRESS ...................             |
       |                                                      |
       --------------------------------------------------------
       |                                                      |
       | ENTER CITY            ...................            |
       |                                                      |
       --------------------------------------------------------
       |                                                      |
       | ENTER STATE & ZIP      ..    .....                   |
       |                                                      |
       --------------------------------------------------------
       |                                                      |
       | ENTER CHECK AMOUNT     ........                      |
       --------------------------------------------------------

                PRESS FUNCTION KEY FOR ALLOCATION
                    IF UNALLOCATED PRESS F6
```

Fig. 8–8. CHECK-SCREEN with borders.

These lines were executed by the following routine:

```
OUTLINE.
    PERFORM ST-LINE VARYING LIN FROM 4 BY 3 UNTIL LIN
                    > 20.
    PERFORM VERT-LINE VARYING LIN FROM 5 BY 1 UNTIL
                    LIN > 19.
ST-LINE.
    DISPLAY (LIN, 21) LONG-LINE.
VERT-LINE.
    DISPLAY (LIN, 20) '¦'.
    DISPLAY (LIN, 65) '¦'.
```

The routine was inserted into the program CH802M.COB or CH802C.COB. The reserved words LIN and COL refer to the line and column placement of the cursor and may be manipulated just as any other numeric integer data item. The PERFORM...VARYING was used to place a horizontal line (defined in working storage):

```
05 LONG-LINE          PIC X(44) VALUE ALL '_'.
```

at six places on the screen, as shown in the routine ST-LINE.

The vertical lines were displayed by the routine VERT-LINE in which the line (LIN) was varied from 5 through 19 and the column remained constant at positions 20 and 65. The vertical line symbol (¦), which is over the backslash (\) on the keyboard, was used for this character.

This routine was executed from the CHECK-ACCEPT routine by inserting the statement.

```
PERFORM OUTLINE.
```

after DISPLAYing the CHECK-SCREEN. Note that using the DISPLAY (LIN, COL) statement after the DISPLAY screen-name statement is workable as long as no characters are positioned in the same screen positions.

The preparation of this screen may be aided by the use of a CRT display layout form similar to that shown in Fig. 8–9.

A version of this program with the lines drawn as above is CH802S.COB on the supplemental disk.

The complete program for CHECKWRITE-2 is shown in Fig. 8–10.

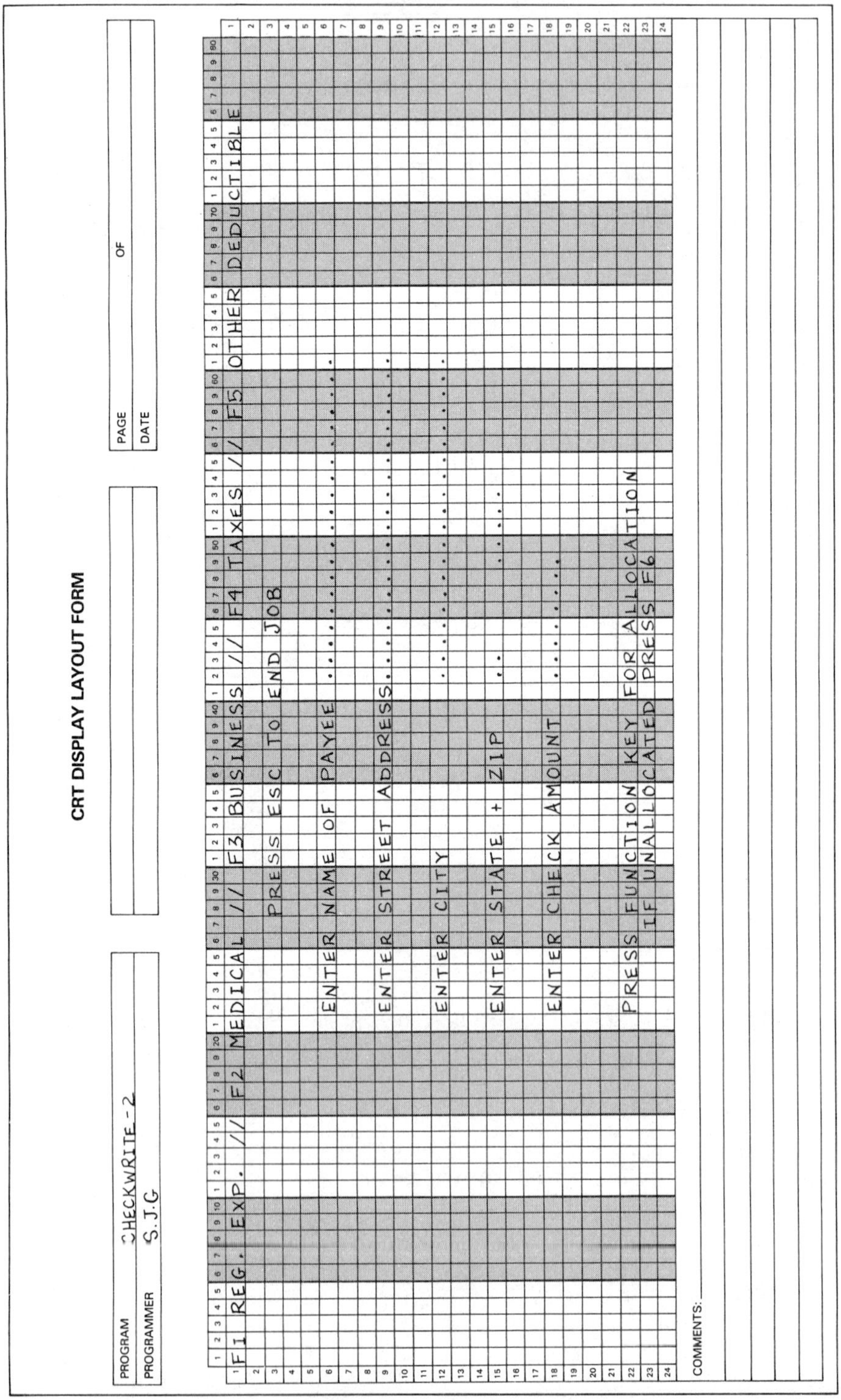

CRT DISPLAY LAYOUT FORM

PROGRAM   CHECKWRITE-2
PROGRAMMER   S.J.G

```
F1 REG. EXP. // F2 MEDICAL // F3 BUSINESS // F4 TAXES // F5 OTHER DEDUCTIBLE

PRESS ESC TO END JOB

ENTER NAME OF PAYEE  . . . . .

ENTER STREET ADDRESS . . . . .

ENTER CITY

ENTER STATE + ZIP  . .  . .

ENTER CHECK AMOUNT  . . . . . . .

PRESS FUNCTION KEY FOR ALLOCATION
IF UNALLOCATED PRESS F6
```

COMMENTS: _____

Fig. 8–9.   CRT layout for CHECK-SCREEN.

```
****************************************************************
IDENTIFICATION DIVISION.
****************************************************************
PROGRAM-ID.
    CHECKWRITE-2.
AUTHOR.
    S.J.GAUGHRAN.
INSTALLATION.
    PERSONAL COMPUTER SYSTEM.
DATE-WRITTEN.
    AUG. 2, 1984.
SECURITY.
    PASSWORD PROTECTED.
****************************************************************
* This program writes checks, keeps a running balance and allows *
* the user to allocate the expenditures to several categories. *
* It includes automatic date insertion and incrementing of check *
* numbers. At the end totals are printed for the account balance,*
* and the allocated categories. Data entry to the program is   *
* through the keyboard with output to both the screen and the  *
* printer. THIS VERSION IS FOR MONOCHROME SCREENS.            *
****************************************************************
ENVIRONMENT DIVISION.
****************************************************************
CONFIGURATION SECTION.
SOURCE-COMPUTER.
    IBM-PERSONAL-COMPUTER.
OBJECT-COMPUTER.
    IBM-PERSONAL-COMPUTER.
INPUT-OUTPUT SECTION.
FILE-CONTROL.
    SELECT PRINTFILE ASSIGN TO PRINTER.
****************************************************************
DATA DIVISION.
****************************************************************
FILE SECTION.
FD  PRINTFILE
    LABEL RECORDS ARE OMITTED.
01  PRINT-REC            PIC X(133).
****************************************************************
WORKING-STORAGE SECTION.
01  WORKAREAS.
    05  STATUS-CODE      PIC 99    VALUE ZERO.
    05  CITY-WS          PIC X(20).
    05  STATE-WS         PIC XX.
    05  ZIP-WS           PIC X(5).
    05  PASSWORD         PIC X(5).
    05  VALID-PASSWORD   PIC X(5)  VALUE 'STEVO'.
    05  F-KEY            PIC X.
    05  DATE-IN.
        10 YR-IN   PIC 99.
        10 MO-IN   PIC 99.
        10 DAY-IN  PIC 99.
****************************************************************
01  ACCUMULATORS   COMP-3.
    05  OPENING-BALANCE  PIC S9(5)V99.
    05  BALANCE          PIC S9(5)V99.
    05  CLOSE-BAL-OUT    PIC $Z,ZZZ.99-.
    05  CHECK-AMOUNT-WS  PIC S9(5)V99.
    05  CHECK-NO-WS      PIC S9(5).
    05  NUM-CHKS-WS      PIC S9(5)    VALUE ZERO.
    05  REG-TOT-WS       PIC S9(5)V99 VALUE ZERO.
    05  MED-TOT-WS       PIC S9(5)V99 VALUE ZERO.
    05  BUS-TOT-WS       PIC S9(5)V99 VALUE ZERO.
    05  TAX-TOT-WS       PIC S9(5)V99 VALUE ZERO.
    05  OTHER-TOT-WS     PIC S9(5)V99 VALUE ZERO.
    05  UNALL-TOT-WS     PIC S9(5)V99 VALUE ZERO.
    05  TOT-WRITTEN-OUT  PIC S9(5)V99 VALUE ZERO.
****************************************************************
01  HDR-1.
    05  FILLER           PIC X(28) VALUE SPACES.
    05  FILLER           PIC X(17) VALUE 'THE F & G COMPANY'.
```

Fig. 8–10. Complete program CHECKWRITE-2.

```
***************************************************************
01  HDR-2.
    05  FILLER              PIC X(28) VALUE SPACES.
    05  FILLER              PIC X(16) VALUE 'GARDEN CITY, NY'.
***************************************************************
01  LINE-1.
    05  FILLER              PIC X(05) VALUE SPACES.
    05  FILLER              PIC X(10) VALUE 'CHECK NO. '.
    05  CHECK-NO-OUT        PIC Z(06).
    05  FILLER              PIC X(44) VALUE SPACES.
    05  FILLER              PIC X(06) VALUE 'DATE  '.
    05  DATE-OUT.
        10  MO-OUT  PIC 99.
        10  FILLER  PIC X  VALUE '/'.
        10  DAY-OUT PIC 99.
        10  FILLER  PIC X  VALUE '/'.
        10  YR-OUT  PIC 99.
***************************************************************
01  LINE-2.
    05  FILLER              PIC X(05) VALUE SPACES.
    05  FILLER              PIC X(20) VALUE
                'PAY TO THE ORDER OF '.
    05  NAME-OUT            PIC X(20).
    05  FILLER              PIC X(17) VALUE SPACES.
    05  FILLER              PIC X(09) VALUE 'EXACTLY  '.
    05  CHECK-AMOUNT-OUT PIC **,***.99.
***************************************************************
01  LINE-3.
    05  FILLER              PIC X(25) VALUE SPACES.
    05  ADDRESS-OUT         PIC X(20).
***************************************************************
01  LINE-4.
    05  FILLER              PIC X(25) VALUE SPACES.
    05  CITY-OUT            PIC X(20).
    05  FILLER              PIC XX    VALUE SPACES.
    05  STATE-OUT           PIC X(02).
    05  FILLER              PIC X(02) VALUE SPACES.
    05  ZIP-OUT             PIC X(05).
***************************************************************
01  LINE-5.
    05  FILLER              PIC X(05) VALUE SPACES.
    05  FILLER              PIC X(18) VALUE
                'LAST NATIONAL BANK'.
***************************************************************
01  LINE-6.
    05  FILLER              PIC X(05) VALUE SPACES.
    05  FILLER              PIC X(16) VALUE
                'SEAFORD,NY 11783'.
***************************************************************
01  DASHES.
    05  FILLER              PIC X(79) VALUE ALL '_'.
***************************************************************
SCREEN SECTION.
***************************************************************
01  INITIAL-SCREEN.
    05  BLANK SCREEN.
    05  LINE 1 COLUMN 25 VALUE 'CHECK WRITING PROGRAM' BLINK.
    05  LINE 2 COLUMN 1  VALUE 'ENTER PASSWORD: ' HIGHLIGHT.
    05  PIC X(5)            TO PASSWORD SECURE  .
    05  LINE 7 COLUMN 1
                    VALUE 'ENTER THE BEGINNING CHECK NUMBER: '.
    05  PIC 9(5)           TO CHECK-NO-WS  .
    05  LINE 11 COLUMN 1  VALUE 'ENTER THE OPENING BALANCE '.
    05  LINE 12 COLUMN 27 VALUE ' WITH SIGN IF NEGATIVE '.
    05  PIC  99999.99-   TO OPENING-BALANCE.
***************************************************************
01  CHECK-SCREEN.
    05  BLANK SCREEN.
    05  LINE 1  COLUMN 1  REVERSE-VIDEO
                        VALUE 'F1 REG. EXP. // F2 MEDICAL //'.
    05  LINE 1  COLUMN 30 REVERSE-VIDEO
                        VALUE ' F3 BUSINESS // F4 TAXES // '.
    05  LINE 1  COLUMN 58 REVERSE-VIDEO
                        VALUE 'F5 OTHER DEDUCTIBLE '.
```

Fig. 8–10. (*continued*)

```
        05  LINE 3  COLUMN 27 REVERSE-VIDEO
                          VALUE ' PRESS ESC TO END JOB '.
        05  LINE 6  COLUMN 21 VALUE ' ENTER NAME OF PAYEE '
                                        UNDERLINE.
        05  LINE 6  COLUMN 43 PIC X(20) TO NAME-OUT BELL.
        05  LINE 9  COLUMN 21 VALUE ' ENTER STREET ADDRESS '.
        05  LINE 9  COLUMN 43 PIC X(20) TO ADDRESS-OUT.
        05  LINE 12 COLUMN 21 VALUE ' ENTER CITY '.
        05  LINE 12 COLUMN 43 PIC X(20) TO CITY-OUT.
        05  LINE 15 COLUMN 21 VALUE ' ENTER STATE & ZIP'.
        05  LINE 15 COLUMN 43 PIC XX    TO STATE-OUT AUTO FULL.
        05  LINE 15 COLUMN 49 PIC X(5) TO ZIP-OUT AUTO FULL.
        05  LINE 18 COLUMN 21 VALUE ' ENTER CHECK AMOUNT '.
        05  LINE 18 COLUMN 43 PIC 9(5)V99 TO CHECK-AMOUNT-WS
                                        REQUIRED.
        05  LINE 22 COLUMN 22 REVERSE-VIDEO VALUE
                          'PRESS FUNCTION KEY FOR ALLOCATION'.
        05  LINE 23 COLUMN 27 REVERSE-VIDEO VALUE
                          'IF UNALLOCATED PRESS F6 '.
*******************************************************************
01  TOTAL-SCREEN.
    05  BLANK SCREEN.
    05  LINE 2 COLUMN 4   REVERSE-VIDEO
                          VALUE 'REG. EXP.    MEDICAL      '.
    05  REVERSE-VIDEO
                  VALUE 'BUSINESS      TAXES        OTHER    '.
    05  REVERSE-VIDEO    VALUE 'UNALLOCATED'.
    05  LINE 4 COLUMN 3   PIC Z,ZZZ.99 FROM REG-TOT-WS.
    05          COLUMN 15  PIC Z,ZZZ.99 FROM MED-TOT-WS.
    05          COLUMN 27  PIC Z,ZZZ.99 FROM BUS-TOT-WS.
    05          COLUMN 39  PIC Z,ZZZ.99 FROM TAX-TOT-WS.
    05          COLUMN 51  PIC Z,ZZZ.99 FROM OTHER-TOT-WS.
    05          COLUMN 63  PIC Z,ZZZ.99 FROM UNALL-TOT-WS.
    05  LINE 6 COLUMN 15 REVERSE-VIDEO VALUE 'OPENING BALANCE'.
    05          COLUMN 39 REVERSE-VIDEO VALUE 'TOTAL WRITTEN'.
    05          COLUMN 58 REVERSE-VIDEO VALUE 'CLOSING BALANCE'.
    05  LINE 8 COLUMN 17  PIC $Z,ZZZ.99- FROM OPENING-BALANCE.
    05          COLUMN 40  PIC $Z,ZZZ.99  FROM TOT-WRITTEN-OUT.
    05          COLUMN 62  PIC $Z,ZZZ.99- FROM BALANCE.
    05  LINE 10 COLUMN 15 REVERSE-VIDEO VALUE 'NUMBER OF CHECKS'.
    05          COLUMN 45 REVERSE-VIDEO
                          VALUE 'NEXT CHECK NUMBER'.
    05  LINE 12 COLUMN 18 PIC Z,ZZZ FROM NUM-CHKS-WS.
    05          COLUMN 49 PIC ZZZZZ FROM CHECK-NO-WS.
*******************************************************************
PROCEDURE DIVISION.
*******************************************************************
BEGIN.
    OPEN OUTPUT PRINTFILE.
    MOVE SPACES TO PRINT-REC.
    WRITE PRINT-REC AFTER ADVANCING PAGE.
    PERFORM INITIAL-ACCEPT.
    PERFORM CHECK-ACCEPT THRU CHECK-ACCEPT-EXIT.
    PERFORM LOOP-RTN UNTIL STATUS-CODE = 01.
    PERFORM TOTAL-RTN.
    CLOSE PRINTFILE.
    STOP RUN.
*******************************************************************
LOOP-RTN.
    WRITE PRINT-REC FROM HDR-1
        AFTER ADVANCING 5 LINES.
    WRITE PRINT-REC FROM HDR-2
        AFTER ADVANCING 1 LINE.
    WRITE PRINT-REC FROM LINE-1
        AFTER ADVANCING 1 LINE.
    WRITE PRINT-REC FROM LINE-2
        AFTER ADVANCING 2 LINES.
    WRITE PRINT-REC FROM LINE-3
        AFTER ADVANCING 2 LINES.
    WRITE PRINT-REC FROM LINE-4
        AFTER ADVANCING 2 LINES.
    WRITE PRINT-REC FROM LINE-5
        AFTER ADVANCING 2 LINES.
```

Fig. 8–10. (*continued*)

```
      WRITE PRINT-REC FROM LINE-6
          AFTER ADVANCING 3 LINES.
      ADD  1        TO CHECK-NO-WS.
      WRITE PRINT-REC FROM DASHES
          AFTER ADVANCING 2 LINES.
      MOVE SPACES TO LINE-3
                     LINE-4.
      PERFORM CHECK-ACCEPT THRU CHECK-ACCEPT-EXIT.
******************************************************************
 INITIAL-ACCEPT.
      DISPLAY INITIAL-SCREEN.
      ACCEPT  INITIAL-SCREEN.
      IF PASSWORD NOT = VALID-PASSWORD
          DISPLAY (3, 1) ' NOT AUTHORIZED USER OF CHECKWRITE '
          STOP RUN.
      ACCEPT DATE-IN FROM DATE.
          MOVE YR-IN       TO YR-OUT.
          MOVE MO-IN       TO MO-OUT.
          MOVE DAY-IN      TO DAY-OUT.
      MOVE OPENING-BALANCE TO BALANCE.
******************************************************************
 CHECK-ACCEPT.
      DISPLAY CHECK-SCREEN.
      ACCEPT  CHECK-SCREEN ON ESCAPE   MOVE 01 TO STATUS-CODE
                                GO TO CHECK-ACCEPT-EXIT.
      ACCEPT (15, 1) F-KEY WITH PROMPT.
      ACCEPT STATUS-CODE FROM ESCAPE KEY.
      PERFORM ALLOCATION-CHECK.
      MOVE CHECK-NO-WS      TO CHECK-NO-OUT.
      ADD 1                 TO NUM-CHKS-WS.
      SUBTRACT CHECK-AMOUNT-WS FROM BALANCE.
      MOVE CHECK-AMOUNT-WS TO CHECK-AMOUNT-OUT.
 CHECK-ACCEPT-EXIT.
      EXIT.
******************************************************************
 ALLOCATION-CHECK.
      IF STATUS-CODE  =  02
                          ADD CHECK-AMOUNT-WS TO REG-TOT-WS
      ELSE  IF STATUS-CODE = 03
                          ADD CHECK-AMOUNT-WS TO MED-TOT-WS
          ELSE IF STATUS-CODE  =  04
                          ADD CHECK-AMOUNT-WS TO BUS-TOT-WS
            ELSE IF STATUS-CODE   =  05
                          ADD CHECK-AMOUNT-WS TO TAX-TOT-WS
              ELSE IF STATUS-CODE  =  06
                          ADD CHECK-AMOUNT-WS TO OTHER-TOT-WS
               ELSE IF STATUS-CODE = 07
                          ADD CHECK-AMOUNT-WS TO UNALL-TOT-WS.
******************************************************************
 TOTAL-RTN.
      SUBTRACT BALANCE     FROM OPENING-BALANCE
              GIVING TOT-WRITTEN-OUT.
      MOVE BALANCE         TO CLOSE-BAL-OUT.
      DISPLAY TOTAL-SCREEN.
      IF BALANCE IS NEGATIVE
          DISPLAY (18, 10) ' GET TO THE BANK, QUICKLY !! '
          DISPLAY (20, 10) ' YOUR BALANCE IS   ' CLOSE-BAL-OUT.
******************************************************************
```

Fig. 8-10. *(continued)*

> *The program CHECKWRITE-2 is available as CH802M.COB on the supplemental disk.*

EXERCISES

1. Using any of the programs you have completed for the preceding chapters, insert the necessary statements to run the program in the DEBUGGING MODE. Use the TRACE and EXHIBIT statements. Run the program with and without the DEBUGGING MODE clause in the SOURCE-COMPUTER entry.

   Note: In the following two exercises the output file will have to be defined in the SELECT as ACCESS MODE IS SEQUENTIAL rather than the previously used LINE SEQUENTIAL. The two programs from previous chapters that read these files will also have to be altered in the same manner.

2. Exercise 4 in Chapter 5 is a Vehicle Fuel Report. The program assumes that an input file has already been created. Write a program using the screen layouts shown to create the data record MILEAGE-DATA. Use the DISPLAY and ACCEPT screen. (See screen layouts shown below and on page 288.)

Output Layout

MILEAGE-DATA						
VEHICLE NUMBER	MAKE	YEAR	ODOMETER INITIAL READING	ODOMETER FINAL READING	GAL USED	COST PER GAL
1 1 1 1		1 1 1 1 1 1	2 2 2 2 2 2	2 2 2	3 3 3 3	
1 2 3 4	5 6 7 8 9 0 1	2 3 4 5 6 7 8 9	0 1 2 3 4 5	6 7 8 9	0 1 2 3	

CRT DISPLAY LAYOUT FORM

PROGRAM CREATE MILEAGE - DATA

PROGRAMMER S.J.G.

PAGE 1 OF 1

DATE 9/21/XX

```
            VEHICLE DATA

    VEHICLE NUMBER  0000

    VEHICLE MAKE            YEAR 00

    INITIAL ODOMETER  000000
    FINAL   ODOMETER  000000
          NEGATIVE MILEAGE - RE-ENTER
    GALLONS USED  000.0
    COST PER GAL  0.000
```

COMMENTS:

LINE 15 IS DISPLAYED IF FINAL ODOMETER ENTRY
IS LESS THAN INITIAL ENTRY. MESSAGE SHOULD
APPEAR IN REVERSE VIDEO.

288

3. Exercise 3 in Chapter 6 is a report summarizing the courses taken by each student during a semester. Write the necessary input program to create these records using the screen layouts shown below and on page 290. If the student number and name are the same for several entries, have these two items repeated in the record without having the user type in the repetitive information. Use the DISPLAY and ACCEPT screen.

Output Layout

STUDENT-REC							
STUDENT NUMBER	STUDENT NAME	COURSE NUMBER		COURSE TITLE	CREDIT	GRADE
		DEPT	NUMB			
	1 1 1 1 1 1 1 1 1 1 2 2 2 2 2 2 2 2 2 2 3 3 3	3 3 3 3 3 3 4 4 4 4 4 4 4 4 4 4 5 5	5 5 5 5 5
1 2 3 4 5 6 7 8 9	0 1 2 3 4 5 6 7 8 9 0 1 2 3 4 5 6 7	8 9 0	1 2 3	4 5 6 7 8 9 0 1 2 3 4 5 6 7 8 9 0 1	2 3	4 5 6

CRT DISPLAY LAYOUT FORM

```
STUDENT COURSE DATA

STUDENT NUMBER  000000000

STUDENT NAME    ...........

COURSE NUMBER
      DEPT ....    NUMBER ......

COURSE TITLE ..............

CREDITS 00

GRADE ...
```

COMMENTS:

9

TABLE HANDLING

Previous chapters have introduced the basic instructions to enable a programmer to ACCEPT and DISPLAY data, READ a file, arithmetically and logically manipulate the data read, and write an output record.

This chapter introduces the use of tables in the COBOL language. A **table** can be defined as a collection or arrangement of data in a fixed form for ready reference. Such data include tax tables, interest tables, insurance rate tables, and so on. Figure 9–1 illustrates a hypothetical table of postal rates.

The cost of sending a package can be found in the second column of this table by choosing a rate in the first column that is closest to, but not less than, the weight of the package. Each weight-cost combination is referred to as an **element** of the table and consists of a **variable** (in this case, the weight of the package) and a **value** (in this case, the cost of mailing the package). The table itself is referred to as a **one-level table**: for a given element of the table the value is determined by one variable—the weight in pounds. It is also possible to define and process two- and three-level tables in a COBOL program. Figure 9–2 illustrates a two-level table. In this table, the value of an element is determined by two variables: the weight of the package and the class of mail by which the package is to be shipped.

ONE-LEVEL POSTAL RATE TABLE

Weight (in pounds)	Rate
1	$ .75
2	.75
3	.75
4	.80
5	.80
6	.85
7	.85
8	.90
9	.95
10	1.00
11	1.10
12	1.20
13	1.30
14	1.50
15	1.75

Fig. 9–1.   Hypothetical one-level postal rate table.

DEFINING A TABLE IN STORAGE

Assume that the table illustrated in Fig. 9–1 is to be defined in the computer program. Tables may be defined in either the FILE SECTION or the WORKING-STORAGE SECTION. Typically they are defined in the WORKING-STORAGE SECTION. As is the case in previous data definitions, the table must be defined within an 01 level and a data-name assigned to the table. The data-name assigned at the 01 level does not allow reference to the elements of the table but only to the table as a whole. Each element in this table is described with a level number from 02 to 49, a data-name, and a corresponding PICTURE clause. The actual number of elements in the table is specified by an OCCURS clause.

TWO-LEVEL POSTAL RATE TABLE

Weight (in pounds)	RATE		
	First Class	**Second Class**	**Third Class**
1	$1.05	$ .90	$ .75
2	1.15	.95	.75
3	1.30	1.00	.75
4	1.55	1.10	.80
5	1.80	1.20	.80
6	2.05	1.35	.85
7	2.45	1.50	.85
8	2.85	1.65	.90
9	3.35	1.80	.95
10	3.95	2.00	1.00
11	4.70	2.20	1.10
12	5.60	2.40	1.20
13	6.85	2.60	1.30
14	8.25	2.80	1.50
15	9.75	3.00	1.75

Fig. 9–2. Hypothetical two-level postal rate table.

THE OCCURS CLAUSE

There are two formats of the OCCURS clause, but only one is considered at this time. The first general format of the OCCURS clause is as follows:

GENERAL FORMAT 1

OCCURS integer TIMES

This clause may be used to describe any data-name *except* one on an 01 or 77 level. **Integer-1** in this clause refers to the number of times a field or group of fields is repeated. The lowest value is, of course, 1. The maximum number of elements is 1023.

For the one-level table, assume that the table is to be called POSTAL-RATE-TABLE and that each element within the table is to be referred to by the data-name RATE. The WORKING-STORAGE SECTION entries would be as follows:

```
WORKING-STORAGE SECTION.
01  POSTAL-RATE-TABLE.
    05  RATE     PIC S9V99  OCCURS 15 TIMES.
```

Fifteen fields are established in storage, each with the PICTURE S9V99. If the values stored in the table are to be used in subsequent computation the USAGE may be specified as COMPUTATIONAL-3 or COMP-3. It is also possible to use the OCCURS clause with a group item. For example, if RATE had been divided into DOLLAR-AMT and CENT-AMT, the WORKING-STORAGE SECTION entries would have been the following:

```
WORKING-STORAGE SECTION.
01  POSTAL-RATE-TABLE.
    05  RATE      OCCURS 15 TIMES.
        10  DOLLAR-AMT    PIC S9.
        10  CENT-AMT      PIC SV99.
```

However, a specific value for each element has not yet been placed in the table. Assume that these values are contained in a file on the disk, one input record per element in the table. Each record contains a weight (variable) in positions 1 and 2 and a mailing cost (value) in positions 3 to 5 for a specific element. It is necessary to read each record and move the value of the element to the appropriate position in the table. For this reason, each element within the table must be uniquely addressable. This is accomplished by a process known as **subscripting**.

SUBSCRIPTING

Subscripting is used to identify and access individual elements within a table. Whenever an OCCURS clause is used within the DATA DIVISION of a COBOL program, a **subscript** must be used to identify individual elements within the table. In the table illustrated in Fig. 9–1, the first value in the table may be defined as RATE (1), the second element as RATE (2), the third as RATE (3), etc., for each value in the table. In each of these cases the number contained within the parentheses is the subscript. Thus, a subscript is a numeric value that can be used to uniquely identify an element within a table. The fourth element in the table described above would be referred to as

```
RATE (4)
```

where RATE is the 05-level data-name and (4) is the subscript. This subscript directs the computer to the fourth element of POSTAL-RATE-TABLE. Similarly, the statement

```
ADD INVOICE-AMOUNT  RATE (7) GIVING COST-TOTAL.
```

would cause the value of the seventh item in POSTAL-RATE-TABLE to be added to INVOICE-AMOUNT and the result stored in COST-TOTAL.

It is also possible to use a data-name as a subscript. For example, if when executed, the data item SUBSCPT-WEIGHT contained the value 7, the statement

```
ADD INVOICE-AMOUNT RATE (SUBSCPT-WEIGHT) GIVING COST-TOTAL.
```

would have the same effect as the previous statement.

The following rules cover the use of subscripts:

1. The subscript must be either a numeric literal greater than zero and less than 1024 or a data-name that contains an integral value greater than zero and less than 1024.

2. The subscript must be enclosed in parentheses and appear to the right of the data-name to which it applies. The subscript must be separated from this data-name by at least one space
    [e.g., RATE (SUBSCPT-WEIGHT)].

3. A subscript may not itself be subscripted.

4. A subscripted data-name must be unique.

5. Any item that has an OCCURS clause or that is subordinate to an item that has an OCCURS clause must have a subscript when referenced. A subscript **may not** be used with an item that is not described with an OCCURS clause.

6. If more than one level of subscript is present, the individual subscripts within the parentheses must be separated by a *comma* and a space [e.g., RATE (CLASS, MAIL, SUBSCPT-WEIGHT)]. Note that this comma is an exception to the authors' practice of not using commas in our program since they are normally not needed in COBOL statements. No more than three levels of subscripts may be used.

A SIMPLE PROGRAM TO CREATE AND REFERENCE A TABLE

Now the actual values of the elements may be placed in POSTAL-RATE-TABLE. These values are being input, one element of the table per record. Figure 9–3 lists a program that establishes the POSTAL-RATE-TABLE shown in Fig. 9–1, uses the table, and prints out the total cost of each article to be sent. Total cost consists of the cost of the items purchased (to be read in) and the cost of mailing the items third class. Figure 9–4 lists sample output from the program.

The program shown in Fig. 9–4 is available on the supplemental disk as CH901.COB.

Note that the variable VARIABLE-WEIGHT of TABLE-RECORD is used as the subscript to assign values to the elements in the table. This is not always possible. It is possible in this case because the field VARIABLE-WEIGHT contains integer values that correspond *exactly* to the position in which the variable is to be placed. If VARIABLE-WEIGHT is 13 pounds, the value contained in VALUE-COST of this record is stored in the thirteenth position in the table.

Note also that the field SHIPPING-WEIGHT of INVOICE-RECORD is not used directly to reference a value from POSTAL-RATE-TABLE. SHIPPING-WEIGHT does not necessarily contain an integer value. The weight of a package to be shipped could be 10.3 pounds. Therefore, it is necessary to convert this weight to the nearest integer weight greater than or equal to SHIPPING-WEIGHT.

This is done by adding .9 to SHIPPING-WEIGHT, causing the integer portion of SHIPPING-WEIGHT to be rounded up to the nearest integer weight greater than or equal to the weight of the package. If the package weighs 10.3 pounds, and .9 is added to this number, the result,

```
IDENTIFICATION DIVISION.
PROGRAM-ID.
    TABLE-PROBLEM-1.
* This Is Figure 9-3.
*********************************************************************
ENVIRONMENT DIVISION.
CONFIGURATION SECTION.
SOURCE-COMPUTER.
    IBM-PERSONAL-COMPUTER.
OBJECT-COMPUTER.
    IBM-PERSONAL-COMPUTER.
INPUT-OUTPUT SECTION.
FILE-CONTROL.
    SELECT TABLE-FILE ASSIGN TO DISK
        ORGANIZATION IS LINE SEQUENTIAL.
    SELECT INPUT-FILE ASSIGN TO DISK
        ORGANIZATION IS LINE SEQUENTIAL.
    SELECT PRINT-FILE ASSIGN TO PRINTER.
*********************************************************************
DATA DIVISION.
FILE SECTION.
FD  TABLE-FILE
    LABEL RECORDS ARE STANDARD
    VALUE OF FILE-ID IS 'CH901T.DAT'.
01  TABLE-REC          PIC X(5).
FD  INPUT-FILE
    LABEL RECORDS ARE STANDARD
    VALUE OF FILE-ID IS 'CH901D.DAT'.
01  IN-REC            PIC X(52).
FD  PRINT-FILE
    LABEL RECORDS ARE OMITTED.
01  PRINT-REC        PIC X(80).
*********************************************************************
WORKING-STORAGE SECTION.
01  WORK-AREAS.
    05  SUBSCPT-WEIGHT        PIC 99        USAGE COMP-0.
    05  COST-TOTAL            PIC S999V99 VALUE ZERO.
    05  EOF                   PIC 9         VALUE ZERO.
01  POSTAL-RATE-TABLE.
    05  RATE                  PIC S9V99 OCCURS 15 TIMES.
01  TABLE-RECORD.
    05  VARIABLE-WEIGHT       PIC S99.
    05  VALUE-COST            PIC S9V99.
01  INVOICE-RECORD.
    05  CUSTOMER-NO           PIC X(5).
    05  CUSTOMER-NAME         PIC X(15).
    05  CUSTOMER-ADDR         PIC X(25).
    05  INVOICE-AMOUNT        PIC S99V99.
    05  SHIPPING-WEIGHT       PIC S99V9.
01  TITLES-1.
    05  FILLER                PIC X(5) VALUE ' CUST'.
    05  FILLER                PIC X(7) VALUE SPACES.
    05  FILLER                PIC X(4) VALUE 'CUST'.
    05  FILLER                PIC X(17) VALUE SPACES.
    05  FILLER                PIC X(8) VALUE 'CUSTOMER'.
    05  FILLER                PIC X(11) VALUE SPACES.
    05  FILLER                PIC X(3) VALUE 'INV'.
    05  FILLER                PIC X(4) VALUE SPACES.
    05  FILLER                PIC X(5) VALUE 'SHIP.'.
    05  FILLER                PIC X(2) VALUE SPACES.
    05  FILLER                PIC X(5) VALUE 'SHIP.'.
    05  FILLER                PIC X(2) VALUE SPACES.
    05  FILLER                PIC X(5) VALUE 'TOTAL'.
01  TITLES-2.
    05  FILLER                PIC X(6) VALUE 'NUMBER'.
    05  FILLER                PIC X(6) VALUE SPACES.
    05  FILLER                PIC X(4) VALUE 'NAME'.
    05  FILLER                PIC X(17) VALUE SPACES.
    05  FILLER                PIC X(7) VALUE 'ADDRESS'.
    05  FILLER                PIC X(11) VALUE SPACES.
    05  FILLER                PIC X(6) VALUE 'AMOUNT'.
    05  FILLER                PIC X(3) VALUE SPACES.
```

Fig. 9-3. Program to create and reference a table.

```
         05  FILLER                 PIC X(2) VALUE 'WT'.
         05  FILLER                 PIC X(4) VALUE SPACES.
         05  FILLER                 PIC X(4) VALUE 'COST'.
         05  FILLER                 PIC X(3) VALUE SPACES.
         05  FILLER                 PIC X(4) VALUE 'COST'.
     01  PRINT-LINE.
         05  CUSTOMER-NO-O          PIC X(5).
         05  FILLER                 PIC X(2) VALUE SPACES.
         05  CUSTOMER-NAME-O        PIC X(15).
         05  FILLER                 PIC X(2) VALUE SPACES.
         05  CUSTOMER-ADDR-O        PIC X(25).
         05  FILLER                 PIC X(2) VALUE SPACES.
         05  INVOICE-AMOUNT-O       PIC $ZZ.99.
         05  FILLER                 PIC X(2) VALUE SPACES.
         05  SHIPPING-WEIGHT-O      PIC 99.9.
         05  FILLER                 PIC X(2) VALUE SPACES.
         05  SHIPPING-COST-O        PIC $Z.99.
         05  FILLER                 PIC X(2) VALUE SPACES.
         05  TOTAL-COST-O           PIC $ZZZ.99.
 ****************************************************************
 PROCEDURE DIVISION.
 MAIN-LINE.
     PERFORM OPEN-RTN.
     PERFORM TABLE-LOAD-RTN 15 TIMES.
     PERFORM HEADING-RTN.
     PERFORM PRIMER-READ.
     PERFORM SHIPPING-COST-RTN UNTIL EOF = 1.
     PERFORM CLOSE-RTN.
     STOP RUN.
 ****************************************************************
 OPEN-RTN.
     OPEN INPUT   TABLE-FILE
                  INPUT-FILE
          OUTPUT PRINT-FILE.
 ****************************************************************
 TABLE-LOAD-RTN.
     READ TABLE-FILE INTO TABLE-RECORD
             AT END DISPLAY 'TABLE LOADING ERROR'
                    PERFORM CLOSE-RTN
                    STOP RUN.
     MOVE VALUE-COST TO RATE (VARIABLE-WEIGHT).
 ****************************************************************
 HEADING-RTN.
     WRITE PRINT-REC FROM TITLES-1 AFTER PAGE.
     WRITE PRINT-REC FROM TITLES-2 AFTER ADVANCING 1 LINE.
 ****************************************************************
 PRIMER-READ.
     READ INPUT-FILE INTO INVOICE-RECORD AT END MOVE 1 TO EOF.
 ****************************************************************
 SHIPPING-COST-RTN.
     ADD .9 SHIPPING-WEIGHT GIVING SUBSCPT-WEIGHT.
     ADD INVOICE-AMOUNT RATE (SUBSCPT-WEIGHT) GIVING COST-TOTAL.
     PERFORM MOVE-RTN.
     WRITE PRINT-REC FROM PRINT-LINE AFTER ADVANCING 1 LINES.
     READ INPUT-FILE INTO INVOICE-RECORD AT END MOVE 1 TO EOF.
 ****************************************************************
 MOVE-RTN.
     MOVE COST-TOTAL TO TOTAL-COST-O.
     MOVE RATE (SUBSCPT-WEIGHT) TO SHIPPING-COST-O.
     MOVE CUSTOMER-NO TO CUSTOMER-NO-O.
     MOVE CUSTOMER-NAME TO CUSTOMER-NAME-O.
     MOVE CUSTOMER-ADDR TO CUSTOMER-ADDR-O.
     MOVE INVOICE-AMOUNT TO INVOICE-AMOUNT-O.
     MOVE SHIPPING-WEIGHT TO SHIPPING-WEIGHT-O.
 ****************************************************************
 CLOSE-RTN.
     CLOSE TABLE-FILE
           INPUT-FILE
           PRINT-FILE.
 ****************************************************************
```

Fig. 9-3. (*continued*)

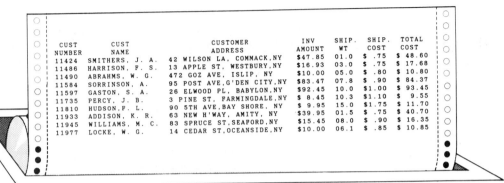

Fig. 9–4. Sample output from table problem 1.

11.2, contains in its integer portion the weight to the nearest pound greater than or equal to the actual weight.

To use this value to reference the table, the .2 or fractional portion must be eliminated from this value. This is done by moving the total to a data item that provides for no decimal places in its description: the 05-level data item SUBSCPT-WEIGHT. The single statement

ADD .9 SHIPPING-WEIGHT GIVING SUBSCPT-WEIGHT.

places an integer value into SUBSCPT-WEIGHT that represents the value contained in SHIPPING-WEIGHT rounded up to the nearest integer. This value is then used as a subscript to reference the appropriate cost of shipping the package from POSTAL-RATE-TABLE so that the shipping cost can be added to INVOICE-AMOUNT to produce COST-TOTAL. This is done with the following statement:

ADD INVOICE-AMOUNT RATE (SUBSCPT-WEIGHT) GIVING COST-TOTAL.

When the value COST-TOTAL is obtained, it is moved to the edited output area TOTAL-COST-O.

Note that SUBSCPT-WEIGHT is specified with USAGE COMP-0. This USAGE is sometimes specified for data items used as subscripts because it generally results in more efficient storage utilization and leads to a more efficient object program than USAGE DISPLAY. If no USAGE clause is specified, USAGE DISPLAY is assumed.

Table values are relatively simple to handle, but the input file described above is tedious to maintain outside the program. When the values to be stored in the computer are not subject to frequent change, the table data may be set up within the COBOL source program, thus eliminating the need to maintain an input table file outside the program. VALUE clauses can be used to eliminate the need for the input file TABLE-FILE, the file and record description entries for TABLE-FILE, and the TABLE-LOAD-RTN in the PROCEDURE DIVISION. In place of these entries and the working storage entries

```
01  POSTAL-RATE-TABLE.
    05  RATE                     PIC S9V99 OCCURS 15 TIMES.
```

would be the following working storage entries:

```
01  POSTAL-RATE-TABLE-VALUES.
    05  FILLER    PIC S9V99   VALUE 0.75.
    05  FILLER    PIC S9V99   VALUE 0.75.
    05  FILLER    PIC S9V99   VALUE 0.75.
    05  FILLER    PIC S9V99   VALUE 0.80.
    05  FILLER    PIC S9V99   VALUE 0.80.
    05  FILLER    PIC S9V99   VALUE 0.85.
    05  FILLER    PIC S9V99   VALUE 0.85.
    05  FILLER    PIC S9V99   VALUE 0.90.
    05  FILLER    PIC S9V99   VALUE 0.95.
    05  FILLER    PIC S9V99   VALUE 1.00.
    05  FILLER    PIC S9V99   VALUE 1.10.
    05  FILLER    PIC S9V99   VALUE 1.20.
    05  FILLER    PIC S9V99   VALUE 1.30.
    05  FILLER    PIC S9V99   VALUE 1.50.
    05  FILLER    PIC S9V99   VALUE 1.75.
01  POSTAL-RATE-TABLE   REDEFINES
                        POSTAL-RATE-TABLE-VALUES.
    05  RATE      PIC S9V99   OCCURS 15 TIMES.
```

Each of the entries in the POSTAL-RATE-TABLE-VALUES record may be assigned a unique data-name, but this is not necessary because the individual elements will be referenced by the data-name RATE together with an appropriate subscript. The data-name FILLER for each entry simplifies the coding. Each element, or FILLER, is assigned a PICTURE and *must* be the same size and description. In addition, each element description contains a VALUE clause.

However, these elements are not coded in a form that allows subscripting. The rules governing subscripting state that only items defined with an OCCURS clause may be subscripted. Since (with the exception of condition-name entries) VALUE clauses cannot be used with items that have OCCURS clauses, it is necessary to redefine the record POSTAL-RATE-TABLE-VALUES as a table. This is done with the REDEFINES clause that was discussed in Chapter 6. The general format of the REDEFINES is:

GENERAL FORMAT 2

data-name-1 REDEFINES data-name-2

The REDEFINES clause is used when it is desirable to refer to the same storage area by multiple data-names or where there is a need to describe a data storage area in more than one manner. That is, it specifies a redefinition of the storage area, not of the contents of the area.

Data-name-2 is the data-name associated with a previous data item-description entry, while **data-name-1** is an alternative name for the same area. The level numbers of both data-names must be identical. There may be no entries having numerically lower-level numbers between the data item description entries of these items.

The following restrictions relate to the use of the REDEFINES clause:

1. It must not be used with 88-level items.

2. It may not be used at the 01 level in the FILE SECTION.

3. A VALUE may not be assigned to a storage area that is redefined.

4. It must contain a PICTURE clause when it redefines an elementary data item.

5. When a group data item is redefined, each subordinate elementary data item must contain a PICTURE clause.

The REDEFINES clause does not reserve additional storage space; it allows a previously defined data area to be described differently. The entire table may now be referenced by using either the 01-level data-name POSTAL-RATE-TABLE-VALUES or POSTAL-RATE-TABLE. Both refer to the same area in storage. Any item in the table may now be referenced by the data-name RATE followed by a space and a subscript (a positive integer or a data-name containing a positive integer) contained within parentheses.

Let's consider the earlier example in which the table values were obtained from an external file (see Fig. 9–3). Only this time, let's assume that the input field VARIABLE-WEIGHT is not contained on each input record. Clearly, some other data item will be needed to serve as the subscript when storing the input values in the table. A method to accomplish this is shown below, provided that the input records are in the same order as they appear in the table.

```
TABLE-LOAD-RTN.
    READ TABLE-FILE INTO TABLE-RECORD
            AT END DISPLAY 'TABLE LOADING ERROR'
                   PERFORM CLOSE-RTN
                   STOP RUN.
    MOVE VALUE-COST TO RATE (VARIABLE-WEIGHT).
    ADD 1 TO SUBSCPT-WEIGHT.
```

In this case the data item SUBSCPT-WEIGHT is being used as a subscript to indicate the position in which the incoming table records are to be stored. Thus, it is essential that when it is defined in working storage, it is given the initial VALUE 1. This will cause the value of the first element input to be placed in the first position in the table. The statement ADD 1 TO SUBSCPT-WEIGHT will vary SUBSCPT-WEIGHT so that each subsequent value input will be placed in the next available space. The table values must be input in the same order as they are to appear in the table. After all the table values have been input, the data item SUBSCPT-WEIGHT is reused to store the rounded-up integer value of the data item SUBSCPT-WEIGHT, as it did in the original version of the program.

In this example, you may have asked yourself why INPUT-FILE could not be read directly into the table with a statement such as

```
READ INPUT-FILE INTO RATE (SUBSCPT-WEIGHT) AT END ...
```

The answer is quite simple. The group item INPUT-REC should not be moved to an elementary data item. For most COBOL compilers, this is an illegal move. Thus the group item INPUT-REC must be moved to a group item or an alphanumeric elementary item, in this case to the group item TABLE-RECORD. The numeric item VALUE-COST can be moved to the numeric item RATE (SUBSCPT-WEIGHT).

THE PERFORM STATEMENT IN TABLE HANDLING

In previous chapters we have discussed the PERFORM with the TIMES and UNTIL options. In table handling, a third option of the PERFORM will prove to be extremely useful—the PERFORM with VARYING option. The general format of this statement is as follows:

GENERAL FORMAT 3

PERFORM range [VARYING $\begin{Bmatrix} \text{index-name} \\ \text{data-name} \end{Bmatrix}$ FROM $\begin{Bmatrix} \text{data-name} \\ \text{literal} \end{Bmatrix}$

BY $\begin{Bmatrix} \text{data-name} \\ \text{literal} \end{Bmatrix}$ UNTIL condition.]

This statement is particularly useful in table handling because it can be used to control the value contained in a data item used as a subscript. For example, in the previous program we considered the situation where the position of the table element was not input with the value of the table element. We simply loaded the table values into the table as they were input. To do this, we used the data item SUBSCPT-WEIGHT to point to the position in the table into which each value input was to be placed. This necessitated that we initialize SUBSCPT-WEIGHT to 1 and that we increment it by 1 each time a new table value is read. This we did 15 times. Using the PERFORM...VARYING option, we could accomplish this task much more easily and directly. We simply could have written

```
PERFORM TABLE-LOAD-RTN VARYING SUBSCPT-WEIGHT
       FROM 1 BY 1 UNTIL SUBSCPT-WEIGHT > 15.
PERFORM HEADING-RTN.
            .
            .
            .
TABLE-LOAD-RTN.
    READ INPUT-FILE INTO TABLE-RECORD
        AT END DISPLAY 'TABLE LOADING ERROR'
               PERFORM CLOSE-RTN
               STOP RUN.
    MOVE VALUE-COST TO RATE (SUBSCPT-WEIGHT).
HEADING-RTN.            .
                       .
                       .
```

This single PERFORM statement will initialize SUBSCPT-WEIGHT to **1,** increment it by 1 each time TABLE-LOAD-RTN is performed, and **terminate** the procedure when it has been done 15 times.

    The last version of the PERFORM that we shall discuss is a direct **extension** of the format above. In this format of the PERFORM, it is **possible** to vary the value of up to three data items (which can be used as subscripts). The general format of this version of the PERFORM is as follows:

GENERAL FORMAT 4

$$\text{\underline{PERFORM} range \underline{VARYING}} \begin{Bmatrix} \text{data-name} \\ \text{index-name} \end{Bmatrix} \underline{\text{FROM}} \begin{Bmatrix} \text{data-name} \\ \text{literal} \end{Bmatrix}$$

$$\underline{\text{BY}} \begin{Bmatrix} \text{data-name} \\ \text{literal} \end{Bmatrix} \underline{\text{UNTIL}} \quad \text{condition-1}$$

$$[\underline{\text{AFTER}} \begin{Bmatrix} \text{data-name} \\ \text{index-name} \end{Bmatrix} \underline{\text{FROM}} \begin{Bmatrix} \text{data-name} \\ \text{literal} \end{Bmatrix}$$

$$\underline{\text{BY}} \begin{Bmatrix} \text{data-name} \\ \text{literal} \end{Bmatrix} \underline{\text{UNTIL}} \quad \text{condition-2}]$$

$$[\underline{\text{AFTER}} \begin{Bmatrix} \text{data-name} \\ \text{index-name} \end{Bmatrix} \underline{\text{FROM}} \begin{Bmatrix} \text{data-name} \\ \text{literal} \end{Bmatrix}$$

$$\underline{\text{BY}} \begin{Bmatrix} \text{data-name} \\ \text{literal} \end{Bmatrix} \underline{\text{UNTIL}} \quad \text{condition-3}]$$

    In this format of the PERFORM, all **identifiers** and **literals** are subject to the rules of the previous format of the PERFORM. **Index-names**, their uses, and their constraints are discussed later in the chapter. Identifiers are varied from the last named to the first named: **identifier-7**, if present is varied first; **identifier-4** is varied second; **identifier-1** is varied last. This process is illustrated in Fig. 9–5.

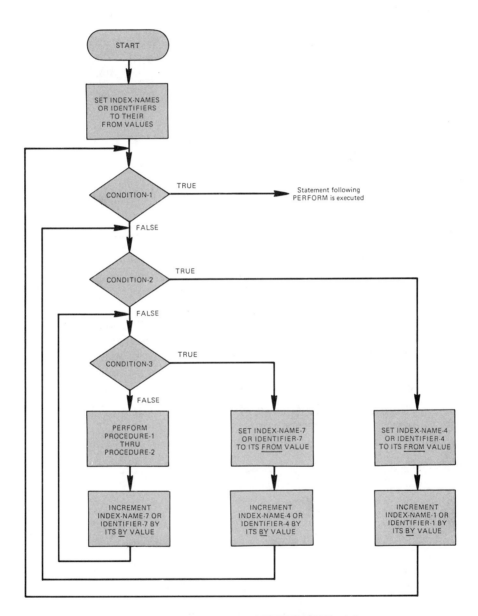

**Fig. 9–5. Flowchart of PERFORM with
VARYING ... AFTER ... AFTER.**

Thus, the following program segment causes the numbers to be displayed as shown at the left:

```
1  1  1          PERFORM DISPLAY-RTN
1  1  2              VARYING SUB-1 FROM 1 BY 1 UNTIL SUB-1 > 4
1  2  1              AFTER SUB-2 FROM 1 BY 1 UNTIL SUB-2 > 3
1  2  2              AFTER SUB-3 FROM 1 BY 1 UNTIL SUB-3 > 2.
1  3  1                                   .
1  3  2                                   .
2  1  1                                   .
2  1  2          DISPLAY-RTN.
2  2  1              DISPLAY SUB-1  SUB-2  SUB-3.

    .
    .
4  2  2
4  3  1
4  3  2
```

Two-Level and Three-Level Tables

Sometimes a particular value in a table is determined by more than one variable. In the table shown in Fig. 9–6, the annual insurance premium due on a particular policy per thousand dollars of insurance is determined by two variables: the age category of the person and the risk class into which the person falls. A person 40 to 44 years of age in

TWO-LEVEL INSURANCE PREMIUM TABLE

Age Category	Risk Class		
	1	2	3
below 18	$38.50	$42.35	$46.59
18–34	36.00	39.60	43.56
35–39	36.75	40.43	44.48
40–44	38.00	41.80	45.98
45–49	39.50	43.45	47.80
50–54	45.00	49.50	54.45
55–59	52.00	57.20	62.92
above 59	70.00	77.00	84.70

Fig. 9–6. Hypothetical two-level insurance premium table.

the third risk class would pay $45.98 per quarter per thousand dollars of insurance. This same rate may be indicated as

CLASS-RATE (4,3)

where 4 is a subscript indicating the fourth age category and 3 is a subscript indicating the third risk class. The rate may also be indicated as

CLASS-RATE (AGE-CAT-SUBSCPT,RISK-CLASS-SUBSCPT)

where AGE-CAT-SUBSCPT is a data-name containing the value 4 and RISK-CLASS-SUBSCPT is a data-name containing the value 3. In the latter case, the data-name AGE-CAT-SUBSCPT and RISK-CLASS-SUBSCPT serve as subscripts. Thus, it is possible to refer to a particular item in a table by more than one subscript. Up to three subscripts may be used to identify an element in a table in COBOL.

Assume that the table shown in Fig. 9–6 is to be placed in storage for reference in a customer billing program. This program reads in data records containing the customer's number, name, address, amount of insurance in thousands of dollars, sex, age category, and risk class. The output of the program is a listing of the information input together with the premium due.

The table may be defined in working storage as follows:

```
WORKING-STORAGE SECTION.
01   INSURANCE-TABLE-VALUES.
     05   FILLER   PIC 99V99   VALUE 38.50
     05   FILLER   PIC 99V99   VALUE 42.35
     05   FILLER   PIC 99V99   VALUE 46.59
     05   FILLER   PIC 99V99   VALUE 36.00
     05   FILLER   PIC 99V99   VALUE 39.60
                          .
                          .
                          .
     05   FILLER   PIC 99V99   VALUE 84.70.
01   INSURANCE-TABLE REDEFINES INSURANCE-TABLE-VALUES.
     05   AGE-CATEGORY   OCCURS 8 TIMES.
          10   CLASS-RATE PIC 99V99   OCCURS 3 TIMES.
```

Now there are 24 fields in storage. Each field is associated with a unique age category and risk classification. For example, the first field defined corresponds to an age category of 1 and a risk class of 1; it can be uniquely referenced by the subscripted name CLASS-RATE (1,1). Similarly, the fourth field defined would correspond to an age category of 2 and a risk class of 1; it can be uniquely identified by the subscripted name CLASS-RATE (2,1). This scheme may be used to uniquely identify every field or element within the table.

To confirm how a particular element is identified, the previous may be *thought of as if it were set up as follows:*

```
01   INSURANCE-TABLE.
     05   AGE-CATEGORY (1).
          10   CLASS-RATE (1,1) PIC 99V99 VALUE 38.50.
          10   CLASS-RATE (1,2) PIC 99V99 VALUE 42.35.
          10   CLASS-RATE (1,3) PIC 99V99 VALUE 46.59.
     05   AGE-CATEGORY (2).
          10   CLASS-RATE (2,1) PIC 99V99 VALUE 36.00.
          10   CLASS-RATE (2,2) PIC 99V99 VALUE 39.60.
          10   CLASS-RATE (2,3) PIC 99V99 VALUE 43.56.
                              .
                              .
                              .
     05   AGE-CATEGORY (8).
          10   CLASS-RATE (8,1) PIC 99V99 VALUE 70.00.
          10   CLASS-RATE (8,2) PIC 99V99 VALUE 77.00.
          10   CLASS-RATE (8,3) PIC 99V99 VALUE 84.70.
```

Of course, it is not possible to define a table in this manner. But if the table is viewed in this way, there is a clear correspondence between a particular table element and a subscripted data-name. The element in the eighth age category and the second risk class can be uniquely referenced as CLASS-RATE (8,2).

Since the elements in the table are not defined as USAGE COMP-3, USAGE DISPLAY is assumed. Whenever a table is created with USAGE DISPLAY, the elements in the table may be assigned values using nonnumeric literals. In many cases, this can greatly reduce the number of entries required to assign values to the table elements. The table above could have been defined in working storage with the following entries:

```
WORKING-STORAGE SECTION.
01   INSURANCE-TABLE-VALUES.
     05   FILLER   PIC X(12) VALUE '385042354659'.
     05   FILLER   PIC X(12) VALUE '360039604356'.
     05   FILLER   PIC X(12) VALUE '367540434448'.
     05   FILLER   PIC X(12) VALUE '380041804598'.
     05   FILLER   PIC X(12) VALUE '395043454780'.
     05   FILLER   PIC X(12) VALUE '450049505445'.
     05   FILLER   PIC X(12) VALUE '520057206292'.
     05   FILLER   PIC X(12) VALUE '700077008470'.
```

```
01  INSURANCE-TABLE  REDEFINES INSURANCE-TABLE-VALUES.
    05  AGE-CATEGORY  OCCURS 8 TIMES.
        10  CLASS-RATE PIC 99V99 OCCURS 3 TIMES.
```

Using nonnumeric literals, initial values are assigned to the table with only eight 05 entries; using the previous method, 24 10-level entries were required. The fewer number of program lines results from excluding three entries, or one complete AGE-CATEGORY entry, in each 05-level entry. This does not change the way the individual elements within the table are addressed. The subscripted name CLASS-RATE (2,1) still corresponds to the element for age category 2 and risk class 1.

A complete listing of the customer billing program using the latter table definition, including sample input and output, is shown in Figs. 9–7 through 9–9. Figure 9–11 illustrates a similar program that reads in a three-level table (Fig. 9–10) and produces a listing that includes customer identifying information and the insurance premium due.

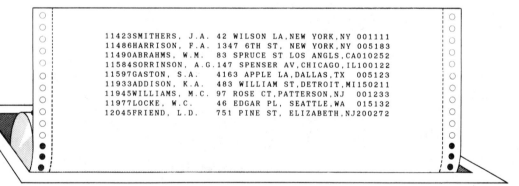

```
11423SMITHERS, J.A. 42 WILSON LA,NEW YORK,NY 001111
11486HARRISON, F.A. 1347 6TH ST, NEW YORK,NY 005183
11490ABRAHMS, W.M.  83 SPRUCE ST LOS ANGLS,CA010252
11584SORRINSON, A.G.147 SPENSER AV,CHICAGO,IL100122
11597GASTON, S.A.   4163 APPLE LA,DALLAS,TX  005123
11933ADDISON, K.A.  483 WILLIAM ST,DETROIT,MI150211
11945WILLIAMS, M.C. 97 ROSE CT,PATTERSON,NJ  001233
11977LOCKE, W.C.    46 EDGAR PL, SEATTLE,WA  015132
12045FRIEND, L.D.   751 PINE ST, ELIZABETH,NJ200272
```

Fig. 9–7. Sample input for two-level customer billing program.

This program is available on the supplemental disk as CH902.COB.

```
        IDENTIFICATION DIVISION.
        PROGRAM-ID. BILLING-PROGRAM.
       * This Is Figure 9-8.
       ***********************************************************
        ENVIRONMENT DIVISION.
        CONFIGURATION SECTION.
        SOURCE-COMPUTER. IBM-PERSONAL-COMPUTER.
        OBJECT-COMPUTER. IBM-PERSONAL-COMPUTER.
        INPUT-OUTPUT SECTION.
        FILE-CONTROL.
            SELECT CUST-FILE ASSIGN TO DISK
                ORGANIZATION IS LINE SEQUENTIAL.
            SELECT LIST-FILE ASSIGN TO PRINTER.
       ***********************************************************
        DATA DIVISION.
        FILE SECTION.
        FD  CUST-FILE
            VALUE OF FILE-ID 'CH902D.DAT'
            LABEL RECORDS ARE STANDARD
            RECORD CONTAINS 51 CHARACTERS.
        01  CUST-REC     PIC X(51).
        FD  LIST-FILE
            LABEL RECORDS ARE OMITTED
            RECORD CONTAINS 80 CHARACTERS.
        01  LIST-RECORD  PIC X(80).
       ***********************************************************
        WORKING-STORAGE SECTION.
        01  WORK-AREAS.
            05  EOF            PIC 9 VALUE ZERO.
        01  TABLE-RECORD.
            05  PREM-VALUE     PIC 99V99.
        01  CUST-RECORD.
            05  CUST-NO        PIC X(5).
            05  CUST-NAME      PIC X(15).
            05  CUST-ADD       PIC X(25).
            05  INS-AMT        PIC 999.
            05  SEX            PIC 9.
            05  AGE-CAT        PIC 9.
            05  RISK-CLASS     PIC 9.
        01  INSURANCE-TABLE-VALUES.
            05  FILLER         PIC X(12) VALUE '385042354659'.
            05  FILLER         PIC X(12) VALUE '360039604356'.
            05  FILLER         PIC X(12) VALUE '367540434448'.
            05  FILLER         PIC X(12) VALUE '380041804598'.
            05  FILLER         PIC X(12) VALUE '395043454780'.
            05  FILLER         PIC X(12) VALUE '450049505445'.
            05  FILLER         PIC X(12) VALUE '520057206292'.
            05  FILLER         PIC X(12) VALUE '700077008470'.
        01  INSURANCE-TABLE REDEFINES INSURANCE-TABLE-VALUES.
            05  AGE-CATEGORY OCCURS 8 TIMES.
                10  CLASS-RATE PIC 99V99 OCCURS 3 TIMES.
        01  REPORT-MAIN-TITLE.
            05  FILLER         PIC X(27) VALUE SPACES.
            05  FILLER         PIC X(25) VALUE 'CUSTOMER PREMIUM DUE LIST'.
        01  REPORT-SUBTITLE-1.
            05  FILLER         PIC X(4) VALUE 'CUST'.
            05  FILLER         PIC X(5) VALUE SPACES.
            05  FILLER         PIC X(8) VALUE 'CUSTOMER'.
            05  FILLER         PIC X(15) VALUE SPACES.
            05  FILLER         PIC X(8) VALUE 'CUSTOMER'.
            05  FILLER         PIC X(12) VALUE SPACES.
            05  FILLER         PIC X(3) VALUE 'INS'.
            05  FILLER         PIC X(2) VALUE SPACES.
            05  FILLER         PIC X(3) VALUE 'AGE'.
            05  FILLER         PIC X(1) VALUE SPACES.
            05  FILLER         PIC X(3) VALUE 'RSK'.
            05  FILLER         PIC X(2) VALUE SPACES.
            05  FILLER         PIC X(7) VALUE 'PREMIUM'.
        01  REPORT-SUBTITLE-2.
            05  FILLER         PIC X(4) VALUE 'NUMB'.
            05  FILLER         PIC X(7) VALUE SPACES.
            05  FILLER         PIC X(4) VALUE 'NAME'.
```

Fig. 9–8. Two-level customer billing program.

```
         05   FILLER        PIC X(17) VALUE SPACES.
         05   FILLER        PIC X(7) VALUE 'ADDRESS'.
         05   FILLER        PIC X(13) VALUE SPACES.
         05   FILLER        PIC X(3) VALUE 'AMT'.
         05   FILLER        PIC X(2) VALUE SPACES.
         05   FILLER        PIC X(3) VALUE 'CLS'.
         05   FILLER        PIC X(1) VALUE SPACES.
         05   FILLER        PIC X(3) VALUE 'CLS'.
         05   FILLER        PIC X(4) VALUE SPACES.
         05   FILLER        PIC X(3) VALUE 'DUE'.
    01   DATA-RECORD.
         05   CUST-NO-O     PIC X(5).
         05   FILLER        PIC X(2) VALUE SPACES.
         05   CUST-NAME-O   PIC X(15).
         05   FILLER        PIC X(2) VALUE SPACES.
         05   CUST-ADD-O    PIC X(25).
         05   FILLER        PIC X(3) VALUE SPACES.
         05   INS-AMT-O     PIC 999.
         05   FILLER        PIC X(3) VALUE SPACES.
         05   AGE-CAT-O     PIC 9.
         05   FILLER        PIC X(3) VALUE SPACES.
         05   RISK-CLASS-O  PIC 9.
         05   FILLER        PIC X(3) VALUE SPACES.
         05   PREM-DUE-O    PIC $ZZZZZ.99.
**************************************************************
    PROCEDURE DIVISION.
    MAIN-LINE.
         PERFORM OPEN-RTN.
         PERFORM HEADING-RTN.
         PERFORM PRIMER-READ-RTN.
         PERFORM COMPUTE-PREMIUM UNTIL EOF = 1.
         PERFORM CLOSE-RTN.
         STOP RUN.
**************************************************************
    OPEN-RTN.
         OPEN INPUT  CUST-FILE
              OUTPUT LIST-FILE.
**************************************************************
    HEADING-RTN.
         WRITE LIST-RECORD FROM REPORT-MAIN-TITLE
              AFTER ADVANCING PAGE.
         WRITE LIST-RECORD FROM REPORT-SUBTITLE-1 AFTER 3.
         WRITE LIST-RECORD FROM REPORT-SUBTITLE-2 AFTER 1.
**************************************************************
    PRIMER-READ-RTN.
         READ CUST-FILE INTO CUST-RECORD
              AT END MOVE 1 TO EOF.
**************************************************************
    COMPUTE-PREMIUM.
         COMPUTE PREM-DUE-O = INS-AMT * CLASS-RATE
                             (AGE-CAT, RISK-CLASS).
         PERFORM MOVE-RTN.
         WRITE LIST-RECORD FROM DATA-RECORD AFTER 1.
         READ CUST-FILE INTO CUST-RECORD
              AT END MOVE 1 TO EOF.
**************************************************************
    MOVE-RTN.
         MOVE CUST-NO        TO CUST-NO-O.
         MOVE CUST-NAME      TO CUST-NAME-O.
         MOVE CUST-ADD       TO CUST-ADD-O.
         MOVE INS-AMT        TO INS-AMT-O.
         MOVE AGE-CAT        TO AGE-CAT-O.
         MOVE RISK-CLASS     TO RISK-CLASS-O.
**************************************************************
    CLOSE-RTN.
         CLOSE CUST-FILE
               LIST-FILE.
**************************************************************
```

Fig. 9–8. (*continued*)

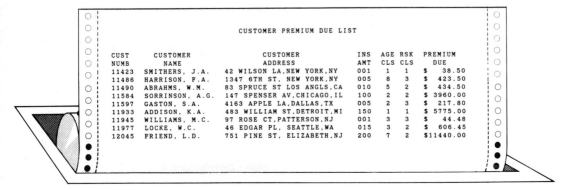

```
                    CUSTOMER PREMIUM DUE LIST

   CUST     CUSTOMER                CUSTOMER            INS  AGE RSK  PREMIUM
   NUMB       NAME                   ADDRESS            AMT  CLS CLS    DUE
   11423  SMITHERS, J.A.   42 WILSON LA,NEW YORK,NY    001   1   1   $    38.50
   11486  HARRISON, F.A.   1347 6TH ST, NEW YORK,NY    005   8   3   $   423.50
   11490  ABRAHMS, W.M.    83 SPRUCE ST LOS ANGLS,CA   010   5   2   $   434.50
   11584  SORRINSON, A.G.  147 SPENSER AV,CHICAGO,IL   100   2   2   $  3960.00
   11597  GASTON, S.A.     4163 APPLE LA,DALLAS,TX     005   2   3   $   217.80
   11933  ADDISON, K.A.    483 WILLIAM ST,DETROIT,MI   150   1   1   $  5775.00
   11945  WILLIAMS, M.C.   97 ROSE CT,PATTERSON,NJ     001   3   3   $    44.48
   11977  LOCKE, W.C.      46 EDGAR PL, SEATTLE,WA     015   3   2   $   606.45
   12045  FRIEND, L.D.     751 PINE ST, ELIZABETH,NJ   200   7   2   $ 11440.00
```

Fig. 9–9.   Output from two-level billing program.

THREE-LEVEL INSURANCE PREMIUM TABLE

Age Category	Male Risk Class			Female Risk Class	
	1	2	3	1	2
below 18	$38.50	$42.35	$46.59	$34.65	$38.12
18–34	36.00	39.60	43.56	32.40	35.64
35–39	36.75	40.43	44.48	33.03	36.38
40–44	38.00	41.80	45.98	34.20	37.62
45–49	39.50	43.45	47.80	35.55	39.11
50–54	45.00	49.50	54.45	40.50	44.55
55–59	52.00	57.20	62.92	46.80	51.48
above 59	70.00	77.00	84.70	63.00	69.30

Fig. 9–10.   Hypothetical three-level insurance table.

```
         IDENTIFICATION DIVISION.
         PROGRAM-ID. BILLING-PROGRAM.
       * This Is Figure 9-11.
       ****************************************************************
         ENVIRONMENT DIVISION.
         CONFIGURATION SECTION.
         SOURCE-COMPUTER. IBM-PERSONAL-COMPUTER.
         OBJECT-COMPUTER. IBM-PERSONAL-COMPUTER.
         INPUT-OUTPUT SECTION.
         FILE-CONTROL.
             SELECT TABLE-FILE ASSIGN TO DISK
                 ORGANIZATION IS LINE SEQUENTIAL.
             SELECT CUST-FILE ASSIGN TO DISK
                 ORGANIZATION IS LINE SEQUENTIAL.
             SELECT LIST-FILE ASSIGN TO PRINTER.
       ****************************************************************
         DATA DIVISION.
         FILE SECTION.
         FD  TABLE-FILE
             LABEL RECORDS ARE STANDARD
             VALUE OF FILE-ID IS 'CH903T.DAT'.
         01  TABLE-REC          PIC X(4).
         FD  CUST-FILE
             VALUE OF FILE-ID IS 'CH902D.DAT'
             LABEL RECORDS ARE STANDARD
             RECORD CONTAINS 51 CHARACTERS.
         01  CUST-REC    PIC X(51).
         FD  LIST-FILE
             LABEL RECORDS ARE OMITTED
             RECORD CONTAINS 80 CHARACTERS.
         01  LIST-RECORD  PIC X(80).
       ****************************************************************
         WORKING-STORAGE SECTION.
         01  WORK-AREAS.
             05  EOF            PIC 9 VALUE ZERO.
         01  SUBSCRIPTS.
             05  SUBSCPT-1      PIC 9 USAGE COMP SYNC.
             05  SUBSCPT-2      PIC 9 USAGE COMP SYNC.
             05  SUBSCPT-3      PIC 9 USAGE COMP SYNC.
         01  TABLE-RECORD.
             05  PREM-VALUE     PIC 99V99.
         01  CUST-RECORD.
             05  CUST-NO       PIC X(5).
             05  CUST-NAME     PIC X(15).
             05  CUST-ADD      PIC X(25).
             05  INS-AMT       PIC 999.
             05  SEX           PIC 9.
             05  AGE-CAT       PIC 9.
             05  RISK-CLASS    PIC 9.
         01  INSURANCE-TABLE.
             05  AGE-CATEGORY OCCURS 8 TIMES.
                 10  SEX-TYPE OCCURS 2 TIMES.
                     15  CLASS-RATE PIC 99V99 OCCURS 3 TIMES.
         01  REPORT-MAIN-TITLE.
             05  FILLER       PIC X(27) VALUE SPACES.
             05  FILLER       PIC X(25) VALUE 'CUSTOMER PREMIUM DUE LIST'.
         01  REPORT-SUBTITLE-1.
             05  FILLER         PIC X(4) VALUE 'CUST'.
             05  FILLER         PIC X(5) VALUE SPACES.
             05  FILLER         PIC X(8) VALUE 'CUSTOMER'.
             05  FILLER         PIC X(15) VALUE SPACES.
             05  FILLER         PIC X(8) VALUE 'CUSTOMER'.
             05  FILLER         PIC X(12) VALUE SPACES.
             05  FILLER         PIC X(3) VALUE 'INS'.
             05  FILLER         PIC X(6) VALUE SPACES.
             05  FILLER         PIC X(3) VALUE 'AGE'.
             05  FILLER         PIC X(1) VALUE SPACES.
             05  FILLER         PIC X(3) VALUE 'RSK'.
             05  FILLER         PIC X(2) VALUE SPACES.
             05  FILLER         PIC X(7) VALUE 'PREMIUM'.
         01  REPORT-SUBTITLE-2.
             05  FILLER         PIC X(4) VALUE 'NUMB'.
```

Fig. 9-11. Three-level customer billing program.

```
          05  FILLER        PIC X(7) VALUE SPACES.
          05  FILLER        PIC X(4) VALUE 'NAME'.
          05  FILLER        PIC X(17) VALUE SPACES.
          05  FILLER        PIC X(7) VALUE 'ADDRESS'.
          05  FILLER        PIC X(13) VALUE SPACES.
          05  FILLER        PIC X(3) VALUE 'AMT'.
          05  FILLER        PIC X(2) VALUE SPACES.
          05  FILLER        PIC X(3) VALUE 'SEX'.
          05  FILLER        PIC X(1) VALUE SPACES.
          05  FILLER        PIC X(3) VALUE 'CLS'.
          05  FILLER        PIC X(1) VALUE SPACES.
          05  FILLER        PIC X(3) VALUE 'CLS'.
          05  FILLER        PIC X(4) VALUE SPACES.
          05  FILLER        PIC X(3) VALUE 'DUE'.
      01  DATA-RECORD.
          05  CUST-NO-O     PIC X(5).
          05  FILLER        PIC X(2) VALUE SPACES.
          05  CUST-NAME-O   PIC X(15).
          05  FILLER        PIC X(2) VALUE SPACES.
          05  CUST-ADD-O    PIC X(25).
          05  FILLER        PIC X(3) VALUE SPACES.
          05  INS-AMT-O     PIC 999.
          05  FILLER        PIC X(3) VALUE SPACES.
          05  SEX-O         PIC 9.
          05  FILLER        PIC X(3) VALUE SPACES.
          05  AGE-CAT-O     PIC 9.
          05  FILLER        PIC X(3) VALUE SPACES.
          05  RISK-CLASS-O  PIC 9.
          05  FILLER        PIC X(3) VALUE SPACES.
          05  PREM-DUE-O    PIC $ZZZZZ.99.
*******************************************************************
  PROCEDURE DIVISION.
  MAIN-LINE.
      PERFORM OPEN-RTN.
      PERFORM TABLE-LOAD-RTN.
      PERFORM HEADING-RTN.
      PERFORM PRIMER-READ-RTN.
      PERFORM COMPUTE-PREMIUM UNTIL EOF = 1.
      PERFORM CLOSE-RTN.
      STOP RUN.
*******************************************************************
  OPEN-RTN.
      OPEN INPUT  TABLE-FILE
                  CUST-FILE
           OUTPUT LIST-FILE.
*******************************************************************
  TABLE-LOAD-RTN.
      PERFORM READ-TABLE
          VARYING SUBSCPT-1 FROM 1 BY 1 UNTIL SUBSCPT-1 > 8
              AFTER SUBSCPT-2 FROM 1 BY 1 UNTIL SUBSCPT-2 > 2
              AFTER SUBSCPT-3 FROM 1 BY 1 UNTIL SUBSCPT-3 > 3.
*******************************************************************
  READ-TABLE.
      READ TABLE-FILE INTO TABLE-RECORD
          AT END DISPLAY 'TABLE READ ERROR'
                  PERFORM CLOSE-RTN
                  STOP RUN.
      MOVE PREM-VALUE TO CLASS-RATE (SUBSCPT-1, SUBSCPT-2,
                  SUBSCPT-3).
*******************************************************************
  HEADING-RTN.
      WRITE LIST-RECORD FROM REPORT-MAIN-TITLE
          AFTER ADVANCING PAGE.
      WRITE LIST-RECORD FROM REPORT-SUBTITLE-1 AFTER 3.
      WRITE LIST-RECORD FROM REPORT-SUBTITLE-2 AFTER 1.
*******************************************************************
  PRIMER-READ-RTN.
      READ CUST-FILE INTO CUST-RECORD
          AT END MOVE 1 TO EOF.
*******************************************************************
  COMPUTE-PREMIUM.
      COMPUTE PREM-DUE-O = INS-AMT * CLASS-RATE
                          (AGE-CAT, SEX, RISK-CLASS).
      PERFORM MOVE-RTN.
```

Fig. 9–11. (*continued*)

```
 ○ ┆     WRITE LIST-RECORD FROM DATA-RECORD AFTER 1.         ○
 ○ ┆     READ CUST-FILE INTO CUST-RECORD                     ○
 ○ ┆             AT END MOVE 1 TO EOF.                       ○
 ○ ┆ ************************************************************ ○
 ○ ┆ MOVE-RTN.                                                ○
 ○ ┆     MOVE CUST-NO        TO CUST-NO-O.                    ○
 ○ ┆     MOVE CUST-NAME      TO CUST-NAME-O.                  ○
 ○ ┆     MOVE CUST-ADD       TO CUST-ADD-O.                   ○
 ○ ┆     MOVE INS-AMT        TO INS-AMT-O.                    ○
 ○ ┆     MOVE SEX            TO SEX-O.                        ○
 ○ ┆     MOVE AGE-CAT        TO AGE-CAT-O.                    ○
 ○ ┆     MOVE RISK-CLASS     TO RISK-CLASS-O.                 ○
 ○ ┆ ************************************************************ ○
 ○ ┆ CLOSE-RTN.                                               ○
 ○ ┆     CLOSE TABLE-FILE                                     ●
 ● ┆           CUST-FILE                                      ●
 ● ┆           LIST-FILE.                                     ●
 ● ┆ ************************************************************ ●
```

Fig. 9–11. (*continued*)

This program is available on the supplemental disk as CH903.COB.

TABLE SEARCHING

To this point, elements in a table have been referenced by the location of the element in the table. However, in many applications it is necessary to search a table until a match is obtained between the data given and the identifying data within the element of the table. This process, a common programming problem, is called **table lookup**. For example, if a table contains a list of the company's salespeople by number and corresponding name, it may be necessary to determine the salespeople's names from their numbers. Since a salesperson's number has little if any correlation with his or her location in the table, it is necessary to search the entire table, element by element, until an element is located that has a matching number. If no match is obtained, an error message is printed out. Figure 9–12 illustrates a program that searches such a table for the name and address of the salespeople whose numbers are input to the program. This program assumes that the number and names of the 35 salespeople employed by this company are read into the table from an external data file.

```
      IDENTIFICATION DIVISION.
      PROGRAM-ID. EMPLOYEE-TABLE-SEARCH.
    * This Is Figure 9-12.
    *****************************************************************
      ENVIRONMENT DIVISION.
      CONFIGURATION SECTION.
      SOURCE-COMPUTER. IBM-PERSONAL-COMPUTER.
      OBJECT-COMPUTER. IBM-PERSONAL-COMPUTER.
      INPUT-OUTPUT SECTION.
      FILE-CONTROL.
          SELECT TABLE-FILE ASSIGN TO DISK
              ORGANIZATION IS LINE SEQUENTIAL.
          SELECT IN-FILE ASSIGN TO DISK
              ORGANIZATION IS LINE SEQUENTIAL.
          SELECT OUT-FILE ASSIGN TO PRINTER.
    *****************************************************************
      DATA DIVISION.
      FILE SECTION.
      FD  TABLE-FILE
          LABEL RECORDS ARE STANDARD
          VALUE OF FILE-ID IS 'CH904T.DAT'.
      01  TABLE-REC          PIC X(40).
      FD  IN-FILE
          LABEL RECORDS ARE STANDARD
          VALUE OF FILE-ID 'CH904D.DAT'.
      01  IN-REC  PIC X(05).
      FD  OUT-FILE
          LABEL RECORDS ARE OMITTED
          RECORD CONTAINS 80 CHARACTERS.
      01  OUT-REC  PIC X(80).
    *****************************************************************
      WORKING-STORAGE SECTION.
      01  SWITCHES-N-COUNTERS.
          05  EOF               PIC 9 VALUE ZERO.
          05  COUNTR            PIC 99 VALUE ZERO.
      01. SALSMN-TABLE.
    *     05  SALSMN-NO-NAME OCCURS 35 TIMES.
          05  SALSMN-NO-NAME OCCURS 5 TIMES.
              10  SALSMN-NO    PIC X(5).
              10  SALSMN-NAME  PIC X(35).
      01  SALSMN-SEARCH-REC.
          05  SALSMN-NO-S    PIC X(5).
      01  TITLE-1.
          05  FILLER          PIC X(19) VALUE SPACES.
          05  FILLER          PIC X(11) VALUE 'SALESMAN NO'.
          05  FILLER          PIC X(18) VALUE SPACES.
          05  FILLER          PIC X(13) VALUE 'SALESMAN NAME'.
      01  PRINT-REC.
          05  FILLER          PIC X(22) VALUE SPACES.
          05  SMN-NO          PIC X(5).
          05  FILLER          PIC X(10) VALUE SPACES.
          05  SMN-NAME        PIC X(35).
    *****************************************************************
      PROCEDURE DIVISION.
      MAIN-LINE.
          PERFORM OPEN-RTN.
          PERFORM TABLE-LOAD-RTN VARYING COUNTR FROM 1 BY 1
                  UNTIL COUNTR > 35.
          PERFORM HEADING-RTN.
          PERFORM PRIMER-READ.
          PERFORM PROCESS-RTN UNTIL EOF = 1.
          PERFORM CLOSE-RTN.
          STOP RUN.
    *****************************************************************
      OPEN-RTN.
          OPEN INPUT  TABLE-FILE
                      IN-FILE
               OUTPUT OUT-FILE.
    *****************************************************************
      TABLE-LOAD-RTN.
          READ TABLE-FILE INTO SALSMN-NO-NAME (COUNTR)
              AT END DISPLAY 'TABLE LOAD ERROR'
```

Fig. 9-12.   Program illustrating table searching using subscripts.

```
                    PERFORM CLOSE-RTN
                    STOP RUN.
  ************************************************************
  HEADING-RTN.
      WRITE OUT-REC FROM TITLE-1 AFTER ADVANCING PAGE.
  ************************************************************
  PRIMER-READ.
      READ IN-FILE INTO SALSMN-SEARCH-REC AT END MOVE 1 TO EOF.
  ************************************************************
  PROCESS-RTN.
      PERFORM DUMMY-RTN VARYING COUNTR FROM 1 BY 1
          UNTIL SALSMN-NO-S = SALSMN-NO (COUNTR) OR COUNTR > 35.
      IF COUNTR > 35 PERFORM ERROR-RTN
      ELSE PERFORM MOVE-RTN
          WRITE OUT-REC FROM PRINT-REC AFTER ADVANCING 2 LINES.
      READ IN-FILE INTO SALSMN-SEARCH-REC AT END MOVE 1 TO EOF.
  ************************************************************
  DUMMY-RTN.
      EXIT.
  ************************************************************
  MOVE-RTN.
      MOVE SALSMN-NO (COUNTR) TO SMN-NO.
      MOVE SALSMN-NAME (COUNTR) TO SMN-NAME.
  ************************************************************
  ERROR-RTN.
      DISPLAY 'NO HIT FOUND FOR SALESMAN NO ' SALSMN-NO-S.
  ************************************************************
  CLOSE-RTN.
      CLOSE TABLE-FILE
            IN-FILE
            OUT-FILE.
```

Fig. 9–12. (continued)

This program is available on the supplemental disk as CH904.COB.

INDEXING

An **index** serves the same general purpose as the subscript in a COBOL program and can be used by the programmer in a similar manner. There are, however, some basic differences between an index and a subscript. First, indexes generally produce more efficient programs than subscripts do. Therefore, where possible, the use of indexes is recommended over the use of subscripts. Second, additional COBOL statements are used when working with indexed tables. For example, when one or more indexes are used to access table elements, this fact is indicated by an INDEXED BY option after the OCCURS clause. The INDEXED BY option causes the index field(s) to be generated automatically by the COBOL compiler and does not require that the index field(s) be defined in the DATA DIVISION by the programmer.

GENERAL FORMAT 5

OCCURS integer TIMES [INDEXED BY index-name . . .]

This format of the OCCURS clause is used whenever indexes are used to access table elements. Up to three OCCURS clauses may be used depending on whether the table being described is a one-, two-, or three-level table.

The DEPENDING ON supported in mainframe versions of COBOL is not supported in IBM COBOL for the PC.

The KEY option is used only with the INDEXED BY option. When this option is indicated, it stipulates whether the data being described is arranged in ASCENDING or DESCENDING order with respect to the values contained in **data-name-2**, **data-name-3**, and so on. If data-name-2 is also the name of the entry containing the OCCURS clause, the specified keys *must not be* subordinate to any other entry containing an OCCURS clause.

When more than one key is listed, they are listed in decreasing order of significance. That is, the items are arranged in sequence by data-name-2, in sequence within data-name-2 by data-name-3, and so on.

The INDEXED BY option is required when the data-name described by an OCCURS clause is referenced by an index. This clause is also required when the data-name described by the OCCURS clause is a group item and the data items subordinate to this item are referenced by indexes. Because the index field(s) are generated automatically by the compiler, the item(s) corresponding to the index-name(s) specified in this option *must not be defined elsewhere in the program.* An index-name must be initialized by a SET statement or PERFORM...VARYING before it can be used in the program. The SET statement will be discussed later in this chapter.

The following segment of a WORKING-STORAGE SECTION contains a table description utilizing the INDEXED BY and KEY options:

```
WORKING-STORAGE SECTION
01   SALSMN-TABLE.
     05   SALSMN-NO-NAME OCCURS 50 TIMES.
          ASCENDING KEY SALSMN-NO
```

```
         INDEXED BY INDEX-NO.
    10   SALSMN-NO      PIC X(5).
    10   SALSMN-NAME    PIC X(35).
```

This program segment accomplishes the following:

1. It defines the table SALSMN-TABLE consisting of 50 SALSMN-NO-NAME elements.

2. It indicates that the elements are in ASCENDING order according to the values contained in the field SALSMN-NO of each element.

3. It indicates that the field INDEX-NO is generated by the compiler and is used as an index for referencing the elements within the table.

THE SEARCH ALL STATEMENT

Figure 9–12 indicated how a table is searched for a particular element. That program utilized subscripts to step through the individual elements in the table to locate the desired element. This process is easier if the table elements are defined with indexes. When table elements are defined using the OCCURS clause with the INDEXED BY option, a SEARCH statement may be used to search the table for a particular element satisfying a specified condition. There are two formats for the SEARCH statement; the first format is referred to as the SEARCH ALL statement, and the second format is referred to as the SEARCH statement.

The general format of the SEARCH ALL statement is as follows:

GENERAL FORMAT 6

SEARCH ALL identifier-1 [AT END imperative-statement-1]

WHEN condition $\left\{ \begin{array}{l} \text{NEXT SENTENCE} \\ \text{imperative-statement-2} \end{array} \right\}$ ...

The SEARCH ALL statement allows the programmer to search an entire table for an element satisfying a particular condition. When an entire table is to be searched using the SEARCH ALL statement, the control field for the table *must* have been specified in either ASCENDING or DESCENDING sequence in the table definition.

In the SEARCH ALL statement, a nonsequential or binary search operation will take place. The setting of the index-name is varied during the search operation in a manner so that at no time will the value of the index be less than the value corresponding to the first element in the table or greater than the value corresponding to the last element in the table. When control passes from the SEARCH ALL statement without condition-1 being satisfied, the final setting of the index is unpredictable.

Identifier-1 must be a data item whose description includes an OCCURS clause with the KEY and INDEXED BY options. The KEY option of the OCCURS clause must be specified when describing a table that is searched using the SEARCH ALL statement. Identifier-1 itself *may not* contain a subscript or index.

The AT END option functions in much the same manner as it does with the READ statement. If, after the entire table has been searched and the particular condition being tested for has not been reached, **imperative-statement-1** following the reserved words AT END is executed. If imperative-statement-1 does not terminate with a statement transferring control elsewhere in the program, control is automatically transferred to the statement immediately following the SEARCH ALL sentence after executing imperative-statement-1. If no AT END clause is present and the entire table has been searched without satisfying the condition being tested, control is transferred to the statement immediately following the SEARCH ALL sentence.

The WHEN entry is required in the SEARCH ALL statement; it indicates the condition that must be satisfied to complete the searching operation and the action to be taken when this condition has been satisfied. **Condition-1** within this entry must consist of one of the following:

1. A simple relational condition or condition-name may be used. The subject data-name in the condition must be entered in the KEY clause of the OCCURS.

2. Only the equality test (= or EQUAL TO) is valid.

3. A condition-name, if used, may have only a single value.

4. The condition may be compounded but only by the AND.

Any data-name that appears in the KEY clause of identifier-1 may appear as the subject or object (not both) of a test, or it may be the name of a conditional variable with which the tested condition-name is associated. However, all data-names that appear in the KEY of identifier-1 before the data-name used as the subject or object of the test must also be included within condition-1. For example, if the description of identifier-1 contains the clause

```
ASCENDING KEY KEY-1, KEY-2
```

and key-2 is to be included in condition-1, key-1 must also appear in condition-1.

If condition-1 is satisfied, control is transferred to **imperative-statement-2** or to the NEXT SENTENCE after the SEARCH ALL statement, depending on which of these options is specified. As with the imperative-statement-1, if imperative-statement-2 does not terminate with a statement transferring control elsewhere in the program, control is transferred to the sentence immediately following the SEARCH ALL sentence after imperative-statement-2 is executed.

Figure 9–13 illustrates a program employing indexing and the SEARCH ALL statement. This program performs the identical function as the program illustrated in Fig. 9–12, which utilized subscripts. All statements added to or changed from Fig. 9–12 have been identified by an asterisk at the far right of the statement. This program also contains a new statement: the SET statement.

THE SET STATEMENT

Indexes differ from subscripts in that they may be initialized and modified by the COBOL statement SET. (When indexes are named in the PERFORM...VARYING statement, the FROM and BY clauses have the same effect as the SET statement, as discussed later in this chapter.) For example, if it is necessary to initialize the subscript SUBSCPT to 1, this may be accomplished with the following statement:

```
MOVE 1 TO SUBSCPT.
```

To accomplish the same thing for the index INDEX-VALUE, it is necessary to use the SET statement

```
SET INDEX-VALUE TO 1.
```

Similarly, to increase the value contained in the index INDEX-VALUE by 1, it is necessary to use the SET statement

```
SET INDEX-VALUE UP BY 1.
```

```
IDENTIFICATION DIVISION.
PROGRAM-ID. EMPLOYEE-TABLE-SEARCH.
* This Is Figure 9-13
*********************************************************************
ENVIRONMENT DIVISION.
CONFIGURATION SECTION.
SOURCE-COMPUTER. IBM-PERSONAL-COMPUTER.
OBJECT-COMPUTER. IBM-PERSONAL-COMPUTER.
INPUT-OUTPUT SECTION.
FILE-CONTROL.
    SELECT TABLE-FILE ASSIGN TO DISK
        ORGANIZATION IS LINE SEQUENTIAL.
    SELECT IN-FILE ASSIGN TO DISK
        ORGANIZATION IS LINE SEQUENTIAL.
    SELECT OUT-FILE ASSIGN TO PRINTER.
*********************************************************************
DATA DIVISION.
FILE SECTION.
FD  TABLE-FILE
    LABEL RECORDS ARE STANDARD
    VALUE OF FILE-ID IS 'CH905T.DAT'.
01  TABLE-REC           PIC X(40).
FD  IN-FILE
    LABEL RECORDS ARE STANDARD
    VALUE OF FILE-ID IS 'CH905D.DAT'.
01  IN-REC              PIC X(05).
FD  OUT-FILE
    LABEL RECORDS ARE OMITTED
    RECORD CONTAINS 80 CHARACTERS.
01  OUT-REC  PIC X(80).
WORKING-STORAGE SECTION.
*********************************************************************
01  SWITCHES-N-COUNTERS.
    05  EOF                PIC 9 VALUE ZERO.
01  SALSMN-TABLE.
    05  SALSMN-NO-NAME OCCURS 35 TIMES
            ASCENDING KEY IS SALSMN-NO                          *
            INDEXED BY INDEX-VALUE.                             *
        10  SALSMN-NO    PIC X(5).
        10  SALSMN-NAME  PIC X(35).
01  SALSMN-SEARCH-REC.
    05  SALSMN-NO-S    PIC X(5).
01  TITLE-1.
    05  FILLER         PIC X(19) VALUE SPACES.
    05  FILLER         PIC X(11) VALUE 'SALESMAN NO'.
    05  FILLER         PIC X(18) VALUE SPACES.
    05  FILLER         PIC X(13) VALUE 'SALESMAN NAME'.
01  PRINT-REC.
    05  FILLER         PIC X(22) VALUE SPACES.
    05  SMN-NO         PIC X(5).
    05  FILLER         PIC X(10) VALUE SPACES.
    05  SMN-NAME       PIC X(35).
*********************************************************************
PROCEDURE DIVISION.
MAIN-LINE.
    PERFORM OPEN-RTN.
    PERFORM TABLE-LOAD-RTN VARYING INDEX-VALUE FROM 1 BY 1       *
            UNTIL INDEX-VALUE > 35.                              *
    PERFORM HEADING-RTN.
    PERFORM PRIMER-READ.
    PERFORM PROCESS-RTN UNTIL EOF = 1.
    PERFORM CLOSE-RTN.
    STOP RUN.
*********************************************************************
OPEN-RTN.
    OPEN INPUT  TABLE-FILE
                IN-FILE
         OUTPUT OUT-FILE.
*********************************************************************
TABLE-LOAD-RTN.
    READ TABLE-FILE INTO SALSMN-NO-NAME (INDEX-VALUE)
```

**Fig. 9-13. Program illustrating the use of the
SEARCH ALL statement.**

```
                 AT END DISPLAY 'TABLE LOAD ERROR'
                       PERFORM CLOSE-RTN
                       STOP RUN.
******************************************************************
     HEADING-RTN.
         WRITE OUT-REC FROM TITLE-1
                 AFTER ADVANCING PAGE.
******************************************************************
     PRIMER-READ.
         READ IN-FILE INTO SALSMN-SEARCH-REC
             AT END MOVE 1 TO EOF.
******************************************************************
     PROCESS-RTN.
         SEARCH ALL SALSMN-NO-NAME                              *
             AT END PERFORM ERROR-RTN                           *
             WHEN SALSMN-NO-S = SALSMN-NO (INDEX-VALUE)         *
                 PERFORM MOVE-RTN
                 WRITE OUT-REC FROM PRINT-REC AFTER 2.
         READ IN-FILE INTO SALSMN-SEARCH-REC AT END MOVE 1 TO EOF.
******************************************************************
     MOVE-RTN.
         MOVE SALSMN-NO (INDEX-VALUE) TO SMN-NO.               *
         MOVE SALSMN-NAME (INDEX-VALUE) TO SMN-NAME.           *
******************************************************************
     ERROR-RTN.
         DISPLAY 'NO HIT FOUND FOR SALESMAN NO ' SALSMN-NO-S.
******************************************************************
     CLOSE-RTN.
         CLOSE TABLE-FILE
               IN-FILE
               OUT-FILE.
```

Fig. 9–13. (*continued*)

This program is available on the supplemental disk as CH905.COB.

The two general formats of the SET statement are as follows:

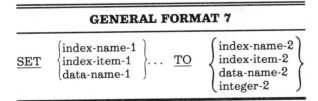

GENERAL FORMAT 7

$$\underline{SET} \left\{ \begin{array}{l} \text{index-name-1} \\ \text{index-item-1} \\ \text{data-name-1} \end{array} \right\} \ldots \ \underline{TO} \left\{ \begin{array}{l} \text{index-name-2} \\ \text{index-item-2} \\ \text{data-name-2} \\ \text{integer-2} \end{array} \right\}$$

GENERAL FORMAT 8

$$\underline{\text{SET}} \text{ index-name-3} \ldots \begin{Bmatrix} \underline{\text{UP}} \text{ BY} \\ \underline{\text{DOWN}} \text{ BY} \end{Bmatrix} \begin{Bmatrix} \text{data-name-4} \\ \text{integer-4} \end{Bmatrix}$$

The first format is used to initialize one or more index-names, the second format is used to increment or decrement the value contained in an index. It has been stated previously that the index-names must be assigned to a given table through the INDEXED BY option of the OCCURS clause. It should be noted that an index may also be described independently of the INDEXED BY clause, in which case it is used in the same manner as a subscript while operating more efficiently. An index that is established independently of a table is described as follows:

```
05  IND    USAGE IS INDEX
```

Note that no PICTURE clause is included in this entry.

In both formats of the SET statement any data names must be described as elementary integer items.

In the first format of the SET statement, **index-name-1**, **index-item-1**, or **data-name-1** (the identifiers after the word SET) receive a value equivalent to the contents of the identifier after the word TO. This is equivalent to a MOVE operation.

In the second format of the SET statement, the contents of **index-name-3** (and **index-name-4**, etc., if present) are reduced (DOWN) or incremented (UP) by the contents of **data-name-4** or **integer-4**. This is equivalent to an ADD or SUBTRACT operation.

In the VARYING option of the PERFORM statement, it is possible to initialize and vary the value contained in an index. References to identifiers in this format also refer to index-names. When index-names are used in this format of the PERFORM statement, the FROM and BY clauses have the same effect as in the SET statement. Thus, it is possible to initialize and vary the value of an index by using either the VARYING option of the PERFORM statement or the SET statement. For example, the following two program segments have the same effect:

```
        PROGRAM SEGMENT 1                      PROGRAM SEGMENT 2
- - - - - - - - - - - - - - - - - - - - -   - - - - - - - - - - - - - - - - - - - - -
                                                 PERFORM PARAG-1,
     SET INDEX-1 TO 1.                            VARYING INDEX-1 FROM 1
     PERFORM PARAG-1 10 TIMES.                    BY 1 UNTIL INDEX-1 > 10.
                    .                                          .
                    .                                          .
                    .                                          .
  PARAG-1.                                    PARAG-1.
                    .                                          .
                    .                                          .
                    .                                          .
     SET INDEX-1 UP BY 1.                                      .
  PARAG-2.                                    PARAG-2.
                    .                                          .
                    .                                          .
                    .                                          .
```

THE SEARCH STATEMENT

The first search format was referred to as the SEARCH ALL; this format is referred to as the SEARCH statement. The general format of the SEARCH statement is as follows:

GENERAL FORMAT 9

SEARCH identifier-1 [VARYING $\begin{Bmatrix} \text{identifier-2} \\ \text{index-name-1} \end{Bmatrix}$]

[AT END imperative-statement-1]

WHEN condition-1 $\begin{Bmatrix} \text{NEXT SENTENCE} \\ \text{imperative-statement-2} \end{Bmatrix}$ ...

The major difference between the SEARCH and SEARCH ALL statements is that in the SEARCH statement, the index is varied sequentially—beginning with the value to which it is initially set—until one of the conditions specified in the SEARCH statement has been satisfied. The next time the SEARCH is executed, it begins testing the indicated conditions with the index value retained from the previously executed SEARCH statement, unless the index value has been changed by a SET statement. The benefit of this feature will be illustrated later.

Identifier-1 must be a data item whose description includes an OC-CURS clause with the INDEXED BY option, or that data item must be subordinate to a data item whose description includes an OCCURS clause with an INDEXED BY option. Identifier-1 itself *may not* contain a subscript or index.

Identifier-2, when specified in the VARYING option, must be a numeric elementary data item described as an integer. When stipulated, identifier-2 is incremented by the same value, at the same time, as the index-name associated with identifier-1. If **index-name-1** is specified in the VARYING option, one of the following rules applies:

1. If index-name-1 is one of the indexes specified in working-storage for identifier-1, it is used as the index for the search.

2. If index-name-1 is one of the indexes specified for another table in working-storage, it is automatically incremented by the same value, at the same time, as the index-name for identifier-1.

The AT END option serves the same purpose and functions the same in the SEARCH statement as it does in the SEARCH ALL statement.

As with the SEARCH ALL statement, the WHEN entry is required; however, in the case of the SEARCH statement, *more than one WHEN entry may be included.* If more than one WHEN entry is stated, the search is considered to be complete when the condition(s) stated in *any* WHEN entry has been satisfied. That is, the first condition to be satisfied, regardless of the WHEN entry in which it occurs, terminates the search. Another difference between the WHEN statement used with the SEARCH and the SEARCH ALL concerns the conditions. Only certain types of conditions could be tested with the SEARCH ALL statement. In the SEARCH statement, however, **condition-1**, **condition-2**, and so on may be any condition (relation condition, class condition, condition-name condition, etc.).

There is one other important condition when using the SEARCH statement. This concerns the value of the index-name associated with identifier-1 when the SEARCH statement is initiated.

If, at the start of execution of the SEARCH statement, the index-name contains a value that is greater than the highest allowable index-value for identifier-1, the SEARCH is immediately terminated. If an AT END statement is present, the imperative statement corresponding to the AT END entry is then executed. If an AT END statement is not present, control is transferred to the next sentence following the SEARCH sentence.

If at the start of the execution of the SEARCH statement, the index-name contains a value that is not greater than the highest allowable index value for identifier-1, the SEARCH begins immediately by evaluating condition-1, condition-1 if present, and so on, in order, making use of the indexes where specified to determine the position of the elements to be tested.

If none of these conditions is satisfied, the index-name for identifier-1 is incremented and the process is repeated. If one of the conditions is satisfied during the process, the search is immediately terminated and the imperative statement associated with the condition satisfied (or NEXT SENTENCE, if specified) is executed. The index-name then *retains the value* it has at the time the condition is satisfied. If no condition is satisfied by the time the entire table is searched, the imperative statement corresponding to the AT END entry is executed. If this imperative statement does not terminate with a statement transferring control elsewhere in the program, control is then transferred to the sentence following the SEARCH statement after the AT END imperative statement is executed.

We have learned that the binary searching method used by the SEARCH ALL is a very efficient method when it is necessary to search an entire table *and* when the data in the table are in sequence (either ascending or descending). There are, however, some situations where it is necessary to search a table serially by examining one element after the other.

First, it is absolutely necessary to search a table serially when it is not in any particular sequence. The binary searching technique employed by the SEARCH ALL will work only if the table is in sequence. For tables where the elements are not in sequence, the SEARCH must be employed. In certain circumstances, a table may be deliberately created out of sequence. For example, where certain elements are more likely to occur than others, it is sometimes advisable to place those elements high in the table and employ the SEARCH.

A SEARCH may also be desirable in certain cases with tables that are in sequence. To illustrate this point, let's assume that we wish to search a tax table that contains at each salary level a tax rate that applies to any salary that falls in the interval. To determine when a hit is found in this table, we would need a WHEN condition, which could be stated as

```
WHEN SALARY NOT < LOW-LIMIT (INDEX-NAME) AND
     SALARY NOT > UPPER-LIMIT (INDEX-NAME)
```

This is not possible with a SEARCH ALL statement, since the WHEN condition used with a SEARCH ALL may not test for GREATER

```
        IDENTIFICATION DIVISION.
        PROGRAM-ID. EMPLOYEE-TABLE-SEARCH.
      * This Is Figure 9-14
      ************************************************************
        ENVIRONMENT DIVISION.
        CONFIGURATION SECTION.
        SOURCE-COMPUTER. IBM-PERSONAL-COMPUTER.
        OBJECT-COMPUTER. IBM-PERSONAL-COMPUTER.
        INPUT-OUTPUT SECTION.
        FILE-CONTROL.
            SELECT TABLE-FILE ASSIGN TO DISK
                   ORGANIZATION IS LINE SEQUENTIAL.
            SELECT IN-FILE ASSIGN TO DISK
                   ORGANIZATION IS LINE SEQUENTIAL.
            SELECT OUT-FILE ASSIGN TO PRINTER.
      ************************************************************
        DATA DIVISION.
        FILE SECTION.
        FD  TABLE-FILE
            LABEL RECORDS ARE STANDARD
            VALUE OF FILE-ID IS 'CH905T.DAT'.
        01  TABLE-REC            PIC X(40).
        FD  IN-FILE
            LABEL RECORDS ARE STANDARD
            VALUE OF FILE-ID 'CH906D.DAT'.
        01  IN-REC PIC X(05).
        FD  OUT-FILE
            LABEL RECORDS ARE OMITTED
            RECORD CONTAINS 80 CHARACTERS.
        01  OUT-REC PIC X(80).
      ************************************************************
        WORKING-STORAGE SECTION.
        01  SWITCHES-N-COUNTERS.
            05  EOF                PIC 9 VALUE ZERO.
        01  SALSMN-TABLE.
            05  SALSMN-NO-NAME OCCURS 35 TIMES.
                    INDEXED BY INDEX-VALUE.
                10  SALSMN-NO   PIC X(5).
                10  SALSMN-NAME PIC X(35).
        01  SALSMN-SEARCH-REC.
            05  SALSMN-NO-S    PIC X(5).
        01  TITLE-1.
            05  FILLER         PIC X(19) VALUE SPACES.
            05  FILLER         PIC X(11) VALUE 'SALESMAN NO'.
            05  FILLER         PIC X(18) VALUE SPACES.
            05  FILLER         PIC X(13) VALUE 'SALESMAN NAME'.
        01  PRINT-REC.
            05  FILLER         PIC X(22) VALUE SPACES.
            05  SMN-NO         PIC X(5).
            05  FILLER         PIC X(10) VALUE SPACES.
            05  SMN-NAME       PIC X(35).
      ************************************************************
        PROCEDURE DIVISION.
        MAIN-LINE.
            PERFORM OPEN-RTN.
            PERFORM TABLE-LOAD-RTN VARYING INDEX-VALUE FROM 1 BY 1
                    UNTIL INDEX-VALUE > 35.
            PERFORM HEADING-RTN.
            PERFORM PRIMER-READ.
            SET INDEX-VALUE TO 1.                              *
            PERFORM PROCESS-RTN UNTIL EOF = 1.
            PERFORM CLOSE-RTN.
            STOP RUN.
      ************************************************************
        OPEN-RTN.
            OPEN INPUT  TABLE-FILE
                        IN-FILE
                 OUTPUT OUT-FILE.
      ************************************************************
        TABLE-LOAD-RTN.
            READ TABLE-FILE INTO SALSMN-NO-NAME (INDEX-VALUE)
```

Fig. 9–14. Program illustrating the SEARCH using a sequential file.

```
                    AT END DISPLAY 'TABLE LOAD ERROR'
                         PERFORM CLOSE-RTN
                         STOP RUN.
************************************************************
    HEADING-RTN.
        WRITE OUT-REC FROM TITLE-1
                    AFTER ADVANCING PAGE.
************************************************************
    PRIMER-READ.
        READ IN-FILE INTO SALSMN-SEARCH-REC
                    AT END MOVE 1 TO EOF.
************************************************************
    PROCESS-RTN.
        SEARCH SALSMN-NO-NAME                               *
            AT END PERFORM ERROR-RTN
            WHEN SALSMN-NO-S = SALSMN-NO (INDEX-VALUE)
                PERFORM MOVE-RTN
                    WRITE OUT-REC FROM PRINT-REC AFTER 2.
        READ IN-FILE INTO SALSMN-SEARCH-REC AT END MOVE 1 TO EOF.
************************************************************
    MOVE-RTN.
        MOVE SALSMN-NO (INDEX-VALUE) TO SMN-NO.             *
        MOVE SALSMN-NAME (INDEX-VALUE) TO SMN-NAME.         *
************************************************************
    ERROR-RTN.
        DISPLAY 'NO HIT FOUND FOR SALESMAN NO ' SALSMN-NO-S.
        SET INDEX-VALUE TO 1.                              *
************************************************************
    CLOSE-RTN.
        CLOSE TABLE-FILE
              IN-FILE
              OUT-FILE.
```

Fig. 9–14. (*continued*)

THAN (>) or LESS THAN (<) conditions. Thus the SEARCH would be appropriate.

As a further illustration of the advantage of employing the SEARCH with a sequential table, let's assume that we wish to access a sequential table a number of times and that the entries are in the same sequence as the table. Using the SEARCH ALL, the entire table would have to be searched for each inquiry. With the SEARCH, the searching process is sequential and may be resumed from the point where it left off in the previous access. As each access is completed, the index is pointing to the spot where the hit occurred. Thus, since the next access is further in the table than the current one, or equal to the current one (there may be multiple entries in a sequential input file), the search may be resumed from the current point. The only difficulty occurs if the element being searched for is not in the table. In such a case, the index would have to be reset to the previous value (if saved) or back to 1 before subsequent accesses may be made. This process is illustrated in Fig. 9–14. This program assumes that the inquiries are in sequential order by salesperson number.

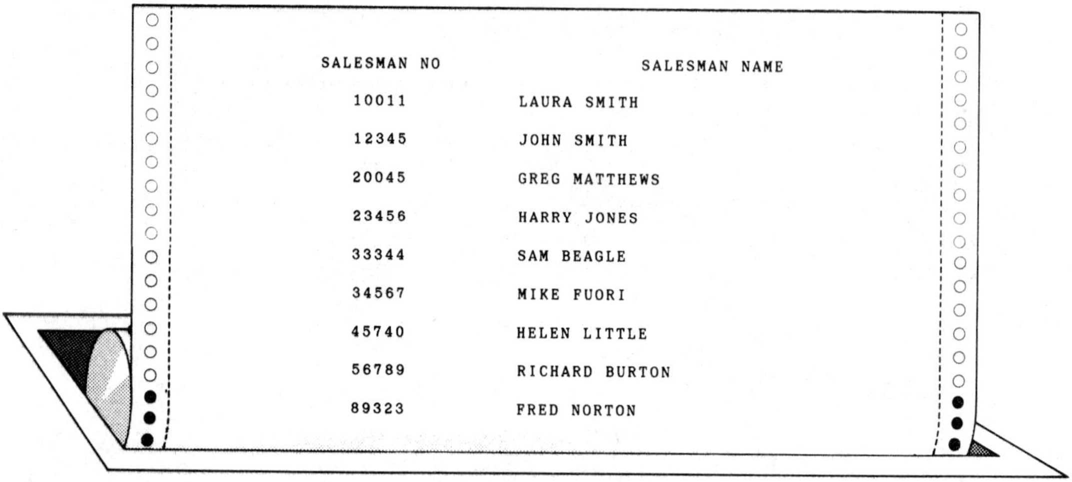

```
        SALESMAN NO                    SALESMAN NAME

           10011          LAURA SMITH

           12345          JOHN SMITH

           20045          GREG MATTHEWS

           23456          HARRY JONES

           33344          SAM BEAGLE

           34567          MIKE FUORI

           45740          HELEN LITTLE

           56789          RICHARD BURTON

           89323          FRED NORTON
```

Fig. 9–15.   Output from CH906.COB.

This program is available on the supplemental disk as CH906.COB.

EXERCISES

---

1. Write a program to produce a list of employees, including a full job title for each. The input record EMPLOYEE-REC described on page 332 contains a code for the job title. The actual job titles are read from the TABLE-REC to create the table. Write this program in two different versions: using the SEARCH ALL verb and using the SEARCH.

2. Write a program that reads current sales data for each salesperson in the company, calculates the average amount of sales for *all* salespeople, and prints out the report described on page 333. Note that the report includes the difference (+ or −) from the average for each. In order to do this, it will be necessary to read all the salesperson's records from the SALES-AMOUNT file prior to printing any of the data. Assume that the company has 25 salespeople.

3. A large national sales organization has divided the country into five districts for its marketing operations. As each sale is recorded, a table is to be constructed that accumulates the sales amount for each month of the year, in each district. After all the sales have been read and accumulated, a report is to be printed as described on page 334.

Solutions to the exercises, together with any necessary data files, are provided on the supplemental disk.

Input Layout

Input Record: TABLE-REC

Output Layout

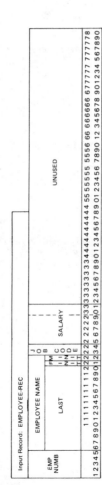

Input Layout

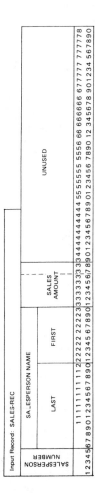

Input Record: SALES-REC

SALESPERSON NUMBER	SA_ESPERSON NAME		SALES AMOUNT	UNUSED
	LAST	FIRST		

```
          1 1 1 1 1 1 1 1 1 1 2 2 2 2 2 2 2 2 2 2 3 3 3 3 3 3 3 3 3 3 4 4 4 4 4 4 4 4 4 4 5 5 5 5 5 5 5 5 5 5 6 6 6 6 6 6 6 6 6 6 7 7 7 7 7 7 7 7 7 7 7 8
1 2 3 4 5 6 7 8 9 0 1 2 3 4 5 6 7 8 9 0 1 2 3 4 5 6 7 8 9 0 1 2 3 4 5 6 7 8 9 0 1 2 3 4 5 6 7 8 9 0 1 2 3 4 5 6 7 8 9 0 1 2 3 4 5 6 7 8 9 0 1 2 3 4 5 6 7 8 9 0
```

Output Layout

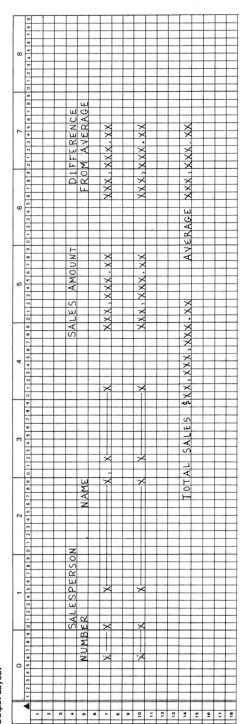

Input Layout

Input Record: SALES-REC

D I S T R I C T	M O N T H	SALES AMOUNT	UNUSED

```
          1 1 1 1 1 1 1 1 1 1 2 2 2 2 2 2 2 2 2 2 3 3 3 3 3 3 3 3 3 3 4 4 4 4 4 4 4 4 4 4 5 5 5 5 5 5  5 5 5 5 6 6  6 6 6 6 6 7 7 7 7  7 7 7 7 7 8
1 2 3 4 5 6 7 8 9 0 1 2 3 4 5 6 7 8 9 0 1 2 3 4 5 6 7 8 9 0 1 2 3 4 5 6 7 8 9 0 1 2 3 4 5 6 7 8 9 0 1 2 3 4 5 6  7 8 9 0 1 2  3 4 5 6 7 8 9 0 1 2  3 4 5 6 7 8 9 0
```

Output Layout

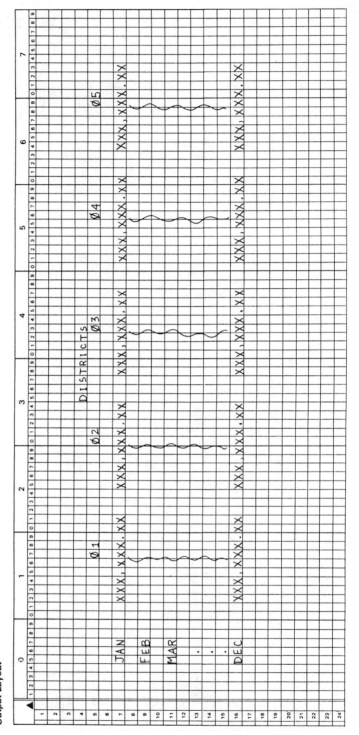

C H A P T E R

10

PROGRAMMING USING SEQUENTIAL FILES

ENVIRONMENT DIVISION

The ENVIRONMENT DIVISION of a COBOL program is concerned with the physical description of the files used by the program. You may remember that in using the ACCEPT and DISPLAY for input/output, no entries were required in this division except for the SPECIAL-NAMES entry designating the PRINTER as the output device for the DISPLAY.

When files were introduced and we began to READ and WRITE data using the disk and to WRITE data on the printer, we needed to add the INPUT-OUTPUT SECTION and the FILE-CONTROL paragraph with the appropriate SELECT entries. The general format is shown on the following page.

The SELECT Clause

The SELECT Clause represents one sentence in the FILE-CONTROL paragraph, which describes various attributes of the file. The possible entries for the ASSIGN TO clause are DISK or PRINTER. No other devices are specified in IBM COBOL. Usually the ASSIGN TO appears right after the SELECT, but it and all the other clauses may be in any order after the filename entry.

GENERAL FORMAT 1

INPUT-OUTPUT SECTION.
FILE-CONTROL.

    SELECT filename ASSIGN TO $\left\{ \begin{array}{l} \text{DISK} \\ \text{PRINTER} \end{array} \right\}$

    $\left[\text{RESERVE integer} \left\{ \begin{array}{l} \text{AREA} \\ \text{AREAS} \end{array} \right\} \right]$

    [FILE STATUS IS data-name-1]

    $\left[\text{ACCESS MODE IS} \left\{ \begin{array}{l} \text{SEQUENTIAL} \\ \text{RANDOM} \\ \text{DYNAMIC} \end{array} \right\} \right]$

    $\left[\text{ORGANIZATION IS} \left\{ \begin{array}{l} \text{SEQUENTIAL} \\ \text{LINE SEQUENTIAL} \\ \text{RELATIVE} \\ \text{INDEXED} \end{array} \right\} \right]$

    [RECORD KEY IS data-name-2]

    [RELATIVE KEY IS data-name-3]

The RESERVE Clause

This clause is permitted but serves no purpose in IBM COBOL. Since proper syntax is required, it is recommended that it be omitted.

The FILE STATUS Clause

Current versions of COBOL offer a method that allows the program to test the result of input/output operations. If the FILE STATUS option is included in the SELECT entry, a two-character, alphanumeric value is placed in the specified field after the input/output operation. The data-name-1 following the FILE STATUS entry refers to this two-byte alphanumeric field in the WORKING-STORAGE SECTION or the LINKAGE SECTION (covered later). The two bytes are referred to as left-hand and right-hand characters. The left byte refers to the type of result:

LEFT-BYTE CODE	MEANING
0	Successful completion
1	End-of-file condition
2	Invalid key (relative and indexed files)
3	Nonrecoverable error
9	Specific conditions

The right-hand byte is set to 0 if no other information is available and to specific characters for more definitive information. The following values are returned to the FILE STATUS data-name for SEQUENTIAL files:

LEFT	RIGHT	MEANING
0	0	Successful completion
1	0	EOF (end of file)
3	0	Permanent error
3	4	Disk space full
9	1	File damaged

If a 30 is returned as a result of an attempt to OPEN an input file, it means that the file was not found. Additional codes will be discussed later regarding RELATIVE and INDEXED files.

The ACCESS MODE Clause

Up to this point, we have been processing data in a sequential mode. In fact, ACCESS IS SEQUENTIAL is the default for all files in COBOL. Previously used SELECT statements such as

```
SELECT INPUT-FILE ASSIGN TO DISK.
```

could also have been written as

```
SELECT INPUT-FILE ASSIGN TO DISK ACCESS MODE IS SEQUENTIAL.
```

Either of the the above SELECT entries are appropriate as long as we are processing sequential files. The other access modes, RANDOM and DYNAMIC, will be discussed in the next chapter.

The ORGANIZATION Clause

Line Sequential Files   You may have noticed that up to this point in the text we have been using disk files only as input files and all output files were going to the printer. The type of files that we have been reading from the disk were designated as ORGANIZATION IS LINE SEQUENTIAL. This is the method of organization used with files that are not the output of COBOL but which have been created using some other method, such as EDLIN or a word processor. The significant characteristic of this type of file is the method used to indicate the length of each record. The records may be variable in length (within the maximum declared in the FD) and are terminated by a carriage return/line feed delimiter initiated by the editor program. LINE SEQUENTIAL files are limited to character (DISPLAY) type data and are consistent with the format expected in files by DOS.

Sequential Files   Regular SEQUENTIAL files are identified by the entry ACCESS IS SEQUENTIAL in the SELECT statement (this entry is the default for all files). Files with this type of access are normally written and read only by COBOL programs. It was noted previously that LINE SEQUENTIAL files were terminated by a carriage return/ line feed; SEQUENTIAL files have their length indicated by a two-byte count field preceding each data record. The records shown below are as they would appear in a dump of the disk record. They are 66-character records preceded by a 2-byte count field—in this case a blank and a B. The B represents the ASCII value 66. The complete set of ASCII codes are described in Appendix G of the IBM BASIC manual you received with your IBM PC. They have ASCII values of 000 to 255. These are not to be confused with hexadecimal representation, which describes how values are actually stored in binary.

```
B1234567LAURA   SMITH    74 E FUNSTON ST  WICHITA    KS66094018
B1345678STANLEY MADISON 2112 FIRST ST     ATLANTA    GA12789038
B1456789JOSEPH GREY      92 MAPLE ST       EUGENE     OR78901068
B2456789MARY    EVANS    93 MESQUITE RD    AMARILLO   TX77801038
```

A complete FILE-CONTROL paragraph for a sequential file might appear as follows:

```
FILE-CONTROL.
      SELECT MASTER-IN ASSIGN TO DISK
      FILE STATUS IS FILE-STAT
      ACCESS MODE IS SEQUENTIAL
      ORGANIZATION IS SEQUENTIAL.
```

The I-O-CONTROL Paragraph

The general format of the I-O CONTROL paragraph is shown here:

GENERAL FORMAT 2

I-O-CONTROL.

   SAME <u>RECORD</u> AREA FOR filename ...

This is an optional clause that states that several files are to share the same physical buffer area in order to conserve memory space. This is useful only when several files are being processed and they are <u>not</u> open at the same time.

```
I-O-CONTROL.
      SAME RECORD AREA FOR  TABLE FILE
                           DETAIL FILE
                           CONTROL-FILE.
```

DATA DIVISION

As in the case of all files in COBOL, sequential files must be defined in the DATA DIVISION.

The FILE SECTION

The FILE SECTION of a COBOL program contains the following two types of entries:

1. File description entries

2. Record description entries

The general format of a file description entry is as follows:

GENERAL FORMAT 3

<u>FD</u> filename

    <u>LABEL</u> <u>RECORDS</u> clause

    [<u>VALUE</u> <u>OF</u> FILE-ID clause]

    [<u>DATA</u> <u>RECORDS</u> clause]

    [<u>RECORD</u> CONTAINS clause]

    [<u>BLOCK</u> CONTAINS clause]

As noted in previous discussions, this clause is required in the FILE SECTION for every file to be used by the program. In IBM COBOL, these would be DISK files and PRINTER files.

The LABEL RECORDS Clause

As noted in the general format above, the only required entry in addition to the FD filename is the LABEL RECORDS clause. This clause does not serve the same function as it does in mainframe computers; it is, however, a required entry for regular sequential disk files and is used to identify the fact that a particular filename is to be read or a new filename is to be written. This clause operates in conjunction with the VALUE OF FILE-ID clause described below.

GENERAL FORMAT 4

<u>LABEL</u> $\begin{Bmatrix} \underline{RECORD} \text{ IS} \\ \underline{RECORDS} \text{ ARE} \end{Bmatrix}$ $\begin{Bmatrix} OMITTED \\ STANDARD \end{Bmatrix}$

The OMITTED option is used with PRINTER files and the STANDARD option is used with DISK files.

The RECORD CONTAINS Clause

GENERAL FORMAT 5

<u>RECORD</u> CONTAINS [integer-1 TO] integer-2 CHARACTERS

This is an optional entry and serves to document the size of the logical records contained in the file. In this version of COBOL, the record size is defined by the data description entries following the 01 level, and the size of the record is not affected by this entry. The entry is somewhat misleading with the use of the integer-1 TO integer-2 option, since SEQUENTIAL files do not support variable length records in this version of COBOL.

The **BLOCK CONTAINS** Clause

GENERAL FORMAT 6

$$\underline{\text{BLOCK}}\text{ CONTAINS}\quad \begin{Bmatrix}\text{integer-1 CHARACTERS}\\\text{integer-2 }\underline{\text{RECORDS}}\end{Bmatrix}$$

This clause is also *optional* and is included in IBM COBOL for consistency with other (mainframe) versions. It is normally associated with tape files, which are not supported by IBM COBOL and direct access files as implemented on mainframe computers. If used, the syntax must be correct. The intent of this entry is to indicate the number of logical records in a physical block of data on tape (or disk). If the CHARACTER option is used, it would indicate the total number of characters in the physical block. It is recommended that the entry be omitted from your program.

The **VALUE OF FILE-ID** Clause

GENERAL FORMAT 7

$$\underline{\text{VALUE}}\ \underline{\text{OF}}\ \underline{\text{FILE-ID}}\text{ IS}\quad \begin{Bmatrix}\text{data-name}\\\text{literal}\end{Bmatrix}$$

This entry is unique to microcomputer versions of COBOL. It is used to identify the drive and the filename to be used as input or output. The SELECT entry merely identifies the assignment of the file to DISK; in mainframe versions of COBOL the SELECT entry would identify the external name of a file assigned by the job-control language. The VALUE OF FILE-ID entry is not used for files assigned to the PRINTER.

If the data-name option is used, the name refers to an alphanumeric data-item described in the WORKING-STORAGE SECTION. The data-item has a maximum of 14 characters in the format ~

with DOS filename conventions:

```
drive:filename.extension
```

```
where drive  =     1 character
      filename =  1 to 8 characters
      extension = 1 to 3 characters
      space     = 1 character (used in data-name option)
```

Examples:

```
  VALUE OF FILE-ID IS 'B:TRANFILE.DAT'
```

or

```
  VALUE OF FILE-ID IS FILENAME
                     .
                     .
                     .
  01   FILENAME.
       05  DRIVE-ID          PIC X.
       05  NEWNAME           PIC X(12).
```

The second example would permit the entry of both the drive and designator and the filename through an ACCEPT entry at execution time, thus allowing considerable flexibility regarding the data to be processed. **Note:** If this second method is used, the name may be shorter than 14 characters but *it must end with a space character.*

Assignment of DISK Files to Other Devices   If the entry CON or USER is assigned to the VALUE OF FILE-ID clause, the output data will be directed to the display console. The difference between the two is that CON will direct the data to the screen as buffered output, blocks at a time, while USER will send the data to the screen character by character. In versions of DOS earlier than 2.0, you must specify CON. In later versions the USER specification is more convenient, because the data appears immediately without waiting for an entire block to fill.

An important entry for the device assignment is NUL. If this entry is used at runtime the file so specified will be considered to be at end of file for an input file and will be ignored if an output file.

Other possible assignments to this clause are LPT1 and PRN, both of which send the output file to the printer. These options are useful in program testing, because they can be altered every time the program is run without recompilation. Best results will be obtained when using

LINE SEQUENTIAL files because the possible control codes contained in the files will be more suitable to the printer and display.

Assignment of PRINTER Files to DISK   Unfortunately, it is not possible in this version of COBOL to direct files that have been assigned to the printer to disk unless there have been no carriage control options such as ADVANCING or LINAGE used. You would also have to change the SELECT entry (requiring recompilation) because files assigned to PRINTER do not allow for a VALUE OF FILE-ID clause. In order, therefore, to assign PRINTER files to DISK, you would create 80 character (or 132 character) disk files, with no carriage return options, write them out on the disk, and print them later using a utility or other program. You can skip lines in this manner by inserting blank records in the file.

The best approach, if the output is to be saved for later printing, would be to create a disk file of the output data and write another program that would read that file and edit it for the printer. In this manner you may use the carriage control features offered for print files.

Procedure Division

Declaratives

An optional entry intended for the processing of input/output errors and for additional processing of the end of file condition is the DECLARATIVES part of a COBOL program. This is included in the program *immediately* after the PROCEDURE DIVISION header.

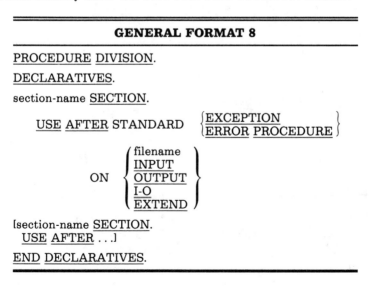

GENERAL FORMAT 8

PROCEDURE DIVISION.

DECLARATIVES.

section-name SECTION.

USE AFTER STANDARD $\begin{Bmatrix} \text{EXCEPTION} \\ \text{ERROR PROCEDURE} \end{Bmatrix}$

ON $\begin{Bmatrix} \text{filename} \\ \text{INPUT} \\ \text{OUTPUT} \\ \text{I-O} \\ \text{EXTEND} \end{Bmatrix}$

[section-name SECTION.
   USE AFTER . . .]

END DECLARATIVES.

The DECLARATIVES sections are processed as a result of input/output errors on a particular file or on all INPUT, OUTPUT files, etc. as specified in the USE sentence. Each section is performed separately and all procedures invoked by a section *must* be contained within that section. The compiler inserts an exit procedure at the end of *each* section to provide for return to the *next sentence after the one that caused the error.*

One of the advantages of using DECLARATIVES is the additional flexibility gained in handling input/output errors. Without this feature, most I/O errors result in program termination. The DECLARATIVES feature allow some action to be taken and the execution of the program resumed.

DECLARATIVES may be used in conjunction with the FILE STATUS clause, and the contents of the FILE STATUS data-item may be tested in the DECLARATIVES section for the file to determine the specific problem. A FILE STATUS entry of 30, which is returned on an attempt to OPEN a file, indicates that the file was not found. Normally this would result in a program termination, but if DECLARATIVES are used alternate action may be initiated.

The AT END condition is also noted in the FILE STATUS data-item, and technically end of file is an error. If the AT END clause is *omitted* from the READ statement, control will be passed to the appropriate DECLARATIVE on the end of file condition.

There will be more discussion of the use of FILE STATUS and DECLARATIVES in the next chapter while describing INDEXED and RELATIVE files.

A typical DECLARATIVES follows:

```
PROCEDURE DIVISION.
  DECLARATIVES.
  INPUT-ERROR SECTION.
      USE AFTER ERROR PROCEDURE ON INFILE.
  INPUT-ERROR-MESSAGES.
      DISPLAY (1,1) ERASE.
      IF FILE-STAT = '30' DISPLAY 'FILE NOT FOUND INFILE'.
      IF FILE-STAT = '10' DISPLAY 'END OF FILE ON INFILE'.
          MOVE 1 TO EOF.
  END DECLARATIVES.
```

The OPEN Statement

As for all files, the OPEN statement must be executed before any access of that file when processing SEQUENTIAL files.

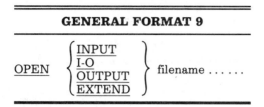

GENERAL FORMAT 9

OPEN $\left\{ \begin{array}{l} \text{INPUT} \\ \text{I-O} \\ \text{OUTPUT} \\ \text{EXTEND} \end{array} \right\}$ filename . . . . . .

INPUT A unique action occurs when SEQUENTIAL files are OPENed as INPUT. The first record is read into memory so that there is no delay when the first READ is issued. This option is available only for files contained on disk.

OUTPUT A file OPENed as OUTPUT will replace a file with the same name so the operator must be sure that previous versions of the sequential file are not available on disk. Or, making use of the variable option of the VALUE OF FILE-ID clause, the procedure should ensure that a new filename is entered. In a monthly update, the filename could be MSTR-JUN.DAT to distinguish it from the previous months MSTR-APR.DAT, etc. Files may be sent to both disk and to the printer using this option.

I-O A file which is OPENed as I-O will have the capability of updating (changing) data on an existing file. It will be possible to do so *without* creating a new file. Of course, if records are to be added or deleted from a SEQUENTIAL file, the entire file will have to be recreated. This type of processing will make use of the READ and REWRITE verbs described below.

EXTEND This option, which is also restricted to output file processing, causes the file to be *added* to the end of an existing sequential file. This is a very useful option when creating a history file and will alleviate the problem of having to merge several files. If a program is run each week and the input transactions are to be saved for an end of month report, this option would allow the adding of each week's records to the previous week's data on the same file.

The CLOSE Statement

Just as the OPEN statement prepares files for subsequent processing, the CLOSE statement removes files from the processing cycle.

GENERAL FORMAT 10

CLOSE filename [WITH LOCK] . . .

After a file has been CLOSEd you may not READ, WRITE, or RE-WRITE to that file; it may, however, be OPENed for subsequent processing. If it has been CLOSEd with the LOCK option it may not be OPENed during the current program.

An example of the CLOSE statement:

```
CLOSE OLD-MAST WITH LOCK
      TRAN-FILE
      PRINT-FILE
      NEW-MAST.
```

PROCESSING SEQUENTIAL FILES

Sequential files are used for many types of applications. It is the most efficient type of file in terms of the use of disk space and in terms of processing time (providing most of the file is to be processed).

The following discussions will be concerned with:

1. creating a sequential file

2. updating a sequential file with recreating

3. updating a sequential file without recreating

Creating a Sequential File

Assume that we are going to create a sequential file, which will be later used to update a master file containing information about magazine subscribers. The input method will be the keyboard, and the data will be output to disk. We will also assume, prior to discussing the COBOL SORT in a later chapter, that all the input data is in ascending sequence by subscriber number. This program is logically equivalent to previously shown programs that input data and write out to the printer. The difference will be in the format of the data being sent to disk (since no editing and no spacing between fields will be required), the assignment of the device to DISK, and the inclusion of the VALUE OF FILE-ID clause in the FD.

```
IDENTIFICATION DIVISION.
PROGRAM-ID. CH1001.
AUTHOR.
    S.J.GAUGHRAN.
***********************************************************************
*                                                                     *
* This program will create a sequential disk file from input          *
* entered from the keyboard. A proof listing is printed and a         *
* control total of the number of records created and a hash           *
* total of the subscription numbers is established.                   *
***********************************************************************
ENVIRONMENT DIVISION.
CONFIGURATION SECTION.
SOURCE-COMPUTER.
    IBM-PERSONAL-COMPUTER.
OBJECT-COMPUTER.
    IBM-PERSONAL-COMPUTER.
FILE-CONTROL.
    SELECT SUB-MAINT ASSIGN TO DISK
        FILE STATUS IS STAT
        ACCESS MODE IS SEQUENTIAL
        ORGANIZATION IS SEQUENTIAL.
    SELECT PRINT-FILE ASSIGN TO PRINTER.
***********************************************************************
DATA DIVISION.
FILE SECTION.
FD  SUB-MAINT
        LABEL RECORDS ARE STANDARD
        VALUE OF FILE-ID IS  NEW-SUB-WS.
01  MAINT-REC                    PIC X(59).
FD  PRINT-FILE
    LABEL RECORDS ARE OMITTED.
01  PRINT-REC                    PIC X(80).
***********************************************************************
WORKING-STORAGE SECTION.
***********************************************************************
01  MAINT-REC-WS.
    05  SUB-NO-MAINT             PIC 9(05).
    05  NAME-MAINT               PIC X(16).
    05  ADDR-MAINT               PIC X(14).
    05  CITY-MAINT               PIC X(12).
    05  STATE-MAINT              PIC XX.
    05  ZIP-MAINT                PIC X(05).
    05  DATE-MAINT.
        10  MONTH-MAINT          PIC 99.
        10  YEAR-MAINT           PIC 99.
    05  DATE-EDIT REDEFINES DATE-MAINT PIC X(04).
    05  CODE-MAINT               PIC X.
***********************************************************************
01  TOTALS-WORKAREAS.
    05  NEW-SUB-WS.
        10  FILENAME             PIC X(14).
        10  FILLER               PIC X       VALUE SPACES.
    05  TOTAL-RECORDS-GOOD       PIC S9(4)   VALUE ZERO.
    05  TOTAL-RECORDS-BAD        PIC S9(4)   VALUE ZERO.
    05  HASH-TOTAL               PIC S9(09)  VALUE ZERO.
    05  STAT                     PIC XX.
    05  END-OF-INPUT             PIC 99      VALUE ZERO.
***********************************************************************
01  TITLE-LINE.
    05  FILLER                   PIC X(02)   VALUE SPACES.
    05  FILLER                   PIC X(03)   VALUE 'NUM'.
    05  FILLER                   PIC X(08)   VALUE SPACES.
    05  FILLER                   PIC X(04)   VALUE 'NAME'.
    05  FILLER                   PIC X(12)   VALUE SPACES.
    05  FILLER                   PIC X(07)   VALUE 'ADDRESS'.
    05  FILLER                   PIC X(07)   VALUE SPACES.
    05  FILLER                   PIC X(04)   VALUE 'CITY'.
    05  FILLER                   PIC X(09)   VALUE SPACES.
    05  FILLER                   PIC X(02)   VALUE 'ST'.
    05  FILLER                   PIC X(03)   VALUE SPACES.
    05  FILLER                   PIC X(03)   VALUE 'ZIP'.
```

Fig. 10–1. Program used to create a sequential disk file.

```
     05   FILLER                   PIC X(03)   VALUE SPACES.
     05   FILLER                   PIC X(03)   VALUE 'EXP'.
     05   FILLER                   PIC X(04)   VALUE SPACES.
     05   FILLER                   PIC X(03)   VALUE 'TYP'.
************************************************************
01   DETAIL-LINE.
     05   FILLER                   PIC X(01)       VALUE SPACES.
     05   SUB-NO-OUT               PIC X(05).
     05   FILLER                   PIC X(02)       VALUE SPACES.
     05   SUB-NAME-OUT             PIC X(16).
     05   FILLER                   PIC X(02)       VALUE SPACES.
     05   ADDR-OUT                 PIC X(14).
     05   FILLER                   PIC X(02)       VALUE SPACES.
     05   CITY-OUT                 PIC X(12).
     05   FILLER                   PIC X(02)       VALUE SPACES.
     05   STATE-OUT                PIC XX.
     05   FILLER                   PIC X(02)       VALUE SPACES.
     05   ZIP-OUT                  PIC X(05).
     05   FILLER                   PIC X(02)       VALUE SPACES.
     05   DATE-OUT                 PIC XX/XX.
     05   FILLER                   PIC X(02)       VALUE SPACES.
     05   MESSAGE-OUT              PIC X(05)       VALUE SPACES.
************************************************************
01   TOTAL-LINE.
     05   FILLER                   PIC X(02)       VALUE SPACES.
     05   FILLER                   PIC X(15)
               VALUE 'TOTAL GOOD REC '.
     05   TOTAL-RECORDS-GOOD-OUT   PIC Z(04).
     05   FILLER                   PIC X(03)       VALUE SPACES.
     05   FILLER                   PIC X(16)
               VALUE 'TOTAL ERROR REC '.
     05   TOTAL-RECORDS-BAD-OUT    PIC Z(04).
     05   FILLER                   PIC X(03)       VALUE SPACES.
     05   FILLER                   PIC X(23)
               VALUE 'HASH TOTAL - GOOD RECS '.
     05   HASH-TOTAL-OUT           PIC Z(09).
************************************************************
SCREEN SECTION.
************************************************************
01   FIRST-SCREEN.
     05   BLANK SCREEN.
     05   LINE 15 COLUMN 10 REVERSE-VIDEO
               VALUE 'Enter Output Filename In DOS Format '.
     05   LINE 17 COLUMN 10 PIC X(14) TO FILENAME.
************************************************************
01   INPUT-SCREEN.
     05   BLANK SCREEN.
     05   LINE 1   COLUMN 11 VALUE '**** '.
     05   LINE 1   COLUMN 16 VALUE 'IF LAST ENTRY PRESS ESC '.
     05   LINE 1   COLUMN 54 VALUE '**** '.
     05   LINE 2   COLUMN 21 VALUE 'SUBSCRIPTION UPDATE - INPUT '.
     05   LINE 4   COLUMN 11 VALUE 'TRANSACTION TYPE: (1 = DELETE'.
     05   LINE 4   COLUMN 40 VALUE ' / 2 = ADD)'.
     05   LINE 4   COLUMN 52 PIC 9 TO CODE-MAINT AUTO.
     05   LINE 6   COLUMN 11 VALUE 'SUBSCRIBER NUMBER: '.
     05   LINE 6   COLUMN 30 PIC 9(5) TO SUB-NO-MAINT.
     05   LINE 8   COLUMN 22 VALUE 'NAME: '.
     05   LINE 8   COLUMN 30 PIC X(16) TO NAME-MAINT.
     05   LINE 10  COLUMN 22 VALUE 'STREET: '.
     05   LINE 10  COLUMN 30 PIC X(14) TO ADDR-MAINT.
     05   LINE 12  COLUMN 22 VALUE 'CITY: '.
     05   LINE 12  COLUMN 30 PIC X(12) TO CITY-MAINT.
     05   LINE 14  COLUMN 22 VALUE 'STATE: '.
     05   LINE 14  COLUMN 30 PIC XX TO STATE-MAINT AUTO.
     05   LINE 14  COLUMN 35 VALUE 'ZIP: '.
     05   LINE 14  COLUMN 39 PIC X(5) TO ZIP-MAINT AUTO.
     05   LINE 16  COLUMN 11 VALUE 'EXPIRATION DATE: '.
     05   LINE 16  COLUMN 30 VALUE 'MONTH: '.
     05   LINE 16  COLUMN 37 PIC 99 TO MONTH-MAINT AUTO.
     05   LINE 16  COLUMN 41 VALUE 'YEAR: '.
     05   LINE 16  COLUMN 47 PIC 99 TO YEAR-MAINT AUTO.
************************************************************
PROCEDURE DIVISION.
DECLARATIVES.
```

Fig. 10-1. (*continued*)

```
FILE-CREATE-ERROR SECTION.
    USE AFTER ERROR PROCEDURE ON SUB-MAINT.
CREATE-ERRORS.
        IF STAT = '34' DISPLAY 'DISK IS FULL'.
        IF STAT = '30' DISPLAY 'UNABLE TO OPEN FILE '
                    DISPLAY 'CHECK NAME:  ' NEW-SUB-WS
                    DISPLAY 'AND RESTART PROGRAM '.
    STOP RUN.
END DECLARATIVES.
******************************************************************
MAIN-LINE.
    DISPLAY FIRST-SCREEN.
    ACCEPT  FIRST-SCREEN.
    OPEN OUTPUT SUB-MAINT
                PRINT-FILE.
    PERFORM HDR-ROUTINE.
    PERFORM CREATE-ROUTINE THRU CREATE-ROUTINE-EXIT
                UNTIL END-OF-INPUT = 01.
    PERFORM TOTAL-ROUTINE.
    CLOSE SUB-MAINT
          PRINT-FILE.
    STOP RUN.
******************************************************************
HDR-ROUTINE.
    WRITE PRINT-REC FROM TITLE-LINE
          AFTER ADVANCING PAGE.
    MOVE SPACES TO PRINT-REC.
    WRITE PRINT-REC
          AFTER ADVANCING 1.
******************************************************************
CREATE-ROUTINE.
    DISPLAY INPUT-SCREEN.
    ACCEPT  INPUT-SCREEN ON ESCAPE
                    MOVE 01 TO END-OF-INPUT
                    GO TO CREATE-ROUTINE-EXIT.
    MOVE SUB-NO-MAINT           TO SUB-NO-OUT.
    MOVE NAME-MAINT             TO SUB-NAME-OUT.
    MOVE ADDR-MAINT             TO ADDR-OUT.
    MOVE CITY-MAINT             TO CITY-OUT.
    MOVE STATE-MAINT            TO STATE-OUT.
    MOVE ZIP-MAINT              TO ZIP-OUT.
    MOVE DATE-EDIT              TO DATE-OUT.
    IF CODE-MAINT = 1       MOVE 'DEL ' TO MESSAGE-OUT
    ELSE
        IF CODE-MAINT = 2  MOVE 'NEW' TO MESSAGE-OUT
        ELSE
                    MOVE 'ERROR' TO MESSAGE-OUT.
    IF CODE-MAINT = 1   OR   2
                WRITE MAINT-REC FROM MAINT-REC-WS
                ADD 1           TO TOTAL-RECORDS-GOOD
                ADD SUB-NO-MAINT TO HASH-TOTAL
    ELSE    ADD 1 TO TOTAL-RECORDS-BAD.
    WRITE PRINT-REC FROM DETAIL-LINE
                AFTER ADVANCING 1.
CREATE-ROUTINE-EXIT.
    EXIT.
TOTAL-ROUTINE.
    MOVE TOTAL-RECORDS-GOOD    TO TOTAL-RECORDS-GOOD-OUT.
    MOVE TOTAL-RECORDS-BAD     TO TOTAL-RECORDS-BAD-OUT.
    MOVE HASH-TOTAL            TO HASH-TOTAL-OUT.
    WRITE PRINT-REC FROM TOTAL-LINE
                AFTER ADVANCING 2.
```

Fig. 10-1. (*continued*)

> *The complete source program shown in Fig. 10–1 is available*
> *on the supplemental disk as filename CH1001.COB.*

Note the addition of the optional clause

```
FILE STATUS IS STAT
```

in the SELECT entry for the output file. This refers to a two-character
data item in working-storage that will contain a specific code reflecting
the outcome of any operation concerning the file. The specific codes
are described above. In the same entry we have

```
ACCESS MODE IS SEQUENTIAL
ORGANIZATION IS SEQUENTIAL
```

both of which are optional, since sequential is the default. We have included them for documentation purposes because in the next chapter
we will be dealing with other options.

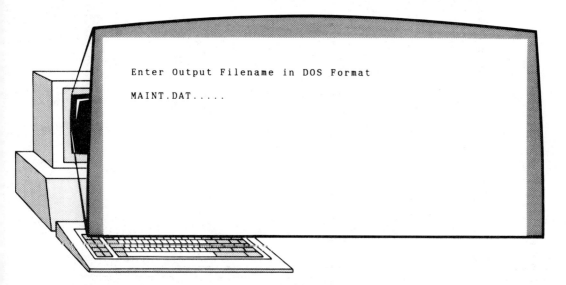

Fig. 10–2. Screen for entry of filename.

In the FD for the file SUB-MAINT the VALUE OF FILE-ID clause specifies another data item, NEW-SUB-WS, which is to contain the actual DOS filename when this program executes. This will make it possible to vary the filename during operation of this series of programs.

The SCREEN SECTION begins with an entry called FIRST-SCREEN. Figure 10-2 shows what will appear when the program begins.

The second entry in the SCREEN SECTION is the INPUT-SCREEN used to enter the data for transfer to the disk. This screen appears in Fig. 10-3.

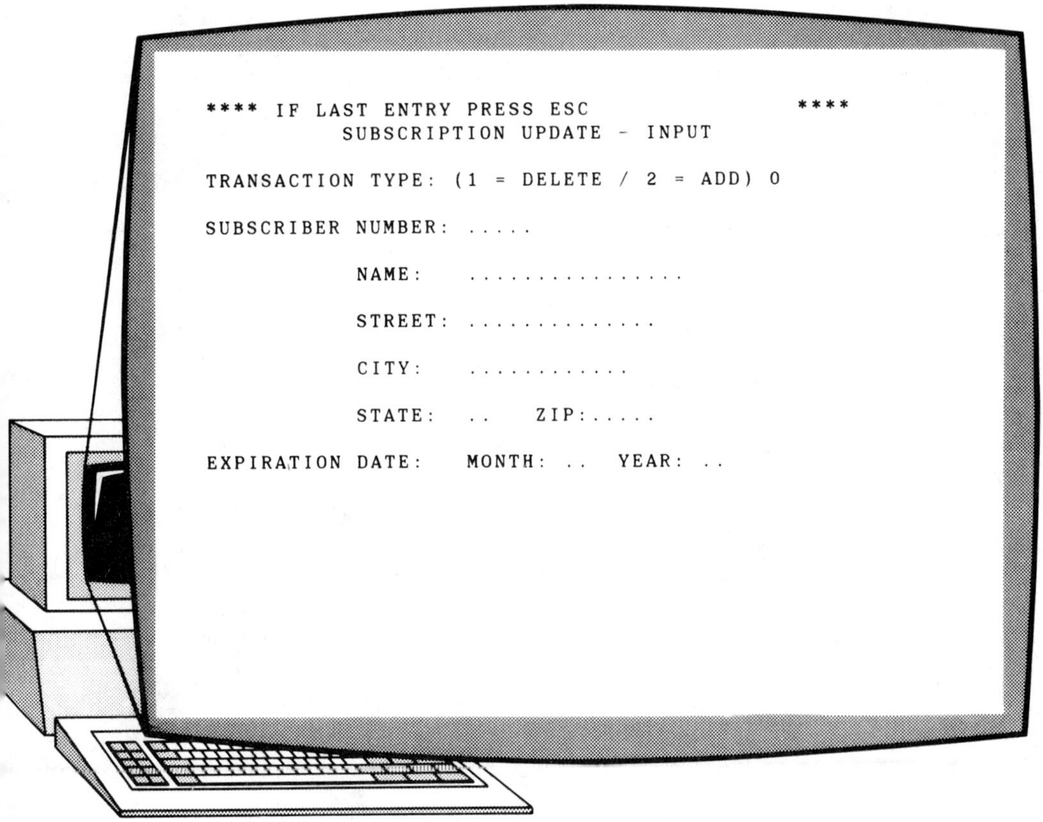

```
**** IF LAST ENTRY PRESS ESC                    ****
            SUBSCRIPTION UPDATE - INPUT

TRANSACTION TYPE: (1 = DELETE / 2 = ADD) 0

SUBSCRIBER NUMBER: .....

          NAME:    ...............

          STREET:  .............

          CITY:    ...........

          STATE:   ..    ZIP:.....

EXPIRATION DATE:   MONTH: ..  YEAR: ..
```

Fig. 10-3. Input screen.

The next new entry is the DECLARATIVES, which must be located immediately after the PROCEDURE DIVISION header. This consists of one section, since we are only concerned with one disk file in this program. If an error condition occurs, control will be transferred to this section. We have included two tests to determine the specific problem. These tests check the contents of STAT (the FILE STATUS entry) and display an appropriate message. Since we are creating a file, the only errors we will test for will be to check if the filename is invalid or if the disk is full. Since both of these would be unrecoverable errors, we have inserted a STOP RUN at this point rather than have control passed back to the statement immediately after the input/output statement that caused the error.

The remainder of this program provides for the input of data from the keyboard using the DISPLAY and ACCEPT screen statements, transfer of the data to the disk and the printer (where a proof list is prepared), and the accumulating of control totals for good records (valid transaction codes), bad records, and a hash total of the subscriber numbers. This hash total can be used in a manual check to ensure that all data has been entered.

Updating a Sequential File—Recreating

The second program required in this little system is one that will allow for the addition or deletion of records from a sequential master file. The term *master file* is used to indicate that it contains data that is being retained because the data is relatively stable. Most systems are built around a master file—the record of our account in a department store, the payroll master, which records the permanent data about out pay, etc.

Most of the processing of master files involves changing the data and adding or deleting records from the file. We will use the technique of adding and deleting records from the file in this example. The ability to change data in an existing record will be shown in the next example. It should be noted that an ability to change existing records could have been included in this program.

The complete source program shown in Fig. 10–4 is available on the supplemental disk as filename CH1002.COB.

```
IDENTIFICATION DIVISION.
PROGRAM-ID.
    CH1002.
AUTHOR.
    S.J.GAUGHRAN.
**********************************************************************
* This program has two input files, in the same sequence and        *
* one output file. It is an example of a simple sequential file     *
* update. A 'file dump' has been included to check whether the      *
* proper updating has been accomplished.                            *
**********************************************************************
ENVIRONMENT DIVISION.
CONFIGURATION SECTION.
SOURCE-COMPUTER.
    IBM-PERSONAL-COMPUTER.
OBJECT-COMPUTER.
    IBM-PERSONAL-COMPUTER.
INPUT-OUTPUT SECTION.
FILE-CONTROL.
    SELECT SUB-MAST-OLD ASSIGN TO DISK
        FILE STATUS IS STAT
        ACCESS IS SEQUENTIAL
        ORGANIZATION IS SEQUENTIAL.
    SELECT SUB-MAST-NEW ASSIGN TO DISK
        FILE STATUS IS STAT
        ACCESS IS SEQUENTIAL
        ORGANIZATION IS SEQUENTIAL.
    SELECT SUB-MAINT  ASSIGN TO DISK
        FILE STATUS IS STAT
        ACCESS IS SEQUENTIAL
        ORGANIZATION IS SEQUENTIAL.
**********************************************************************
DATA DIVISION.
FILE SECTION.
FD  SUB-MAST-OLD
    LABEL RECORDS ARE STANDARD
    VALUE OF FILE-ID IS OLD-MAST-DOS.
01  OLD-REC.
    05  SUB-NO-OLD-IN     PIC X(05).
    05  NAME-OLD-IN       PIC X(16).
    05  ADDR-OLD-IN       PIC X(14).
    05  CITY-OLD-IN       PIC X(12).
    05  STATE-OLD-IN      PIC XX.
    05  ZIP-OLD-IN        PIC X(05).
    05  DATE-OLD-IN       PIC X(04).
**********************************************************************
FD  SUB-MAST-NEW
    LABEL RECORDS ARE STANDARD
    VALUE OF FILE-ID IS NEW-MAST-DOS.
01  NEW-REC.
    05  SUB-NO-NEW-OUT    PIC X(05).
    05  NAME-NEW-OUT      PIC X(16).
    05  ADDR-NEW-OUT      PIC X(14).
    05  CITY-NEW-OUT      PIC X(12).
    05  STATE-NEW-OUT     PIC XX.
    05  ZIP-NEW-OUT       PIC X(05).
    05  DATE-NEW-OUT      PIC X(04).
**********************************************************************
FD  SUB-MAINT
    LABEL RECORDS ARE STANDARD
    VALUE OF FILE-ID IS SUB-MAINT-DOS.
01  MAINT-REC.
    05  SUB-NO-MAINT      PIC X(05).
    05  NAME-MAINT        PIC X(16).
    05  ADDR-MAINT        PIC X(14).
    05  CITY-MAINT        PIC X(12).
    05  STATE-MAINT       PIC XX.
    05  ZIP-MAINT         PIC X(05).
    05  DATE-MAINT        PIC X(04).
    05  CODE-MAINT        PIC X.
**********************************************************************
```

Fig. 10-4. Sequential update program.

```
WORKING-STORAGE SECTION.
01  WORKAREAS.
    05  EOF              PIC 9   VALUE 0.
    05  STAT             PIC XX  VALUE SPACES.
    05  OLD-MAST-DOS.
        10  FILLER       PIC X(14).
        10  FILLER       PIC X(01) VALUE SPACE.
    05  NEW-MAST-DOS.
        10  FILLER       PIC X(14).
        10  FILLER       PIC X(01) VALUE SPACE.
    05  SUB-MAINT-DOS.
        10  FILLER       PIC X(14).
        10  FILLER       PIC X(01) VALUE SPACE.
****************************************************************
 SCREEN SECTION.
****************************************************************
01  FIRST-SCREEN.
    05  BLANK SCREEN.
    05  LINE 15 COLUMN 24 REVERSE-VIDEO
                VALUE ' Enter Filenames In DOS Format '.
    05  LINE 17 COLUMN 28 VALUE 'OLD MASTER :'.
    05  LINE 17 COLUMN 41 PIC X(14) TO OLD-MAST-DOS.
    05  LINE 19 COLUMN 28 VALUE 'NEW MASTER :'.
    05  LINE 19 COLUMN 41 PIC X(14) TO NEW-MAST-DOS.
    05  LINE 21 COLUMN 28 VALUE 'MAINT UPDATE :'.
    05  LINE 21 COLUMN 42 PIC X(14) TO SUB-MAINT-DOS.
****************************************************************
 PROCEDURE DIVISION.
 DECLARATIVES.
 OLD-MASTER SECTION.
     USE AFTER ERROR PROCEDURE SUB-MAST-OLD.
 OLD-MAST-ERROR.
     IF STAT = '10' MOVE HIGH-VALUES TO SUB-NO-OLD-IN
     ELSE IF STAT = '30' DISPLAY 'ERROR ON OLD MASTER '.
 NEW-MASTER SECTION.
     USE AFTER ERROR PROCEDURE SUB-MAST-NEW.
 NEW-MAST-ERROR.
     IF STAT = '30' DISPLAY 'ERROR ON NEW-MASTER'
     ELSE IF STAT = '34' DISPLAY 'DISK FULL '.
 SUB-MAINT-FILE SECTION.
     USE AFTER ERROR PROCEDURE SUB-MAINT.
 SUB-MAINT-ERROR.
     IF STAT = '10' MOVE HIGH-VALUES TO SUB-NO-MAINT
     ELSE IF STAT = '30' DISPLAY 'ERROR ON SUB-MAINT'.
 END DECLARATIVES.
 FILE-ENTRY.
     DISPLAY FIRST-SCREEN.
     ACCEPT  FIRST-SCREEN.
 BEGIN.
     OPEN INPUT  SUB-MAST-OLD
                 SUB-MAINT
          OUTPUT SUB-MAST-NEW.
     PERFORM READ-MASTER.
     PERFORM READ-MAINT.
     PERFORM LOOP-RTN UNTIL
             SUB-NO-OLD-IN = HIGH-VALUES
         AND
             SUB-NO-MAINT  = HIGH-VALUES.
     CLOSE SUB-MAST-OLD
           SUB-MAINT
           SUB-MAST-NEW.
     PERFORM DUMP-RTN.
     STOP RUN.
****************************************************************
 LOOP-RTN.
     IF SUB-NO-OLD-IN  EQUAL TO SUB-NO-MAINT
         PERFORM DELETE-RTN
     ELSE  IF SUB-NO-OLD-IN  LESS THAN SUB-NO-MAINT
             PERFORM NO-CHANGE-RTN
           ELSE PERFORM ADD-RTN.
****************************************************************
 DELETE-RTN.
     IF CODE-MAINT  NOT   EQUAL TO '1'
         DISPLAY 'DELETE CODE ERROR'
```

Fig. 10–4. (*continued*)

354

```
                    MOVE OLD-REC      TO NEW-REC
                    PERFORM READ-MAINT
                    PERFORM NO-CHANGE-RTN
               ELSE PERFORM READ-MASTER
                    PERFORM READ-MAINT.
*********************************************************************
     NO-CHANGE-RTN.
          MOVE OLD-REC          TO NEW-REC.
          PERFORM WRITE-MASTER.
          PERFORM READ-MASTER.
*********************************************************************
     ADD-RTN.
          IF CODE-MAINT  NOT  EQUAL TO '2'
                    DISPLAY 'ADD CODE ERROR'
                    PERFORM READ-MAINT
          ELSE MOVE MAINT-REC  TO NEW-REC
               PERFORM WRITE-MASTER
               PERFORM READ-MAINT.
*********************************************************************
     READ-MASTER.
          READ SUB-MAST-OLD.
*********************************************************************
     READ-MAINT.
          READ SUB-MAINT.
*********************************************************************
     WRITE-MASTER.
          WRITE NEW-REC.
*********************************************************************
     DUMP-RTN.
          OPEN INPUT SUB-MAST-NEW.
          READ SUB-MAST-NEW AT END MOVE 1 TO EOF.
          PERFORM READ-IT UNTIL EOF = 1.
          CLOSE SUB-MAST-NEW.
*********************************************************************
     READ-IT.
          DISPLAY NEW-REC.
          READ SUB-MAST-NEW AT END MOVE 1 TO EOF.
```

Fig. 10–4. (*continued*)

This program does not introduce any new COBOL statements but is principally concerned with specific programming techniques. We have chosen to simplify this program and have it deal only with adding and deleting records from the file in order to more clearly demonstrate the principal of sequential update logic.

This is a "classic" programming problem, and prior to the advent of direct access devices (disks) this was the only method for maintaining master files. One major difficulty lies in dealing with several end of file possibilities while matching the master and detail (transaction) records so that a new file in the proper sequence may be created. Sequential files do not have specific addresses on the disk; they are processed successfully on the basis of the records in each file being in the same sequence.

In our sample program, the master file (SUB-MAST-OLD) is to be updated on the basis of records contained in the detail file (SUB-

MAINT) and the *entire* new master file is to be created as SUB-MAST-NEW. This creation of a complete new master is an important consideration. One of the advantages of sequential processing is its speed—but only when a major portion of the file is involved.

The program differs from previous programs in that it involves three files, all assigned to DISK. The DECLARATIVES, therefore, have entries and appropriate error routines for three files. You will note that each file has its own section, a requirement when using DECLARATIVES. You may use the option of establishing a section for all INPUT or OUTPUT rather than for specific files. Note in the DECLARATIVES that we are also testing for a '10'. This is the value in the FILE STATUS entry for end of file. We have chosen to demonstrate this method rather than using the AT END clause of the READ statement. The end of file signal is considered to be an error by the operating system and a value of '10' is entered into FILE STATUS. There is no particular advantage to treating the end of file in this manner but it does allow us to use the DECLARATIVES for any exception to the specified input/output operation.

Program Logic   As shown in Fig. 10-5, this program will have three files, which must be named before operation can begin. A small problem arises at this point regarding the *first* time that this program is run—there will be no SUB-MAST-OLD. IBM COBOL provides for

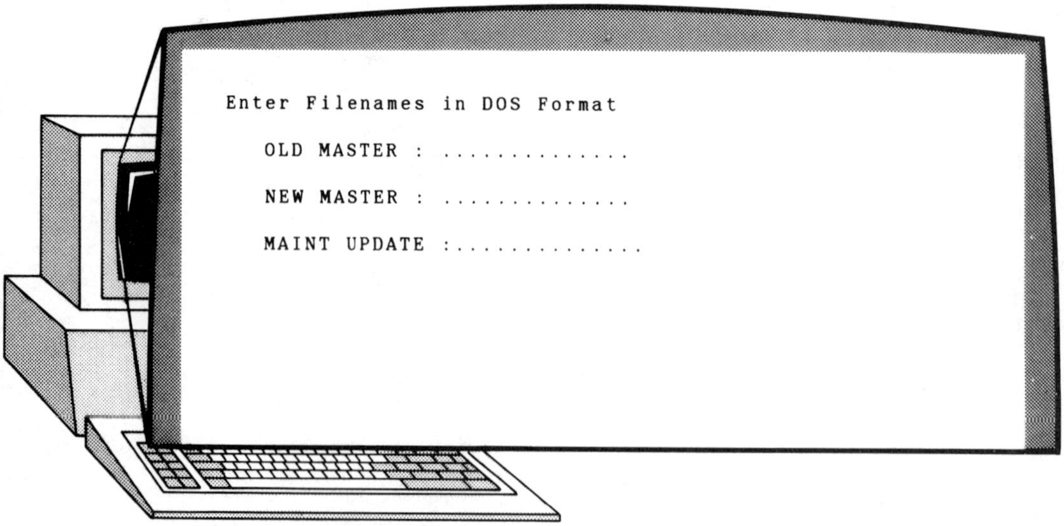

Fig. 10–5.   Screen for entry of filenames.

this situation in allowing us to specify a filename of NUL. This will cause *all* references to the file to be ignored—in fact, a file given the DOS name of NUL will be considered to be at end of file immediately. This works very well during the first update cycle when we are creating the master file, and could, of course, be used in any situation in which a program is to be run without one of the files being used.

Once the filenames have been established, the initialization part of the program, called BEGIN in this example, is executed. Note that since there are two input files we will have a priming READ for both files:

```
PERFORM READ-MASTER.
PERFORM READ-MAINT.
```

Note also that the main loop of this program is controlled by the end of file condition in *both* input files.

```
PERFORM LOOP-RTN UNTIL
        SUB-NO-OLD-IN = HIGH-VALUES
   AND
        SUB-NO-MAINT  = HIGH-VALUES.
```

This involves placing the figurative constant HIGH-VALUES into the field SUB-NO-OLD-IN in the master file at end of the file and placing HIGH-VALUES into the field SUB-NO-MAINT in the detail file when it reaches the end. Thus, depending on which file reaches an end of file condition first, the value HIGH-VALUES is placed in the key field (the one on which the file is sequenced). Since HIGH-VALUES will always test greater than the key field value in the record being tested against it in the other file, the actual record will always be processed. In essence, we will have forced the processing of the remaining file to completion after the first file reaches end of file.

If SUB-MAST-OLD reaches end of file first, the remaining records in SUB-MAINT will be processed. If SUB-MAINT reaches end of file first, the remaining records in SUB-MAST-OLD will be processed. Regardless of which file reaches the end first, this procedure will guarantee the processing of the remaining records from the other file. When both have reached end of file, both will contain HIGH-VALUES in the key field and the condition of the PERFORM...UNTIL will be satisfied.

It should be noted that since *HIGH-VALUES is alphanumeric*, it was necessary to define the key fields used in the comparison (SUB-NO-OLD-IN and SUB-NO-MAINT) as alphanumeric so that when either reaches an end HIGH-VALUES may be moved to the appropriate field.

Note that in this program, this move is done in the DECLARATIVES; an alternative is to do it in the AT END clause.

The paragraph LOOP-RTN is used to determine the relationship between SUB-NO-OLD-IN and SUB-NO-MAINT. In the first IF statement, the condition SUB-NO-OLD EQUAL TO SUB-NO-MAINT is tested. If the condition is equal, it is assumed that the record is to be deleted, since this program only adds and deletes records from the master file. Note that in DELETE-RTN we check to see if the code is a 1, for deleting a record, and if it is not the record is written on the new master (SUB-MAST-NEW) and an error message is shown on the console. If the comparison shows that SUB-NO-OLD-IN IS LESS THAN SUB-NO-MAINT there is no delete and the current master record is written to the new master on disk.

The only possible condition if none of the above were true is that the key field in the master file is greater than the key in the detail, indicating that a *new* record is to be added to the file. Here again, the code is checked. If it is not a 2 for an added record, an error message is displayed and the record is *not* written on the new master file.

To keep this program simple, we did not include a printout, but we have included a routine called DUMP-RTN, which will be executed after the end of file on both the master and the detail files. This routine will OPEN the new master file (SUB-MAST-NEW) as INPUT, read the file, and display it on the console. As noted in previous chapters, the program could be altered to cause this display to be directed to the printer.

The logic of this program should be studied carefully; many problems require similar logical reasoning for their solution. In addition, the concepts illustrated in this simplified update program apply to virtually every update of a standard sequential organized file.

Updating a Sequential File—Without Recreating

When sequential files are stored on disk, which is the normal situation with the IBM PC, it is possible to make changes to *existing* records without recreating the entire file. Two COBOL statements make this possible:

1. Opening a file as I-O

2. Use of the REWRITE verb

The program shown in Fig. 10–6 is an example of such a program. This program has been written to allow for changes to the master file (SUB-MAST).

```
        IDENTIFICATION DIVISION.
        PROGRAM-ID. CH1003.
**************************************************************
*                                                          *
* This program will update a sequential disk file from input *
* entered from the keyboard. This program allows for changes in *
* existing records on a sequential file. It is referred to as *
* updating a sequential file 'in place' without recreating the *
* entire file.                                             *
**************************************************************
        ENVIRONMENT DIVISION.
        CONFIGURATION SECTION.
        SOURCE-COMPUTER.
            IBM-PERSONAL-COMPUTER.
        OBJECT-COMPUTER.
            IBM-PERSONAL-COMPUTER.
        FILE-CONTROL.
            SELECT SUB-MAST ASSIGN TO DISK
                FILE STATUS IS STAT
                ACCESS MODE IS SEQUENTIAL
                ORGANIZATION IS SEQUENTIAL.
            SELECT PRINT-FILE ASSIGN TO PRINTER.
**************************************************************
        DATA DIVISION.
        FILE SECTION.
        FD  SUB-MAST
                LABEL RECORDS ARE STANDARD
                VALUE OF FILE-ID IS  SUB-MAST-WS.
        01  MAST-REC                  PIC X(58).
        FD  PRINT-FILE
            LABEL RECORDS ARE OMITTED.
        01  PRINT-REC                 PIC X(80).
**************************************************************
        WORKING-STORAGE SECTION.
**************************************************************
        01  MAST-REC-WS.
            05  SUB-NO-MAST           PIC X(05).
            05  NAME-MAST             PIC X(16).
            05  ADDR-MAST             PIC X(14).
            05  CITY-MAST             PIC X(12).
            05  STATE-MAST            PIC XX.
            05  ZIP-MAST              PIC X(05).
            05  DATE-MAST.
                10  MONTH-MAST        PIC 99.
                10  YEAR-MAST         PIC 99.
            05  DATE-EDIT REDEFINES DATE-MAST PIC X(04).
**************************************************************
        01  TOTALS-WORKAREAS.
            05  FIND-NO               PIC X(05).
            05  SUB-MAST-WS.
                10  FILENAME-MAST     PIC X(14).
                10  FILLER            PIC X       VALUE SPACES.
            05  TOTAL-RECORDS-GOOD    PIC S9(4)   VALUE ZERO.
            05  TOTAL-RECORDS-BAD     PIC S9(4)   VALUE ZERO.
            05  HASH-TOTAL            PIC S9(09)  VALUE ZERO.
            05  STAT                  PIC XX.
            05  END-OF-INPUT          PIC 99      VALUE ZERO.
**************************************************************
        01  TITLE-LINE.
            05  FILLER                PIC X(02)   VALUE SPACES.
            05  FILLER                PIC X(03)   VALUE 'NUM'.
            05  FILLER                PIC X(08)   VALUE SPACES.
            05  FILLER                PIC X(04)   VALUE 'NAME'.
            05  FILLER                PIC X(12)   VALUE SPACES.
            05  FILLER                PIC X(07)   VALUE 'ADDRESS'.
            05  FILLER                PIC X(07)   VALUE SPACES.
            05  FILLER                PIC X(04)   VALUE 'CITY'.
            05  FILLER                PIC X(09)   VALUE SPACES.
            05  FILLER                PIC X(02)   VALUE 'ST'.
            05  FILLER                PIC X(03)   VALUE SPACES.
            05  FILLER                PIC X(03)   VALUE 'ZIP'.
            05  FILLER                PIC X(03)   VALUE SPACES.
```

Fig. 10–6. Program used to change existing records.

```
      05  FILLER                        PIC X(03)  VALUE 'EXP'.
      05  FILLER                        PIC X(04)  VALUE SPACES.
*******************************************************************
01  DETAIL-LINE.
      05  FILLER                        PIC X(01)     VALUE SPACES.
      05  SUB-NO-OUT                    PIC X(05).
      05  FILLER                        PIC X(02)     VALUE SPACES.
      05  SUB-NAME-OUT                  PIC X(16).
      05  FILLER                        PIC X(02)     VALUE SPACES.
      05  ADDR-OUT                      PIC X(14).
      05  FILLER                        PIC X(02)     VALUE SPACES.
      05  CITY-OUT                      PIC X(12).
      05  FILLER                        PIC X(02)     VALUE SPACES.
      05  STATE-OUT                     PIC XX.
      05  FILLER                        PIC X(02)     VALUE SPACES.
      05  ZIP-OUT                       PIC X(05).
      05  FILLER                        PIC X(02)     VALUE SPACES.
      05  DATE-OUT                      PIC XX/XX.
      05  FILLER                        PIC X(02)     VALUE SPACES.
*******************************************************************
01  TOTAL-LINE.
      05  FILLER                        PIC X(02)     VALUE SPACES.
      05  FILLER                        PIC X(15)
                      VALUE 'TOTAL GOOD REC '.
      05  TOTAL-RECORDS-GOOD-OUT        PIC Z(04).
      05  FILLER                        PIC X(03)     VALUE SPACES.
*******************************************************************
SCREEN SECTION.
*******************************************************************
01  FIRST-SCREEN.
      05  BLANK SCREEN.
      05  LINE 15 COLUMN 10 REVERSE-VIDEO
              VALUE ' Enter Master Filename In DOS Format '.
      05  LINE 17 COLUMN 10 PIC X(14) TO FILENAME-MAST.
*******************************************************************
01  INPUT-SCREEN.
      05  BLANK SCREEN.
      05  LINE 6   COLUMN 11 VALUE 'SUBSCRIBER NUMBER: '.
      05  LINE 6   COLUMN 30 PIC 9(5) USING SUB-NO-MAST.
      05  LINE 8   COLUMN 22 VALUE 'NAME: '.
      05  LINE 8   COLUMN 30 PIC X(16) USING NAME-MAST.
      05  LINE 10  COLUMN 22 VALUE 'STREET: '.
      05  LINE 10  COLUMN 30 PIC X(14) USING ADDR-MAST.
      05  LINE 12  COLUMN 22 VALUE 'CITY: '.
      05  LINE 12  COLUMN 30 PIC X(12) USING CITY-MAST.
      05  LINE 14  COLUMN 22 VALUE 'STATE: '.
      05  LINE 14  COLUMN 30 PIC XX USING STATE-MAST AUTO.
      05  LINE 14  COLUMN 35 VALUE 'ZIP: '.
      05  LINE 14  COLUMN 39 PIC X(5) USING ZIP-MAST AUTO.
      05  LINE 16  COLUMN 11 VALUE 'EXPIRATION DATE: '.
      05  LINE 16  COLUMN 30 VALUE 'MONTH: '.
      05  LINE 16  COLUMN 37 PIC 99 USING MONTH-MAST AUTO.
      05  LINE 16  COLUMN 41 VALUE 'YEAR: '.
      05  LINE 16  COLUMN 47 PIC 99 USING YEAR-MAST AUTO.
      05  LINE 20 COLUMN 10 REVERSE-VIDEO VALUE
          'If data Is not to be changed In any field press RETURN '.


*******************************************************************
PROCEDURE DIVISION.
DECLARATIVES.
FILE-CREATE-ERROR SECTION.
    USE AFTER ERROR PROCEDURE ON SUB-MAST.
CREATE-ERRORS.
        DISPLAY (5, 5) ' '
        IF STAT = '34' DISPLAY (, ) 'DISK IS FULL'.
        IF STAT = '30' DISPLAY (, ) 'UNABLE TO OPEN FILE '
                       DISPLAY (, ) 'CHECK NAME:  ' SUB-MAST-WS
                       DISPLAY (, ) 'AND RESTART PROGRAM '.
        IF STAT = '10' DISPLAY (, ) 'END OF FILE on Master File '
                       DISPLAY (, ) 'Acct ' FIND-NO ' NOT FOUND '
                       DISPLAY (, ) 'CHECK AND RESTART PROGRAM '.
```

Fig. 10–6. (*continued*)

```
        STOP RUN.
    END DECLARATIVES.
***************************************************************
MAIN-LINE.
        DISPLAY FIRST-SCREEN.
        ACCEPT  FIRST-SCREEN.
        OPEN I-O    SUB-MAST
            OUTPUT PRINT-FILE.
        PERFORM HDR-ROUTINE.
        PERFORM CREATE-ROUTINE THRU CREATE-ROUTINE-EXIT
                    UNTIL END-OF-INPUT = 01.
        PERFORM TOTAL-ROUTINE.
        CLOSE SUB-MAST
            PRINT-FILE.
        STOP RUN.
***************************************************************
HDR-ROUTINE.
        WRITE PRINT-REC FROM TITLE-LINE
            AFTER ADVANCING PAGE.
        MOVE SPACES TO PRINT-REC.
        WRITE PRINT-REC
            AFTER ADVANCING 1.
***************************************************************
CREATE-ROUTINE.
        DISPLAY (1, 1) ERASE.
        DISPLAY (2, 5) 'Enter Subscription Number to be changed '.
        DISPLAY (3, 9) ' or 99999 to end program '.
        ACCEPT (, ) FIND-NO WITH PROMPT LENGTH-CHECK.
        IF FIND-NO = 99999 MOVE 01 TO END-OF-INPUT
                    GO TO CREATE-ROUTINE-EXIT.
        PERFORM FIND-IT UNTIL SUB-NO-MAST  = FIND-NO
                    OR
                    SUB-NO-MAST  >  FIND-NO.
        IF SUB-NO-MAST  > FIND-NO  PERFORM ERROR-RTN
                    GO TO CREATE-ROUTINE-EXIT.
        DISPLAY INPUT-SCREEN.
        ACCEPT  INPUT-SCREEN ON ESCAPE
                    MOVE 01 TO END-OF-INPUT
                    GO TO CREATE-ROUTINE-EXIT.
        MOVE SUB-NO-MAST     TO SUB-NO-OUT.
        MOVE NAME-MAST            TO SUB-NAME-OUT.
        MOVE ADDR-MAST            TO ADDR-OUT.
        MOVE CITY-MAST            TO CITY-OUT.
        MOVE STATE-MAST           TO STATE-OUT.
        MOVE ZIP-MAST             TO ZIP-OUT.
        MOVE DATE-EDIT            TO DATE-OUT.
        REWRITE MAST-REC FROM MAST-REC-WS.
        WRITE PRINT-REC FROM DETAIL-LINE
                    AFTER ADVANCING 1.
CREATE-ROUTINE-EXIT.
        EXIT.
FIND-IT.
        READ SUB-MAST INTO MAST-REC-WS.
TOTAL-ROUTINE.
        MOVE TOTAL-RECORDS-GOOD   TO TOTAL-RECORDS-GOOD-OUT.
        WRITE PRINT-REC FROM TOTAL-LINE
                    AFTER ADVANCING 2.
ERROR-RTN.
        DISPLAY (20, 15) 'File Not Found or Out of Sequence '.
        MOVE 01 TO END-OF-INPUT.
```

Fig. 10-6. (*continued*)

The complete source program is available on the supplemental disk under the filename CH1003.COB.

The description of the master file, SUB-MAST, in the ENVIRONMENT and DATA DIVISIONs is the same as in CH1002.COB, except that only one file is described—it may be either the old or new master file that is being changed. Procedurally we would assume that it is the most recent version of the file that is being changed and corrected.

The OPEN statement, therefore, refers to only one disk file and the printer:

```
OPEN I-O    SUB-MAST
     OUTPUT PRINT-FILE.
```

The OPEN I-O statement may only be used with disk data. We will see it used in the next chapter when processing indexed and relative files. Here it is used with sequential files in conjunction with the REWRITE statement. It is assumed that files opened in this manner will be accessed by a READ statement. Then, after changing some (or none) of the data in a record, it is rewritten back to the disk in the same place. You may READ a record without following it with a REWRITE, in which case the original data on the disk remains the same. You may not, however, issue a REWRITE without first having issued a READ. To do so would cause unpredictable results—at best you would cause the current data to be written over whatever record was the last one read.

GENERAL FORMAT 11

REWRITE record-name [FROM data-name]

The record that was most recently accessed by a READ statement is replaced on the disk. It is assumed that the replacement is the same size as the record read. A longer record will be truncated but an attompt to REWRITE a rocord ohortor than tho ono READ will oauoo unpredictable results.

```
REWRITE MAST-REC FROM MAST-REC-WS.
```

EXERCISES

1. The LOBOC Department Stores have requested the preparation of a program to produce their monthly bills. Two sequential files are used as input. The first, called NAME-FILE, contains the name and address information for each customer. The second, called BAL-FWD, contains the financial data for the bill. Both files are in ascending sequence by customer number. If no money is owed, there is *no* BAL-FWD record for that customer. *All* customers are on the NAME-FILE. (**Note:** The STRING statement should be used to make the name line and the city, state, zip line more compact on the bill. Use the SPACE character as a delimiter.) (See the print layout on page 365.)

2. The First National Bank needs a program to update customer checking accounts. The file CUST-MAST will be updated by data read from the file CUST-TRAN. Both sequential files are in sequence by account number, with the possibility of more than one transaction for a customer. The deposits (code 23) will precede the withdrawals (code 44) for that customer. If, after all transactions have been processed for a given customer and the account is overdrawn, print out the balance, with a sign, and also print as indicated on the print layout shown on page 366. The status of all accounts will be shown on the Account Register summary. The new CUST-MAST is also output. You may either recreate the entire file or update the CUST-MAST "in place" as shown in the text.

3. A program is required to print student transcripts. The program reads the following three files:

   a. TABLE-FILE is a table in course-number sequence that contains the number (to be used as a subscript), the department name, the course name, and the number of credits.
   b. STUD-MAST is the student master file that contains the names and addresses of currently enrolled students.
   c. STUD-GRADE is the transaction file that contains the grades for each course a student has taken.

Both STUD-MAST and STUD-GRADE are sequential files in sequence by student number. The output for this program is the TRANSCRIPT report described on page 367. Include in the program the grading scheme and grade point average of your own choosing.

Solutions to the exercises, together with any necessary data files, are provided on the supplemental disk.

NAME-FILE (100 Characters)

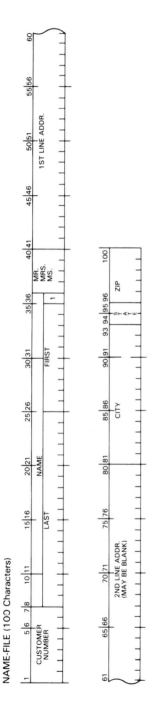

BAL-FWD (19 Characters)

Output Layout

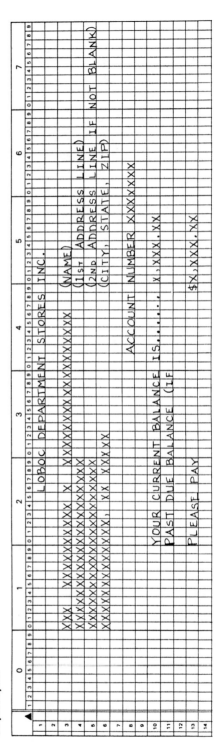

365

Input Layouts

CUST-MAST (Old and New—29 Characters)

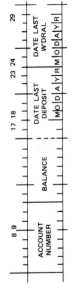

ACCOUNT NUMBER	BALANCE	DATE LAST DEPOSIT	DATE LAST W'DRAL
		MO DA YR	MO DA YR

8 9   17 18   23 24   29

CUST-TRAN (25 Characters)

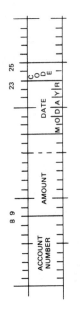

ACCOUNT NUMBER	AMOUNT	DATE	CODE
		MO DA YR	

8 9   23   25

Output Layout

	0	1	2	3	4	5	6	7
1	ACCOUNT NUMBER	BALANCE	LAST DEPOSIT	LAST W'DRAWL	O'DRAWN
2					
3	XXXXXXX	X,XXX,XXX.XX-	XX/XX/XX	XXXXXXXXXX	***
4					
5	XXXXXXX	X,XXX,XXX.XX	XX/XX/XX	XXXXXXXXXX	
6	.				

Input Layouts

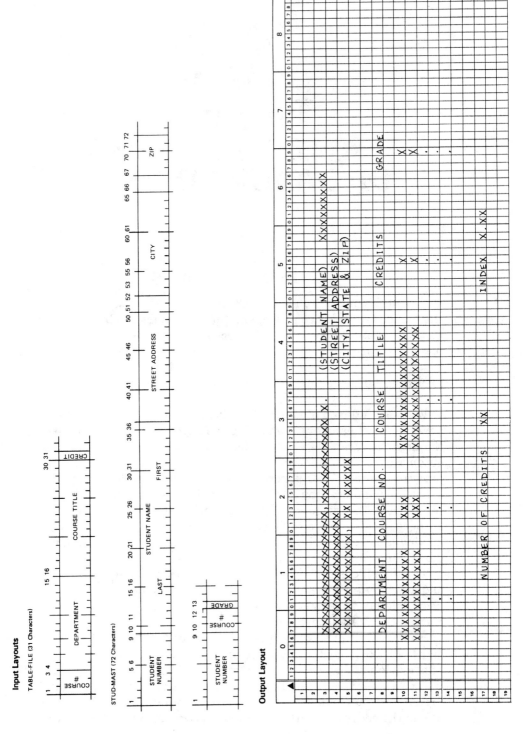

Output Layout

CHAPTER

11

INDEXED AND RELATIVE ORGANIZED FILES

INDEXED FILES

One of the most often used methods of file organization in COBOL is the indexed or index sequential method. As indicated by the name, this method combines the ability to access files sequentially, in the same manner as previous programs, and through the use of an index. This index is created by the operating system when the file is created and may then be used to access *specific* records in the file in a random manner.

When an indexed file is created, DOS actually creates two files, a file containing data and one containing the keys and pointers to the data in the data file. This file is given the same name as the data file but it is automatically assigned the filename extension of .KEY. The COBOL program contains no reference to this file; its creation and processing are done completely by DOS. This key file is very complex and beyond the scope of this discussion. We must be aware of its existence, however, because if we were to delete it from our disk or fail to copy it when making a backup of the data file, we would no longer have a valid indexed file.

The data file contains each data record preceded by a two-byte field and a one-byte reference count that indicates whether the record has been deleted. This delete code is used only by DOS and is of no concern to the COBOL program.

Each record in the file must have a specific field designated as the **key** field. This may be a numeric or an alphanumeric entry. Typically it is the field used as the unique identifier of the record—the Social Security Number, account number, part number, etc. When the file is created, as shown in Fig. 11-1, this field is identified as the record key. When the record is written to the disk, two files are actually created—

one file containing the data and a second file containing the keys. Figure 11–2 shows the screen listing of the data used to create the file.

Let's begin by examining a program to create an indexed file.

```
        IDENTIFICATION DIVISION.
        PROGRAM-ID. CREATE-INDEX-FILE.
********************************************************
        ENVIRONMENT DIVISION.
        CONFIGURATION SECTION.
        SOURCE-COMPUTER. IBM-PERSONAL-COMPUTER.
        OBJECT-COMPUTER. IBM-PERSONAL-COMPUTER.
        FILE-CONTROL.
            SELECT IN-FILE ASSIGN TO DISK
                ORGANIZATION IS LINE SEQUENTIAL.
            SELECT INDEX-FILE ASSIGN TQ DISK
                ORGANIZATION IS INDEXED
                ACCESS IS SEQUENTIAL
                RECORD KEY IS ITEM-NO.
********************************************************
        DATA DIVISION.
        FILE SECTION.
        FD  IN-FILE
            LABEL RECORDS ARE STANDARD
            VALUE OF FILE-ID IS 'DATAFILE.111'
            RECORD CONTAINS 80 CHARACTERS.
        01  IN-REC  PIC X(80).
        FD  INDEX-FILE
            LABEL RECORDS ARE STANDARD
            RECORD CONTAINS 50 CHARACTERS
            VALUE OF FILE-ID 'INDFILE.111'.
        01  DISK-RECORD.
            05  ITEM-NO        PIC X(3).
            05  OTHER-DATA     PIC X(47).
********************************************************
        WORKING-STORAGE SECTION.
        01  INDICATORS-N-SWITCHES.
            05  EOF            PIC 9 VALUE 0.
********************************************************
        PROCEDURE DIVISION.
        MAIN-LINE.
            PERFORM OPEN-RTN.
            PERFORM READ-RTN.
            PERFORM PROCESS-RTN UNTIL EOF = 1.
            PERFORM CLOSE-RTN.
            DISPLAY 'RUN COMPLETE'.
            STOP RUN.
        OPEN-RTN.
            OPEN INPUT  IN-FILE
                 OUTPUT INDEX-FILE.
        READ-RTN.
            READ IN-FILE INTO DISK-RECORD AT END MOVE 1 TO EOF.
        PROCESS-RTN.
            DISPLAY DISK-RECORD.
            WRITE DISK-RECORD INVALID KEY PERFORM CANT-WRITE.
            PERFORM READ-RTN.
        CANT-WRITE.
            DISPLAY 'UNABLE TO WRITE RECORD, ITEM-NO ', ITEM-NO.
            PERFORM CLOSE-RTN.
            STOP RUN.
        CLOSE-RTN.
            CLOSE IN-FILE
                  INDEX-FILE.
```

Fig. 11–1. Program used to create an indexed file.

> *The complete source program shown in Fig. 11–1 is available on the supplemental disk as filename CH1101.COB.*

Note: The index sequential method is also known as VSAM (Virtual Storage Access Method) on IBM mainframe systems. An older version of indexed file access was known as ISAM (Indexed Sequential Access Method). The method we will be describing in this chapter is, from the COBOL source program standpoint, almost identical to VSAM and to the ANS standard for indexed files. The authors have run these programs on the IBM PC and on an IBM 4381 with very little change.

The INPUT-OUTPUT SECTION

This program is similar to those in the previous chapter that created sequential files. The first difference that we see is a new clause, which has been used in the FILE-CONTROL paragraph—ORGANIZATION IS INDEXED. This clause is required with *all* indexed files. There are several other clauses that may be used with indexed files; these are given below in the general format of the FILE-CONTROL paragraph.

GENERAL FORMAT 1

INPUT-OUTPUT SECTION.
FILE-CONTROL.

SELECT filename ASSIGN TO $\left\{ \begin{array}{l} \text{DISK} \\ \text{PRINTER} \end{array} \right\}$

RESERVE integer $\left\{ \begin{array}{l} \text{AREA} \\ \text{AREAS} \end{array} \right\}$

FILE STATUS IS data-name-1

ACCESS MODE IS $\left\{ \begin{array}{l} \text{SEQUENTIAL} \\ \text{RANDOM} \\ \text{DYNAMIC} \end{array} \right\}$

ORGANIZATION IS $\left\{ \begin{array}{l} \text{SEQUENTIAL} \\ \text{LINE SEQUENTIAL} \\ \text{RELATIVE} \\ \text{INDEXED} \end{array} \right\}$

RECORD KEY IS data-name-2

RELATIVE KEY IS data-name-3

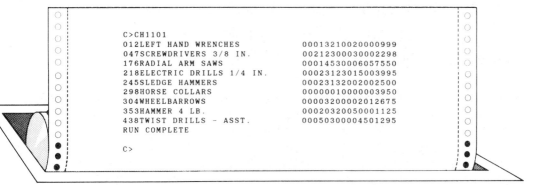

```
C>CH1101
012LEFT HAND WRENCHES            0001321002000999
047SCREWDRIVERS 3/8 IN.          0021230003002298
176RADIAL ARM SAWS               0001453000605750
218ELECTRIC DRILLS 1/4 IN.       0002312301500399
245SLEDGE HAMMERS                0002313200200250
298HORSE COLLARS                 0000001000000395
304WHEELBARROWS                  0000320000201267
353HAMMER 4 LB.                  0002032005000112
438TWIST DRILLS - ASST.          0005030000450129
RUN COMPLETE

C>
```

Fig. 11–2. Screen with file data.

There are new options in the ACCESS MODE IS clause that we have not discussed before. These are RANDOM and DYNAMIC. When files are processed randomly, the record to be accessed must be located by DOS through the use of some method other than merely reading the next available record. We will see how RANDOM is used in the next program. The DYNAMIC access mode will be discussed later.

The FILE STATUS clause, described in the previous chapter, allows the program to monitor the execution of each input/output operation. When this clause is specified, a value is moved into the data-name indicated after each input/output operation that refers to this file. The value placed into the data-name by the system indicates the status of the execution of the statement. The values that the system may place in this data-name and their corresponding meanings are given in Chapter 10. The FILE STATUS is really needed in dealing with indexed files because of the increased number of error conditions that can occur with this type of organization and the additional access modes.

The RECORD KEY Clause

Another very important entry in the SELECT statement is the identification of the RECORD KEY. This clause names the field in the disk record description that is to be used by DOS in establishing the index. Every indexed file must have a RECORD KEY and every program that accesses an index file (either SEQUENTIAL or RANDOM) must include this clause in the SELECT.

The program shown above creates an indexed file with data from a LINE SEQUENTIAL file that was entered through a word processor. The output is the indexed file that will be used in the next several programs.

Sequential Processing of an Indexed File

The sequential processing of an indexed file is the same as for a sequential file except for the two items noted above with respect to the creation of an indexed file—the presence of an ORGANIZATION IS INDEXED clause and the identification of the RECORD KEY.

After it has been created, an indexed file may be processed sequentially, one record after the other, just as with a sequential file. After the initial creation of the indexed file, however, sequential access would normally involve using the file for input. It is possible to change existing records in an indexed file while processing it sequentially by using the REWRITE verb, but it would *not* be possible to add or delete records. In sequential processing of an indexed file, it may be opened as INPUT, I-O, or OUTPUT.

The START Statement

Because of the presence of the index and the identification of the RECORD KEY, an indexed file may be processed sequentially beginning at other than the first record of the file. One method to accomplish this is by using the START command.

In the program shown in Fig. 11–3, the value of the key field for the first record to be processed must be placed into the field specified in the RECORD KEY clause prior to processing. The START statement is then issued, causing DOS to search the index for the key contained in the RECORD KEY field and make this the first record available for sequential processing. Sequential processing could then continue until the end of file, until another START statement is issued, moving the index to another record, or until terminated for some other reason. A similar situation will be described below regarding the ACCESS IS DYNAMIC option.

GENERAL FORMAT 2

START filename [KEY $\begin{Bmatrix} \text{IS \underline{GREATER} THAN} \\ \text{\underline{NOT} \underline{LESS} THAN} \\ \text{\underline{EQUAL} TO} \end{Bmatrix}$ data-name]

[INVALID KEY imperative-statement . . .]

```
            IDENTIFICATION DIVISION.
            PROGRAM-ID. PRINT-INDEX-FILE.
      **********************************************************
            ENVIRONMENT DIVISION.
            CONFIGURATION SECTION.
            SOURCE-COMPUTER. IBM-PERSONAL-COMPUTER.
            OBJECT-COMPUTER. IBM-PERSONAL-COMPUTER.
            FILE-CONTROL.
                SELECT INDEX-FILE ASSIGN TO DISK
                    ORGANIZATION IS INDEXED
                    FILE STATUS IS STAT
                    RECORD KEY IS ITEM-NO.
                SELECT PRINT-FILE ASSIGN TO PRINTER.
      **********************************************************
            DATA DIVISION.
            FILE SECTION.
            FD  INDEX-FILE
                LABEL RECORDS ARE STANDARD
                RECORD CONTAINS 50 CHARACTERS
                VALUE OF FILE-ID 'INDFILE.111'.
            01  DISK-RECORD.
                05  ITEM-NO        PIC X(3).
                05  ITEM-NAME      PIC X(30).
                05  QUANT-ON-HAND  PIC 9(7).
                05  REORDER-PT     PIC 9(5).
                05  UNIT-PRICE     PIC 999V99.
            FD  PRINT-FILE
                LABEL RECORDS ARE OMITTED
                RECORD CONTAINS 80 CHARACTERS.
            01  PRINT-REC          PIC X(80).
      **********************************************************
            WORKING-STORAGE SECTION.
            01  INDICATORS-N-WORKAREAS.
                05  EOF            PIC 9 VALUE 0.
                05  STAT           PIC XX.
                05  START-NO       PIC X(03).
            01  PRINT-TITLES.
                05  FILLER         PIC X(03) VALUE SPACES.
                05  FILLER         PIC X(05) VALUE 'ITEM '.
                05  FILLER         PIC X(10) VALUE SPACES.
                05  FILLER         PIC X(09) VALUE 'ITEM NAME'.
                05  FILLER         PIC X(09) VALUE SPACES.
                05  FILLER         PIC X(14) VALUE 'QUANT. ON HAND'.
                05  FILLER         PIC X(04) VALUE SPACES.
                05  FILLER         PIC X(11) VALUE 'REORDER PT.'.
                05  FILLER         PIC X(03) VALUE SPACES.
                05  FILLER         PIC X(10) VALUE 'UNIT PRICE'.
            01  PRINT-RECORD.
                05  FILLER            PIC X(04) VALUE SPACES.
                05  ITEM-NO-O         PIC X(03).
                05  FILLER            PIC X(02) VALUE SPACES.
                05  ITEM-NAME-O       PIC X(30).
                05  FILLER            PIC X(01) VALUE SPACES.
                05  QUANT-ON-HAND-O   PIC ZZZZZZ9.
                05  FILLER            PIC X(10) VALUE SPACES.
                05  REORDER-PT-O      PIC ZZZZ9.
                05  FILLER            PIC X(07) VALUE SPACES.
                05  UNIT-PRICE-O      PIC $ZZ9.99.
      **********************************************************
            PROCEDURE DIVISION.
            MAIN-LINE.
                PERFORM OPEN-RTN.
                PERFORM START-RTN.
                PERFORM HEADING-RTN.
                PERFORM READ-RTN.
                PERFORM MOVE-WRITE UNTIL EOF = 1.
                PERFORM CLOSE-RTN.
                STOP RUN.
      **********************************************************
            OPEN-RTN.
                OPEN INPUT  INDEX-FILE
                     OUTPUT PRINT-FILE.
```

Fig. 11-3. Sequential processing of an indexed file beginning at a predetermined record.

```
*****************************************************************
START-RTN.
    DISPLAY 'ENTER BEGINNING PART NUMBER '.
    ACCEPT START-NO.
    MOVE START-NO TO ITEM-NO.
    START INDEX-FILE
                KEY IS EQUAL TO ITEM-NO
                INVALID KEY
                DISPLAY
                'INVALID RECORD KEY ' ITEM-NO ' FOR START'
                DISPLAY 'STAT = ' STAT
                PERFORM CLOSE-RTN
                STOP RUN.
*****************************************************************
HEADING-RTN.
    WRITE PRINT-REC FROM PRINT-TITLES
                AFTER ADVANCING PAGE.
*****************************************************************
READ-RTN.
    READ INDEX-FILE AT END MOVE 1 TO EOF.
*****************************************************************
MOVE-WRITE.
    PERFORM MOVE-RTN.
    PERFORM WRITE-RTN.
    PERFORM READ-RTN.
*****************************************************************
MOVE-RTN.
    MOVE ITEM-NO         TO ITEM-NO-O.
    MOVE ITEM-NAME       TO ITEM-NAME-O.
    MOVE QUANT-ON-HAND   TO QUANT-ON-HAND-O.
    MOVE REORDER-PT      TO REORDER-PT-O.
    MOVE UNIT-PRICE      TO UNIT-PRICE-O.
*****************************************************************
WRITE-RTN.
    WRITE PRINT-REC FROM PRINT-RECORD
                AFTER ADVANCING 2 LINES.
*****************************************************************
CLOSE-RTN.
    CLOSE INDEX-FILE
          PRINT-FILE.
```

Fig. 11–3. (*continued*)

*The complete source program shown in Fig. 11–3 is available
on the supplemental disk as filename CH1102.COB.*

Updating an indexed file when ACCESS IS SEQUENTIAL is specified is almost identical to the updating of a sequential file without recreating, as shown in the previous chapter. In neither case can records
be added when ACCESS IS SEQUENTIAL is specified.

RANDOM PROCESSING OF AN INDEXED FILE

This is the principal reason that we have the ORGANIZATION IS INDEXED option: the ability to access specific records in any order, one at a time. Any type of inquiry system depends on this ability since the time required to search sequential files to find a specific record would be prohibitive.

The differences, noted in Fig. 11–4, in a program to randomly update an indexed file, will be the use of the ACCESS IS RANDOM clause in the SELECT statement and the program logic involved with obtaining the key for the record to be processed. Since most of the logic necessary to find and make available the desired record is executed by DOS, the actual program logic for updating this type of file is relatively simple. It is certainly less complicated than that required to update a sequential file (as seen in the previous chapter).

The REWRITE Statement

As seen in the previous program using the START statement, the key to the record that is to be accessed from the indexed file is made available to the RECORD KEY field in the disk record description. The READ statement is issued; if it is successfully completed, the proper record is available for processing. After the necessary changes are made to the record, a REWRITE statement is issued to ensure that the record is returned to the *same place in the file* that it came from. The REWRITE statement can be used only with files OPENed as I-O and only after a READ statement has been executed. To issue a REWRITE without a previous READ would yield unpredictable results, since DOS would attempt to write it on top of the data for whatever key was last present in the RECORD KEY field.

GENERAL FORMAT 3

REWRITE record-name FROM data-name

INVALID KEY imperative-statement . . .

```
        IDENTIFICATION DIVISION.
        PROGRAM-ID. UPDATE-IND-FILE.
        *********************************************************
        ENVIRONMENT DIVISION.
        CONFIGURATION SECTION.
        SOURCE-COMPUTER. IBM-PERSONAL-COMPUTER.
        OBJECT-COMPUTER. IBM-PERSONAL-COMPUTER.
        FILE-CONTROL.
            SELECT UPDATE-FILE ASSIGN TO DISK
                ORGANIZATION IS LINE SEQUENTIAL.
            SELECT  INDEX-FILE ASSIGN TO DISK
                ORGANIZATION IS INDEXED
                ACCESS IS RANDOM
                FILE STATUS IS STAT
                RECORD KEY IS ITEM-NO.
        *********************************************************
        DATA DIVISION.
        FILE SECTION.
        FD  INDEX-FILE
            LABEL RECORDS ARE STANDARD
            RECORD CONTAINS 50 CHARACTERS
            VALUE OF FILE-ID 'INDFILE.111'.
        01  DISK-RECORD.
            05  ITEM-NO          PIC X(3).
            05  ITEM-NAME        PIC X(30).
            05  QUANT-ON-HAND    PIC 9(7).
            05  REORDER-PT       PIC 9(5).
            05  UNIT-PRICE       PIC 999V99.
        FD  UPDATE-FILE
            LABEL RECORDS ARE STANDARD
            VALUE OF FILE-ID IS 'DETAIL.113'
            RECORD CONTAINS 51 CHARACTERS.
        01  UPDATE-REC        PIC X(51).
        *********************************************************
        WORKING-STORAGE SECTION.
        01  INDICATORS-N-KEYS.
            05  EOF                PIC 9    VALUE 0.
            05  STAT               PIC XX   VALUE SPACES.
        01  UPDATE-RECORD.
            05  UPDATE-CODE        PIC 9.
            05  UPDATE-DATA.
                10  ITEM-NO-U        PIC X(3).
                10  ITEM-NAME-U      PIC X(30).
                10  QUANT-ON-HAND-U PIC 9(7).
                10  REORDER-PT-U     PIC 9(5).
                10  UNIT-PRICE-U     PIC 999V99.
        *********************************************************
        PROCEDURE DIVISION.
        *********************************************************
        *                                                       *
        * THIS PROGRAM IS TO UPDATE AN INDEXED FILE.            *
        * IF UPDATE-CODE = 1, ONLY QUANTITY ON HAND IS TO       *
        * BE UPDATED FROM UPDATE-RECORD. IF UPDATE-CODE =       *
        * 2, THE ENTIRE CONTENTS OF THE DISK RECORD ARE TO      *
        * BE REPLACED BY UPDATE-RECORD. IF UPDATE-CODE = 3,     *
        * THE CORRESPONDING OLD RECORD IS TO BE DELETED,        *
        * AND IF UPDATE-CODE = 4 A NEW RECORD IS TO BE ADDED    *
        * TO THE FILE.                                          *
        *********************************************************.
        DECLARATIVES.
        INDEX-FILE-ERROR SECTION.
            USE AFTER ERROR PROCEDURE ON INDEX-FILE.
        ERROR-MESSAGES.
            IF STAT = '22' DISPLAY 'DUPLICATE RECORD '
                        ITEM-NO-U
            ELSE IF STAT = '23' DISPLAY 'NO RECORD FOUND FOR '
                        ITEM-NO-U
                ELSE IF STAT = '30' DISPLAY 'FILE NOT FOUND FOR '
                        ITEM-NO-U
                    ELSE DISPLAY STAT ' FILE ERROR ' ITEM-NO-U.
        END DECLARATIVES.
        *********************************************************
```

Fig. 11–4. Program used to randomly update an indexed file.

```
MAIN-LINE.
    PERFORM OPEN-RTN.
    PERFORM READ-RTN.
    PERFORM UPDATE-TEST UNTIL EOF = 1.
    PERFORM CLOSE-RTN.
    STOP RUN.
****************************************************************
OPEN-RTN.
    OPEN INPUT UPDATE-FILE
         I-O   INDEX-FILE.
****************************************************************
READ-RTN.
    READ UPDATE-FILE INTO UPDATE-RECORD
                     AT END MOVE 1 TO EOF.
****************************************************************
READ-DISK-RTN.
    MOVE ITEM-NO-U      TO ITEM-NO.
    READ   INDEX-FILE.
****************************************************************
UPDATE-TEST.
        IF UPDATE-CODE = 1
                  PERFORM UPDATE-QUANT-ON-HAND
        ELSE IF UPDATE-CODE = 2
                  PERFORM UPDATE-ENTIRE-RECORD
            ELSE IF UPDATE-CODE = 3
                  PERFORM DELETE-OLD-RECORD
                ELSE IF UPDATE-CODE = 4
                      PERFORM ADD-NEW-RECORD
                      ELSE PERFORM UPDATE-CODE-ERROR.
    PERFORM READ-RTN.
****************************************************************
UPDATE-QUANT-ON-HAND.
    PERFORM READ-DISK-RTN.
    IF STAT = '00'
       MOVE QUANT-ON-HAND-U TO QUANT-ON-HAND
       REWRITE DISK-RECORD.
****************************************************************
UPDATE-ENTIRE-RECORD.
    PERFORM READ-DISK-RTN.
    IF STAT = '00'
       MOVE UPDATE-DATA   TO DISK-RECORD
       REWRITE DISK-RECORD.
****************************************************************
DELETE-OLD-RECORD.
    MOVE ITEM-NO-U      TO ITEM-NO.
    DELETE INDEX-FILE.
****************************************************************
ADD-NEW-RECORD.
    MOVE ITEM-NO-U       TO ITEM-NO.
    MOVE ITEM-NAME-U     TO ITEM-NAME.
    MOVE QUANT-ON-HAND-U TO QUANT-ON-HAND.
    MOVE REORDER-PT-U    TO REORDER-PT.
    MOVE UNIT-PRICE-U    TO UNIT-PRICE.
    WRITE DISK-RECORD.
****************************************************************
UPDATE-CODE-ERROR.
    DISPLAY 'UPDATE CODE ' UPDATE-CODE
            ' BAD, RECORD ' ITEM-NO.
****************************************************************
CLOSE-RTN.
    CLOSE   INDEX-FILE
            UPDATE-FILE.
****************************************************************
```

Fig. 11-4. (*continued*)

The complete source program shown in Fig. 11–4 is available on the supplemental disk as filename CH1103.COB.

The DELETE Statement

It is possible to remove records from the indexed file through use of the DELETE statement. The key of the record to be removed is placed in the RECORD KEY field in the same manner as when a READ is being executed. The statement must contain the filename, just as in a READ statement.

The result of issuing a DELETE statement is to have a special code placed in the first position of the record (provided for by DOS, not by the programmer) which indicates that the record has been deleted. Neither RANDOM nor SEQUENTIAL access to the file will make such a record available again. Some of the deleted records will be replaced by subsequent WRITE operations—adding new records to the file. Reorganization of the file to recover the areas containing deleted records is discussed later in the section on the REBUILD utility.

GENERAL FORMAT 4

DELETE filename RECORD

[INVALID KEY imperative-statement]

If ACCESS IS RANDOM or ACCESS IS DYNAMIC is specified, the INVALID KEY option *must* be specified (see General Format 5 of the READ statement below) or the DECLARATIVES option must be included in the PROCEDURE DIVISION. This is because the DELETE statement does not have to be preceded by a READ statement. It is possible that the RECORD KEY will contain the key for a record that is not on the file, causing an error condition.

SEQUENTIAL AND RANDOM PROCESSING OF AN INDEXED FILE

Should it be necessary to process a file both sequentially and randomly in the same program, the indexed organization is ideal. By specifying ACCESS IS DYNAMIC, both access methods are possible and determined by the form of the READ statement used. The general formats of the READ statement for use with indexed files where either ACCESS IS RANDOM or ACCESS IS DYNAMIC has been specified are given below.

The READ Statements

GENERAL FORMAT 5

READ filename [INTO identifier]

[INVALID KEY imperative-statement]

GENERAL FORMAT 6

READ filename [NEXT] [INTO identifier]

[AT END imperative-statement]

If a record is to be accessed randomly, General Format 5 *must* be used regardless of whether ACCESS IS RANDOM or ACCESS IS DYNAMIC has been specified. However, if a record is to be accessed sequentially when ACCESS IS DYNAMIC has been specified, General Format 6 of the READ statement *must* be used. A record cannot be accessed sequentially when ACCESS IS RANDOM has been specified.

Note that General Format 6 of the READ statement is very similar to the format of the READ statement used to read a sequential file. The only difference is the presence of the optional clause NEXT. Using this option specifies that we wish to sequentially read a record from an indexed file where ACCESS IS DYNAMIC has been specified. This causes the file to be accessed sequentially from the point where the last record was accessed. If no record was previously accessed from the file, the file will be accessed sequentially beginning with the first record on the file.

If, after one or more sequential READ statements have been executed, a random access READ statement is encountered (General Format 5), the record corresponding to the value in the RECORD KEY will be randomly accessed. Thus, one would have to make certain that the key value corresponding to the desired record is placed in the RECORD KEY prior to the execution of the random access READ.

Figure 11–5 illustrates a program that accesses an indexed file randomly to find a specific record and then lists the file sequentially from that record to the end of the file.

```
            IDENTIFICATION DIVISION.
            PROGRAM-ID. PRINT-INDEX-FILE.
            AUTHOR. S.J. GAUGHRAN.
            ****************************************************************
            ENVIRONMENT DIVISION.
            CONFIGURATION SECTION.
            SOURCE-COMPUTER. IBM-PERSONAL-COMPUTER.
            OBJECT-COMPUTER. IBM-PERSONAL-COMPUTER.
            FILE-CONTROL.
                SELECT INDEX-FILE ASSIGN TO DISK
                    ORGANIZATION IS INDEXED
                    FILE STATUS IS STAT
                    ACCESS IS DYNAMIC
                    RECORD KEY IS ITEM-NO.
                SELECT PRINT-FILE ASSIGN TO PRINTER.
            ****************************************************************
            DATA DIVISION.
            FILE SECTION.
            FD  INDEX-FILE
                LABEL RECORDS ARE STANDARD
                RECORD CONTAINS 50 CHARACTERS
                VALUE OF FILE-ID 'INDFILE.111'.
            01  DISK-RECORD.
                05  ITEM-NO         PIC X(3).
                05  ITEM-NAME       PIC X(30).
                05  QUANT-ON-HAND   PIC 9(7).
                05  REORDER-PT      PIC 9(5).
                05  UNIT-PRICE      PIC 999V99.
            FD  PRINT-FILE
                LABEL RECORDS ARE OMITTED
                RECORD CONTAINS 80 CHARACTERS.
            01  PRINT-REC           PIC X(80).
            ****************************************************************
            WORKING-STORAGE SECTION.
            01  INDICATORS-N-WORKAREAS.
                05  EOF             PIC 9 VALUE 0.
                05  STAT            PIC XX.
                05  START-NO        PIC X(03).
            01  PRINT-TITLES.
                05  FILLER          PIC X(11) VALUE 'ITEM NUMBER'.
                05  FILLER          PIC X(08) VALUE SPACES.
                05  FILLER          PIC X(09) VALUE 'ITEM NAME'.
                05  FILLER          PIC X(09) VALUE SPACES.
                05  FILLER          PIC X(14) VALUE 'QUANT. ON HAND'.
                05  FILLER          PIC X(03) VALUE SPACES.
                05  FILLER          PIC X(11) VALUE 'REORDER PT.'.
                05  FILLER          PIC X(03) VALUE SPACES.
                05  FILLER          PIC X(10) VALUE 'UNIT PRICE'.
            01  PRINT-RECORD.
                05  FILLER          PIC X(04) VALUE SPACES.
                05  ITEM-NO-O       PIC X(03).
                05  FILLER          PIC X(02) VALUE SPACES.
                05  ITEM-NAME-O     PIC X(30).
                05  FILLER          PIC X(01) VALUE SPACES.
                05  QUANT-ON-HAND-O PIC ZZZZZZ9.
                05  FILLER          PIC X(10) VALUE SPACES.
                05  REORDER-PT-O    PIC ZZZZ9.
                05  FILLER          PIC X(07) VALUE SPACES.
                05  UNIT-PRICE-O    PIC $ZZ9.99.
            ****************************************************************
            PROCEDURE DIVISION.
            ****************************************************************
            DECLARATIVES.
            INDEX-FILE-ERROR SECTION.
                USE AFTER ERROR PROCEDURE ON INDEX-FILE.
            ERROR-MESSAGES.
                IF STAT = '23' DISPLAY 'NO RECORD FOUND FOR '
                            START-NO
                ELSE IF STAT = '30' DISPLAY ' FILE NOT FOUND '
                        ELSE DISPLAY STAT ' FILE ERROR ' ITEM-NO.
                STOP RUN.
            END DECLARATIVES.
```

**Fig. 11-5. Program used to access an indexed file
randomly and sequentially.**

```
********************************************************
MAIN-LINE.
    PERFORM OPEN-RTN.
    PERFORM START-RTN.
    PERFORM HEADING-RTN.
    PERFORM MOVE-WRITE UNTIL EOF = 1.
    PERFORM CLOSE-RTN.
    STOP RUN.
********************************************************
OPEN-RTN.
    OPEN INPUT  INDEX-FILE
         OUTPUT PRINT-FILE.
********************************************************
START-RTN.
    DISPLAY 'ENTER BEGINNING PART NUMBER '.
    ACCEPT START-NO.
    MOVE START-NO TO ITEM-NO.
    READ INDEX-FILE.
********************************************************
HEADING-RTN.
    WRITE PRINT-REC FROM PRINT-TITLES
                    AFTER ADVANCING PAGE.
********************************************************
READ-RTN.
    READ INDEX-FILE NEXT
                AT END MOVE 1 TO EOF.
********************************************************
MOVE-WRITE.
    PERFORM MOVE-RTN.
    PERFORM WRITE-RTN.
    PERFORM READ-RTN.
********************************************************
MOVE-RTN.
    MOVE ITEM-NO         TO ITEM-NO-O.
    MOVE ITEM-NAME       TO ITEM-NAME-O.
    MOVE QUANT-ON-HAND   TO QUANT-ON-HAND-O.
    MOVE REORDER-PT      TO REORDER-PT-O.
    MOVE UNIT-PRICE      TO UNIT-PRICE-O.
********************************************************
WRITE-RTN.
    WRITE PRINT-REC FROM PRINT-RECORD
                    AFTER ADVANCING 2 LINES.
********************************************************
CLOSE-RTN.
    CLOSE INDEX-FILE
          PRINT-FILE.
```

Fig. 11-5. (continued)

The complete source program shown in Fig. 11-5 is available on the supplemental disk as filename CH1104.COB.

FILE STATUS CLAUSE

We noted above that the number of errors that can occur while processing indexed files makes the use of DECLARATIVES or the INVALID KEY clause necessary.

The possible FILE STATUS codes and their meaning regarding indexed files are as follows:

File Status Code	Meaning
00	Successful completion
10	End of file
21	Key not in sequence (possible during create)
22	Attempt to write a duplicate (trying to add a record already on the file)
23	Not found (random access of record not on disk)
24	Disk space full
30	File not found
91	File structure destroyed

THE REBUILD UTILITY

When an indexed file has been opened as I-O for the purpose of updating existing records, deleting records, and/or adding records it is particularly vulnerable to any type of interrupt. The possible causes of such an interrupt are a power failure, a system reset caused by some other reason, or even a DISK FULL condition while adding records to the file. It is not possible for the program to be merely restarted because some of the file would already have been updated. If we were updating a sequential file when such an event occurred, we would merely restart the job, ignoring the "new" master file which had been partially created. But with an indexed file there is no "old" master and no "new" master—they are one and the same.

The IBM COBOL compiler contains a program called **REBUILD.EXE,** which is used to recover from one of these conditions.

The procedure (with a two-disk system) is to place the disk with REBUILD in disk B and the one with the indexed file in A. The necessary procedure is displayed by REBUILD, but we have summarized it here.

Type B:REBUILD and if there is no room on the data disk in A you may place a scratch diskette in B. The program will prompt you for the

Input Key Length

which is the length of the key field in bytes. The responses must be a positive integer representing the number of bytes in the RECORD KEY field. The second prompt:

Input Key Position

requires a response with a positive integer stating how far the RECORD KEY field is away from the beginning of the record; this would be 1 if it were the first field. If either of these responses is incorrect there is no way for REBUILD to check, so the program will continue but the new file created will *not* be usable.

The next prompt is for the

Input Source Filename

which will be the name of the data file as specified in the VALUE OF FILE-ID clause and *not* the name of the .KEY file. This name may be preceded by a drive designator if it is not on A. If this file is not found, a message is displayed and the prompt appears again.

The final prompt is

Input Target Filename

which will be the name of the new data file and new key. If this is to be written on the same disk as the source, you will have to make it unique. But if it is to be directed to another disk (or another directory), it may be the same as the name of the source file. If it has been necessary to create a unique name, you may RENAME it after the recovery operation is complete. If there is not enough room for the new file, a message will be displayed and you will be able to re-enter the target filename, directing it to a different disk.

If all the entries are correct, a message will be displayed indicating that the conversion was successful and giving the record count for the source and target files—these should be identical. If there were deleted records on the source file, they will not be counted. The REBUILD program continues with a repeat of the Input Key Length prompt. Pressing the enter key with no data entry will terminate REBUILD; any other response will allow you to start the process over on the same or other file.

FILE REORGANIZATION

One of the problems encountered with indexed files is a lack of efficient use of storage on the disk as a result of frequent DELETE and WRITE operations. Considerable blank space may be left and the file will become larger, even if files are being deleted, since the space for those files is not completely recovered. As this occurs you may use the REBUILD utility, as detailed above, to reorganize the file into more efficient form by eliminating blank spaces and recovering space from deleted records. You may try the REBUILD program on any indexed file, regardless of whether it has been damaged, to see how it works.

RELATIVE FILE ORGANIZATION

A second method of organization for direct access of disk files is available called relative file organization. The indexed file organization described above depended on an index, contained in a separate file, to provide the means of direct access to a record. It further depended on the record itself containing the key value in a field called RECORD KEY. Relative organization does not depend on either of these two factors: there is no index on a separate file or anywhere else, and it is not necessary for the record to contain any value indicating its key.

Each record is allocated a fixed length area in the file by a key that refers to that *position*. For example, the key used to locate the 129th record in a relative file is the value 129. This is quite similar to referencing data contained in a table, where the subscript (or index) will refer to the "relative" location of the field in the table. The difference **here is that** the data is not contained in RAM, as with a table, but in a file on the disk. In IBM COBOL the keys may be positive integers from 1 to 32767—so even with a fixed disk there is some limit to the number of records.

Access modes

Just as with indexed files, the records in a relative file may be accessed as SEQUENTIAL, RANDOM, or DYNAMIC. The program logic for sequential access is the same as for files whose organization is SEQUENTIAL, LINE SEQUENTIAL, or INDEXED. Access in a RANDOM or DYNAMIC mode will depend on the key that is identified in the program as the RELATIVE KEY.

A typical SELECT clause for the creation (sequential access) of a relative file is:

```
SELECT REL-FILE ASSIGN TO DISK
       ORGANIZATION IS RELATIVE
       ACCESS IS SEQUENTIAL
       RELATIVE KEY IS REL-KEY.
```

The field called REL-KEY must be an unsigned integer in the range 1 to 32767 that is *not* contained in the relative file being described. It may be in working storage or in some other file (RELATIVE, SEQUENTIAL, or INDEXED). During creation of a relative file this key must be incremented by one each time a record is written. It is possible to write records containing blanks to reserve space for future additions.

The most convenient use of a relative file is for an application that has key fields represented by a continuous sequence of integer numbers. An example would be a file created for the recording of invoices or other records that are assigned a continuous number series. Even if the numbers did not begin at 1 but at perhaps 2000, the program could subtract 2000 from the actual number in order to create a continuous series of numbers from 1 to n.

In this instance, one might ask why not create an indexed file for this purpose? The answer is that one of the advantages of a relative file is speed—the calculation of the location of the record is done in RAM without any additional disk access. Because of the .KEY file in an indexed organization, there are two disk accesses required; one to the .KEY file and one to the data file. If a file were going to be subject to many RANDOM accesses, the relative file would be faster.

EXAMPLE OF A RELATIVE FILE

In Chapter 7 we included a program to create checks interactively in order to demonstrate the use of the screen capabilities of IBM COBOL. We have altered that program so that a disk file is created that records the check number, the date written, the payee, the amount, and the type of expenditure. The following program segments indicate those parts of CH701.COB that have been changed to include this feature in the program.

```
FILE-CONTROL.
    SELECT PRINTFILE ASSIGN TO PRINTER.
    SELECT CHECKFILE ASSIGN TO DISK
            ORGANIZATION IS RELATIVE
            ACCESS IS SEQUENTIAL
*           ACCESS IS RANDOM
            RELATIVE KEY IS CHECK-NO-KEY.
```

The additional SELECT entry for the relative file is shown above. Note that the specification ACCESS IS SEQUENTIAL is used *only* for the initial creation of the relative file—after the first run a new version of the program must be used with ACCESS IS RANDOM. We have included this other entry in the program with an asterisk in column 7 so that it is treated as a comment. After creating the file the first time, you may move the asterisk to column 7 of the ACCESS IS SEQUENTIAL entry—or make a copy of the program and save two versions.

The additional FILE SECTION and WORKING-STORAGE SECTION entries are shown below:

```
FD   CHECKFILE
     LABEL RECORDS ARE STANDARD
     VALUE OF FILE-ID IS 'CHECKS,DAT'.
01   CHECK-REC              PIC X(41).

WORKING-STORAGE SECTION.
             .
             .
             .
01   RELATIVE-KEY-WS.
     05   CHECK-NO-KEY      PIC 9(05).
01   CHECK-RECON.
     05   CHECK-NO-R        PIC 9(05).
     05   DATE-OUT-R        PIC X(06).
     05   NAME-OUT-R        PIC X(20).
```

```
05   CHECK-AMOUNT-R   PIC S9(5)V99.
05   STATUS-CODE-R    PIC 99.
05   RECON-R          PIC 9  VALUE ZERO.
```

This will describe a 41-character record with the essential information needed for check reconciliation. The program is run in the same manner as program CH701.COB in Chapter 7.

> *The complete source program containing the above is available on the supplemental disk as filename CH1105.COB.*

RANDOM PROCESSING OF A RELATIVE FILE

The RELATIVE KEY Clause

As noted above, access to individual records in a RELATIVE file requires that the RELATIVE KEY contain an integer number representing the position of the record *relative* to the other records in the file.

The program shown in Fig. 11–6 is intended to be run when the statement and cleared checks are received from the bank. The check number is entered (this becomes the RELATIVE KEY), and the record for that check is read from the file. The check data are listed as shown in Fig. 11–7. A 1 is placed in the last position of the record to indicate that this check has cleared, and the record is rewritten in the same place on the disk. A total of all checks that have cleared is accumulated and printed when all checks have been entered.

A second part of this programs begins after all cleared checks have been entered. The program again accesses the relative file but this time in a sequential mode. You will note that there are two SELECT entries and two FD's for the relative file—one with RANDOM access and one with SEQUENTIAL. This second part of the program reads every record in the file sequentially, bypassing those that have a code 1 in the last position, indicating that they have been cleared by the bank, and listing those that are still outstanding along with a total as shown in Fig. 11–8. Since this file contains several fields of information about each check, it could be used for other purposes, such as analysis of expenditures, etc.

```
IDENTIFICATION DIVISION.
PROGRAM-ID.
    CHECKRECON.
AUTHOR.
    S.J.GAUGHRAN.
SECURITY.
    NONE.
************************************************************
* This program accesses the relative check reconcilition file  *
* to record those checks which have been cleared and to list   *
* those which are still outstanding.                           *
************************************************************
ENVIRONMENT DIVISION.
CONFIGURATION SECTION.
SOURCE-COMPUTER.
    IBM-PERSONAL-COMPUTER.
OBJECT-COMPUTER.
    IBM-PERSONAL-COMPUTER.
INPUT-OUTPUT SECTION.
FILE-CONTROL.
    SELECT PRINTFILE ASSIGN TO PRINTER.
    SELECT CHECKFILE ASSIGN TO DISK
           ORGANIZATION IS RELATIVE
           ACCESS IS RANDOM
           RELATIVE KEY IS CHECK-NO-KEY.
    SELECT CHECKFILE-1 ASSIGN TO DISK
           ORGANIZATION IS RELATIVE
           ACCESS IS SEQUENTIAL.
************************************************************
DATA DIVISION.
FILE SECTION.
FD  PRINTFILE
    LABEL RECORDS ARE OMITTED.
01  PRINT-REC            PIC X(133).
FD  CHECKFILE
    LABEL RECORDS ARE STANDARD
    VALUE OF FILE-ID IS 'CHECKS.DAT'.
01  CHECK-REC            PIC X(41).
FD  CHECKFILE-1
    LABEL RECORDS ARE STANDARD
    VALUE OF FILE-ID IS 'CHECKS.DAT'.
01  CHECK-REC-1          PIC X(41).
************************************************************
WORKING-STORAGE SECTION.
01  WORKAREAS.
    05  PASSWORD         PIC X(5).
    05  VALID-PASSWORD   PIC X(5)   VALUE 'STEVO'.
    05  F-KEY            PIC X.
    05  EOF              PIC 9      VALUE ZERO.
01  ACCUMULATORS    COMP-3.
    05  CHECKS-TOTAL     PIC S9(5)V99  VALUE ZERO.
01  RELATIVE-KEY-WS.
    05  CHECK-NO-KEY     PIC 9(05).
01  CHECK-RECON.
    05  CHECK-NO-R       PIC 9(05).
    05  DATE-OUT-R       PIC X(06).
    05  NAME-OUT-R       PIC X(20).
    05  CHECK-AMOUNT-R   PIC S9(5)V99.
    05  STATUS-CODE-R    PIC 99.
    05  RECON-R          PIC 9  VALUE ZERO.
01  TITLE-1.
    05  FILLER           PIC X(29)  VALUE SPACES.
    05  TYPE-RPT         PIC X(18)  VALUE
                         'CHECKS CLEARED    '.
01  TITLE 2.
    05  FILLER           PIC X(10)  VALUE SPACES.
    05  FILLER           PIC X(12)  VALUE 'CHECK NUMBER'.
    05  FILLER           PIC X(05)  VALUE SPACES.
    05  FILLER           PIC X(04)  VALUE 'DATE'.
    05  FILLER           PIC X(08)  VALUE SPACES.
    05  FILLER           PIC X(05)  VALUE 'PAYEE'.
    05  FILLER           PIC X(16)  VALUE SPACES.
```

Fig. 11-6. Random and sequential access of a relative file.

388

```
                05   FILLER              PIC X(06)   VALUE 'AMOUNT'.
          01   DETAIL-1.
                05   FILLER              PIC X(13)   VALUE SPACES.
                05   CHECK-NO-OUT        PIC X(05).
                05   FILLER              PIC X(08)   VALUE SPACES.
                05   DATE-OUT            PIC XX/XX/XX.
                05   FILLER              PIC X(04)   VALUE SPACES.
                05   NAME-OUT            PIC X(20).
                05   FILLER              PIC X(02)   VALUE SPACES.
                05   AMOUNT-OUT          PIC ZZ,ZZ9.99.
          01   TOTAL-LINE.
                05   FILLER              PIC X(10)   VALUE SPACES.
                05   FILLER              PIC X(06)   VALUE 'TOTAL '.
                05   CHECKS-TOTAL-OUT PIC $$$$,$$$.99.
     ***********************************************************
     PROCEDURE DIVISION.
     BEGIN.
          OPEN OUTPUT PRINTFILE
                 I-O     CHECKFILE.
          PERFORM HEADING-RTN.
          PERFORM INITIAL-ACCEPT.
          PERFORM LOOP-RTN THRU LOOP-RTN-EXIT
                           UNTIL CHECK-NO-KEY = 0.
          PERFORM TOTAL-RTN.
          CLOSE CHECKFILE.
          OPEN INPUT CHECKFILE-1.
          MOVE 'CHECKS OUTSTANDING' TO TYPE-RPT.
          PERFORM HEADING-RTN.
          PERFORM SEQ-READ.
          PERFORM RECON-RTN UNTIL EOF = 1.
          PERFORM TOTAL-RTN.
          CLOSE PRINTFILE
                 CHECKFILE-1.
          STOP RUN.
     ***********************************************************
     INITIAL-ACCEPT.
          DISPLAY (1, 1) ERASE.
          DISPLAY (2, 20) 'CHECK RECONCILIATION '.
          DISPLAY (5, 15) 'If End of Job enter 0 '.
          DISPLAY (8, 15) 'ENTER CHECK NUMBER '.
          ACCEPT  (8, 37) CHECK-NO-KEY WITH PROMPT EMPTY-CHECK.
     ***********************************************************
     LOOP-RTN.
          READ CHECKFILE INTO CHECK-RECON
                        INVALID KEY DISPLAY
                        'NUMBER NOT FOUND'
                           GO TO LOOP-RTN-EXIT.
          PERFORM MOVE-DATA-WRITE.
          MOVE 1            TO RECON-R.
          REWRITE CHECK-REC FROM CHECK-RECON.
          DISPLAY (8, 1) ERASE.
          DISPLAY (8, 15) 'ENTER CHECK NUMBER '.
          ACCEPT  (8, 37) CHECK-NO-KEY WITH PROMPT EMPTY-CHECK.
     LOOP-RTN-EXIT.
          EXIT.
     ***********************************************************
     RECON-RTN.
          IF RECON-R = ZERO
              PERFORM MOVE-DATA-WRITE.
          PERFORM SEQ-READ.
     ***********************************************************
     SEQ-READ.
          READ CHECKFILE-1 INTO CHECK-RECON
               AT END MOVE 1 TO EOF.
     ***********************************************************
     MOVE-DATA-WRITE.
          MOVE CHECK-NO-R       TO CHECK-NO-OUT.
          MOVE DATE-OUT-R       TO DATE-OUT.
          MOVE NAME-OUT-R       TO NAME-OUT.
          MOVE CHECK-AMOUNT-R   TO AMOUNT-OUT.
          WRITE PRINT-REC FROM DETAIL-1.
          ADD  CHECK-AMOUNT-R   TO CHECKS-TOTAL.
     ***********************************************************
```

Fig. 11–6. (*continued*)

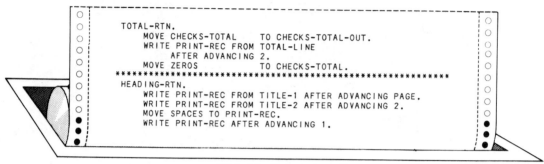

```
TOTAL-RTN.
    MOVE CHECKS-TOTAL      TO CHECKS-TOTAL-OUT.
    WRITE PRINT-REC FROM TOTAL-LINE
        AFTER ADVANCING 2.
    MOVE ZEROS            TO CHECKS-TOTAL.
*************************************************************
HEADING-RTN.
    WRITE PRINT-REC FROM TITLE-1 AFTER ADVANCING PAGE.
    WRITE PRINT-REC FROM TITLE-2 AFTER ADVANCING 2.
    MOVE SPACES TO PRINT-REC.
    WRITE PRINT-REC AFTER ADVANCING 1.
```

Fig. 11-6. (continued)

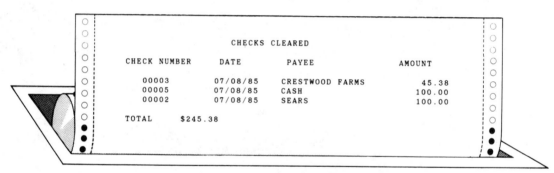

```
                    CHECKS CLEARED

   CHECK NUMBER      DATE        PAYEE              AMOUNT

      00003       07/08/85    CRESTWOOD FARMS        45.38
      00005       07/08/85    CASH                  100.00
      00002       07/08/85    SEARS                 100.00

   TOTAL     $245.38
```

Fig. 11-7. Listing of cleared checks.

```
                    CHECKS OUTSTANDING

   CHECK NUMBER      DATE        PAYEE              AMOUNT

      00001       07/08/85    LOCAL ELECTRIC CO      97.25
      00004       07/08/85    JOHN JACKSON, MD       50.00
      00006       07/08/85    AJAX OFFICE SUPPLY    398.50
      00007       07/08/85    AT & T                 78.90
      00008       07/08/85    COMPUTERPLACE INC     120.00

   TOTAL     $744.65
```

Fig. 11-8. Listing of outstanding checks.

> *The complete source program shown in Fig. 11–6 is available on the supplemental disk as filename CH1106.COB.*

EXERCISES

1. This exercise consists of three programs to create, update, and access an indexed file, as shown in the systems diagram below. The system will record the sales and returns amounts for any number of salespersons.

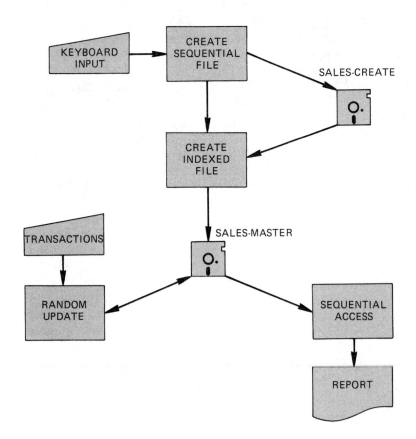

a. Create an indexed sequential file called SALES-MASTER from the input sequential file called SALES-CREATE.

b. Randomly update SALES-MASTER depending on the input received from the sequential files SALES-TRAN, which is in random order. The type of transactions on SALES-TRAN are as follows:

Type 1 = sale, add to YR-TO-DATE-SALES

Type 2 = return, add to YR-TO-DATE-RETURNS

Type 3 = addition, a new salesperson's record is to be added to the file

Type 4 = deletion, a salesperson has been terminated and his/her record is to be deleted

c. The file SALES-MASTER, after having been updated, is used to prepare the report described on the opposite page. This report is printed in salesperson number sequence.

$$YR\text{-}TO\text{-}DATE\text{-}SALES - YR\text{-}TO\text{-}DAT\text{-}RETURNS$$
$$= NET\text{-}SALES$$

The files needed for this program are described in the print layout shown on the opposite page.

Input Record: SALES-CREATE

SALESPERSON NAME				YR-TO-DATE SALES	YR-TO-DATE RETURNS
SALESPERSON NUMBER	LAST	FIRST INIT	MIDDLE INIT	DEPT		

```
                    1111111111222222222233333333 33
1234567890123456789012345678901234567 89
```

Disk Record: SALES-MASTER

SALESPERSON NUMBER	SALESPERSON NAME				YR-TO-DATE SALES	YR-TO-DATE RETURNS
	LAST	FIRST INIT	MIDDLE INIT	DEPT		

```
           1111111111111112222222222 223333333333
1234567890123456789012345678901234567 89
```

Input Record: SALES-TRAN

SALESPERSON NUMBER	AMOUNT	SALESPERSON NAME			
		LAST	FIRST INIT	MIDDLE INIT	DEPT

```
           1111 11111122222222223 33
1234567890 1234567890123456789012345678901
```

Output Layout

```
        0         1         2         3         4         5         6         7
 123456789012345678901234567890123456789012345678901234567890123456789012345678901234567890

 1
 2                         SALES REPORT
 3      DEPT              SALESPERSON              YR-TO-DATE       YR-TO-DATE
 4      NO.    NUMBER       NAME                     SALES          RETURNS          NET
 5                                                                                  SALES
 6
 7      XX    XXXXX    X.X.              X.X.      X,XXX,XXX.XX   X,XXX,XXX.XX   X,XXX,XXX.XX
 8             ~~~~     ~~~               ~~          ~~~~           ~~~~           ~~~~
 9
10
11      XX    XXXXX    X.X.              X.X.      X,XXX,XXX.XX   X,XXX,XXX.XX   X,XXX,XXX.XX
12
13
14             TOTALS                            $XX,XXX,XXX.XX $XXX,XXX,XXX.XX $XX,XXX,XXX.XX
15                                               $XX,XXX,XXX.XX  $XX,XXX,XXX.XX  $XX,XXX,XXX.XX
16
17
18
```

2. a. Write a program to create an indexed file with names, addresses, and telephone numbers that will be used as an address book. The RECORD KEY should be the name field. (Note that the name is entered last name first.)

b. Write a second program that will allow adding, deleting, and looking up of information in this file by the use of the name field.

c. What are the limitations of using the name as the index?

Disk Record: ADDRESS-BOOK

NAME	STREET ADDRESS	CITY	STATE	ZIP	AREA CODE	PHONE
111111111 11222222	2222333333333334444444	4444 5555555 5556	66	666666	67	7777 7777
123456789012345678901234 5	67890123456789012345	6789 01 23456 7890	12	345678	90	1234 5678

3. a. Write a program to create a relative file to store data regarding unpaid invoices. The invoice numbers are to begin at 2000.

b. Write a program to update this file in a random order as invoices are paid by placing a code P in the PAID field and by adding new invoices at the end of the file as new numbers are assigned.

c. Write a program to print a listing of outstanding invoices as shown in the print layout on the opposite page.

The solutions to the exercises, together with any necessary data files, are provided on the supplemental disk.

Input Layout

INV. NO.	CUST. NO.	DATE MM/DD/YY	AMOUNT	PAID
1 2 3 4 5 6 7	8 9 0	1 2 3 4 5 6 7	8 9 0 1 2 3 4 5	6 7

Input Record: INVOICES

Output Layout

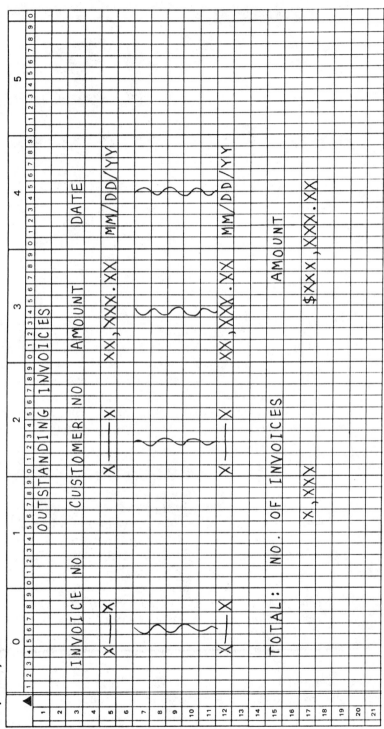

12

THE COBOL SORT

It may be necessary to sort an input file or merge several input files prior to the processing of these files. This can generally be accomplished by one of two means: the required operation can be accomplished by employing a special utility program, such as PCSORT, prior to using the file(s) with a COBOL program; or the file(s) can be sorted or merged within a COBOL program using the SORT or MERGE features. The latter methods will be described in this chapter.

THE SORT OPERATION

Sorting is a relatively slow process compared to other computer operations because of the large percentage of input/output operations involved. The COBOL sort is a file sort and is quite different from other methods of sorting, such as the Bubble Sort, Shell Sort, etc., which are internal sorts and use tables to first read in *all* the data, rearrange it in the table, and finally process it. A file sort reads one data record at a time, places it in a special sort file on the disk, and then proceeds to read in each record and write out strings of records in several disk work areas. This process is continued until all the records have been rearranged into the desired sequence and the sort is completed. The advantage of this type of sort is that the size of the file is limited by the amount of disk space available rather than the amount of RAM, as would be the case with an internal sort.

The Collating Sequence

The character sequence used by the IBM COBOL SORT is the ASCII collating sequence, which is described in Fig. 6-5 (page 174).

INSTALLING THE IBM COBOL SORT

Only two changes are required to run the COBOL SORT.

1. Your COBOL diskette (or the directory on your hard disk containing your COBOL compiler) must contain a file called COBSRT.LIB. If you have a single-sided disk system, this file must be on the disk containing the COBOL LIBRARIES. The linker will search for this file when you have used the SORT or MERGE in your COBOL program.

2. You must run a program called FIXLIB.COM, which will alter your COBOL compiler to accept a SORT/MERGE operation.

The easiest way to install the SORT/MERGE is to copy these two files onto the same disk or directory as your other COBOL files. With the drive containing these files as the default drive, type FIXLIB, which will cause the following messages to appear:

```
The Sort interface module in COBOL1.LIB has been updated.
The COBOL memory management has been updated for Sort.

Save this one as your new COBOL1.LIB library master.
```

Of course, as in all cases where you are altering important software, run this on a duplicate copy of your COBOL compiler and library disk.

The coding requirements of the SORT feature are described below, division by division.

THE ENVIRONMENT DIVISION

The ENVIRONMENT DIVISION is the first division affected by the SORT feature. The IDENTIFICATION DIVISION of a COBOL program is concerned only with identifying the program and is not affected by the incorporation of the SORT feature.

The FILE-CONTROL Paragraph

The programs dealt with previously have been concerned with two basic types of files: input files and output files. A COBOL program utilizing the SORT feature, however, is concerned with a third type of file: a **sort file**. A sort file is a work file, as mentioned above, used by the system to facilitate the sorting operation. As with any other file used with a COBOL program, a sort file must be identified in a SELECT statement. ASSIGN clauses for sort files are similar to input or output files, except that a sort file, of course, must always be assigned to DISK and that sort files have an optional clause naming a SORT STATUS data field, which is similar in operation to the FILE STATUS clause described in previous chapters.

GENERAL FORMAT 1

SELECT filename ASSIGN TO DISK

[SORT STATUS IS identifier]

The SORT STATUS Clause

At the completion of the sort, a two-character alphanumeric code is placed in the field named in the SORT STATUS clause indicating the result of the sort. The data-name included in this clause must be a two-character alphanumeric field defined in working storage. As with the FILE STATUS clause, the SORT STATUS allows the program to check the result of the sort and take whatever action is appropriate. Without the use of the SORT STATUS option, execution of the program will terminate if an error occurs at runtime.

The codes used and their meanings are shown below:

Status Code	Description
00	Successful completion
10	Sort needs more memory
11	Program attempted to execute a SORT statement from within an INPUT or OUTPUT PROCEDURE (nested sorts are NOT permitted)
71	OPEN error

72	CLOSE error
73	WRITE error
74	READ error
76	DELETE error
80	{
81	{Internal sort error
82	{

A typical SELECT entry would be:

```
SELECT SORT-FILE ASSIGN TO DISK
    SORT STATUS IS SORT-STAT.
```

The I-O CONTROL Paragraph

This is an optional entry that can be used in IBM COBOL to conserve memory, an important consideration in this version of COBOL. The purpose of this clause is to add to the efficiency of memory utilization by having the same input/output or sort areas shared by more than one file. All the files may be opened simultaneously, but only one set of data may be present at any given time.

GENERAL FORMAT 2

$$\left[\text{SAME} \left\{ \begin{array}{l} \text{RECORD} \\ \text{SORT} \\ \text{SORT-MERGE} \end{array} \right\} \text{AREA FOR filename-1, filename-2, [filename-3 ...] ...} \right]$$

THE DATA DIVISION

Any input or output files used with a COBOL program must have appropriate file and record description entries in the DATA DIVISION. In the case of a program utilizing the SORT feature, the programmer must provide sort file description and record description entries for each sort file used in the program. The general format of the sort file description (SD) entry is as follows:

GENERAL FORMAT 3

SD sort-filename

[RECORD CONTAINS [integer-1 TO] integer-2 CHARACTERS]

[DATA $\begin{Bmatrix} \text{RECORD IS} \\ \text{RECORDS ARE} \end{Bmatrix}$ data-name-1 [data-name-2] ...]

[VALUE OF FILE-ID IS $\begin{Bmatrix} \text{data-name} \\ \text{literal} \end{Bmatrix}$]

A sort file description entry must begin with the required word SD beginning in the A Area. This must be followed immediately by a programmer-supplied name describing the records to be sorted. This sort-filename must correspond to the sort-filename stipulated in the SELECT clause, may not be qualified or subscripted, and must adhere to the rules for the formation of data-names.

The DATA RECORDS and RECORD CONTAINS clauses are the same as those used with file description (FD) entries and are optional.

The sort file description must be followed immediately by the record description entry. The same rules that apply to the record description entries for input or output files apply to records within a sort file. Only the fields that are specifically referenced by the PROCEDURE DIVISION need be described separately. Unreferenced fields may be grouped together and assigned the name FILLER. One or more of the explicitly described fields must be used to determine the order in which the records are to be sorted. This field(s) is referred to as the **sort key(s)**.

The Sort Key

Each record in a file to be sorted must be identified by a code called its key. A key may be a part number, employee number, department number, a person or company name, and so on. Keys were also employed when records were being recorded on or returned from indexed and relative organized files. The key in these cases served to verify or control the order in which records were recorded on and retrieved from a file. In the case of a sort file, however, the key is used only in sorting the records into key sequence.

In some cases a file may be sorted according to several different keys contained within the record. For example, an employee file that may be normally sorted into employee number sequence may be re-sorted according to name, department code, and so on.

It is possible that more than one key may be used in the same sort operation. Figure 12-1 illustrates employee records that are sorted on three keys: plant number, department number, and employee number. When more than one key is used in sorting a file, the keys are referred to as a **major key**, an **intermediate key**, and a **minor key**. If more than one of these is written into the SORT statement, the importance of the keys is from major key to minor key, with the major key being the first listed in the SORT statement, the intermediate key being the second listed, and the minor key being the third listed in the SORT statement. Since there may be more than 3 keys (12 are permitted in IBM COBOL), all except the first and the last are referred to as inter-mediate keys and their importance (hierarchy) will be determined by the order in which they are entered in the SORT statement.

The file listed in Fig. 12-1 is sorted into plant number sequence (major key). Within each plant group, individual records are sorted into department number sequence (intermediate key). Then within

Plant-No	Dept-No	Employee-No	Employee-Name
1	12	1249	SMITHERS, JOHN A.
1	12	1592	HARRISON, FRED S.
1	12	3345	ABRAMS, WILLIAM M.
1	18	0145	SAGER, HAMILTON S.
1	18	1337	GORIN, STEPHEN A.
1	27	1992	PACILLIO, JAMES P.
1	27	2001	HICKEY, MARY T.
1	27	2009	ADINOLF, KATHERINE E.
1	27	2158	WILLIAMS, MARTIN L.
2	15	1477	LOCKE, RICHARD G.
2	15	1553	FIECCO, LAWRENCE T.
2	23	0194	PATTEN, GEORGE R.
2	23	0957	FURY, THOMAS J.
2	23	1942	AHERN, WILBUR L.
2	48	1056	ATHERS, SEAN C.
2	48	2083	WILSON, SUZANNE M.

Fig. 12-1. Records sorted into ascending sequence according to three sort keys—minor key employee *number*.

```
============================================================
 Plant-No        Dept-No        Employee-No    Employee-Name
------------------------------------------------------------
    1              12              3345         ABRAMS, WILLIAM M.
    1              12              1592         HARRISON, FRED S.
    1              12              1249         SMITHERS, JOHN A.
    1              18              1337         GORIN, STEPHEN A.
    1              18              0145         SAGER, HAMILTON S.
    1              27              2009         ADINOLF, KATHERINE E.
    1              27              2001         HICKEY, MARY T.
    1              27              1992         PACILLIO, JAMES P.
    1              27              2158         WILLIAMS, MARTIN L.
    2              15              1553         FIECCO, LAWRENCE T.
    2              15              1477         LOCKE, RICHARD G.
    2              23              1942         AHERN, WILBUR L.
    2              23              0957         FURY, THOMAS J.
    2              23              0194         PATTEN, GEORGE R.
    2              48              1056         ATHERS, SEAN C.
    2              48              2083         WILSON, SUZANNE M.
============================================================
```

Fig. 12–2. Records sorted into ascending sequence according to three sort keys—minor key employee *name*.

each department records are sorted into employee number sequence (minor key). Figure 12–2 shows this same group of data with employee name as the minor key instead of employee number.

The following basic rules govern the use of sort key items:

1. They must describe data-names associated with filename-1 of the SORT statement (the file described by the SD).

2. Key data-names can be qualified.

3. When more than one record description appears, the key items need only be described in one of the record descriptions.

4. None of the data-names described as keys may be described by an entry that contains an OCCURS clause or is subordinate to an entry that contains an OCCURS.

5. A maximum of 12 keys can be specified and each may have a length of from 1 to 256 characters.

THE PROCEDURE DIVISION

This division must contain a SORT statement describing the sorting operation. This statement may also indicate any input and output procedures that are to be followed in the process of executing the sorting operation.

The SORT Statement

The general format of the SORT is as follows:

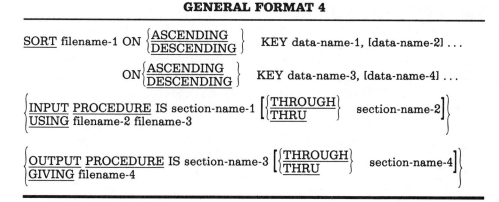

GENERAL FORMAT 4

Filename-1 is the name assigned to the file in the sort description (SD) entry in the DATA DIVISION.

The ASCENDING and DESCENDING Options
These options allow the programmer to specify whether the records are to be sorted into an ascending or descending collating sequence, respectively, depending on one or more sort keys. At least one ASCENDING or DESCENDING clause must be specified in a SORT statement. Each data-name associated with an ASCENDING or DESCENDING option refers to a key data item and must appear in at least one record description entry associated with the sort file identified as filename-1. It is possible to have both an ASCENDING and a DESCENDING option specified for a particular file. For example, execution of the SORT statement

```
SORT INPUT-FILE-S
     ON DESCENDING KEY PLANT-NO
                        DEPT-NO
        ASCENDING     KEY EMPLOYEE-NO
        USING  IN-FILE
        GIVING OUT-FILE.
```

causes the records released to the file INPUT-FILE-S to be sorted into descending sequence on the key PLANT-NO. Within PLANT-NO, records are sorted into descending sequence on the key DEPT-NO. And finally, within DEPT-NO, records are sorted into ascending sequence on the key EMPLOYEE-NO. Note that the relative significance of the keys is determined *only* by the order in which they appear.

The INPUT PROCEDURE Option

This option, when present, indicates to the program that one or more consecutive *sections* appear in the PROCEDURE DIVISION that are to process records *before* they are sorted. As records are processed by the INPUT PROCEDURE, they are released to the sort file one record at a time. Generally, the INPUT PROCEDURE includes any procedures necessary to select, create, or modify records prior to being sorted.

Section-name-1 and section-name-2 are the names of the first and last of the *consecutive* sections that are contained in the INPUT PROCEDURE. If only one section is present, THRU section-name-2 is omitted.

It should be noted that the sort merely passes control to the INPUT PROCEDURE section. The normal repetition required for processing will be controlled within the section, as we will see below in the sample programs.

The following rules govern the use of the INPUT PROCEDURE option:

1. The section(s) specified in an INPUT PROCEDURE must not be contained in an OUTPUT PROCEDURE.

2. An INPUT PROCEDURE must contain at least one RELEASE statement. The purpose of the RELEASE statement is to transfer records from the input file to the sort file; it is described later in this chapter.

3. The INPUT PROCEDURE may not have any statement referring to the sort file such as an OPEN, etc.

4. Control must not be passed to the INPUT PROCEDURE except as a result of executing a SORT statement in which the INPUT PROCEDURE is specified. If such a situation were to occur, the RELEASE statement would not function, since no sort file has been specified to receive the data.

5. The INPUT PROCEDURE may not contain any SORT statements.

6. If the INPUT PROCEDURE is to input a file (the normal situation), the file must be OPENed prior to the SORT or within the INPUT PROCEDURE and must be CLOSEd within the INPUT PROCEDURE or outside the SORT after the sorting is completed.

7. The INPUT PROCEDURE must not contain any statements that transfer control outside the INPUT PROCEDURE.

8. Control must not be transferred from elsewhere in the program to within the INPUT PROCEDURE.

9. When all records have been RELEASEd to filename-1 (the sort file), control must be transferred to the *last statement* within the range of the INPUT PROCEDURE. After this statement has been executed, the compiler inserts a routine to initiate the sorting of all records RELEASEd to filename-1.

Note this last requirement regarding the INPUT PROCEDURE. It is quite different from other COBOL logical constructs and many find it confusing. The execution of what is physically the last statement within the range of the INPUT PROCEDURE (and the OUTPUT PROCEDURE) is required before the INPUT PROCEDURE is complete. This will also be demonstrated in the sample programs.

The USING Option This option, when used *instead of the INPUT PROCEDURE*, causes all records in filename-2, filename-3, etc., to be transferred automatically to the sort file, filename-1. Unlike the INPUT PROCEDURE, no processing may take place between the reading of the record and this automatic transfer.

The following considerations apply to filename-2 (and filename-3, . . .):

1. The files may be any type of file organization, but for INDEXED and RELATIVE files the ACCESS mode must be SEQUENTIAL.

2. The input files must not be OPENed prior to execution of the SORT.

3. The file(s) must be described in the DATA DIVISION with standard FD entries and record descriptions.

4. The file(s) must be ASSIGNed in the ENVIRONMENT DIVISION with SELECT statements.

The OUTPUT PROCEDURE Option   This option indicates that one or more consecutive *sections* appear in the PROCEDURE DIVISION to process records *after* they have been sorted. After the file is sorted, the sorted records are returned to the OUTPUT PROCEDURE one record at a time for processing. As with the INPUT PROCEDURE, the OUTPUT PROCEDURE includes any procedures needed to select, modify, or copy records—but in this case *after* the records have been sorted.

Section-name-3 and section-name-4 are the names of the first and last of the consecutive sections that are contained in the OUTPUT PROCEDURE. If only one section is present, THRU section-name-4 is omitted.

The following rules govern the use of the OUTPUT PROCEDURE option:

1. The section(s) specified in an OUTPUT PROCEDURE must not be contained in an INPUT PROCEDURE.

2. An OUTPUT PROCEDURE must contain at least one RETURN statement. The purpose of the RETURN statement is to transfer records from the sort file to the output file; it is described later in this chapter.

3. The OUTPUT PROCEDURE may not have any statement referring to the sort file such as an OPEN, etc.

4. Control must not be passed to the OUTPUT PROCEDURE except as a result of executing a SORT statement in which the OUTPUT PROCEDURE is specified. If such a situation were to

occur, the RETURN statement would not function, since no sort file has been specified to receive the data.

5. The OUTPUT PROCEDURE may not contain any SORT statements.

6. If the OUTPUT PROCEDURE is to output a file (the normal situation), the file must be OPENed prior to the SORT or within the OUTPUT PROCEDURE and must be CLOSEd within the OUTPUT PROCEDURE or outside the SORT after the sorting is completed.

7. The OUTPUT PROCEDURE must not contain any statements that transfer control outside the OUTPUT PROCEDURE.

8. Control must not be transferred from elsewhere in the program to within the OUTPUT PROCEDURE.

9. When all records have been RETURNed to filename-1 (the sort file), control must be transferred to the *last statement* within the range of the OUTPUT PROCEDURE. After this statement has been executed, the compiler inserts a routine to terminate the sort and to pass control to the next sentence after the SORT statement.

The GIVING Option   This option causes all sorted records in the sort file, filename-1, to be transferred *automatically* to filename-3. Unlike the OUTPUT PROCEDURE, no processing takes place between the completion of the sort and the writing of the record to an output file. In addition, this option may be chosen only when the sorted records are to be output on one file. If, for example, a new disk file is to be created and a printed report is required, the OUTPUT PROCEDURE option would have to be used.

The considerations that apply to filename-3 are the same as those that apply to filename-2 (filename-3, . . .) in the USING option:

1. The files may have any type of organization, but for INDEXED and RELATIVE files the ACCESS mode must be SEQUENTIAL. This would be used in creating INDEXED or RELATIVE files.

2. The output files must not be OPENed prior to execution of the SORT.

3. The file(s) must be described in the DATA DIVISION with standard FD entries and record descriptions.

4. The file(s) must be ASSIGNed in the ENVIRONMENT DIVISION with SELECT statements.

The RELEASE Statement

This statement transfers records from the INPUT PROCEDURE to the sort file named in the sort description (SD) entry. The general format of the statement is as follows:

GENERAL FORMAT 5

RELEASE sort-record-name [FROM identifier]

This statement may be used *only* within the range of an INPUT PROCEDURE associated with a SORT statement, and must appear at least once within the INPUT PROCEDURE. Logically this statement is similar to a WRITE, since it causes the sort record to be "written" onto the sort work file.

Sort-record-name refers to the name of the logical record within the associated SD entry. If the FROM option is specified, the RELEASE statement is equivalent to the following two statements:

```
MOVE identifier TO sort-record-name
RELEASE sort-record-name
```

with the MOVE statement subject to the restraints that apply to a simple alphanumeric MOVE statement.

Note that the RELEASE statement uses the sort-record-name just as a WRITE would use the record-name. Once a record has been RELEASED, it is no longer available, and the sort-file contains only those records passed to it by a RELEASE statement in the INPUT PROCEDURE.

The RETURN Statement

This statement transfers sorted records from the sort work file to the OUTPUT PROCEDURE for processing and output. The general format of this statement is as follows:

GENERAL FORMAT 6

RETURN sort-filename RECORD [INTO identifier]

AT END imperative-statement

This statement may be used only within the range of an OUTPUT PROCEDURE associated with a SORT statement and must appear at least once within an OUTPUT PROCEDURE.

Sort-filename refers to the name assigned to the sort file in the sort file description (SD) entry. Identifier must be the name of a working storage area or an output area. The INTO option, if specified, is equivalent to a RETURN statement followed by an alphanumeric MOVE. The imperative-statement stipulated in the AT END option is executed when all the records have been RETURNed to the OUTPUT PROCEDURE for processing and output. After the imperative-statement has been executed, no further RETURN statements may be executed within the current OUTPUT PROCEDURE.

You will note that the RETURN statement is logically similar to a READ statement, including the required AT END clause. It causes the sorted records to be "read" from the sort work area on the disk for further processing.

The EXIT Statement

This statement is commonly used as the last statement or exit point in an INPUT or OUTPUT PROCEDURE, in much the same way as it is used with the PERFORM statement. The general format is as follows:

GENERAL FORMAT 7

paragraph-name.

EXIT.

When used as an exit point for an INPUT or OUTPUT PROCEDURE, the EXIT statement must appear as the only statement in the last paragraph of the procedure. Execution of the EXIT in this manner satisfies the requirement that to terminate either an INPUT or OUTPUT PROCEDURE, the last statement in the procedure must be executed.

Sorting with Indexed and Relative Files

In many versions of COBOL, it is only possible to process sequentially organized files with the USING and GIVING options of the SORT. IBM COBOL allows both types of organization with the USING and GIVING options providing that the ACCESS MODE IS SEQUENTIAL. We have significantly altered the index file creation program from Chapter 11 (Fig. 11–1, program CH1101.COB) to make use of this feature. You can see in Fig. 12–3 that this greatly simplifies the creation of the indexed file and also ensures that the file will be created in ascending sequence—a requirement for the creation of indexed files.

SAMPLE SORT APPLICATION WITH VARIATIONS

The Basic Problem

The initial problem is to write a program to sort a disk file (INPUT-FILE) currently in EMPLOYEE-NO sequence into ASCENDING sequence by DEPT-NO, and within DEPT-NO by EMPLOYEE-NO. The sorted records are to be recorded sequentially on a disk file called DISK-FILE. The following layout describes the records to be sorted:

Character Positions	Contents	
1–5	Employee number,	PIC 9(5)
6–30	Employee name,	PIC X(25)
31–33	Department number,	PIC X(3)
34–60	Other relevant data,	PIC X(27)

Within the ENVIRONMENT DIVISION the only changes necessary to implement the sort are the SELECT and ASSIGN clauses related to the sort-work file SORT-FILE. The FILE-CONTROL entry is as follows:

```
FILE-CONTROL.
    SELECT INPUT-FILE ASSIGN TO DISK
           ORGANIZATION IS LINE SEQUENTIAL.
    SELECT DISK-FILE ASSIGN TO DISK.
    SELECT SORT-FILE ASSIGN TO DISK.
    SELECT PRINT-FILE ASSIGN TO PRINTER.
```

```
*******************************************************************
      IDENTIFICATION DIVISION.
*******************************************************************
      PROGRAM-ID. CREATE-INDEX-FILE.
      AUTHOR.   S.J.GAUGHRAN
******************************************************
      ENVIRONMENT DIVISION.
*******************************************************************
      CONFIGURATION SECTION.
      SOURCE-COMPUTER. IBM-PERSONAL-COMPUTER.
      OBJECT-COMPUTER. IBM-PERSONAL-COMPUTER.
      FILE-CONTROL.
           SELECT IN-FILE ASSIGN TO DISK
                ORGANIZATION IS LINE SEQUENTIAL.
           SELECT INDEX-FILE ASSIGN TO DISK
                ORGANIZATION IS INDEXED
                ACCESS IS SEQUENTIAL
                RECORD KEY IS ITEM-NO.
           SELECT SORT-FILE ASSIGN TO DISK.
      ***********************************************
      DATA DIVISION.
      *******************************************************************
      FILE SECTION.
      FD   IN-FILE
           LABEL RECORDS ARE STANDARD
           VALUE OF FILE-ID IS 'DATAFILE.111'
           RECORD CONTAINS 80 CHARACTERS.
      01   IN-REC  PIC X(80).
      FD   INDEX-FILE
           LABEL RECORDS ARE STANDARD
           PECORD CONTAINS 50 CHARACTERS
           VALUE OF FILE-ID IS 'INDSORT.121'.
      01   DISK-RECORD.
           05   ITEM-NO        PIC X(3).
           05   OTHER-DATA     PIC X(47).
      SD   SORT-FILE.
      01   SORT-REC.
           05   ITEM-NO-S      PIC X(3).
           05   FILLER         PIC X(47).
      *******************************************
      PROCEDURE DIVISION.
      *********************************************************
      MAIN-LINE.
           SORT SORT-FILE ASCENDING KEY ITEM-NO-S
                USING IN-FILE
                GIVING INDEX-FILE.
           DISPLAY 'RUN COMPLETE'.
           STOP RUN.
      *******************************************
      *******************************************
```

Fig. 12–3. SORT and creation of an indexed file.

*The complete source program shown in Fig. 12–3 is available
on the supplemental disk as filename CH1201.COB.*

The DATA DIVISION must contain a sort file description entry for SORT-FILE together with a record description entry for the SORT-RECORDs. In addition, this division will also contain the descriptions for the input INPUT-FILE and the output DISK-FILE. The DATA DIVISION for the sample program could be as follows:

```
DATA DIVISION.
FILE SECTION.
FD   INPUT-FILE
     LABEL RECORDS ARE STANDARD
     VALUE OF FILE-ID IS 'IN-DATA.DAT'.
01   INPUT-RECORD          PIC X(60).
FD   DISK-FILE
     LABEL RECORDS ARE STANDARD
     VALUE OF FILE-ID IS 'DISK-REC.DAT'.
01   DISK-RECORD           PIC X(60).
SD   SORT-FILE
01   SORT-RECORD.
     05   EMPLOYEE-NO       PIC 9(5).
     05   EMPLOYEE-NAME     PIC X(25).
     05   DEPT-NO           PIC X(3).
     05   OTHER-DATA        PIC X(27).
```

Note that no detail record description is included for either INPUT-RECORD or for DISK-RECORD; there is no need to identify or access the individual fields within these records. The fields on which the sort is based *must be identified*, but these fields need only be described in the record description of the sort record SORT-RECORD. A SORT statement with the USING option causes INPUT-RECORD to be moved directly to SORT-RECORD. Once all the records in INPUT-RECORD have been copied into SORT-FILE, this file is sorted. Then the GIVING option of the SORT statement causes the sorted records to be transferred without any changes directly to DISK-FILE, in the new sequence. The PROCEDURE DIVISION entries that accomplish this are as follows:

```
PROCEDURE DIVISION.
SORT-RTN.
    SORT SORT-FILE
         ASCENDING KEY DEPT-NO
                       EMPLOYEE-NO
         USING INPUT-FILE
         GIVING DISK-FILE.
    STOP RUN.
```

Variation I of the Basic Problem

Assume that in addition to what was done above, a report is to be printed with appropriate titles, containing the EMPLOYEE-NO, EMPLOYEE-NAME, and DEPT-NO for each employee record on the file. Employees listed on this report are to appear in the same order as they are written on DISK-FILE.

In order to solve this problem a print routine must be placed at a logical point in the program. Two possibilities exist. First, a routine could be inserted at the end of the previous program to re-OPEN, READ, WRITE to the printer and CLOSE the sorted output file, DISK-FILE. Second, as the records are being recorded on the output file DISK-FILE from SORT-FILE, they could be printed out in a report. This latter approach is good because it eliminates the necessity of having to read the entire DISK-FILE. There are, however, a couple of problems with adding the writing of the print file to the program as shown above. The GIVING option only allows the creation of one file, in this case DISK-FILE. In order for the printout to be edited and have titles printed, some small amount of processing is required. You will remember that the USING and GIVING options can only be used when there is to be no processing. A program for Variation I is shown in Fig. 12–4.

Additional statements are required to create the new file PRINT-FILE. These statements have been used many times in previous programs, and they appear in this program in the file and record descriptions associated with PRINT-FILE as well as in the WORKING-STORAGE SECTION.

Also, additional statements result from the change in the SORT statement. Because the sorted output records are no longer simply transcribed onto an output file, the GIVING option of the SORT statement must not be used. An OUTPUT PROCEDURE must be coded that produces both a sorted disk file (DISK-FILE) and a listing (PRINT-FILE) in the same sequence. This OUTPUT PROCEDURE is identified in the SORT statement as the PROCESS-OUTPUT SECTION.

In the OPEN-RTN and the CLOSE-RTN of the PROCESS-OUTPUT SECTION, both DISK-FILE and PRINT-FILE are OPENed and CLOSEd, respectively. These procedures are necessary because they are no longer automatically handled by the SORT statement. (The opening and closing of a file are handled automatically by the SORT statement when the file is specified in a USING or a GIVING clause.)

```
*****************************************************************
IDENTIFICATION DIVISION.
*****************************************************************
PROGRAM-ID. BASIC-SORT-PROGRAM-VARIATION-1.
AUTHOR.  S. J. GAUGHRAN
*****************************************************************
ENVIRONMENT DIVISION.
*****************************************************************
CONFIGURATION SECTION.
SOURCE-COMPUTER.
     IBM-PERSONAL-COMPUTER.
OBJECT-COMPUTER.
     IBM-PERSONAL-COMPUTER.
FILE-CONTROL.
     SELECT INPUT-FILE ASSIGN TO DISK
             ORGANIZATION IS LINE SEQUENTIAL.
     SELECT DISK-FILE  ASSIGN TO DISK.
     SELECT SORT-FILE  ASSIGN TO DISK.
     SELECT PRINT-FILE ASSIGN TO PRINTER.
*****************************************************************
DATA DIVISION.
*****************************************************************
FILE SECTION.
FD  INPUT-FILE
     LABEL RECORDS ARE STANDARD
     VALUE OF FILE-ID IS 'IN-DATA.DAT'.
01  INPUT-RECORD         PIC X(60).
FD  DISK-FILE
     LABEL RECORDS ARE STANDARD
     VALUE OF FILE-ID IS 'DISK-REC.DAT'.
01  DISK-RECORD          PIC X(60).
SD  SORT-FILE
01  SORT-RECORD.
     05  EMPLOYEE-NO       PIC 9(5).
     05  EMPLOYEE-NAME     PIC X(25).
     05  DEPT-NO           PIC X(3).
     05  OTHER-DATA        PIC X(27).
FD  PRINT-FILE
     LABEL RECORDS ARE OMITTED.
01  PRINT-RECORD          PIC X(80).
*****************************************************************
WORKING-STORAGE SECTION.
01  SWITCHES-N-INDICATORS.
     05  EOF              PIC 9 VALUE ZERO.
01  PRINT-TITLES.
     05  FILLER           PIC X(13) VALUE SPACES.
     05  FILLER           PIC X(15) VALUE 'EMPLOYEE NUMBER'.
     05  FILLER           PIC X(06) VALUE SPACES.
     05  FILLER           PIC X(13) VALUE 'EMPLOYEE NAME'.
     05  FILLER           PIC X(06) VALUE SPACES.
     05  FILLER           PIC X(17) VALUE 'DEPARTMENT NUMBER'.
01  PRINT-RECORD-WS.
     05  FILLER           PIC X(18) VALUE SPACES.
     05  EMPLOYEE-NO-O    PIC 9(5).
     05  FILLER           PIC X(05) VALUE SPACES.
     05  EMPLOYEE-NAME-O  PIC X(25).
     05  FILLER           PIC X(07) VALUE SPACES.
     05  DEPT-NO-O        PIC X(03).
*****************************************************************
PROCEDURE DIVISION.
*****************************************************************
SORT-IT SECTION.
*****************************************************************
SORT-RTN.
     SORT SORT-FILE
         ASCENDING KEY DEPT-NO
                       EMPLOYEE-NO
         USING INPUT-FILE
         OUTPUT PROCEDURE PROCESS-OUTPUT.
     STOP RUN.
*****************************************************************
PROCESS-OUTPUT SECTION.
*****************************************************************
```

Fig. 12–4. COBOL program for Variation I of the simple SORT program.

```
OUT-PROC-MAIN-LINE.
    PERFORM OPEN-RTN.
    PERFORM HEADING-RTN.
    PERFORM RETURN-RTN.
    PERFORM WRITE-RETURN-RTN UNTIL EOF = 1.
    PERFORM CLOSE-RTN.
    GO TO OUT-PROC-EXIT.
************************************************************
OPEN-RTN.
    OPEN OUTPUT DISK-FILE
                PRINT-FILE.
************************************************************
HEADING-RTN.
    WRITE PRINT-RECORD FROM PRINT-TITLES
        AFTER ADVANCING PAGE.
************************************************************
RETURN-RTN.
    RETURN SORT-FILE AT END
                MOVE 1 TO EOF.
************************************************************
WRITE-RETURN-RTN.
    PERFORM MOVE-RTN.
    WRITE PRINT-RECORD FROM PRINT-RECORD-WS
        AFTER ADVANCING 1 LINE.
    WRITE DISK-RECORD.
    PERFORM RETURN-RTN.
************************************************************
MOVE-RTN.
    MOVE SORT-RECORD       TO DISK-RECORD.
    MOVE EMPLOYEE-NO       TO EMPLOYEE-NO-O.
    MOVE EMPLOYEE-NAME     TO EMPLOYEE-NAME-O.
    MOVE DEPT-NO           TO DEPT-NO-O.
************************************************************
CLOSE-RTN.
    CLOSE DISK-FILE
            PRINT-FILE.
************************************************************
OUT-PROC-EXIT.
    EXIT.
************************************************************
************************************************************
```

Fig. 12–4. (*continued*)

The complete source program shown in Fig. 12–4 is available on the supplemental disk as filename CH1202.COB.

In the RETURN-RTN, a RETURN statement is used to RETURN the sorted records, one at a time, for processing. The RETURN of records from the sorting operation, as with the opening and closing of an output file, is handled automatically by the SORT only when the GIVING option has been specified. Otherwise, it must be handled by the programmer within the OUTPUT PROCEDURE. Normally, once a record has been RETURNed, it is available only in the sort-record (unless directed elsewhere with the INTO option). It can then be moved to an output record (area) and written out as required by the program.

The paragraph OUT-PROC-EXIT is not absolutely necessary; CLOSE-RTN could serve as the exit point from the OUTPUT PROCEDURE. However, it is a good practice to include an EXIT paragraph in any INPUT or OUTPUT PROCEDURE; this clearly indicates the end of the procedure and aids in the readability and documentation of the program.

You may be wondering why a GO TO statement was used to transfer control to OUT-PROC-EXIT instead of a PERFORM statement. The explanation is quite simple. A PERFORM statement would cause control to return to the statement following the PERFORM upon its completion. This would mean that the EXIT statement would not be the last statement executed in the OUTPUT PROCEDURE, since its execution would be followed by execution of the statement following the PERFORM (the OPEN statement in our case). One must always keep in mind that to complete the execution of an INPUT or OUTPUT PROCEDURE, the last statement within its range must be executed *sequentially and not under control of a PERFORM statement*. Realizing this fact, structured programming advocates consider this an allowable use of the GO TO command.

Variation II of the Basic Problem

Assume that, in addition to what was done in Variation I, the input file INPUT-FILE must be updated and sorted to produce DISK-FILE and the listing. Variation II is concerned with the addition, updating and deletion of records from INPUT-FILE. The update records are recorded on an additional file called UPDATE-FILE in sequence by EMPLOYEE-NO. The update code is in position 61 of each record. A code 1 indicates a new employee, a code 2 indicates an employee to be deleted, a code 3 indicates that a particular field (OTHER-DATA) is to be updated, and a code 4 indicates that the entire record is to be replaced with the incoming update record. The format of the update is as follows:

Character Positions	Contents
1–5	Employee number
6–30	Employee name
31–33	Department number
34–60	Other relevant data
61	Update code (numeric field)

As with the addition of the printed report in Variation I, a logical point in the program must be found for this update routine. Again, two possibilities exist. First, the entire disk file may be updated *prior* to its use by the sort. This will also necessitate an additional reading of the disk file. Second, the disk records may be updated as they are released to SORT-FILE. This latter method is more efficient because the entire file does not have to be read an extra time. New records are released to SORT-RECORD for sorting, but records to be deleted are merely not released to the sort. A program for Variation II is shown in Fig. 12–5 (page 418).

One group of changes results from the addition of the new file UPDATE-FILE. In addition to the changes relating directly to the inclusion of UPDATE-FILE, a detailed record description is given for DISK-RECORD. This is done so that records to be deleted may be identified. The identifying field in DISK-RECORD is EMPLOYEE-NO-D; it is necessary for this field to be specifically described in DISK-RECORD. The other fields are described to increase the documentation of the program.

The remaining changes result from the altering of the SORT statement. Because the disk file is no longer being transferred directly onto the work file SORT-FILE for subsequent sorting, the USING option of the SORT statement may not be used. The INPUT PROCEDURE must be included in the PROCEDURE DIVISION. The INPUT PROCEDURE is specified in the SORT statement as the PROCESS-INPUT SECTION.

As was the case when using the OUTPUT PROCEDURE in Variation I, it is necessary for the programmer to include, either prior to the SORT statement or within the INPUT PROCEDURE, a statement to open the files used by the INPUT PROCEDURE that have not been opened previously. In addition, these files must be CLOSEd within or after the INPUT PROCEDURE. These operations are handled in the paragraphs OPEN-RTN-1 and CLOSE-RTN-1.

```
*****************************************************************
IDENTIFICATION DIVISION.
*****************************************************************
PROGRAM-ID. BASIC-SORT-PROGRAM-II.
AUTHOR. S.J.GAUGHRAN
*****************************************************************
ENVIRONMENT DIVISION.
*****************************************************************
CONFIGURATION SECTION.
SOURCE-COMPUTER.
    IBM-PERSONAL-COMPUTER.
OBJECT-COMPUTER.
    IBM-PERSONAL-COMPUTER.
SPECIAL-NAMES.
    PRINTER IS PRTOUT.
FILE-CONTROL.
    SELECT INPUT-FILE  ASSIGN TO DISK
           ORGANIZATION IS LINE SEQUENTIAL.
    SELECT DISK-FILE   ASSIGN TO DISK.
    SELECT SORT-FILE   ASSIGN TO DISK.
    SELECT PRINT-FILE  ASSIGN TO PRINTER.
    SELECT UPDATE-FILE ASSIGN TO DISK
           ORGANIZATION IS LINE SEQUENTIAL.
*****************************************************************
DATA DIVISION.
*****************************************************************
FILE SECTION.
FD  INPUT-FILE
    LABEL RECORDS ARE STANDARD
    VALUE OF FILE-ID IS 'INPUT.DAT'.
01  INPUT-RECORD.
    05  EMPLOYEE-NO-I    PIC X(5).
    05  EMPLOYEE-NAME-I  PIC X(25).
    05  DEPT-NO-I        PIC X(3).
    05  OTHER-DATA-I     PIC X(27).
FD  DISK-FILE
    LABEL RECORDS ARE STANDARD
    VALUE OF FILE-ID IS 'DISK-REC.DAT'.
01  DISK-RECORD.
    05  EMPLOYEE-NO-D    PIC X(5).
    05  EMPLOYEE-NAME-D  PIC X(25).
    05  DEPT-NO-D        PIC X(3).
    05  OTHER-DATA-D     PIC X(27).
SD  SORT-FILE.
01  SORT-RECORD.
    05  EMPLOYEE-NO      PIC X(5).
    05  EMPLOYEE-NAME    PIC X(25).
    05  DEPT-NO          PIC X(3).
    05  OTHER-DATA       PIC X(27).
FD  PRINT-FILE
    LABEL RECORDS ARE OMITTED.
01  PRINT-RECORD        PIC X(80).
FD  UPDATE-FILE
    LABEL RECORDS ARE STANDARD
    VALUE OF FILE-ID IS 'UPDATE.DAT'.
01  UPDATE-RECORD.
    05  EMPLOYEE-NO-U    PIC X(5).
    05  EMPLOYEE-NAME-U  PIC X(25).
    05  DEPT-NO-U        PIC X(3).
    05  OTHER-DATA-U     PIC X(27).
    05  UPDATE-CODE-U    PIC 9.
*****************************************************************
WORKING-STORAGE SECTION.
01  SWITCHES-N-INDICATORS.
    05  EOF              PIC 9 VALUE ZERO.
01  PRINT-TITLES.
    05  FILLER           PIC X(13) VALUE SPACES.
    05  FILLER           PIC X(15) VALUE 'EMPLOYEE NUMBER'.
    05  FILLER           PIC X(06) VALUE SPACES.
    05  FILLER           PIC X(13) VALUE 'EMPLOYEE NAME'.
    05  FILLER           PIC X(06) VALUE SPACES.
    05  FILLER           PIC X(17) VALUE 'DEPARTMENT NUMBER'.
```

Fig. 12-5. COBOL program for Variation II of the simple SORT program.

```
     01   PRINT-RECORD-WS.
          05   FILLER              PIC X(18) VALUE SPACES.
          05   EMPLOYEE-NO-O       PIC X(5).
          05   FILLER              PIC X(05) VALUE SPACES.
          05   EMPLOYEE-NAME-O     PIC X(25).
          05   FILLER              PIC X(07) VALUE SPACES.
          05   DEPT-NO-O           PIC X(03).
     ************************************************************
     PROCEDURE DIVISION.
     ************************************************************
     SORT-IT SECTION.
     ************************************************************
     SORT-RTN.
D        READY TRACE.
         SORT SORT-FILE
              ASCENDING KEY DEPT-NO
                              EMPLOYEE-NO
              INPUT  PROCEDURE PROCESS-INPUT
              OUTPUT PROCEDURE PROCESS-OUTPUT.
         STOP RUN.
     ************************************************************
     PROCESS-INPUT SECTION.
     ************************************************************
     IN-PROC-MAIN-LINE.
         PERFORM OPEN-RTN-1.
         PERFORM READ-UPDATE-RTN.
         PERFORM READ-INPUT-RTN.
         PERFORM COMPARE-RTN UNTIL
                      EMPLOYEE-NO-U = HIGH-VALUES
                  AND
                      EMPLOYEE-NO-I = HIGH-VALUES.
         PERFORM CLOSE-RTN-1.
         GO TO IN-PROC-EXIT.
     ************************************************************
     OPEN-RTN-1.
         OPEN INPUT  UPDATE-FILE
                     INPUT-FILE.
     ************************************************************
     READ-UPDATE-RTN.
         READ UPDATE-FILE AT END
                  MOVE HIGH-VALUES TO EMPLOYEE-NO-U.
     ************************************************************
     READ-INPUT-RTN.
         READ INPUT-FILE AT END
                  MOVE HIGH-VALUES TO EMPLOYEE-NO-I.
     ************************************************************
     COMPARE-RTN.
D        EXHIBIT EMPLOYEE-NO-U  EMPLOYEE-NO-I.
         IF EMPLOYEE-NO-U GREATER THAN EMPLOYEE-NO-I
              PERFORM NO-UPDATE
              PERFORM READ-INPUT-RTN
         ELSE IF EMPLOYEE-NO-U LESS THAN EMPLOYEE-NO-I
                  PERFORM NEW-EMPLOYEE
                  PERFORM READ-UPDATE-RTN
              ELSE      PERFORM UPDATE-OR-DELETE
                        PERFORM READ-INPUT-RTN
                        PERFORM READ-UPDATE-RTN.
     ************************************************************
     NO-UPDATE.
         RELEASE SORT-RECORD FROM INPUT-RECORD.
         DISPLAY SORT-RECORD UPON PRTOUT.
     ************************************************************
     NEW-EMPLOYEE.
         RELEASE SORT-RECORD FROM UPDATE-RECORD.
         DISPLAY SORT-RECORD UPON PRTOUT.
     ************************************************************
     UPDATE-OR-DELETE.
         IF UPDATE-CODE-U = 2
                  NEXT SENTENCE
         ELSE IF UPDATE-CODE-U = 3
                  PERFORM UPDATE-OTHER-DATA
              ELSE IF UPDATE-CODE-U = 4
                        PERFORM UPDATE-ENTIRE-RECORD
                   ELSE PERFORM UPDATE-CODE-ERROR-RTN.
```

Fig.12–5. (continued)

419

```
***************************************************************
 UPDATE-OTHER-DATA.
     MOVE OTHER-DATA-U     TO OTHER-DATA-I.
     RELEASE SORT-RECORD FROM INPUT-RECORD.
     DISPLAY SORT-RECORD UPON PRTOUT.
***************************************************************
 UPDATE-ENTIRE-RECORD.
     RELEASE SORT-RECORD FROM UPDATE-RECORD.
     DISPLAY SORT-RECORD UPON PRTOUT.
***************************************************************
 UPDATE-CODE-ERROR-RTN.
     DISPLAY 'BAD UPDATE CODE (' UPDATE-CODE-U
          ') FOR EMPLOYEE NUMBER = ' EMPLOYEE-NO-U.
***************************************************************
 CLOSE-RTN-1.
     CLOSE INPUT-FILE
           UPDATE-FILE.
***************************************************************
 IN-PROC-EXIT.
     EXIT.
***************************************************************
 PROCESS-OUTPUT SECTION.
***************************************************************
 OUT-PROC-MAIN-LINE.
     PERFORM OPEN-RTN.
     PERFORM HEADING-RTN.
     PERFORM RETURN-RTN.
     PERFORM WRITE-RETURN-RTN UNTIL EOF = 1.
     PERFORM CLOSE-RTN.
     GO TO OUT-PROC-EXIT.
***************************************************************
 OPEN-RTN.
     OPEN OUTPUT DISK-FILE
                 PRINT-FILE.
***************************************************************
 HEADING-RTN.
     WRITE PRINT-RECORD FROM PRINT-TITLES
           AFTER ADVANCING PAGE.
***************************************************************
 RETURN-RTN.
     RETURN SORT-FILE AT END
                      MOVE 1 TO EOF.
***************************************************************
 WRITE-RETURN-RTN.
     PERFORM MOVE-RTN.
     WRITE PRINT-RECORD FROM PRINT-RECORD-WS
           AFTER ADVANCING 1 LINE.
     WRITE DISK-RECORD.
     PERFORM RETURN-RTN.
***************************************************************
 MOVE-RTN.
     MOVE SORT-RECORD     TO DISK-RECORD.
     MOVE EMPLOYEE-NO     TO EMPLOYEE-NO-O.
     MOVE EMPLOYEE-NAME   TO EMPLOYEE-NAME-O.
     MOVE DEPT-NO         TO DEPT-NO-O.
***************************************************************
 CLOSE-RTN.
     CLOSE DISK-FILE
           PRINT-FILE.
***************************************************************
 OUT-PROC-EXIT.
     EXIT.
***************************************************************
***************************************************************
```

Fig. 12-5. (*continued*)

420

> *The complete source program shown in Fig. 12–5 is available on the supplemental disk as filename CH1203.COB.*

The main body of this section deals with the actual update of the input file INPUT-FILE using the transaction file UPDATE-FILE. Since updating was discussed in previous chapters, it will not be discussed again here.

It is a good practice to indicate the end of an INPUT or OUTPUT PROCEDURE with an EXIT statement. This is done in IN-PROC-EXIT.

THE MERGE OPERATION

The COBOL MERGE statement makes it possible to combine two or more input files with identical record formats sorted in the same sequence. During the process, records are made available in a single merged sequence to an OUTPUT PROCEDURE or to an output file. The same results could be achieved by sorting these files. The advantage to using the merge over the sort for this operation is that the merge will generally execute faster, since its logic recognizes that the files being combined are already in the same sequence.

The general format of the MERGE statement is as follows:

GENERAL FORMAT 8

MERGE filename-1 ON $\left\{\begin{array}{l}\text{ASCENDING}\\\text{DESCENDING}\end{array}\right\}$ KEY data-name-1 data-name-2 . . .

ON $\left\{\begin{array}{l}\text{ASCENDING}\\\text{DESCENDING}\end{array}\right\}$ KEY data-name-3 data-name-4 . . . . . .

USING filename-2 filename-3 filename-4 . . .

$\left\{\begin{array}{l}\text{OUTPUT PROCEDURE IS section-name-1}\left[\left\{\begin{array}{l}\text{THROUGH}\\\text{THRU}\end{array}\right\}\text{section-name-2}\right]\\\text{GIVING filename-5}\end{array}\right\}$

Filename-1 must be specified in an SD in the FILE SECTION. The rules governing the use of the ASCENDING/DESCENDING KEY clause, the USING/GIVING clauses, and the OUTPUT PROCEDURE are identical to those for the sort.

It should be noted that no provision is made in the MERGE statement for an INPUT PROCEDURE.

The process that takes place during the execution of a MERGE statement is as follows:

1. Control enters the MERGE statement.

2. The merge-file (filename-1) and all the files being merged (filename-2, filename-3, . . .) are opened and positioned at their beginning.

3. The records from the files being merged are copied onto the merge-file according to the key field(s) and sequence(s) specified in the MERGE statement.

4. All input files are then closed.

5. The GIVING or OUTPUT PROCEDURE option is then executed. If the GIVING option is specified in the MERGE statement, the output file (filename-3) is opened, the merge-file is copied onto it, the output file is closed, and control passes to the statement following the MERGE statement. If the OUTPUT PROCEDURE option is specified, the merge-file is positioned at its beginning and control is passed to the section(s) specified in the OUTPUT PROCEDURE where RETURN statements access the merged records in sequence and make them available for processing. After the last statement within the range of the OUTPUT PROCEDURE has been executed, control passes to the statement following the MERGE statement.

To illustrate this process, let's assume that a company wishes to merge its four quarterly sales files into a single yearly sales file. We shall also assume that each of these quarterly sales files is in ascending sequence by department number, and in ascending sequence by salesman number within each department. A program that could accomplish this task utilizing the MERGE feature is shown in Fig. 12–6.

The complete source program shown in Fig. 12–6 is available on the supplemental disk as filename CH1204.COB.

```
**********************************************************
 IDENTIFICATION DIVISION.
**********************************************************
 PROGRAM-ID. QUARTERLY-SALES-MERGE.
 AUTHOR. S.J.GAUGHRAN
**********************************************************
 ENVIRONMENT DIVISION.
**********************************************************
 CONFIGURATION SECTION.
 SOURCE-COMPUTER.
     IBM-PERSONAL-COMPUTER.
 OBJECT-COMPUTER.
     IBM-PERSONAL-COMPUTER.
 FILE-CONTROL.
     SELECT FIRST-QUARTER  ASSIGN TO DISK
            ORGANIZATION IS LINE SEQUENTIAL.
     SELECT SECOND-QUARTER ASSIGN TO DISK
            ORGANIZATION IS LINE SEQUENTIAL.
     SELECT THIRD-QUARTER  ASSIGN TO DISK
            ORGANIZATION IS LINE SEQUENTIAL.
     SELECT FOURTH-QUARTER ASSIGN TO DISK
            ORGANIZATION IS LINE SEQUENTIAL.
     SELECT MERGE-FILE     ASSIGN TO DISK.
     SELECT YEARLY-SALES   ASSIGN TO DISK.
**********************************************************
 DATA DIVISION.
**********************************************************
 FILE SECTION.
 FD  FIRST-QUARTER
     LABEL RECORDS ARE STANDARD
     VALUE OF FILE-ID IS FILE-1.
 01  FIRST-QUARTER-REC   PIC X(60).
 FD  SECOND-QUARTER
     LABEL RECORDS ARE STANDARD
     VALUE OF FILE-ID IS FILE-2.
 01  SECOND-QUARTER-REC  PIC X(60).
 FD  THIRD-QUARTER
     LABEL RECORDS ARE STANDARD
     VALUE OF FILE-ID IS FILE-3.
 01  THIRD-QUARTER-REC   PIC X(60).
 FD  FOURTH-QUARTER
     LABEL RECORDS ARE STANDARD
     VALUE OF FILE-ID IS FILE-4.
 01  FOURTH-QUARTER-REC  PIC X(60).
 SD  MERGE-FILE.
 01  MERGE-REC.
     05  DEPARTMENT-NO  PIC X(5).
     05  SALESMAN-NO    PIC X(5).
     05  SALES-AMOUNT   PIC 9(5)V99.
     05  OTHER-DATA     PIC X(43).
 FD  YEARLY-SALES
     LABEL RECORDS ARE STANDARD
     VALUE OF FILE-ID IS YEARLY-OUT.
 01  YEARLY-REC         PIC X(60).
**********************************************************
 WORKING-STORAGE SECTION.
 01  FILE-NAMES.
     05  FILE-1       PIC X(14).
     05  FILE-2       PIC X(14).
     05  FILE-3       PIC X(14).
     05  FILE-4       PIC X(14).
     05  YEARLY-OUT   PIC X(14).
**********************************************************
 PROCEDURE DIVISION.
**********************************************************
 MAIN-LINE.
     PERFORM ENTER-FILE-NAMES.
     PERFORM MERGE-OPERATION.
     DISPLAY 'MERGE OPERATION COMPLETE '.
     STOP RUN.
**********************************************************
 ENTER-FILE-NAMES.
```

**Fig. 12–6. Program used to merge four files utilizing the
COBOL MERGE feature.**

```
          DISPLAY ' ENTER NAMES OF QUARTERLY FILES '.
          ACCEPT FILE-1.
          ACCEPT FILE-2.
          ACCEPT FILE-3.
          ACCEPT FILE-4.
          DISPLAY ' ENTER NAME OF YEARLY-OUT'.
          ACCEPT YEARLY-OUT.
********************************************************************
     MERGE-OPERATION.
          MERGE MERGE-FILE ASCENDING KEY DEPARTMENT-NO
                                         SALESMAN-NO
               USING FIRST-QUARTER
                     SECOND-QUARTER
                     THIRD-QUARTER
                     FOURTH-QUARTER
               GIVING YEARLY-SALES.
********************************************************************
********************************************************************
```

Fig. 12–6. (*continued*)

EXERCISES

1. The sequential employee file described in the print layout at the top of page 425 is to be read, sorted by employee name within department, and written to the printer in the format shown.

2. Exercise 1 above requires a program to create an indexed file. Change this program to sort the file SALES-CREATE into ascending sequence by the salesperson number, which is the key used in creating the index.

3. Mailing labels are to be prepared for a portion of the files shown at the bottom of page 425. They are to be used for a promotional letter to only those customers who have spent less than $50 during the last year. The labels must be printed in zip code sequence for bulk mailing purposes. The input file is to remain in sequence by customer number.

The solutions to the exercises, together with any necessary data files, are provided on the supplemental disk.

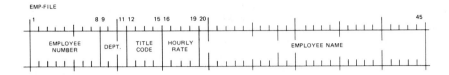

EMP-FILE

EMPLOYEE NUMBER	DEPT.	TITLE CODE	HOURLY RATE	EMPLOYEE NAME

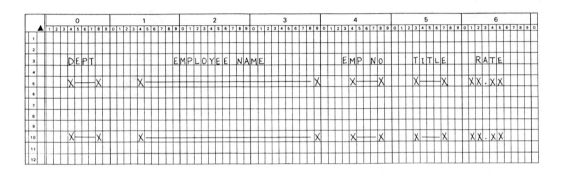

	0	1	2	3	4	5	6

DEPT   EMPLOYEE NAME   EMP NO   TITLE   RATE

X——X   X————————X   X——X   X——X   XX.XX

X——X   X————————X   X——X   X——X   XX.XX

Input Layout

CUSTOMER-MAILING

CUST. NO.	NAME	STREET ADDRESS	TOWN	S T A T E	ZIP	CURRENT YEAR PURCHASES

Output Layout

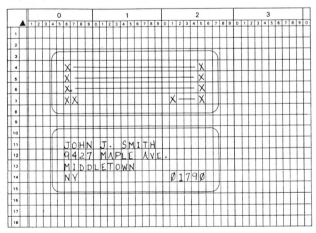

	0	1	2	3

X————————————X
X————————————X
X————————————X
XX   X——X

JOHN J. SMITH
9427 MAPLE AVE.
MIDDLETOWN
NY   Ø1790

13

SUBPROGRAMS, CHAINING, AND SEGMENTATION

INTRODUCTION TO SUBPROGRAMS

Thus far, we have utilized the PERFORM statement to facilitate a modular program structure. In each case we have made the modules an integral part of a single program. It is, however, possible in COBOL to solve a problem by utilizing one main program together with one or more **subprograms**. In such a case, the main program is the executable program. During the execution of this program, it may reference one or more previously written and compiled other programs referred to as subprograms. These subprograms cannot be executed alone but only in conjunction with a main program. These subprograms may be written in COBOL or assembly language, and they must be compiled before they can be called by a main program.

WHY USE A SUBPROGRAM?

There are a number of reasons why one might choose to solve a problem utilizing subprograms. Some of them are:

1. If the task is too large for one programmer to handle in the time available, the task can be assigned to a team of programmers who can concurrently work on separate subprograms. Generally, a chief programmer is assigned to the team and it is his or her job

to direct the overall activities of the team and effectively and efficiently interface with the various members of the team.

2. It is often necessary to incorporate the same routine or procedure in a number of programs. In such cases, this routine or procedure can be written in the form of a subprogram, compiled, and stored in the program library for use by one or more other programs.

3. Some routines or procedures can be written more efficiently in one language than another, and some routines or procedures cannot be written at all in certain languages. Subprograms can be written in virtually any language, as they must be converted to object form and stored on the program library before they can be accessed by a main program. Therefore, the most appropriate language can be selected for each subprogram.

For reasons such as these, the use of subprograms has become so commonplace in business and industry that it is worthy of our consideration.

SAMPLE PROGRAM

To illustrate how one might solve a problem utilizing a subprogram, let's assume that we wish to program a solution to the following problem:

Problem: To write a program to determine the average of each student in a given course. Assume that for each student a nine-digit student number, five examination grades, and a final examination grade are to be input from disk and that each student's grades and average (ROUNDED to the nearest integer) are to be output with appropriate identification on the printer. The following formula is to be used to determine each student's average:

$$STUD\text{-}AV = .3333[.4(GRD\text{-}1 + GRD\text{-}2 + GRD\text{-}3 + GRD\text{-}4 + GRD = 5) + GRD\text{-}FINAL]$$

WRITING A SUBPROGRAM IN COBOL

Let us begin by writing the subprogram to calculate student averages. It should be apparent that if this subprogram is to calculate a student's average, there must be some means by which the main program

```
IDENTIFICATION DIVISION.
PROGRAM-ID. CALC-SUB.
ENVIRONMENT DIVISION.
CONFIGURATION SECTION.
SOURCE-COMPUTER. IBM-PERSONAL-COMPUTER.
OBJECT-COMPUTER. IBM-PERSONAL-COMPUTER.
DATA DIVISION.
WORKING-STORAGE SECTION.
01   WORK-AREAS.
     05   GRD-TOTAL  PIC 9(4).
LINKAGE SECTION.
01   GRD-1        PIC 9(3).
01   GRD-2        PIC 9(3).
01   GRD-3        PIC 9(3).
01   GRD-4        PIC 9(3).
01   GRD-5        PIC 9(3).
01   GRD-FINAL  PIC 9(3).
01   STUD-AVER  PIC 9(3).
PROCEDURE DIVISION USING GRD-1 GRD-2 GRD-3 GRD-4 GRD-5
                         GRD-FINAL STUD-AVER.

STUD-AVER-CALC.
    COMPUTE GRD-TOTAL = GRD-1 + GRD-2 + GRD-3 + GRD-4 + GRD-5.
    COMPUTE STUD-AVER ROUNDED = .3333 * (.4 * GRD-TOTAL +
                                GRD-FINAL).

SUBPROG-EXIT.
    EXIT PROGRAM.
```

Fig. 13-1.   COBOL subprogram to calculate student average.

can communicate the values of the required data items (GRD-1, GRD-2, GRD-3, GRD-4, GRD-5, and GRD-FINAL) to the subprogram and by which the subprogram can communicate the results (STUD-AV) back to the main program. This is accomplished through appropriate entries in the LINKAGE SECTION of the DATA DIVISION (see Fig. 13-1).

The complete source program shown in Fig. 13-1 is available on the supplemental disk as filename CH1301.COB.

The LINKAGE SECTION

Note that in the LINKAGE SECTION, a data item description entry is provided for each value that has to be communicated to or from the main program and the subprogram. The data-names selected for these items do not have to agree with the names selected in the main program but the order in which they are listed in the subprogram and their descriptions must exactly match the order and descriptions which will appear in the main program. In IBM COBOL the entries in the LINKAGE SECTION *must* be either 01-level or 77-level entries.

In addition to the entries in the LINKAGE SECTION, you have probably observed that in the subprogram shown in Fig. 13–1, the PROCEDURE DIVISION entry contains a new clause—the USING clause.

The USING Statement

This statement is used to indicate the *entry point* into the subprogram. Every subprogram must provide an entry point and an exit point. The general format of the USING statement is given below:

GENERAL FORMAT 1

PROCEDURE DIVISION [USING data-name-1 . . .]

In the USING option, data-name-1, etc., represents the data items that will be communicated between the main program and the subprogram. As stated above, the names selected do not have to agree with the names used in the main program, but the order of their appearance and their descriptions must be the same in the main program and the subprogram. The data names listed in the USING option must, however, be described in the LINKAGE SECTION of the subprogram. And they must be individually named (not a group item name), since they must be 01-level or 77-level entries.

In addition to an entry point, a subprogram must have an exit point. This is accomplished with the EXIT PROGRAM statement.

The EXIT PROGRAM Statement

The general format of the EXIT PROGRAM statement is given below:

GENERAL FORMAT 2

EXIT PROGRAM.

The EXIT PROGRAM statement must be preceded by a paragraph-name and be the only statement in the paragraph. Its execution causes control to be returned to the statement in the main or calling program immediately following the statement that called the subprogram—the **CALL statement**. This statement can be seen in Fig. 13–2.

WRITING A MAIN OR CALLING PROGRAM IN COBOL

The main or calling program for the sample problem is shown in Fig. 13–2.

> *The complete source program shown in Fig. 13–2 is available on the supplemental disk as filename CH1302.COB.*

The CALL Statement

The statement required in a main or calling program to call a subprogram is the CALL statement. The general format of the CALL statement is:

GENERAL FORMAT 3

CALL literal [USING data-name . . .]

Literal as used in the above statement is the name of the subprogram, and it should be noted that the name of the subprogram must appear in single or double quotes. As with a program-name, the first eight characters of the literal in a CALL statement are the only characters considered by the system; thus they must be unique. Data-name, etc. are the names of the data items that are to be communicated to or from the main or calling program and the subprogram or called program. As stated earlier, the names do not have to agree with the names used in the subprogram or called program, but they must agree in the order in which they appear and in their descriptions.

```
                    IDENTIFICATION DIVISION.
                    PROGRAM-ID. STUD-AVER-PROG.
                    ENVIRONMENT DIVISION.
                    CONFIGURATION SECTION.
                    SOURCE-COMPUTER. IBM-PERSONAL-COMPUTER.
                    OBJECT-COMPUTER. IBM-PERSONAL-COMPUTER.
                    INPUT-OUTPUT SECTION.
                    FILE-CONTROL.
                        SELECT INPUT-FILE ASSIGN TO DISK
                              ORGANIZATION IS LINE SEQUENTIAL.
                        SELECT PRINT-FILE ASSIGN TO PRINTER.
                    DATA DIVISION.
                    FILE SECTION.
                    FD   INPUT-FILE
                        VALUE OF FILE-ID IS 'CH1302.DAT'
                        LABEL RECORDS ARE STANDARD.
                    01   INPUT-REC        PIC X(80).
                    FD   PRINT-FILE
                        LABEL RECORDS ARE OMITTED.
                    01   PRINT-REC        PIC X(80).
                    WORKING-STORAGE SECTION.
                    01   SWITCHES-N-WORKAREAS.
                        05   EOF           PIC 9 VALUE ZERO.
                        05   STUD-AVER     PIC 9(3).
                    01   DETAIL-INPUT-REC.
                        05   STUD-ID-NO    PIC 9(9).
                        05   GRD-1         PIC 9(3).
                        05   GRD-2         PIC 9(3).
                        05   GRD-3         PIC 9(3).
                        05   GRD-4         PIC 9(3).
                        05   GRD-5         PIC 9(3).
                        05   GRD-FINAL     PIC 9(3).
                    01   DETAIL-OUTPUT-LINE.
                        05   FILLER        PIC XX VALUE SPACES.
                        05   STUD-NO-O     PIC 9(9).
                        05   FILLER        PIC X(8) VALUE SPACES.
                        05   GRD-1-O       PIC ZZ9.
                        05   FILLER        PIC X(3) VALUE SPACES.
                        05   GRD-2-O       PIC ZZ9.
                        05   FILLER        PIC X(3) VALUE SPACES.
                        05   GRD-3-O       PIC ZZ9.
                        05   FILLER        PIC X(3) VALUE SPACES.
                        05   GRD-4-O       PIC ZZ9.
                        05   FILLER        PIC X(3) VALUE SPACES.
                        05   GRD-5-O       PIC ZZ9.
                        05   FILLER        PIC X(5) VALUE SPACES.
                        05   GRD-FINAL-O   PIC ZZ9.
                        05   FILLER        PIC X(5) VALUE SPACES.
                        05   STUD-AVER-O   PIC ZZ9.
                    01   TITLE-ONE.
                        05   FILLER        PIC X VALUE SPACES.
                        05   FILLER        PIC X(11) VALUE 'STUDENT NO.'.
                        05   FILLER        PIC X(15) VALUE SPACES.
                        05   FILLER        PIC X(11) VALUE 'TEST GRADES'.
                        05   FILLER        PIC X(12) VALUE SPACES.
                        05   FILLER        PIC X(5) VALUE 'FINAL'.
                        05   FILLER        PIC X(5) VALUE SPACES.
                        05   FILLER        PIC X(7) VALUE 'AVERAGE'.
                    PROCEDURE DIVISION.
                    100-MAIN-LINE.
                        PERFORM 200-OPEN-RTN.
                        PERFORM 300-HEADING-RTN.
                        PERFORM 400-PRIMER-READ.
                        PERFORM 500-PROCESS-RTN UNTIL EOF = 1.
                        PERFORM 600-CLOSE-RTN.
                        STOP RUN.
                    200-OPEN-RTN.
                        OPEN INPUT INPUT-FILE OUTPUT PRINT-FILE.
                    300-HEADING-RTN.
                        WRITE PRINT-REC FROM TITLE-ONE AFTER PAGE.
                    400-PRIMER-READ.
```

Fig. 13-2.   Main or calling program for the sample problem.

431

```
    READ INPUT-FILE INTO DETAIL-INPUT-REC
                 AT END MOVE 1 TO EOF.
500-PROCESS-RTN.
    PERFORM 550-MOVE-INPUT-RTN.
    CALL "CALC-SUB" USING GRD-1 GRD-2 GRD-3 GRD-4 GRD-5
                          GRD-FINAL STUD-AVER.
    MOVE STUD-AVER TO STUD-AVER-O.
    WRITE PRINT-REC FROM DETAIL-OUTPUT-LINE AFTER ADVANCING 1.
    READ INPUT-FILE INTO DETAIL-INPUT-REC
                 AT END MOVE 1 TO EOF.
550-MOVE-INPUT-RTN.
    MOVE STUD-ID-NO TO STUD-NO-O.
    MOVE GRD-1 TO GRD-1-O.
    MOVE GRD-2 TO GRD-2-O.
    MOVE GRD-3 TO GRD-3-O.
    MOVE GRD-4 TO GRD-4-O.
    MOVE GRD-5 TO GRD-5-O.
    MOVE GRD-FINAL TO GRD-FINAL-O.
600-CLOSE-RTN.
    CLOSE INPUT-FILE PRINT-FILE.
```

Fig. 13–2. (continued)

COMPILING AND LINKING CALLING PROGRAMS AND SUBPROGRAMS

The main program and any subprograms are compiled as individual programs, just as any previous program we have discussed. The joining of the main and subprograms occurs at link time. In the example shown above the procedure to link the two modules is as follows:

```
LINK CH1302 CH1301;
```

This procedure requires that the main program be entered first, followed by any subprograms, and in this case a semicolon (;). The semicolon indicates to the linker that it is to default to the name of the main program for the .EXE name and omit the .MAP. If you leave out the semicolon the following prompts appear before the link begins:

```
Run File [CH1302.EXE]:
List File [NUL.MAP]:
Libraries [.LIB]:
```

After each of the colons (:), you could enter another name or press enter to accept the default shown in brackets. It might be desirable to name the .EXE file differently from the original main (calling) program, in which case the desired program name would be entered in response **to the prompt:**

```
Run File [CH1302.EXE]:CH13MAIN
```

and the executable program would be CH13MAIN.

SUBPROGRAM REVIEW

The main (calling) program and all subprograms (called programs) are written and compiled separately—the COBOL step in the compilation process. After separate .OBJ modules have been created, the main program and all subprograms are joined into one executable program (.EXE). If you were to ask for a DIR of the programs in the above example it might look like the following:

```
Volume in drive C has no label
 Directory of C:\cob

CH1301    COB    1024    7-22-85     3:37p
CH1301    OBJ    2540    7-22-85     3:41p
CH1301    LST    1408    7-22-85     3:41p
CH1302    COB    3712    7-22-85     3:36p
CH1302    OBJ    3834    7-22-85     3:40p
CH1302    LST    4608    7-22-85     3:40p
CH1302    EXE   14720    7-22-85    12:07p
         7 File(s)    4169728 bytes free
```

Note that where CH1301 has a .COB, a .OBJ, and a .LST, it does not have a .EXE. This is because it is a subprogram. The .EXE is only for the main program (CH1302.EXE). It is quite large, since it contains the executable code for CH1301 and CH1302. If these programs were never to change, the .EXE could continue to be used indefinitely, since it now contains all the code for *both* programs. Subprograms are desirable for their operating efficiency at execution time, but since they contain all the necessary code this may be a less desirable technique in terms of program size. IBM COBOL has a limit of 64K for code and 60K for data; the main program and *all* subprograms must fit in the 64K limit.

INTRODUCTION TO CHAINING

As noted above, the use of subprograms involves creating a large executable program at link time. Chaining is a technique in which one program calls in another program at execution time and in which the first program is *completely replaced* by the second (and subsequent) programs. The exception to the complete replacement is that it is possible to pass data from the chaining (first) program to the chained (second) program. There is no limit to the number of programs that may be executed in this manner.

One advantage of this type of interprogram communication is the efficiency of storage utilization. Unlike the subprogram technique, the chained program is not added to the program that invokes it. Rather, it replaces it so that in using this technique each program is limited to the 64K maximum.

The general format of the CHAIN statement is as follows:

GENERAL FORMAT 4

CHAIN $\begin{Bmatrix} \text{literal} \\ \text{identifier} \end{Bmatrix}$ [USING identifier-2 . . .]

A major difference between the CHAIN and the CALL is that the CHAIN is completely effective at runtime; you will remember that the CALL was effective at link time. When using the CHAIN it is possible to alter the name of the chained program at runtime without recompilation, similar to the way that file names are changed by entering, perhaps through an ACCEPT, the new name. If the identifier option of the CHAIN is used, the program name of the .EXE module to be used may be entered through an ACCEPT or other convenient method. If the literal option is used, the literal must be included in the original program in DOS format and enclosed in quotes. The chained program need not be a COBOL program but may be an executable module originated from some other language.

Remember that the chained program does not return control to the chaining (original) program as with the CALL. The chained program must contain the end of processing logic, chain to another program, or *chain back to the original program.*

USE OF CHAINING WITH SYSTEM MENU

In Chapter 11 we have included four programs that are used to carry out various functions for an indexed inventory file. It would be very convenient to set up a menu as shown in Fig. 13–3 that can be used by the operator to select any of these four programs to be run.

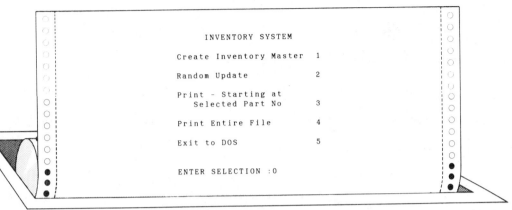

Fig. 13–3. Menu used in chaining inventory programs.

The operator would have to know only the name of the menu program as shown in Fig. 13–4 to run any of the other programs.

The only changes necessary in the programs being chained is to replace the STOP RUN statement with a CHAIN statement, which will pass control back to the menu program, in this example CH1303.EXE. This can be seen below in a segment from the index file create program CH1101.COB, which is shown in Fig. 11–1. If a progam were being chained and it was *not* necessary to pass control back to the chaining program, it would not be necessary to make any changes to the chained program.

```
************************************************
PROCEDURE DIVISION.
MAIN-LINE.
     PERFORM OPEN-RTN.
     PERFORM READ-RTN.
     PERFORM PROCESS-RTN UNTIL EOF = 1.
     PERFORM CLOSE-RTN.
     DISPLAY 'RUN COMPLETE'.
     CHAIN 'CH1303.EXE'.
************************************************
```

Note that the CHAIN statement requires that the .EXE version of the program be named and that the name be enclosed in quotes.

```
      IDENTIFICATION DIVISION.
      ****************************************************************
      PROGRAM-ID. MENU-PROG.
      ****************************************************************
      * This program creates a menu which allows the selection of one  *
      * of a series of programs, the execution of those programs and   *
      * the return to the menu program.                                *
      ****************************************************************
      ENVIRONMENT DIVISION.
      ****************************************************************
      CONFIGURATION SECTION.
      SOURCE-COMPUTER.
          IBM-PERSONAL-COMPUTER.
      OBJECT-COMPUTER.
          IBM-PERSONAL-COMPUTER.
      ****************************************************************
      DATA DIVISION.
      ****************************************************************
      WORKING-STORAGE SECTION.
      01  WORKAREAS.
          05  SEL-PROGRAM      PIC 9   VALUE ZERO.
      ****************************************************************
      SCREEN SECTION.
      01  MENU-SCREEN.
          05  BLANK SCREEN.
          05  LINE  3 COLUMN 26 VALUE 'INVENTORY SYSTEM '.
          05  LINE  5 COLUMN 21 VALUE 'Create Inventory Master  1'.
          05  LINE  7 COLUMN 21 VALUE 'Random Update            2'.
          05  LINE  9 COLUMN 21 VALUE 'Print - Starting at'.
          05  LINE 10 COLUMN 29 VALUE ' Selected Part No 3'.
          05  LINE 12 COLUMN 21 VALUE 'Print Entire File        4'.
          05  LINE 14 COLUMN 21 VALUE 'Exit to DOS              5'.
          05  LINE 17 COLUMN 21 VALUE 'ENTER SELECTION :'.
          05          COLUMN 38 PIC 9 TO SEL-PROGRAM AUTO REQUIRED.
      ****************************************************************
      PROCEDURE DIVISION.
      ****************************************************************
      BEGIN.
          DISPLAY MENU-SCREEN.
          ACCEPT MENU-SCREEN.
          DISPLAY (21, 80) SPACES.
          PERFORM MENU-LOOP THRU MENU-LOOP-EXIT
                          UNTIL SEL-PROGRAM = 5.
          STOP RUN.
      ****************************************************************
      MENU-LOOP.
          IF SEL-PROGRAM = 1 CHAIN 'CH1303A.EXE'
          ELSE IF SEL-PROGRAM = 2 CHAIN 'CH1303B.EXE'
              ELSE IF SEL-PROGRAM = 3 CHAIN 'CH1303C.EXE'
                  ELSE IF SEL-PROGRAM = 4 CHAIN 'CH1303D.EXE'
                      ELSE IF SEL-PROGRAM = 5
                                  GO TO MENU-LOOP-EXIT.
          DISPLAY MENU-SCREEN.
          ACCEPT MENU-SCREEN.
          DISPLAY (21, 80) SPACES.
      MENU-LOOP-EXIT.
          EXIT.
      ****************************************************************
```

Fig. 13-4.   Program used to create menu for program chaining.

> *The complete source program shown in Fig. 13–4 is available on the supplemental disk as filename CH1303.COB.*

PASSING DATA BETWEEN PROGRAMS WHEN CHAINING

It is possible to pass data between programs without writing the data to a file when using the CHAIN statement, just as it was possible with subprograms. In fact, the method is similar. The CHAIN statement would include the USING option followed by the name(s) of the data items to be passed to the chained program.

```
CHAIN 'PROGTWO.EXE' USING GRAND-TOTAL DEPT-TOTAL RUN-DATE.
```

The data items identified in the chaining program may be in the WORKING-STORAGE SECTION, FILE SECTION, or LINKAGE SECTION. The LINKAGE SECTION is possible because the chaining program may be itself a subprogram.

The chained program must include an identification of these data items after the PROCEDURE DIVISION entry:

```
PROCEDURE DIVISION CHAINING GRAND-TOTAL DEPT-TOTAL RUN-DATE.
```

or

```
PROCEDURE DIVISION CHAINING FINAL-TOTAL DEPT-TOTAL DATE-OUT.
```

As with subprograms, the data-names do not have to be identical but they must be identified in the same order. These data names must be defined in the WORKING-STORAGE SECTION of the chained program. One important type of data that could be passed between programs are DOS filenames that may have been established in one program through an ACCEPT and must be passed to the chained program in order for processing of the same file to take place.

INTRODUCTION TO SEGMENTATION

A third method for linking programs is through segmentation. In this method the PROCEDURE DIVISION of a *single* program, which is too large for the 64K limit, is broken into several parts. Some of these parts are always contained in main memory, and some of them are stored on disk. The principle is similar to the virtual storage concept in mainframe computers except that in IBM COBOL the source program itself must identify the segments. The number of segments is 100 (0 to 99), although we will see that there are some restrictions to their use. One particular advantage of segmentation is that the data areas are *not* included and are therefore *always* available to all segments of the program.

SEGMENTS

The PROCEDURE DIVISION is divided into SECTIONS when using this technique and each SECTION is assigned a segment number. Several SECTIONs may have the same segment number, but they must be physically grouped together in the source program.

```
PROCESS-MASTER-FILE SECTION 5.
                    .
                    .
                    .
PROCESS-DETAIL-FILE SECTION 5.
```

Segments that have numbers in the range 0 through 49 are **fixed segments** and are *always* in main memory. Segments that have numbers from 50 through 99 are **independent segments** and are stored on the disk to be loaded into main memory as needed for execution. There is only *one* independent segment in main memory at a time.

Control is passed between segments by the use of PERFORM statements, just as in previous programs. However, it is important to note that there are restrictions. Control may be passed between any of the fixed segments and between any fixed segment and any independent segment. Control may *not* be passed between independent segments. In other words, the main program (fixed segments) may call in, one at a time, any of the independent segments, but independent segments may only pass control back to a fixed segment. The way that we have been describing our program logic is consistent with this restriction, but it does mean that we may not have any "nested" independent segments— although an independent segment may have several sections and paragraphs that are subject to normal program logic *within* the independent segment.

We have again used the check-writing program from Chapter 7 (CH1105.COB) to illustrate this concept. The following excerpt from the PROCEDURE DIVISION of this program shows the changes that were made:

```
************************************************************
 PROCEDURE DIVISION
MAIN SECTION 1.
BEGIN.
      OPEN OUTPUT PRINTFILE
                  CHECKFILE.
      MOVE SPACES TO PRINT-REC.
      WRITE PRINT-REC AFTER ADVANCING PAGE.
      PERFORM INITIAL-ACCEPT.
      PERFORM CHECK-ACCEPT THRU CHECK-ACCEPT-EXIT.
      PERFORM LOOP-RTN UNTIL STATUS-CODE = 01.
      PERFORM TOTAL-RTN.
      CLOSE PRINTFILE
            CHECKFILE.
      STOP RUN.
************************************************************
 LOOP-RTN.
                        .
                        .
                        .
      PERFORM CHECK-ACCEPT THRU CHECK-ACCEPT-EXIT.
************************************************************
 CHECK-ACCEPT.
                        .
                        .
                        .
 CHECK-ACCEPT-EXIT.
      EXIT.
************************************************************
************************************************************
INITIALIZATION SECTION 51.
INITIAL-ACCEPT.
      DISPLAY (1, 1) ERASE.
                        .
                        .
                        .
************************************************************
FINAL SECTION 52.
TOTAL-RTN.
      MOVE REG-TOT-WS       TO REG-TOT-OUT.
                        .
                        .
                        .
************************************************************
```

Three segments have been created with the three sections:

```
MAIN SECTION 1.
INITIALIZATION SECTION 51.
FINAL SECTION 52.
```

The MAIN SECTION 1 contains the fixed segment of this program, which will always be in main memory during execution. The INITIAL-ACCEPT paragraph has been included in its own section, numbered 51 to show that it is an independent segment. The same procedure was followed in having TOTAL-RTN contained in independent segment numbered 52.

The choosing of an initialization routine and an end of job routine as independent segments was a logical one. There is execution time involved in reading in independent segments. It would be quite wasteful to make the main processing routine, in this case LOOP-RTN, an independent segment because this would require that this segment of code be read in from the disk for every iteration. Such an occurrence is called **thrashing**, since frequently used code would be constantly read in from disk. It is important, therefore, to be sure that the independent segments are infrequently used code such as the initialization and end of job routines used above or error routines, exception routines, etc.

> *The complete source program for the segment shown above is available on the supplemental disk as filename CH1304.COB.*

EXERCISES

1. **Subprograms:** The program used to print a list of employees (Program 1, Chapter 9—page 299) contains a table used to provide the employee's title when the title code is input. Since this table is typical of the kind of information that would be needed for many programs in a firm's systems, it would be useful to have this table stored in a subprogram. Write (or revise) the original program so that the table data and the routine that accesses this data for each transaction is contained in a subprogram.

2. **Chaining:** Program 1, Chapter 12 (page 411) consists of three separate programs to create, update, and randomly access an indexed file. Using CHAINING, write a program that will allow the execution of any of these three programs through the use of a menu.

3. **Segmentation:** Take any program that you have already written and segment it into a primary and at least two independent segments.

Solutions to the exercises, together with any necessary data files, are available on the supplemental disk.

INDEX

To Obtain the Diskette

A supplementary diskette containing the complete source listing to all programs illustrated in the book, all challenge programs, selected end-of-chapter exercises, and to specially provided BATch files (more than 100 complete COBOL programs) is available for only $19.95 (New York residents add 7½% sales tax).

Please send me the supplementary diskette for COBOL: *Elements of Programming Style*. I have enclosed $19.95, plus the applicable tax for each diskette I want.

NAME _____

ADDRESS _____

CITY _____STATE _____ ZIP _____

QUANTITY _____ AMOUNT ENCLOSED $ _____

Make check or money order payable to FUORI COMPUTER CONSULTANTS, INC.

Mail to:

Fuori Computer Consultants, Inc.
P.O. Box 446
Commack, N.Y. 11725

Please allow 4 weeks for processing.

Please send me the supplementary diskette for COBOL: *Elements of Programming Style*. I have enclosed $19.95, plus the applicable tax for each diskette I want.

NAME _____

ADDRESS _____

CITY _____STATE _____ ZIP _____

QUANTITY _____ AMOUNT ENCLOSED $ _____

Make check or money order payable to FUORI COMPUTER CONSULTANTS, INC.

Mail to:

Fuori Computer Consultants, Inc.
P.O. Box 446
Commack, N.Y. 11725

Please allow 4 weeks for processing.